Gesturing Toward Reality

Gesturing Toward Reality

David Foster Wallace and Philosophy

Edited by
Robert K. Bolger and Scott Korb

Bloomsbury Academic
An imprint of Bloomsbury Publishing Plc

B L O O M S B U R Y
NEW YORK · LONDON · NEW DELHI · SYDNEY

Bloomsbury Academic
An imprint of Bloomsbury Publishing Inc

1385 Broadway	50 Bedford Square
New York	London
NY 10018	WC1B 3DP
USA	UK

www.bloomsbury.com

BLOOMSBURY and the Diana logo are trademarks of Bloomsbury Publishing Plc

First published 2014
Reprinted 2014

Library of Congress Cataloging-in-Publication Data
A catalog record for this book is available from the Library of Congress.

ISBN: HB: 978-1-4411-2835-5
PB: 978-1-4411-6265-6
ePub: 978-1-4411-9206-6
ePDF: 978-1-4411-6408-7

Typeset by Deanta Global Publishing Services, Chennai, India

For Dave
and
for Kate

Contents

Notes on Contributors

Jon Baskin is a graduate student at the University of Chicago's Committee on Social Thought. He is also a founding editor of *The Point*. He is the author of "Death is Not the End" (*The Point*, 2009) and "Coming to Terms" (*The Point*, 2012), both works about David Foster Wallace. Baskin has other articles that can be found at thepointmag.com.

Andrew Bennett is a professor of English at the University of Bristol. He has published many books and articles on a variety of topics including: *Ignorance: Literature and Agnoiology* (Manchester University Press, 2009) and *An Introduction to Literature, Criticism and Theory*, 4th edn, with Nicholas Royle (Pearson Education, 2009), and *Wordsworth Writing* (Cambridge University Press, 2007).

Robert K. Bolger is the author of *Kneeling at the Altar of Science: The Mistaken Path of Religious Scientism* (Wipf and Stock, 2012). His research interests include philosophy of religion, Wittgenstein, and science and religion. He lives near Seattle, Washington.

Alexis Burgess is an assistant professor of philosophy at Stanford University. His books include *About Being* (forthcoming, Harvard University Press), *New Essays in Metasemantics*, co-edited with Brett Sherman (Oxford University Press, 2014), and *Truth*, co-written with John P. Burgess (Princeton University Press, 2011). He has also written many other articles and contributed chapters to various anthologies.

Maria Bustillos is the author of *Act Like a Gentleman, Think Like a Woman: A Woman's Response to Steve Harvey's Act Like a Lady, Think Like a Man* (Accidental Books, 2009), *Dorkismo: the Macho of the Dork* (Accidental Books, 2009), and "Inside David Foster Wallace's Private Self-Help Library" (*The Awl*, 2011). Maria is a regular contributor to the blog at *The New Yorker*. She lives in Los Angeles.

Leland de la Durantaye is a professor of literature at Claremont McKenna College. He is the author of *Style is Matter: The Moral Art of Vladimir Nabokov* (2007), *Giorgio Agamben: A Critical Introduction* (2009), and the translator of Jacques Jouet's *Upstaged* (2011).

Allard den Dulk is tenured lecturer in philosophy, literature, and film at Amsterdam University College. In 2012, he completed his dissertation at the VU University of Amsterdam, analyzing the shared philosophical dimension of the novels of David Foster Wallace, Dave Eggers, and Jonathan Safran Foer. He has published several articles on the philosophical themes in Wallace's work and in the contemporary fiction it has inspired. For more information, see: www.allarddendulk.nl.

Patrick Horn is the executive director of the Office of Graduate Student Support Services at Azusa Pacific University in Azusa, California. He is the author of *Gadamer and Wittgenstein on the Unity of Language: Reality and Discourse without Metaphysics* (Ashgate, 2005) and several articles in philosophy of religion.

Robert C. Jones is assistant professor of philosophy at California State University, Chico. He is the author of "A Review of the Institute of Medicine's Analysis of using Chimpanzees in Biomedical Research," co-authored with Ray Greek, *Science and Engineering Ethics*, April 2013, and "Science, Sentience, and Animal Welfare," *Biology & Philosophy*, January 2013, 28(1): 1–30. Robert has also published other essays on ethics and animal rights.

Scott Korb teaches writing at New York University's Gallatin School of Individualized Study and Eugene Lang The New School for Liberal Arts. He's also on the faculty of Pacific University's MFA program. His books include *The Faith Between Us: A Jew and a Catholic Search for the Meaning of God* (Bloomsbury, 2007), *Life in Year One: What the World Was Like in First-Century Palestine* (Riverhead, 2010), and *Light without Fire: The Making of America's First Muslim College* (Beacon, 2013). He is associate editor of *The Harriet Jacobs Family Papers* (UNC Press, 2008), which was awarded the 2009 J. Franklin Jameson Prize by the American Historical Association.

Ryan David Mullins is currently completing his Master's Degree in philosophy at the University of Bonn as part of the Europhilosophie Mundus. He is the author of a number of articles in the field of autism studies. His interests comprise metaphysics, philosophy of physics, and philosophy of film. He also has an impressive Pez collection, which is nothing to sneeze at.

Randy Ramal is an assistant professor of theories and philosophy of religion at Claremont Graduate University. He is the editor of *Metaphysics, Analysis, and the Grammar of God: Process and Analytic Voices in Dialogue* (Mohr Siebeck, 2010), as well as various other essays.

Kevin Timpe is professor of philosophy at Northwest Nazarene University. He is the author of *Free Will in Philosophical Theology* (Bloomsbury, 2013), *Virtues and Their Vices*, co-edited with Craig Boyd (Oxford University Press, 2014), *Arguing about Religion* (Routledge, 2009), and *Metaphysics and God* (Routledge, 2009). He has also published articles in the area of metaphysics and free will.

Thomas Tracey is an independent scholar who holds degrees in literature from Trinity College Dublin, the University of York (UK), and St John's College, Oxford. He has presented at conferences exploring the work of David Foster Wallace at the University of Liverpool and CUNY. He has also published an essay on Wallace and trauma in *Consider David Foster Wallace: Critical Essays*. He lives and teaches in Dublin.

Blakey Vermeule is an associate professor of English at Stanford University. She is the author of *Why Do We Care About Literary Characters* (The Johns Hopkins University Press, 2010) and *The Party of Humanity: Writing Moral Psychology in Eighteenth-Century Britain* (The Johns Hopkins University Press, 2000).

Acknowledgements

Robert thanks his co-editor Scott Korb for all his hard work and expertise without which this volume would have never been born. He also thanks his wife Lara and dog Annie for making life livable and wondrous. Thanks to professor Robert Coburn for providing the art for the cover of the book and for continuing to be an extraordinary friend. Finally, thanks to Dave for his friendship, kindness, and help in guiding me toward a spirituality of the "tummy."

Scott thanks Robert in turn, along with his colleagues and friends, and students at NYU's Gallatin School of Individualized Study, Eugene Lang The New School for Liberal Arts, and Pacific University. Many thanks to all the contributors to this volume. And, as always, for everything, thanks to Kate Garrick.

The editors would also like to thank everyone at Bloomsbury Academic, Haaris Naqvi most especially.

Love, and What You Will, Do:
An Introduction

Scott Korb

In April 2011, I received an email from Robert Bolger—"from the Old days at Union," he reminded me—asking whether I'd be interested in helping him pull together a collection of essays about David Foster Wallace and philosophy. More than a decade earlier, in the year we overlapped at NYC's Union Theological Seminary, Robert had known me as a reader of Wallace's work. I'd known him as a fellow Catholic in our liberal Protestant seminary, and he was studying philosophy. Since we'd last seen each other, Robert explained, he'd earned his PhD in philosophy of religion, written a book about religion and science, and, while living in Claremont, California, had come to know Dave, as he called him, through regular gatherings in "a meeting hall at a local church." In time they became friends.[1] I said I'd be happy to help out.

That's basically how this book came to be.

Now, I'm no philosopher. (You'll see there's no full essay from me collected here.) Since leaving seminary, which I followed with a degree in literature, I've been writing books about religion, while also teaching undergraduate and MFA writing courses. And as long as I've been teaching I've been teaching essays by Wallace.

Each semester, no matter what sort of writing we're about to undertake, my students and I first turn to Wallace's 2001 essay "Tense Present" (later published as "Authority and American Usage"). Here we read of the "Democratic Spirit," which, Wallace writes, "combines rigor and humility, i.e., passionate conviction plus a sedulous respect for the convictions of others."[2] This is not easy, Wallace warns—"you will have to be willing to look honestly at yourself and at your motives for believing what you believe, and to do it more or less continually"—and, admittedly, there is sometimes little evidence of such a spirit in our classroom discussions. But we try. Anyway, it's always struck me as a good idea to begin each term with a commitment—and for

---

[1] Robert intersperses some of their correspondence in his essay contained here, "A Less 'Bullshitty' Way To Live: The Pragmatic Spirituality of David Foster Wallace."
[2] Wallace, "Authority and American Usage," in *Consider the Lobster and Other Essays* (New York: Back Bay Books, 2005), 72.

me, a recommitment—to this democratic ideal and, with Wallace's choice of "Spirit," to the possibility of what religion scholar Karen Armstrong has identified as a modern "spiritual attitude": "to see beyond our immediate requirements, and enable us to experience a transcendent value that challenges our solipsistic selfishness."[3]

An undergraduate once put this all very succinctly: "Just remember," she said to the class, "you might be wrong."

Teaching "Tense Present"—and in certain courses about food writing, Wallace's 2004 "Consider the Lobster"—has led me this year to organize an entire course around Wallace's nonfiction. Again, we address the Democratic Spirit. Again, we ask, as Wallace does in the context of the Maine Lobster Festival, "Is it all right to boil a sentient creature alive just for our gustatory pleasure?"[4]

But there's also this question: "Am I the only one who had this queer deep sense as a kid?—that everything exterior to me existed only insofar as it affected me somehow?—that all things were somehow, via some occult adult activity, specially arranged for my benefit? Does anybody else identify with this memory?"[5] And this: "Is it possible really to love other people?"[6] Plus: "Are some things worth dying for?"[7] And they have to deal with this too: "I find myself, in my comfortable navy blue seat, going farther and farther away inside my head."[8]

Questions without answers. Endless recursiveness. Life and death. And so on, twice a week, for sixteen weeks. It's a lot. By midterm, some of the students say that they have a better sense of the inside of Wallace's head than they do any of the topics he covers in his essays. And while going "farther away"[9] inside Wallace's head offers the students many great pleasures, some of them remark that they like him less than they did at the beginning of the term. A few of them say that the work leaves them feeling a little hopeless. (There's no denying that his suicide—the end to his own despair—plays into this thinking.)

[3] Karen Armstrong, *A Short History of Myth* (New York: Canongate, 2005), 137.
[4] Wallace, *Consider the Lobster*, 243.
[5] Wallace, "Getting Away from Already Being Pretty Much Away from It All," in *A Supposedly Fun Thing I'll Never Do Again* (New York: Little, Brown & Co., 1997), 89.
[6] Wallace, "Joseph Frank's Dostoevsky," in *Consider the Lobster*, 265.
[7] Wallace, "Just Asking," in *Both Flesh and Not: Essays* (New York: Little, Brown & Co., 2012), 321.
[8] Wallace, "A Supposedly Fun Thing I'll Never Do Again," in *A Supposedly Fun Thing I'll Never Do Again*, 352.
[9] Jonathan Franzen seems to have borrowed this phrase for his 18 April 2011, *New Yorker* essay about his reaction to Wallace's suicide.

All this makes me eager for my students to see this present volume, for it's filled with hope. It's filled with the Democratic Spirit. And, to be frank, I think it's filled with a love, even in moments of sharp critique, that Wallace would have appreciated.

Individual writers collected here may disagree with my sense that there's some "transcendent value" in bringing a Democratic Spirit to their consideration of Wallace's writing. Indeed, each of the essays collected here has a simpler goal in common—to present Wallace's work as one of the many places where philosophical ideas reside. And collected as they are here, these essays reveal Wallace's work as a series of reminders of how life is and how it could be.

Wallace used as his epigraph to "Tense Present" a line from St Augustine: *Dilige et quod vis fac*. Love, and what you will, do. Although I might be wrong, I've often considered this line a sort of gloss on his entire body of work. Essays and novels, stories, and reviews, that present life as it is and ask how it could be different, better, if our actions were always preceded by love.[10]

---

[10] Fitting how love–love is the score in tennis, a game Wallace loved and wrote beautifully about, before the action starts.

1

How We Ought To Do
Things with Words[1]

Alexis Burgess

Plenty of ink has already been spilled over David Foster Wallace's apology
for prescriptive linguistics in "Authority and American Usage," which was
ostensibly meant to be a review of Brian Garner's *A Dictionary of Modern
American Usage,* but unsurprisingly wound up a constellation of anecdotes,
arguments, allegories, and (let's be honest, occasionally abusive) analyses
of antecedent salvos in those harrowing debates between linguistic liberals
and conservatives—Descriptivists and Prescriptivists—about how we use
language, how we ought to use language, who ought to say how we ought to
use language; not to mention, or *now to* mention (amending the alliterative
list initiated by "constellation of" above): announcements in applied ethics,
like his perplexing pro-life/choice synthesis; an autobiographical analysis
of SNOOT; various afterthoughts and appendices, railing, for example,
against political correctness; and of course the compulsory footnotes,
including an approving reconstruction of the private language argument,
of all things.

But I'd like to spill some more. Because, although, as we'll see, there's a lot I
want to take issue with in this piece of Wallace (henceforth, DFW), his "thesis
statement for [the] whole article"—which is frustratingly hard to locate, by
the way, despite explicit references to it in several section headings[2]—has

---

[1] Thanks to Lanier Anderson, David Hills, Josh Landy, and Adwait Parker for helpful
discussion of this material surrounding a presentation to Stanford's Program in
Philosophy and Literature.

[2] I think it might be this: "I submit, then, that it is indisputably easier to be Dogmatic than
Democratic, especially about issues that are both vexed and highly charged. I submit
further that the issues surrounding 'correctness' in contemporary American usage are
both vexed and highly charged, and that the fundamental questions they involve are ones
whose answers have to be literally *worked out* instead of merely found." Even in context,
though, that leaves a lot of room for interpretation. Wallace, *Consider the Lobster and
Other Essays* (New York: Back Bay Books, 2005), 72.

that rare pair of qualities, {Truth, Significance}, that generally ought to help a thought percolate up through the muddiest intellectual waters to the surface of public consciousness, but, regrettably, so far as I can tell, hasn't here. The unvarnished fact is that *our linguistic choices matter*, for all sorts of reasons. (The main one DFW highlights has to do with the dynamics of group inclusion/exclusion, but hang on, we'll get there.) More people—philosophers, authors, students, fans, teachers, dentists, whoever—should know that "merely verbal" or "semantic" issues can actually be quite important, and that we can accordingly pursue the ethics of diction and other linguistic decisions without being excessively snooty.

If you think you've already internalized this moral, here's a quick diagnostic. Upon first hearing right-wing arguments against same-sex "marriage" based on premises about the meaning of the word, were you inclined to dismiss them more or less out of hand, on something like the ground that semantic considerations are simply irrelevant to social justice? I'll admit that I was. But I was wrong.[3] Now wait, don't get me wrong! I support same-sex marriage every bit as much as the next coast-dwelling, Sunday-*NYT*-subscribing, liberal academic elitist. But the soundness of our arguments is more important than the truth of our conclusions, if only because the former strictly entails the latter. Which is kind of the whole point of my revisiting DFW on the Usage Wars: he got the right answer for (largely) the wrong reasons. So the bulk of this paper is going to be critical. Someone must have said that criticism is a higher form of flattery than imitation. Anyway: end stylistic homage. Pretty much.

The players, the stage

Like the present article, DFW's essay starts negatively but ends more positively. Readers eager to arrive at the Significant Truth on which he and I agree can always skim or skip to my final section. But before he argues *for* a thesis I'll follow him in calling Prescriptivism (P), DFW argues *against* an opposing thesis, Descriptivism (D). Now, this dialectical distinction would just collapse if our two -isms were logically contradictory—any argument against D would be a back-handed argument for P—but in fact they're only logically contrary. In other words: P and D are inconsistent with each other,

---

[3] See, for example, Sally Haslanger, "What Are We Talking About? The Semantics and Politics of Social Kinds," *Hypatia* 20, 4 (November 2005): 10–26, for an illustration of the potential significance of semantic considerations to social justice (though obviously and emphatically *not* for an indictment of same-sex marriage).

but could both be false. Or so it seems to me. DFW never explicitly defines our -isms. But his discussion suggests the following first approximations:

(P) One should (sometimes) make prescriptions about language use.
(D) One should *not* (ever) make prescriptions about language use.

I take it that P and D can't both be true, because it's not possible to sometimes-and-never do any given thing. (Two tacit premises: if one should do A and one should do B, then one should do A-and-B; and if one should do C, then it's possible to do C.) But as I say, P and D might both be false. It could turn out that there just aren't any "shoulds" about linguistic prescriptions.

We can of course define weaker forms of Prescriptivism and Descriptivism—entailed by P and D respectively (but not entailing them)—which do in fact logically contradict D and P respectively, just by negation:

(WP) It's not the case that one should not make prescriptions about language use.
(WD) It's not the case that one should make prescriptions about language use.

WD is easy enough to read, but WP is a bit tortuous. Under standard assumptions about the relationship between obligation and permission, it's equivalent to the more legible:

(WP*) One can permissibly make prescriptions about language use.

If DFW just wanted to establish WP or WP*, arguments against D would suffice; but, again, it seems to me that he's after the somewhat more ambitious P. The irony here is that his positive case for P is, as we'll see, quite clear, concise, and compelling. But he frontloads his review essay with a long string of tricky and ultimately less successful arguments against D. This is a pretty big rhetorical slip in an often masterful paper on, among other things, the rhetoric of lexicography.[4]

Having completed this somewhat tedious exercise in deontic logic, one might like to know what P and D actually *mean*. To begin with, we can say that "prescriptions" are claims about what one should or ought to do. So Prescriptivism is itself a prescription. And insofar as omissions are actions, Descriptivism is a prescription too. This isn't just ironic, it's actually borderline paradoxical. For D is arguably "about" language use—insofar as it's about prescriptions, which are typically expressed using language. So, being a prescription about language use, D falls under its own scope. If it's

---

[4] Of course, my paper structure exhibits a similar mistake. But, well, he started it.

true, one shouldn't say so. But DFW doesn't try to win on this technicality. His glosses on D effectively skirt paradox by qualifying the "One" they address. (One could equally qualify the relevant kind of language use.) He actually distinguishes two main kinds of Descriptivism: Methodological and Philosophical.[5]

Methodological Descriptivism (MD) targets practical lexicography: the dirty business of writing dictionaries, grammar books, and style manuals. Philosophical Descriptivism (ΦD), on the other hand, targets academic linguistics, especially syntax, semantics, and pragmatics. I'm really not at all sure why DFW uses these labels. (I can tell you that "Methodological" is meant to evoke "the scientific method—clinically objective, value-neutral, based on direct observation and demonstrable hypothesis" (83); but of course, linguists are scientists too.)[6] Suffice it to say for present purposes that there's nothing paradoxical about the following claims—

(MD) Lexicographers should not make prescriptions about language use.
(ΦD) Linguists should not make prescriptions about language use.

—so long as they're made by people outside the respective fields (or, again, if language use is somehow circumscribed so that MD and ΦD turn out not to be "about" it). And of course there are corresponding versions of Prescriptivism, plus weakenings of all four new views, after the pattern of the Ws above, for a total of twelve (!) balls in the air. The next two sections take up DFW's arguments against MD and ΦD in turn. I'll argue that they fail, and even suggest some countervailing considerations in favor of MD and ΦD.

Before we get going, though, let me address one last stage-setting question you might be asking yourself. Why does DFW focus on these two special cases of Descriptivism? Because, you might think, lexicographers and linguists are the principal actors in the Usage Wars. And why is that? Because they've been charged with the study of language, and the Usage Wars are all about whether the study of language ought to be partly prescriptive or purely descriptive. But this rationale has a couple of holes in it. First, philosophers

---

[5]   Before he starts using these terms, and intermittently afterward, DFW talks about methodological and philosophical *arguments* for Descriptivism, rather than methodological and philosophical versions of the view. In the interest of consistency, I think we should pick one way of talking or the other. (Though of course we should still distinguish arguments for a given thesis from the thesis itself.) I've found it easier to think and talk in terms of "versions" of Descriptivism, but much of the discussion below could be recast the other way.

[6]   I think he chooses "Philosophical" just to dignify these latter opponents. He could equally have called them sophisticated Descriptivists.

of language are also charged with (part of) the study of language. Second, English and expository writing teachers are also embroiled in the Wars. In fact, they're at the front lines. And as we'll see, DFW actually mounts his main campaign for P from this very outpost. Maybe he means to fold pedagogues in with practical lexicographers; and maybe, as the adjective "Philosophical" suggests, he means to lump linguists together with people like me.[7] If so, it's not clear from the text. More importantly, though, his emphasis on MD and ΦD obscures a third (or fifth) party one might have thought would want to weigh in on normative issues like these. A party that's philosophical, practical, pedagogical, and prescriptive all at once: ethicists.[8] We'll come back to this suggestion.

Methodological Descriptivism

MD says that dictionaries should refrain from issuing prescriptions about the use of language. I can make out at least three separable arguments against MD in DFW's article. What follows are two paragraphs on each, the first expositing the argument and the second replying to it. My overarching complaint will be that DFW tries to prove too much. For in all three cases he reaches (vainly for) the extreme conclusion that a purely descriptive lexicography is *impossible*, in practice and in principle, and therefore that MD absurdly implores dictionary writers to do what simply can't be done. As one might expect, and as we'll verify later, there are more modest and more successful ways to establish the desired anti-Descriptivist result (WP*) that one *can* permissibly make prescriptions about language use.

Here's a reconstruction of DFW's first argument against MD. If MD were true, then lexicography should be exclusively concerned with describing actual language use. The best, most comprehensive way to describe actual language use would simply be to list all of it—to provide an exhaustive catalogue of our linguistic behavior, past, present, and onward. But that's obviously not feasible. (And even if new technology eventually allowed for it, how/why would we use such an unwieldy list?) So, the argument continues, dictionary writers will inevitably have to choose which bits of usage to include and which to exclude. In other words, they'll have to decide what *should* go in their books. Which is of course to make a normative judgment

---

[7] I'm a philosopher of language, not a linguist or lexicographer (and rarely a writing instructor).

[8] I don't mean to suggest that how we write and talk is a *moral* issue (though it might be, occasionally). Moral philosophy is just a fragment of ethics, on my understanding of these terms. Ethics is the broad business of figuring out what we should or ought to do.

about language use. And the resultant dictionary will reflect this judgment, implicitly endorsing or prescribing the uses of language it includes and tacitly censuring the rest. Descriptive lexicography is therefore self-undermining. To pursue it in earnest is ultimately to abandon it. So, demanding the impossible, MD must be wrong.

This argument fails at almost every step. First of all, listing every instance of something is not usually the best way to describe that thing. The best way to describe our use of forks, for example (or covalent bonding, for another), is not to enumerate every historical fork deployment (or to catalogue every covalent bond). Good descriptions are illuminating because they are, among other things, suitably general. Which, second, is not to concede that dictionary writers will have to make inegalitarian divisions among uses of language. For they can simply choose not to include *any* individual uses in their books. After all, the primary kind of "description of language use" we actually find in dictionaries is *definition*. Definitions tell us that a word or phrase is used—by some linguistic community, at some period in time—to mean more or less the same thing as another, typically longer but more familiar phrase. Of course, dictionaries often supplement their definitions with illustrative sentences in which the defined terms appear. But the point is: they needn't. Third, even when they do, the choice to include one example rather than another needn't involve any judgment about what *should* be in the dictionary. Absent some heavy-duty meta-normative theorizing (e.g., Allan Gibbard's 2003 book *Thinking How to Live*), it would seem that I can choose which dessert to have without thereby deciding which dessert I should or ought to have.[9]

DFW's next argument against MD is a bit more formidable, but it overreaches for the same impossibility theorem. I'll give you some of his own words this time. Just to put them in context, recall that he wants to saddle his opponent with the view that lexicographic description ought to be properly "scientific." In the second argument against MD, we're told that it "involves an incredibly crude and outdated understanding of what *scientific* means. It requires a naive belief in scientific Objectivity, for one thing" (85). Which belief is then said to have been undermined "in the physical sciences, [by] everything from quantum mechanics to Information Theory," and a bit later, to have been "thoroughly confuted and displaced—in Lit by the rise of post-structuralism . . . [and] in linguistics by the rise of Pragmatics" (86). Now, I very much doubt that any *one* thing was challenged, let alone refuted, in all of these diverse areas. But I suppose DFW's thought is just that observation

---

[9] Moreover, such normative judgments don't have to be informed by views about which uses of language are good or bad, right or wrong. The criteria for inclusion could simply be statistical representativeness of actual usage and/or likely promotion of comprehension.

and description—however sober, systematic, scholarly, and/or scientific—are ultimately things that *people* do; and people are inevitably "biased" by their "ideologies," to use a couple of his go-to terms. Summing up this second argument against MD, he writes: "To presume that dictionary-making can somehow avoid or transcend ideology is simply to subscribe to a particular ideology, one that might aptly be called Unbelievably Naive Positivism" (86). So, just as with his first argument against MD, we're invited to conclude that there can be no such thing as a purely objective/descriptive lexicography, because lexicography is a human endeavor, and like all such endeavors, it's essentially, inextricably subjective.

Never mind the dubious identification of Positivism with the quest for objectivity. The best response to this argument is just to reject the identification of the objective and the descriptive—or more to the point: the subjective and the prescriptive. Let's grant DFW that all human inquiry is laden with "ideology" and therefore subjective. (I take it one's ideology is supposed to be something like a system of core values and beliefs, resistant, if not impervious, to rational reappraisal.) This hardly guarantees that the fruits of such inquiry will be prescriptions rather than descriptions. Look, I relied (however tacitly) on a lot of different values and beliefs to decide what to buy at the grocery store yesterday. But I can tell you what I bought and why I bought it without saying you should buy the same—without saying anything at all about what one should or ought to do. If Reader-Response Criticism or Jaussian Reception Theory implies otherwise, then so much the worse for them! Our common sense conviction that there's a nontrivial descriptive/prescriptive line to be drawn should carry more weight than the conjunction of the premises in some abstruse philosophical argument to the contrary.

DFW's third argument against MD is comparatively simple. Never mind whether all human inquiry is inherently subjective; and never mind whether you can cram all of our linguistic behavior between two covers. Dictionaries have to be prescriptive simply because they make claims about meanings, and such claims are inextricably normative.[10] Here DFW farms out most of the work to Wittgenstein (note 32; a long one), but I think we can actually appreciate his point without dipping into the private language quagmire. If you say that word W means M in language L, you may not be semantically expressing a normative proposition, but you're sure as heck going to convey—pragmatically, or in some other way—that to use W with any meaning other than M, in a context where L is the presumptive language of discourse, is to

---

[10] For reasons not altogether clear to me, DFW often prefers to write in terms of "grammar and usage" rather than "meanings." I'm fairly confident, however, that this distinction doesn't make a difference to his arguments.

misuse the word, to make a mistake, to do something wrong. What's more, this implication is hard to cancel. Just imagine a book in the reference section with a preface that read: "Proceed at your own risk. The definitions herein are emphatically *not* offered as guides to the usage of any actual language." The idea is basically just that dictionaries function in society as "authorities" on meaning and usage.[11]

Okay, but we might just as well have said that physics textbooks function in society as "authorities" on mass and universal gravitation. DWF's third argument was supposed to target lexicography specifically, not all human inquiry indiscriminately.[12] Yet it lapses into anti-Descriptivism about absolutely everything:

> If a physics textbook operated on Descriptivist principles, the fact that some Americans believe electricity flows better downhill (based on the observed fact that power lines tend to run high above the homes they serve) would require the Electricity Flows Better Downhill Hypothesis to be included as a "valid" theory in the textbook—just as, for Dr. Fries [a proponent of MD], if some Americans use *infer* for *imply* or *aspect* for *perspective*, these usages become ipso facto "valid" parts of language. (89)

This is so stupid it practically drools—to recycle one of DFW's replies to Fries. Or more charitably: so funny one might easily miss its fatuousness on first read. Why in the world would a Descriptivist be impelled to think that *physics is a branch of psychology*, devoted to studying people's *beliefs* about electricity and other physical phenomena? By the same token, why would a proponent of MD be obliged to say that dictionaries should record people's false views about the meanings of public language expressions? I just don't get it. I wish I had something more constructive to say about this third argument against MD, but I'm afraid it might be fundamentally confused.

---

[11] Incidentally, one of the main themes of DFW's review (which I haven't tried to treat) has to do with the rhetorical ingenuity Garner demonstrates in cultivating his own authority here.

[12] As he puts it: "Even if, as a thought experiment, we assume a kind of nineteenth-century scientific realism—in which, even though some scientists' interpretations of natural phenomena might be biased, the natural phenomena themselves can be supposed to exist wholly independent of either observation or interpretation—it's still true that no such realist supposition can be made about 'language behavior,' because such behavior is both *human* and fundamentally *normative*" (86–7). I let it slide earlier, but for the record, DFW is just plain wrong about the state of mainstream philosophy of science. At the time he was writing, and still today, subjective or mind-dependent phenomena in the physical sciences are widely thought to be exceptions that prove the rule.

At any rate, none of the considerations we've surveyed in this section tell against the view that lexicography can and should refrain from issuing prescriptions about the use of language. Anecdotally, for what it's worth, the dictionary on my Kindle isn't very pushy at all, and I have to say I like it that way. But let's move on to DFW's second target in this negative part of his article.

Philosophical Descriptivism

Again, I'm not sure why ΦD is so-called, but best I can tell, the view is supposed to be that academic linguists—and perhaps philosophers of language—shouldn't issue prescriptions about language use. DFW's comparatively brief treatment of ΦD is pivotal to his project in the review, as it transitions us from criticisms of Descriptivism to a positive case for Prescriptivism. So let me be clear about the structure of the present section. First I mount an argument *for* ΦD, loosely inspired by some of DFW's expository remarks. Then I assemble a line of response from his discussion of utility and interpretive labor. Next I show that this line doesn't actually defeat the original argument. Finally, I argue that prescriptivists like DFW shouldn't be bothered by this result, for two reasons. First, restricted forms of descriptivism like ΦD are of course compatible with special cases of P (generated from different restrictions). In particular, we might rest content with the conclusion that *ethicists* should issue prescriptions about language use. Second, and more likely to satisfy DFW, we can actually reconcile P in full generality with ΦD (and MD), by distinguishing what one ought to do *qua* linguist (or lexicographer) from what a linguist or anyone else ought to do *qua* citizen of her linguistic community.

For ΦD. By charter or definition, linguistics is in the business of *explaining* our linguistic behavior.[13] Now, explanation does come in a dizzying variety of (blendable) flavors: causal, historical, statistical, deductive, nomological, teleological, and more. But, crucially, all of these are purely descriptive enterprises. So, given their mission statement, linguists *qua* linguists simply

---

[13] Not every individual action will be amenable to systematic, scientific explanation. Some of the data are just noise. Explanation in morphology and phonology has to leave room for more or less "arbitrary" historical contingencies. Hyperbolically: "there's no particular metaphysical reason why our word for a four-legged mammal that gives milk and goes moo is *cow* and not, say, *prtlmpf*" (91). Explanation in syntax and semantics has to leave room for performance errors—deviations from the behavior dictated by linguistic competence.

have no business issuing prescriptions. After all, the whole point of making a "should" claim is to try to *change* someone's behavior (or at least ensure it stays on a desired course). Whereas the whole point of explanation in a science like linguistics is to try to understand our behavior *as we find it*. All of this is compatible with the logical possibility that generalizations encoded in traditional schoolhouse rules of grammar and usage might turn out to play some role in the production or explanation of our linguistic behavior. However, adding insult to injury, the more we actually learn about the causal/historical underpinnings of our speech and writing, the more these rules look like *ad hoc* conventions imposed after the fact. Like rules of etiquette, they lack explanatory value: "prescriptions against dangling participles or mixed metaphors are basically the linguistic equivalent of whalebone corsets and short forks for salad" (92). And as DFW acknowledges, the sorts of "rules" posited in generative linguistics are no more prescriptive than the "laws" governing chemical composition.

Of course, one might counter that, on a reasonably accommodating conception of "linguistic behavior," the fact that a given schoolhouse rule was taught and enforced in a given country or region, at a certain period in its history, is itself a datum falling under the explanatory purview of linguistics as we demarcated the discipline above. Charitably construed, one of DFW's central points in this portion of the article is that sociolinguistic facts like these can often be explained teleologically, by adverting to the utility of the rules in question. Most of his illustrations have to do with communicative virtue of saving your audience work; whether it's the work involved in resolving indeterminacy in surface syntax, or just the work required to process gratuitous verbiage. (Incidentally, it's hard to believe the irony presented by DFW's own prose styling was lost on him here.)[14]

---

[14] Confession: I never finished *Infinite Jest*. Dog-earing evidence reveals that I stopped at page 531 of the first paperback edition, at the section titled "0450H., 11 November. . . ." Part of the problem is obviously that the book's so long; but I've finished comparably long novels. Another part of the problem is sentences like this one, picked more or less at random: "The student engineer, a pre-doctoral transuranial metallurgist working off massive G.S.L. debt, locks the levels and fills out the left side of his time sheet and ascends with his bookbag through a treillage of industrial stairways with semitic ideograms and developer-smell and past snack bar and billiard hall and modem-banks and extensive Student Counseling offices around the rostral lamina, all the little-used many-staired neuroform way up to the artery-red fire door of the Union's rooftop, leaving Madame Psychosis, as is S.O.P., alone with her show and screen in the shadowless chill" (185). Granted, it's not as bad as the worst of Joyce, say, but sentences like this one make those of us with tastes for desert landscapes pine for the sparse elegance of Hemingway, or even just the flat-footed storytelling of Paul Auster. Every time I have to use my Kindle's dictionary, or restart a sentence because I parsed it incorrectly, I get thrown out of the narrative.

Here's one list: "The injunction against two-way adverbs ('People who eat this often get sick') is an obvious example, as are rules about other kinds of misplaced modifiers ('There are many reasons why lawyers lie, some better than others') and about relative pronouns' proximity to the nouns they modify ('She's the mother of an infant daughter who works twelve hours a day')" (93).

To his credit, DFW doesn't accuse the academy of simply overlooking the role that expedience plays in our linguistic self-regulation: "doubtless there are whole books in Pragmatics or psycholinguistics or something devoted to unpacking this point" (96). But what he fails to make clear is that none of this really tells against ΦD—or even against the specific argument for it we developed above. After all, the mere *study* of linguistic prescriptions doesn't logically entrain *making* any. More generally: the scientific study of a practice needn't involve participation. (We can learn as much as we care to about cannibalism, for example, without engaging in it ourselves.) Of course, calling a rule or prescription "useful" certainly sounds like an endorsement. But utility can be unpacked in purely descriptive terms. Cutting back on big words is useful insofar as more people will be able to understand you. That doesn't mean you *ought* to cut back. I can report the statistical facts about sophisticated diction and audience uptake, and then immediately go on to say—quite sincerely, and without any infelicity—that you can talk however you like.

DFW would actually ultimately agree with most of this, I'd hazard. His real beef with ΦD has less to do with the business of workaday linguistics or philosophy of language, and much more to do with the fact that its philosophical/linguistic proponents implicitly (and occasionally explicitly) underestimate the importance of normative issues about how we write and talk. Reacting to a barb of Steven Pinker's, DFW writes: "from the fact that linguistic communication is not strictly [better: causally] dependent on usage and grammar it does *not* necessarily follow that the traditional rules of usage and grammar are nothing but 'inconsequential decorations'" (94). Simply put: ΦD does not entail D. Even if linguists *qua* linguists have no business issuing prescriptions about language use, someone else might. Who? Well, as I mentioned earlier, one might think ethicists would be well suited to the job. But DFW has other ideas.

He wants to argue for P, which mandates that *every*one participate in the messy business of regulating our linguistic behavior.[15] As it turns out, however, this needn't preclude ΦD (or MD, for that matter). The trick to reconciliation has to do with the "*qua*"s I've been dropping recently. We all play lots of

---

[15] Hence the stuff about the Democratic Spirit (see n2).

different social roles. Even if the job description for linguists (or lexicographers) excludes issuing prescriptions about language use, it can't dictate what they do in their private lives, or more to the point, in their public lives as members of our shared linguistic community. What DFW really cares about establishing is that we all, *qua* citizens of this community—*qua* possible interlocutors—take responsibility for shaping linguistic communication. No matter how we earn our livings, we should be prepared to evaluate how we write and talk, and make prescriptions about language use if and when the need arises.

Stop and think about how you're saying what you're saying

If you're just joining us—perhaps having taken up my early invitation to skim or skip—welcome. Over the last two sections, I've been trying to establish that DFW's offensive against Methodological and Philosophical Descriptivism founders on the actual facts about lexicography and linguistics. But for all we've said thus far, it might still be true that some or all of us (*qua* linguistic citizens) ought to make prescriptions about language use. The aim of this final section is to initiate a positive argument for some such species of Prescriptivism. The general strategy DFW and I both favor involves establishing that our linguistic choices can often have nonlinguistic consequences of pretty obvious practical or ethical significance. In other words, given what we already care about, we should also care about how we express ourselves.[16]

DFW sort of sneaks up on this point in the discussion of interpretive labor we reviewed above, but there are lots of other ways in which our linguistic decisions matter. Elsewhere, together with Professor David Plunkett, PhD, and force of nature, I've tried to catalogue some of these different ways, sketching a basic framework for what we there call "conceptual ethics"—that is, normative/evaluative theorizing about thought and talk Burgess and Plunkett, manuscript.[17] Consider, for example, the tangible harm done by the

---

[16] Case in point. One could easily get negative attention on the blogs for referring in a book review to The Saul Kripke Center as CUNY's Center for Kripkiana. Readers might gloss "-iana" as an expression of derision, implying in this instance that the organization is somehow trifling. Offended parties might well stop reading before the review is even really underway, lending four errant letters excessive influence over the size of one's audience. "This reviewer acknowledges that there seems to be some, umm, personal stuff getting dredged up and worked out here; but the stuff is germane" (104).

[17] A. Burgess and D. Plunkett, "Conceptual Ethics I." *Philosophy Compass*, 8 (2013): 1091–101. doi: 10.1111/phc3.12086; A. Burgess and D. Plunkett, "Conceptual Ethics II." *Philosophy Compass*, 8 (2013): 1102–10. doi: 10.1111/phc3.12085

use of racial slurs. Or, to cash in my titular allusion, think about the practical upshot of a speech act like promising. Once we get going, illustrations start flooding in; for there's no obvious way to cordon our linguistic behavior off from everything else we do.

Plunkett and I focus mostly on the ethics of individual terms or concepts of special philosophical interest, like "personal identity" and "truth." But one of our original inspirations was DFW's observation that how we use language directly affects our chances of gaining membership into various social and professional groups. "The point here is obvious," he admits; and maybe it is, once you've had it pointed out to you: "People really do judge one another according to their use of language. Constantly. . . . [And] at least one component of all this interpersonal semantic judging involves *acceptance*, meaning not some touchy feely emotional affirmation but actual acceptance or rejection of someone's bid to be regarded as a peer, a member of somebody else's collective or community or Group" (97).

DFW sketches various thought experiments involving decisions about diction or grammar that seem to virtually guarantee exclusion from a given group. But the most compelling example in the essay derives from his own experiences teaching black students the mechanics of conventional, academic, expository prose—the dialect of SWE or "Standard Written English, which we might just as well call 'Standard White English' because it was developed by white people and is used by white people, especially educated, powerful white people" (108-9). Here's an excerpt from the relevant lecture summary:

> In this country, SWE is perceived as the dialect of education and intelligence and power and prestige, and anybody of any race, ethnicity, religion, or gender who wants to succeed in American culture has got to be able to use SWE. This is just How It Is. You can be glad about it or sad about it or deeply pissed off. You can believe it's racist and unfair and decide right here and now to spend every waking minute of your adult life arguing against it, and maybe you should, but I'll tell you something—if you ever want those arguments to get listened to and taken seriously, you're going to have to communicate them in SWE, because SWE is the dialect our nation uses to talk to itself. (109)

One of the reasons this can be so hard to read, I submit, is that it's (still) painfully true. I can't put the point any better than DFW has, but I can say that I thought about it every day I tutored the middle-school children of Spanish-speaking Angelinos at 826LA.[18] The tragic fact is that these kids

---

[18] If you don't know about the organization, it's a beautiful, national nonprofit founded by Dave Eggers, one of DFW's literary peers, accepting volunteers at a major US city near you.

are just too young to comprehend the best rationale for the undeniably tedious—and yes, tacitly prescriptive—worksheets their English teachers habitually impose upon them. How do you tell a twelve-year-old that the real danger of being "left behind" is actually, ultimately, that you'll just be left out?

You don't. But here are a couple of things we *can* do, as academics and members of the hyper-educated, linguistic elite. In the first place, we can accept the Significant kernel of Truth in David Foster Wallace's "Authority and American Usage," that prescriptions about language use are socially, even morally necessary—if only as a matter of nonideal theory—and disseminate it throughout our social networks with enough force to permeate the PC membrane that still strangles action around this issue. Cut and paste a passage from DFW to your Facebook page, for starters. Call out friends and colleagues on their deviations from SWE, and outright errors like mispronunciation. They may well take you for a snoot, given the current state of verbal etiquette.[19] But that seems like a small price to pay for the chance to spare the people you care about further linguistic judgment—to improve their prospects for acceptance among the powerful and prestigious peer groups who fetishize this stuff.

Second, and probably more important: rather than leaving the fight to the victims, we can try to combat Linguistic Discrimination by recognizing it for what it is, and censuring it when we see it. It should be illegal to rule out a job candidate for using "urban" slang in an interview; but I expect it happens every day, without comment. The hope would be that we eventually won't need so many rules and regulations about communication. Not because we'll all be raised as expert users of SWE or Esperanto, but because we'll outgrow the tendency to negatively prejudge each other on the basis of objectively insignificant verbal quirks. Some prejudicial heuristics might be hard-wired, but the inference rule from "infinitive splitter" to "ignoramus" surely isn't among them.

---

[19] Incidentally, it's always seemed quite strange to me just how offended people get when you correct their usage. I've gotten reactions akin to what you'd expect for calling someone a pervert. My father tells me that the socially appropriate way to point out a linguistic mistake is to use the target word or phrase correctly oneself, shortly after the offending utterance. But that seems pretty passive-aggressive.

2

The Subsurface Unity of All Things, or David Foster Wallace's Free Will[1]

Leland de la Durantaye

I

Ships as far as the eye can see. The rising sun glittering on the Aegean. Wind rippling the sails, water lapping the bows, fear, excitement, vengeance, glory, the favor of the gods, the order contemplated, the order given.

Or, expressed differently:

> Since obviously under any analysis I have to do either O or O' (since O' is not-O), that is, since $\Box$(O v O'); and since by (I-4) it is either not possible that I do O or not possible that I do O', ($\sim\Diamond$O v $\sim\Diamond$O'), which is equivalent to ($\sim\Diamond\sim\sim$O v $\sim\Diamond\sim$O), which is equivalent to ($\Box\sim$O v $\Box$O), we are left with $\Box$ ($\Box$O v $\Box\sim$O); so that it is necessary that whatever I do, O or O', I do necessarily, and cannot do otherwise.[2]

Both of these remarks are about fate and free will, necessity and contingency. The first is the scene Aristotle sets in *On Interpretation*; the second is David Foster Wallace's reformulation in his exceptionally promising, and sole, contribution to technical philosophy: his senior honors thesis, "Richard Taylor's 'Fatalism' and the Semantics of Physical Modality," submitted in 1985 and published posthumously in 2011 as *Fate, Time, and Language: An Essay on Free Will*.

---

[1] A version of this essay originally appeared as "How to Be Happy: The Ethics of David Foster Wallace," *Boston Review*, March/April 2011: 41–4.

[2] Wallace, *Fate, Time, and Language: An Essay on Free* Will, eds. Steven M. Cahn and Maureen Eckert (New York: Columbia University Press, 2011), 146.

In *On Interpretation* Aristotle defends a view about fate, free will, necessity, and contingency that is at once logical, metaphysical, and naval:

> It is necessary for there to be or not to be a sea-battle tomorrow; but it is not necessary for a sea-battle to take place tomorrow, nor for one not to take place—though it is necessary for one to take place or not to take place.[3]

This seems clear enough, and is. Nothing in Aristotle's example is necessary except that something take place or not take place; a sea battle, after all, cannot both happen and not happen. But what, we might ask, are the metaphysical implications of this logical necessity? How are we to understand contingency and potentiality, if such things could truly be said to exist? Is the general free to give the order for battle, or is all foreordained to happen, fixed in future place by natural law and supernatural will?

When Leibniz took up the same question two millennia later, he asked whether Aristotle's pupil, Alexander the Great, was fated to command, live, and die as he did.

"When we carefully consider the connection of things," Leibniz wrote,

> we see the possibility of saying that there was always in the soul of Alexander marks of all that had happened to him and evidences of all that would happen to him and traces even of everything which occurs in the universe, although God alone could recognize them all.[4]

This leads Leibniz fitfully close to fatalism, the idea that free will is an illusion. He escapes, if escape he does, from this logic-locked world by means of a distinction between "necessary necessity" and "contingent necessity." (Yes, this is suspiciously slippery, and is very much a story unto itself.) Given the metaphysical thickets encountered when we talk about fate and free will, contingency and necessity, it is no surprise that logicians have sought to clarify the question, or that, to that end, they have crafted specialized tools.

In the fullness of time, Aristotle's sea battle gave rise to modal logic—the branch of formal logic concerned with possibility and necessity—and thereby to David Foster Wallace's youthful attempt to use modal logic to refute arguments in favor of fatalism. Sea battles are full of accident and adventure, and thus the sort of thing that generally appeals to budding novelists. Modal logic, however, is a less intuitive choice, and invites some special explanation.

---

[3] Aristotle, *Categories and De Interpretatione*, trans. J. L. Ackrill (Oxford: Oxford University Press, 1963), 53 (9 19a32-6).

[4] G. W. Leibniz, *Discourse on Metaphysics and The Monadology*, trans. George R. Montgomery (New York: Dover, 2005), 9.

Readers of academic philosophy may be interested in the modal logic of "Richard Taylor's 'Fatalism' and the Semantics of Physical Modality," but what is there for Wallace's (large) nonphilosophical readership, used as it is to a very different tone and very different topics, in his thesis? A ready answer is nothing whatsoever. But a better, if hidden, one is that in it is the most important idea of all, the one that links together all his works, all his most passionate thinking. This is the question of how to be truly free—or, as he more colorfully expressed it, of how to be "a fucking human being."[5]

Wallace's thesis is a dense, formula-filled, 80-page examination, restatement, and refutation of the distinguished philosopher (and bee-keeper) Richard Taylor's 1962 paper "Fatalism." When the thesis was submitted to Amherst College's philosophy department in 1985, it was awarded the Gail Kennedy Memorial Prize in Philosophy (the same prize that Wallace's father, James, had won 26 years earlier). As the passage cited above suggests, it is not an easy read—one of the reasons it is surrounded in *Fate, Time, and Language: An Essay on Free Will* by so much ancillary material (the reader doesn't reach the thesis itself until page 141 of the volume) and why James Ryerson's introduction is indispensable for nonspecialist readers. But despite its technical language, the thesis is relatively easy to characterize: it aspires to refute the idea, advanced in Taylor's paper, that free will is an illusion.

Wallace is responding, he explains, specifically to Taylor's "semantic argument out of six seemingly inoffensive presuppositions [that] appears to force upon us a strange and unhappy metaphysical doctrine that does violence to some of our most basic intuitions about human freedom" (146).[6] The "strange and unhappy" doctrine in question is fatalism. Wallace focuses on Taylor's "move from semantics to metaphysics," from claims about language and meaning to claims about the world, and finds the necessary resolution in modal logic.

Early in his thesis, Wallace notes, "I am going to try to bend over backwards to accept Taylor's premises, to grant him everything he seems to want in the argument, and then to show that the conclusion he desires still does not follow validly from that argument" (151). The skilled rhetorician takes the opposing view and states it in its best, brightest, most seductive terms—and then roundly refutes it. In this respect Wallace's thesis is

---

[5] Wallace, "An Interview with David Foster Wallace," by Larry McCaffery, *Review of Contemporary Fiction* 13, 2 (Summer 1993): 127–51; 131.

[6] The principal tool employed is "a formal semantic device" Wallace calls "system J" (presumably because its guiding intuition came from the philosopher Jay Garfield) and which has as its chief merit, according to Wallace, that it "captures nicely the ways in which we all actually do think and talk about physical possibility and time in the course of everyday life" (168).

masterly. He expends a good deal of time and energy distinguishing, in logical terms, something that seems to be in no need of distinguishing, and for which a special semantic device seems wildly superfluous: that "physical possibility is . . . properly understood in a significantly different way from logical possibility" (197). This is perfectly intuitive: a 60-foot man is logically possible, but not physically possible. It thus seems supremely strange that the author would go to such pains to argue it, and that it would need to be argued (with the aid of formulae!) at all.

Aristotle wanted, like his teacher, to "save the phenomena": he thought that philosophy should not stray too far from our considered opinions. Taylor seems to move in a different direction, presenting an argument for something that seems counterintuitive—that we are *not* free to think and act, that nothing can be done about future sea battles. The debate provoked by Taylor's fatalism was focused more on saving logic than saving the phenomena. That is, the problem seems to be philosophy's—how philosophy can coincide with its world, how it can express our basic intuitions, how it can pass the test of accurately reflecting the world in which it is written.

What Wallace does in his thesis—with the same understanding incisiveness of his later analyses of cruise ships, the porn industry, lobster biology, tennis, David Lynch, and a host of other matters—is show how to resist the seemingly compelling premises that led Taylor to that unhappy, fatalist conclusion. Wallace argues that Taylor has made a category mistake, presenting what is ultimately "a *semantic* argument for a *metaphysical* conclusion" (213).[7] Wallace can thus end on a lucid, heartening, and elegant note: "If Taylor and the fatalists want to force upon us a metaphysical conclusion, they must do metaphysics, *not* semantics. And this seems entirely appropriate" (213).

II

The first readers of "Richard Taylor's 'Fatalism' and the Semantics of Physical Modality" knew that it was one of two honors theses its young author was writing. They thought the other—a 500-page novel entitled *The Broom of the System* (1987)—was a sideline, albeit a vast one, the hobby of a man clearly destined, as his father had been, for philosophy.

---

[7] There is a sense in which the thesis thus says something about an endemic confusion—a sort of occupational hazard that comes with a certain kind of philosophy, maybe all philosophy, and which is to confuse logical and metaphysical matters. Wallace is particularly good at unmasking the metaphysical arguments contained in or concealed by logical ones; years later, for instance, in his *Everything and More: A Compact History of Infinity* (2003), he discussed how "implicit in all mathematical theories . . . is some sort of metaphysical position" ([New York: Norton, 2010], 10).

Wallace began graduate work in philosophy at Harvard University a few years later, but he soon abandoned the undertaking after suffering an emotional breakdown. He then dedicated his intellectual energy to fiction and to a series of incomparably brilliant, funny, compassionate, kind, strange, insightful, and moving essays (collected in *A Supposedly Fun Thing I'll Never Do Again* [1997], *Consider the Lobster* [2006], and the posthumous *Both Flesh and Not* [2012]). He wrote no further works of technical philosophy, but he did go on to write a novel, *Infinite Jest*, that made *The Broom of the System* seem short by comparison.

In the wake of the fame these works brought him, Wallace was asked to give Kenyon College's 2005 commencement address. Here he again focused on free will, but this time he took a radically different approach from "Richard Taylor's 'Fatalism' and the Semantics of Physical Modality." The speech—published posthumously as *This Is Water: Some Thoughts, Delivered on a Significant Occasion, about Living a Compassionate Life* (2009)—is a masterpiece. It is friendly, fond, and very, very funny. In his 2004 essay on lobsters, Wallace had expressed his concern "not to come off as shrill or preachy when what I really am is more like confused."[8] In "Consider the Lobster," in *This Is Water*, and in so many other places in his nonfiction, his confusion is expressed with rare lucidity. He did not write with what George Steiner once called "the serene malice of age and work done."[9] He wrote, instead, with the feverish curiosity of youth and of work to be done.[10]

---

[8] Wallace, *Consider the Lobster and Other Essays* (New York: Little, Brown, 2006), 253.

[9] George Steiner, *In Bluebeard's Castle: Some Notes Towards the Redefinition of Culture* (New Haven: Yale University Press, 1971), 93.

[10] What seems to have made, and to make, Wallace so appealing to so many—particularly younger—readers is not how he presents a sheer rock face or magic mountain of knowledge and certainty that the younger or less well-informed reader might hope one day to scale, but how he presents his insights alongside, and interwoven with, his uncertainties. His essays are essayistic in the etymological sense of the word: they are *experiments*; they are *attempts* at understanding. Correspondingly, there are extremely few peremptory announcements of the sort that Steiner—to name a single great example—is a past master of pronouncing. In my limited, but not so very limited, teaching experience, this seems to account for the greater proximity to, affection for, interest in, and desire to imitate Wallace among undergraduates than that felt for other great essayists of his age, whether it be someone of the monumental learning of Steiner or Guy Davenport, or the less academically inflected styles of Joan Didion, Anne Fadiman, Adam Gopnik, Louis Menand, or many, many others.

It bears noting in this context that this searching, provisional element that is the hallmark of Wallace's essay style accounts for their most distinctive formal elements. The first is long, breathless sentences with cascading qualifying clauses. The second of these is the extensive use of long footnotes even, and especially, in periodicals—such as *Esquire*, *Rolling Stone*, or *Gourmet*—that do not normally allow footnotes. This searching quality in form and content means that among the great essayists of the past, the one Wallace most resembles is the modern founder of the genre, the highly associative and uncertain and insightful—and undeniably *free*—Montaigne (with much of the warmth of Lamb and the wit of Chesterton).

The tone of Wallace's Kenyon address is, as all such addresses must be, avuncular, but the voice is that of the uncle who gets high with you, the uncle who says that your father loves you but that when he was your age he made lots of mistakes and is still to this day a whole lot less sure about things than he lets on. Although Wallace was nearly twice as old as 2005's graduates, he spoke on their level; he cares and communicates that care. The speech is jocular, disarming, and open; its attitude is you-might-think-I'm-just-a-ridiculous-old-loser-for-saying-this- but-I-*actually*-believe-it-so-here-goes.[11]

Wallace's argument—for he has one—is that the goal of undergraduate education, and of all education, is free will. He holds that education's greatest benefit consists in "being conscious and aware enough to *choose* what you pay attention to and to *choose* how you construct meaning from experience."[12] The reason he gives is simple and absolutely typical: "Because if you cannot or will not exercise this kind of choice in adult life, you will be totally hosed" (55).

Much of his address is thus advice on how not to get totally hosed, which is to say on how to be happy, which is to say, ethics. From Aristotle onward, ethics has been about how not to get totally hosed—on the highest level. Learning this is the most desirable thing of all. It is what another great essayist of the twentieth century, Guy Davenport, speaking of Montaigne called "the inviolable privacy" of the mind.[13]

Whereas Wallace's thesis aimed to explain the rightness of something that we knew was right from the outset, the commencement address aimed to explain the necessity of something we think either does not exist or we have long since acquired. He argues that if this ultimate goal of a liberal arts education has been reached, "if you've really learned how to think, how to pay attention," you will have unparalleled freedom (92). He then broaches the central topics of the novel he had been at work on for several years and was never to finish (*The Pale King*): boredom, tedium, and alienation. "It will actually be within your power," he continues in his Kenyon address,

---

[11] This seems to me another reason for the great appeal Wallace holds for younger readers: the linked desires for guidance and fellowship. The best essayists feel like friends, and Wallace feels like a good friend to many readers of all ages. That said, his intact earnestness gives hope to young readers alarmed by the cynicism of other intellectual heroes. That he has achieved a sort of wisdom while maintaining a sort of freshness is not the least reason why he is so appealing to younger readers. Another way of saying this is that his avowed, embraced, uncoolness feels, and therefore is, cool to many younger readers.

[12] Wallace, *This Is Water: Some Thoughts, Delivered on a Significant Occasion, about Living a Compassionate Life* (New York: Little, Brown, 2009), 54.

[13] Guy Davenport, *Every Force Evolves a Form* (San Francisco: North Point Press, 1987), 42.

"to experience a crowded, hot, slow, consumer-hell-type situation as not only meaningful, but sacred, on fire with the same force that lit the stars—compassion, love, the subsurface unity of all things" (93). As we might expect, the goal of such freedom is not personal pleasure, not merely "the freedom all to be lords of our tiny skull-sized kingdoms," but what Wallace calls "real freedom": "the really important kind of freedom involves attention, and awareness, and discipline, and effort, and being able truly to care about other people and to sacrifice for them, over and over, in myriad petty little unsexy ways, every day" (117, 120, 125). That is to say, freedom is not about having as few fetters as possible; it is about leading an examined life. Freedom is being a good person, choosing to be a good person, every day.

One thing that Wallace is then underlining is the potentiality alive in and at every moment. That even—and, who knows, maybe especially—in those places that seem most calculated to limit our freedom, to limit our sense of possibility in ourselves and others (such as a "consumer-hell-type situation" of the sort described here—what more peremptory essayists such as Guy Debord and Walter Benjamin respectively called the "society of the spectacle" and "the destruction of experience") we can, and should, keep alive and awake in ourselves a sense of what makes life meaningful—compassion, love, "the subsurface unity of all things"—and to see them not only as what might make us less annoying people to stand next to in the mall, but as embodying the ethical imperatives both at the root of education and that constitute our most basic, and most rewarding, freedom. This entails distinguishing what is in essence good self-consciousness from what Wallace called elsewhere "toxic, paralyzing, raped-by-psychic-Bedouins self-consciousness."[14] To be free is to act ethically, to keep yourself awake and alive even in the most mind-numbing of circumstances to the necessity of kindness and the possibility for change—which is the need to keep alive a sense for change even in circumstances crafted by exploitative forces and situations to create the impression that nothing can be changed on a large scale, and so that one should simply aim to better one's local hedonistic situation.[15] Wallace's

---

[14] David Lipsky, *Although Of Course You End Up Becoming Yourself: A Road Trip With David Foster* Wallace (New York: Broadway Books, 2010), 19.

[15] Cf.: "There is something that all people, whether they admit it or not, know in their heart of hearts: that things could have been different, that that would have been possible. They could not only live without hunger and also probably without fear, but also freely. And yet at the same time—and all over the world—the social apparatus has become so hardened that what lies before them as a means of possible fulfillment presents itself as radically impossible." Theodor Wiesengrund Adorno and Ernst Bloch, "Etwas fehlt: Über die Widersprüche der utopischen Sehnsucht," in Ernst Bloch (ed.), *Tendenz, Latenz, Utopie: Werkausgabe Ergänzungsband* (350–68) (Frankfurt: Suhrkamp, 1985), 353.

position on liberal arts education is that it teaches you not how to perform some set of tasks, but how to attend to yourselves and your world, and how such attention leads to awareness and from awareness to a kind of discipline which is, in turn, the prerequisite for true caring, and true sacrifice. Which is all to say, there is an idea of ethics contained in this single sentence and one with everything in common with Wallace's first philosophical writing.

Wallace once remarked that the most beautiful beginning in all of Western literature is that of Wittgenstein's *Tractatus*: "The world is everything that is the case." With this in mind, our aim should be to see the world, to attend to everything that is the case around us. We should imagine our way into the lives those around us lead, to reflect on what wild contingencies led to our state and to theirs, to reason our way into their beliefs and imagine our way into their fears. To not get totally hosed is to see that the cashier in the consumer-hell-type situation has this soul-crushing job not because it is in the cashier's character to have a crappy job, in the same way that Leibniz thought it was in Alexander's character to conquer Darius and die by poison. It is not divine ordinance that has put things in these places. That this person has a dreadfully boring job while you might have an interesting one is not because that is the right and true order of things in this, the best of all possible worlds, but because of contingent, crooked reasons that no logic—formal, modal, or other—will straighten.

Discussions of free will inevitably touch upon its limits, logical or otherwise—particularly on last refusals. Isaac Bashevis Singer once called suicide "the highest way a man can tell the Almighty, 'I don't agree with the way you are managing the world, and because I don't agree, take back Your gift.'"[16] In *Infinite Jest* Wallace's tennis prodigy Hal says something kindred when he confides to his brother that, "God seems to have a kind of laid-back management style I'm not crazy about."[17] One form of final freedom might indeed be to find, to judge, the management of the world utterly unacceptable and to give back the gift.

Wallace committed suicide in September of 2008, for reasons impossible to know. But the freedom that he writes about in *This Is Water* is focused elsewhere. It is entirely on the living—on life, on the sweet insistence of its fullness and its detail. To be free in the world, as opposed to being merely free in your skull-sized kingdom, you must wonder into the finer reasons for things—you must look, as Jules Verne said, "with all your eyes" at everything around you all the time.

---

[16] Quoted in Cornelia Baulsom-Löwy, *Hure oder Hüterin des Hauses: Das Bild der jüdischen Frau in I. B. Singers Werk* (Trier: WVT, 2004), 345.

[17] Wallace, *Infinite Jest* (New York: Little, Brown, 1996), 27.

Wallace's remark about being totally hosed is a signature stylistic trait and at the same time an absolutely serious, an almost technical, term in his philosophy—and the motivation for his fiction. Because fiction concerns what it is to be "a fucking human being," he aspired to write "morally passionate, passionately moral fiction."[18] He longed to give "CPR to those elements of what's human and magical that still live and glow despite the times' darkness."[19] To be totally hosed is not to come out with less of something, such as money or recognition; it is to be riveted in place by your circumstances, to find yourself incapable of thinking beyond them. Our most human freedom is that of consciousness, of being able to turn our thoughts where we will. And a compassionate life involves learning that certain movements are difficult and yet right, and rewarding beyond all measure. Like that of his modal logic thesis, the end of Wallace's address is artful. "Your education really *is* the job of a lifetime," he says, "and it commences—now. I wish you way more than luck" (136-7). In view of the fact he took his own life three years later, these parting words carry a special sweetness, and sadness.

III

The two posthumous publications, *This Is Water* and *Fate, Time, and Language* are—in truly maximally different ways—books about freedom and contingency. Or, alternately, they are both about how not to get totally hosed. They are both works of philosophy, at opposite ends of the philosophical spectrum. One is highly technical and conceptually sophisticated; the other could not be more vernacular or broadly-aimed. One aims to explain to us the rightness of something we knew from the outset was right. The other aims to explain to us the necessity of something we think either does not exist or that we have long since acquired.

There is a final consideration to be noted in connection with Wallace's early and late, technical and popular, reflections on free will. We care everywhere and always about freedom—except, perhaps, as concerns one thing: love.

So as to distinguish different types of necessity in his refutation of fatalism, Wallace asks, "In order for me to play tennis, it is necessary that I have a tennis racket, but does the absence of a racket mean that I lack the ability to play tennis?"[20] The answer is clearly no, and it should come as no surprise

---

[18] *Consider the Lobster*, 273.
[19] "An Interview with David Foster Wallace," 131.
[20] *Fate, Time, and Language*, 153.

to Wallace's readers that he uses tennis as an example in his investigation of fate and freedom. His finest writing circles around the sport he called, in *Infinite Jest*, a hybrid of chess and boxing. When he watches a professional tennis player—as he does in a 1996 essay on Michael Joyce, a promising player who never broke into the top ranks—Wallace soon turns to questions of free will and choice. "Can you '*choose*' something," he asks, "when you are forcefully and enthusiastically immersed in it at an age when the resources and information necessary for choosing are not yet yours?"[21] Although his reflection begins at that unknowable point, it ends elsewhere—in love. "When Michael Joyce speaks of tennis," Wallace writes:

> the eyes get round and the pupils dilate and the look in them is one of love. . . . It's the sort of love you see in the eyes of really old people who've been happily married for an incredibly long time, or in religious people who are so religious they've devoted their lives to religious stuff.[22]

Are we free to love? Doubtless. Are we free in love? We don't know. Being in love is either freedom itself, or its opposite. And the question is not limited to romantic love. Am I, for instance, free to love dogs? Because my first memories are of dogs, because I confided in them when I was confused and frightened, because mine licked away my earliest tears, am I free in my affection? The reason this sounds silly is that it is silly. The obvious point is that I don't care. Stated philosophically, I have a marked preference for the belief that I actually love dogs. Stated more simply, conditional love is no love at all. And so I love what I love with all the fierceness I can, with every beat of my heart, or not at all.

Wallace's conclusion is simple. "Whether there's '*choice*' involved is, at a certain point, of no interest . . . since it's the very surrender of choice and self that informs the love in the first place" (228). This is radical and right and ultimately his last word on free will and choice. Whatever love is, we do not choose it. In the case of Michael Joyce, it means to "consent to live in a world that, like a child's world, is very serious and very small" (237). Whether Joyce chose the life he is leading cedes to another concern, whether it matters, and whether any of us really chooses.

Wallace doesn't pose the latter question, and professional tennis is admittedly a world unto itself, a special activity, rapturously rich and joyous,

---

[21] Wallace, *A Supposedly Fun Thing I'll Never Do Again: Essays and Arguments* (New York: Little, Brown, 1996), 228.
[22] *A Supposedly Fun Thing*, 228.

as well as potentially limited and limiting on a scale difficult to imagine. Wallace ends his essay on Michael Joyce, "He will say he is happy and mean it. Wish him well" (255). Which is to say, we are free to speculate on the fates of others, about the degree to which others are conditioned by their circumstances and the degree to which they condition those circumstances, but where we should end, ethically, is simple and clear, and everyone has always known it. We should wish them well.

3

A Less "Bullshitty" Way To Live:
The Pragmatic Spirituality of
David Foster Wallace

Robert K. Bolger

All men seek happiness. This is without exception. . . . This is the motive
of every action of every man, even of those who hang themselves.

—Blaise Pascal

Email from Wallace: 7 March 2007

R: Your second paragraph basically sums up my own fidelity to AA. I
feel, think better; I'm less hypersensitive. I'm nicer to people. I'm less
depressed. . . . I wish I could get it as well in other ways (exercise helps, too,
slightly).

/dw/

Philosophical reflection, when it does occur, takes place in the midst of the
warp and woof of everyday life. Much like building a fence in a hurricane,
the philosopher *qua* human must construct arguments with their whole
life whirling and buzzing around them. Even when, as Descartes famously
managed, we can slow life down to practice our philosophical musing alone
by a fire, our past worries and future concerns tend to come along for the
ride. This claim doesn't simply amount to the simplistic fact that thinking is
done by living rational beings (of course that's true); it's rather the substantive
claim that all we are, all we fear, and all we hope for, is brought to bear on
what we think is valid, believe is advantageous, and argue is true. Philosophy,
for better or worse, is a human endeavor, and this fact must not be forgotten
when we are reflecting on an individual's intellectual achievements. I think

something like this must be what the Spanish philosopher Miguel de Unamuno had in mind when he wrote, "In most of the histories of philosophy that I know philosophic systems are presented to us as if growing out of one another spontaneously, and their authors, the philosophers, appear as mere pretexts. The inner biography of the philosophers, of the men [and woman] who philosophized, is assigned a secondary place. And yet it is precisely that inner biography which can mean most to us."[1]

Like all intellectuals—and, in fact, like all of us who are, to use Wallace's term "flesh-sacs"—David Foster Wallace had a life to live. While he was indeed an impressive walking lexicon and accomplished postmodern prophet adored by the literarily savvy Northeast intelligentsia, he was also a friend (of mine), husband, depressed person, lover of tennis, and Alcoholics Anonymous (AA) member. Wallace, at least since his undergraduate days at Amherst, eschewed the pristine world of logic and rationality for descriptions of the contingencies and vicissitudes of human life. His writing oozed the puss of life in all its variety and grossness from consumerism to recovery to depression to boredom. It is this sort of literary pluralism that makes it nearly impossible to ascertain clearly where Wallace's own human stain is bleeding through to the lives of his fictional characters.[2] As with most fiction, the authorial Wallace tends to hide in the shadows with only occasional peeps and pokes through the curtain of language. But that's how it should be right? The writer creates the fiction, which in turn re-creates the writer . . . (repeat till death).

Happily, Wallace's inner biography was not always shrouded behind linguistic subterfuge or post-structuralist word-games; there are times when Wallace thrusts *himself* to the forefront allowing all to view (or listen). This is kenspeckle in his Kenyon College commencement address, later published as *This Is Water*. It is in this work that Wallace presents not only a spiritual way of living, but *his* own spiritual philosophy of life, a philosophy that I believe he tried to live out in his day-to-day existence. A philosophy that also represents his attempt to try and squeeze some modicum of peace from a life that was often fraught with self-doubt and a torturous desire to please. Sadly, his neurotransmitters made maintaining such a view impossible at the end.

---

[1] Miguel de Unamuno, *The Tragic Sense of Life in Men and Nations* (Princeton: Princeton University Press, 1971), 4.

[2] This is true with a bit of a caveat. Surely Wallace's personal life can be seen in some of the recovery and tennis stuff in *Infinite Jest* and we also probably see parts of the philosophy of the real Wallace in the boredom theme in *The Pale King*. The difficulty is that Wallace is so topically diverse that it is hard to tell what is autobiographical to some extent and what is pure fiction (I imagine it is usually an admixture of both).

While *This Is Water* is couched in the folksy language of a quaint commencement address delivered on a hot summer day in a picturesque Ohio town, it contains an account of the process of self-realization that, in some key ways, resembles a fairly straightforward and orthodox explanation of the religious path from self to God. Wallace, in a linear and serial manner, which betrays his wordy and circuitous stylistic tendencies, presents a sort of tripartite theology that begins with an account of the innate problem of human selfishness (an interpretation of the "sinful" human condition), presents a practical way to begin to overcome this "fallen state" (an interpretation of "conversion"), and finally offers suggestions on how we can begin to see the divine presence in the mundane stuff of the world—including in the other people we regularly bump up against (an interpretation of "salvation"). If we wanted to sound a bit more Medieval, we could interpret *This Is Water* as a modern account of the mystical path to God that was spelled out by Dionysius (or maybe Bernard of Clairvaux with some latter emendations by Ignatius) and codified in the concepts of *purgation, illumination,* and *unification*.[3] More probably, however—and as a way of forcing me away from theological speculation—what Wallace offers in *This Is Water* is a sort-of practical/theological account of the program of AA. The recognition of selfishness, the need to learn to turn away from self-obsession and turn toward others, and the traversing of a path that culminates in an ongoing practical experience of a higher power, is something Wallace knew well as an active member of AA, sober for more than fifteen years and the sponsor of many other addicts. Of course, because AA arose out of the context of the Christian holiness movement known as the Oxford Group and under the direct influence of many of the ideas outlined in William James's *Varieties of Religious Experience*, it's no wonder that Wallace's tone is somewhat religious in nature. Whatever Wallace's actual influences, what should not be overlooked is the fact that what he is offering is a set of practical steps (*his* practical steps) that must be applied rather than a series of beliefs that must be assented to.

The speculative nature of the origins and influences of *This Is Water* is not, for better or worse, my concern here; my goal is simply to present Wallace's pragmatic approach to spirituality in a clear way that dissects it into its philosophically and theologically interesting component parts. In doing this, I hope to show the practical reasons for taking Wallace's theology seriously.

---

[3] For a nice discussion of these ideas, see Jean-Marc Laporte, S. J., "Understanding the spiritual journey: from the classical tradition to the Spiritual Exercises of Ignatius," 2009. http://www.jesuits.ca/orientations/stages%20in%20the%20spiritual%20journey.pdf

---

Email from Wallace: 18 October 2005

Work is not going well, and some days I get very depressed and anxious about it. The AA stuff is about the only thing that helps when my thoughts get in obsessive, boring, anxious fear-loops ... I find myself REALLY praying instead of just saying words. ...

X, Dave W.

Email from Wallace: 6 January 2006

I have not written on religion per se—don't know how I would, since even the kimndergarten [sic] stuff in AA seems mindbendingly [sic] complex to me.

Stage setting: Two parables one point

Wallace begins *This Is Water* with a set of parables that, taken together, lay the foundation for the entirety of his argument (if argument is the appropriate term, maybe *presentation* would be more apt). For the sake of simplicity I will refer to the two parables as the "Fish Parable" and the "Eskimo Parable" ("Inuit Parable" for our Canadian friends). First the fish:

> There are these two young fish swimming along and they happen to meet an older fish swimming the other way, who nods at them and says, "Morning, boys. How's the water?" And the two young fish swim on for a bit, and then eventually one of them looks over at the other and goes, "What the hell is water?"[4]

Wallace tells us "clearly" what this parable means: "the immediate point of the fish story is merely that the most obvious, ubiquitous, important realities are often the ones that are hardest to see and talk about."[5] This hermeneutical helpmate, while sufficiently clear (at least as an English sentence goes), is still a bit unsatisfying because we are not yet told what these most "obvious, ubiquitous, important realities" are? What is it that is as close to us as water to fish, so close, that is, that we do not easily recognize its existence? As it turns out, what is so close is not one thing but a variety of things, but more about this as we progress.

---

[4] Wallace, *This Is Water: Some Thoughts, Delivered on a Significant Occasion, about Living a Compassionate Life* (New York: Little, Brown and Company, 2009), 3–4. Kindle Edition.
[5] Wallace, *This is Water*, 8. Kindle Edition.

Now the Eskimo Parable:

There are these two guys sitting together in a bar in the remote Alaskan wilderness. One of the guys is religious, the other's an atheist, and they're arguing about the existence of God. . . . And the atheist says, "Look, it's not like I don't have actual reasons for not believing in God. It's not like I haven't ever experimented with the whole God-and-prayer thing. Just last month, I got caught off away from the camp in that terrible blizzard, and I couldn't see a thing, and I was totally lost, and it was fifty below, and so I did, I tried it: I fell to my knees in the snow and cried out, 'God, if there is a God, I'm lost in this blizzard, and I'm gonna die if you don't help me!'" And now, in the bar, the religious guy looks at the atheist all puzzled: "Well then, you must believe now," he says. "After all, here you are, alive." The atheist rolls his eyes like the religious guy is a total simp: "No, man, all that happened was that a couple Eskimos just happened to come wandering by and they showed me the way back to the camp."[6]

Wallace, recognizing that his audience is composed of a bunch of freshly minted graduating college kids from one of America's premiere liberal arts colleges (what old people and the middle-aged like to call "know-it-alls"), is keenly aware that some may simply take this parable as another hackneyed example of the fact that a single event is open to multiple interpretations ("my truth is not your truth," "everything is relative," yada, yada, yada). Wallace responds that such an interpretation is fine, "except we also never end up talking about just where these individual templates and beliefs come from, meaning, where they come from *inside* the two guys. . . . As if how we construct meaning were not actually a matter of personal, intentional choice, of conscious decision. Plus, there's the matter of arrogance."[7] This little, seemingly insignificant, response to the liberal arts simp (to use Wallace's shortened version of simpleton) actually turns out to be quite important for Wallace's overall project, for it is in this response that Wallace shows the intimate link between the possibility of epistemological freedom (the freedom to choose how we interpret certain events, i.e., the Eskimo Parable) and the ontological price we pay for being human (the things that are hardest to recognize while being the "most obvious, ubiquitous, important realities", i.e., human "arrogance").[8] Here is the same point made with a bit more perspicuity.

[6] Ibid., 17–23. Kindle Edition.
[7] Ibid., 26. Kindle Edition.
[8] There is lot of philosophical dispute swimming in these waters; at the forefront are issues about whether or not we can freely choose our beliefs.

If constructing meaning is a matter of forming beliefs about the world by peering through an inner "interpretive filter," and if we are *free* to choose (with certain normative constraints) which beliefs we are going to entertain and which beliefs we are going to ignore, then it appears that we can *both* freely choose to see the world in a variety of ways (some ways being less stress-producing than others) and we can disregard (or change) our "interpretive filter." This freedom to choose how we interpret certain aspects of reality is the *epistemological* point Wallace is making in the Eskimo parable. But this is not the whole story. It may be that there is something that is part and parcel of being human, something so close to our nature that—like our noses—we rarely notice, but something that is also capable of frustrating and thwarting our *actual* freedom to choose how we interpret reality. This is the *ontological* point of the Fish Parable. Wallace's whole argument, as well as his move toward a pragmatic spirituality, rests on these two issues: epistemological freedom and ontological constraint. And it is, according to Wallace, when we recognize the latter (ontological constraint) that we begin to learn to practice the former (epistemological freedom). So what is as close to us as water to a fish? It is our *ability* to choose and our *inability* to choose how we interpret the things that happen around us every day. It is this paradox that must be investigated.

Email from Wallace: 22 April 2006

I don't take rejection well, either. My ego is very large and fragile. I think one idea behind AA is that it helps make our egos slightly smaller and also slightly denser, more resilient and immune to Shattering from the rejections/criticisms that come to everyone at times. I.e., the end goal is Reduced Suffering.

/dw/

The epistemic effects of a life curved inward

In his book *Saving God*, Mark Johnston describes the propensity of humans to prefer their own needs and desires over those of others by referencing Kant's concept of "radical evil." Johnston writes:

> Kant's doctrine that we are radically evil is not the doctrine that we are
> bad to the bone, bad through and through; it is the manifestly true claim

that there is something at the root of human nature that disposes each one of us to favor himself or herself over the others . . . this is something in the very structure of our consciousness, a profound asymmetry of the evaluational affect, which privileges what is HERE over those things THERE.[9]

In *This Is Water*, Wallace presents a view of human selfishness that has some affinities with Kant's idea of "radical evil." The initial challenge in Wallace's discussion is getting clear about just what he is claiming because he, like Kant, is actually making two different but intimately related points. Wallace writes:

Think about it: There is no experience you've had that you were not the absolute center of. The world as you experience it is there in front of you, or behind you, to the left or right of you, on your TV, or your monitor or whatever. Other people's thoughts and feelings have to be communicated, but your own are so immediate, urgent real. You get the idea.[10]

I do indeed, but this does not yet get us anywhere near "radical evil"; it only describes a cursory and obvious fact about what it means to be human. A simple statement about the privacy of personal experience (or what Lynne Rudder Baker refers to as the "first-person perspective")[11] does not *entail* that the conscious person having the experience is selfish. These first-person statements are true for all human beings, but it is also obviously true that I may use my first-person point of view to help meet others' needs. I may decide to give my life in service for others or even die trying to save another person's life with absolutely no regard for my own well-being. Again, the mere fact that human consciousness *essentially* entails a first-person perspective does not itself *necessitate* selfishness (if it did, handicapped parking spaces would be fruitless). Wallace seems to understand this fact in *This Is Water* when he notes, "Everything in my own immediate experience supports my deep belief that I am the absolute center of the universe, the realest, most vivid and important person in existence."[12] Much like Kant's account of radical evil, Wallace's selfishness, while being parasitic on the fact of human consciousness, also claims that such a privileged point of view lends itself quite naturally to bending all of our thoughts and interests inward on themselves (*incurvatus in se*). We begin to think that *our* interests, *our* wants, and *our*

---

[9] Mark Johnston, *Surviving Death* (Princeton: Princeton University Press), 157–8.
[10] Wallace, *This is Water*, 39–42. Kindle Edition.
[11] See, Lynne Rudder Baker, *Naturalism and the First-Person Perspective* (Oxford: Oxford University Press, 2013).
[12] Ibid., 36.

needs are *the most important* things in the world. We may call this idea *innate selfishness*, "innate" because as Wallace describes it, this is the "default setting" most human beings operate on. Here is how Wallace describes the situation: "It's the automatic, unconscious way that I experience the boring, frustrating, crowded parts of adult life when I'm operating on the automatic, unconscious belief that I am the center of the world and that my immediate needs and feelings are what should determine the world's priorities."[13] Here is the same sort of thing in the words of *Alcoholics Anonymous*: "Selfishness—self-centeredness! That, we think, is the root of our troubles. Driven by a hundred forms of fear, self-delusion, self-seeking, and self-pity, we step on the toes of our fellows and they retaliate."[14]

This account of selfishness is not benign; it rather has very real and practical consequences for the way we live our lives. Here is how this works. Wallace asks us to imagine a seemingly normal trip to the grocery store, one that adults living in the humdrum, Déjà vu-like repetitive nature of day-to-day existence tend to experience *ad infinitum*. Wallace then points out a variety of ways in which this seemingly mundane trip to the market can, if we are aware of our thoughts, reveal to us just how automatic, how annoyingly natural, and how cunningly ubiquitous our selfish thinking tends to be.

Wallace's description of shopping for supper ("supper" being Wallace's homey Midwest synonym for what coastal people call "dinner") involves a litany of normal activities: bad traffic, crowds at the store, aisles filled with tired people, and ADHD kids blocking the way. When we finally do make it to the checkout, we are met with a hideously long Disneyland-like line, people talking on their cell phones and, at the end, a cashier's farewell that Wallace describes as "a voice that is the absolute voice of death." The point is that if we let our "default setting" do the job of interpreting these events (and it does so quite effortlessly), we end up focusing endlessly on "I" and "me" and "mine," the end result being certain frustration and anger. Wallace continues:

> If I don't make a conscious decision about how to think and what to pay attention to, I'm gonna be pissed and miserable every time I have to food shop, because my natural default setting is that situations like this are really all about me, about my hungriness and my fatigue and my desire to just get home, and it's going to seem, for all the world, like everybody is just *in my way*, and who the fuck are all these people in my way?[15]

---

[13] Ibid., 83.
[14] Anonymous, *Alcoholics Anonymous*, 4th edn (New York: Alcoholics Anonymous World Services Inc., 2009), 62.
[15] Wallace, *This Is Water*, 77. Kindle Edition. Emphasis in the original.

Wallace's point is interesting because he makes a distinction between how the world is and how we perceive it to be when we look at it through the lens of selfishness. It is not that everyone else is *actually* in my way or *really* out to make my trip miserable, it is just that when my focus is on my own little plans and desires, this is how things appear; these are the beliefs I automatically form. My beliefs create a reality, a reality that drives me to frustration, but these beliefs are not necessarily true; they are just beliefs filtered through a selfish narrative.

In Wallace's first novel *The Broom of the System*, Jay asks, "The truth is there's no difference between a life and a story? But a life pretends to be something more? But it really isn't more?" Wallace, in *This Is Water*, answers Jay in the affirmative. Wallace writes, "If you're automatically sure that you know what reality is and who and what is really important—if you want to operate on your default setting—then you, like me, probably will not consider possibilities that aren't pointless and annoying. But if you've really learned how to think, how to pay attention, then you will know that you have other options."[16]

Our lives are lived through the filter of stories that we've either been born into, been educated into, or simply come to accept as true, but the stories can always be changed. Stories themselves are not true or false; they are rather the contexts in which statements are judged as true or false. It is not that other possibilities are not possible; it is just that given the apparatus that is helping form some of our beliefs—that is, our own selfishness—these other possibilities are simply not available without some story-changing work being done. The Buddhist scholar David Loy writes, "concepts in themselves are fragments, meaningful as parts of stories. . . . We do not see our stories as stories because we see through them: the world we experience is constructed with them."[17] We may call these stories "life-orienting stories" (following philosopher David Holley), "forms of life" (following Wittgenstein), or simply "world-views"; the important point is to remember that it is from these stories that our beliefs about the world arise. Loy writes, "Our joys and sorrow, laughter and tears, pleasures and pains, loves and fears, epiphanies and despairs—all are storied. They are meaningful within the context of a narrative."[18] In a more overtly theological context, David Holley writes, "people who believe in God are convinced, not by a process of reasoning from publicly available evidence to the conclusion that God exists, but

---

[16] Ibid., 91–2. Kindle Edition.
[17] David Loy, *The World is Made of Stories* (Somerville, MA: Wisdom Publication, 2010), Loc. 17. Kindle Edition.
[18] Ibid., Loc. 225. Kindle Edition.

by a *narrative* vision in which the idea of God plays a fundamental role. When they are able to use this *narrative* to orient themselves in life by discerning the kinds of significance it highlights, the conception of reality it presupposes become believable."[19] When we operate from within a default setting of selfishness, other epistemic possibilities become difficult at best and impossible at worst. Selfishness has epistemic consequences because we naturally have a narrative in place telling us that we are "the absolute center of the universe, the realest, most vivid and important person in existence."

But that's not all; innate selfishness also has pragmatic effects, effects that I refer to as *practical solipsism*. If we take solipsism to be the belief that we are the only things in the world that really exist and all else is a mere figment of my (*really real*) mind, then I submit that there are probably very few real solipsists. But solipsism can be more sinister. If I believe that my needs are more important than the needs of others and that others are simply obstacles in my way then I have, for all practical purposes, cut myself off from being able to see others as *really real*. When we operate on our default setting, other people become mere objects: obstacles to be overcome and babbling entities to be endured. What we have lost is the ability to see other people as people. I as the *really real* am all alone in a world of objects, objects that are constantly thwarting my plans. This type of judgment about the worth of others alienates us from them. Richard Rohr writes, "The small 'I' [ego] knows itself by comparison. . . . As long as were comparing and differentiating from the other, we can't love the other. We judge it."[20] This is why Wallace can tell the group of graduating students assembled in front of him that the real "no-shit value of your liberal arts education is supposed to be about: How to keep from going through your comfortable, prosperous, respectable adult life dead, unconscious, a slave to your head and to your natural default setting of being uniquely, completely, *imperially alone*, day in and day out."[21] This type of aloneness is existential not ontological and it is something that probably should be overcome if we are going to live fulfilling happy lives.

Wallace instinctively seemed to recognize the importance of other people. In an email where I had mentioned how much I liked the Philip Larkin poem "Aubade," Wallace wrote, "Larkin is often bleaker 'on the surface' than he really is (for instance, what do you make of the last line? Notice that the dreadful fear of death afflicts him most when he's ALONE. Is there

---

[19] David M. Holley, *Meaning and Mystery: What it Means to Believe in God* (Malden, MA: Wiley-Blackwell, 2010), 5. Emphasis added.
[20] Richard Rohr, *Everything Belongs* (New York: The Crossroad Publishing Company, 1999), 55.
[21] Wallace, *This Is Water*, 60. Kindle Edition. Emphasis added.

some suggestion that 'treatment' for the fear (not for the death, which is unstoppable) consists of interhuman connection? Is the last line not hopeful, in some way?"[22] Connecting with others, however, is impossible until we can restore a relationship whereby we look upon them with a certain amount of care, respect, or even love. In order for this to happen, a certain conversion away from selfishness must take place.

Email from Wallace: 17 January 2006

We're quite alike, so I know it's true: you have them [T. S. Eliot-like "tremors of bliss"] all the time. The trick is noticing them, which requires thinking less and trying to notice more. It's very hard. This kind of awareness appears to me to be the real goal (and perhaps the promised "4th Dimension") of the sort of spirituality with which AA is concerned. But they really are there all the time; think about it: The anglre [sic] of light through a bus window at certain times, the feeling of the the [sic] first swallow of water when you're thirsty, the [sight of our wives] doing something small that delights you without her knowing, etc. All sorts of tremors. The good days are the days I'm awake and aware enough to feel them.

Overcoming epistemic obstacles:
Or, how to care about the stranger

Wallace's suggestion for overcoming the epistemological and solipsistic effects of innate selfishness is twofold. First, we must learn to be aware enough of our thoughts to recognize that some of our beliefs are utterly selfish and, quite possibly, wrong. This involves an act of attentive awareness to what we think and a certain amount of epistemic humility about what we think we are certain of. Second, we must be able to *make up* (or construct) a set of new and "plausible" stories about other people that acknowledges not only their right to exist but also explains why they justifiably do the things they do and act the way they act.[23] In short, we must develop *compassion* for other people. This sort of stuff—humility and compassion—is rarely an act of

---

[22] Personal email, 20 October 2005.
[23] Of course, these types of stories will have their limits. We do not want to justify all acts to the point where there is no real culpability for behavior that is truly harmful.

simple ratiocination but more likely the product of our will. Because these
ideas form the guts of Wallace's way of overcoming the browbeating effects of
selfishness, I should say a bit more about them.

When Wallace talks of "paying attention," he is not simply referring
to concentrating harder on what is going on around us but rather paying
attention to what is going on inside of us. He says, "Probably the most
dangerous thing about an academic education, at least in my own case, is
that it enables my tendency to over-intellectualize stuff. To get lost in abstract
thinking instead of simply paying attention to what's going on in front of me.
Instead of paying attention to what's going on *inside* me."[24] Of course, we have
already seen that the type of thinking going on inside us is (often) tainted by
innate selfishness; nevertheless, it's good to remember that innate selfishness
is also something arising from our storied lives and is therefore under our
volition. So paying "attention" for Wallace isn't simply some sort of New Age
faux-Buddhism; it isn't the "attention for attention's sake" stuff like feeling the
heat of the mug of tea we are drinking or being acutely and painfully aware
of each and every bite and chew of our meal. Wallace is talking about being
on the lookout for thoughts that automatically and ferociously preference
our desires and our needs over those of others. If we recognize these beliefs as
selfish byproducts of our humanity, then we may be able to *will* other beliefs
in their place.

What we are being asked to do is no less than "die to ourselves." It is
learning to practice a little bit of epistemological humility. We are being asked
to jettison our cocksureness that we are absolutely correct and entertain the
possibility that we may not know everything (even things we are sure we
know). Wallace continues, "The point here is that I think this is one part of
what the liberal arts mantra of 'teaching me how to think' is really supposed
to mean: to be just a little less arrogant, to have some 'critical awareness'
about myself and my certainties . . . because a huge percentage of the stuff
that I tend to be automatically certain of is, it turns out, totally wrong and
deluded."[25] If we can recognize—really recognize—our epistemic fallibility,
we will begin to open the door to considering other possibilities, considering
that there just may be some really good explanations for why other people
are shopping, driving, walking their dog, and working out at the exact
moment I decide to do the same. Our attentiveness to our beliefs permits us
to be open to a plurality of epistemic possibilities; that is, we can tell stories
that explain and justify others' actions, and, if we can consider some of these

---

[24] Wallace, *This Is Water*, 48–9. Kindle Edition. Emphasis in original.
[25] Ibid., 33. Kindle Edition.

stories as if they are *really* possible (but not necessarily true), we may be able to short-circuit our selfish default-setting allowing us to reboot (to keep the computer analogy going) the system as a whole [BTW: does anybody *reboot* anything anymore?]).

In *Everything Belongs*, Richard Rohr writes, "As we observe our mental and emotional flow over a period of disciplined time, we recognize that we largely create our own experiences. . . . We have the power to decide what the moment means and how we will respond to it. We have the power when we have the ability to respond freely. We can decide if we're going to respond to something hatefully or lovingly."[26] Compare Rohr's ideas to the following two statements from Wallace:

> "Learning how to think" really means learning how to exercise some control over *how* and *what* you think. It means being conscious and aware enough to choose what you pay attention to and to choose how you construct meaning from experience.
>
> The really important kind of freedom involves attention, and awareness, and discipline, and effort, and being able truly to care about other people . . .[27]

If the freedom to choose a new story is within our capabilities, then, simply on pragmatic grounds (e.g., choosing a belief for its advantageous results), we may want to begin to change the way we think about others. David Loy, employing a version of the Fish Parable, writes, "Like the proverbial fish who cannot see the water they swim in, we do not notice the medium we dwell within. Unaware that our stories are stories, we experience them as the world. But we can change the water. When our accounts of the world become different the world becomes different."[28]

Now let's harken back to the drudgery of the people who had the nerve to cohabit with us at the supermarket making our life (at least momentarily) miserable. Wallace, recognizing that his opinion of their existence flows from his own selfishness, realizes he can freely choose to change the story.

> [I]f you're aware enough to give yourself a choice, you can choose to look differently at this fat, dead-eyed, over-made-up lady who just screamed at her kid in the checkout line—maybe she's not usually like this; maybe she's been up three straight nights holding the hand of her husband, who's dying of bone cancer, or maybe this very lady is the low-wage

---

[26] Rohr, *Everything Belongs*, 91.
[27] Wallace, *This Is Water*, 53–4, 120. Kindle Edition. Emphasis in original.
[28] Loy, *The Word is Made of Stories*, Loc. 59. Kindle Edition.

clerk at the motor vehicles department who just yesterday helped your spouse resolve a nightmarish red-tape problem through some small act of bureaucratic kindness. Of course, none of this is likely, but it's not impossible—it just depends what you want to consider.[29]

Regarding the traffic problems encountered on the freeway and the maddeningly gigantic gas guzzling vehicles that race through traffic with little care for basic safety, Wallace says, "In this traffic, all these vehicles stuck and idling in my way: It's not impossible that some of these people in SUVs have been in horrible auto accidents in the past and now find driving so traumatic that their therapist has all but ordered them to get a huge, heavy SUV so they can feel safe enough to drive; or that the Hummer that just cut me off is maybe being driven by a father whose little child is hurt or sick in the seat next to him, and he's trying to rush to the hospital."[30]

This sort of "self-deception" is Wallace's Eskimo Parable in practice. If we realize that those beliefs that separate us from others are simply the manifestation of innate selfishness, then we can begin to tell ourselves new stories that not only respect others' right to exist but also release us from the petty frustrations that consume us at a gut level.

While this suggestion appears trivial and simplistic, it isn't. Our selfishness is so ingrained and natural that thinking in a new, non-selfish way takes an act of the will. This is made even more difficult by the fact that we do not choose most of our beliefs. But Wallace isn't simply proposing that we reinterpret the events of life in order to create beliefs we can *justify* as true. He is asking us to create sensible epistemic possibilities (tell ourselves new stories) *that could be true for all we know*. These are possibilities that, if true, would allow us to be less frustrated and more peaceful. This is close to what William James has in mind when he writes, "Pragmatism, on the other hand, asks its usual question. 'Grant an idea or belief to be true,' it says, 'what concrete difference will its being true make in anyone's actual life? How will the truth be realized? What experiences will be different from those that would obtain if the belief were false? What, in short, is the truth's cash-value in experiential terms?'"[31] The conversion that Wallace is advocating is conversion *away* from ourselves, but it is also a conversion that we bring about volitionally and possibly circularly; we create new beliefs and change our inner narrative, which changes our beliefs, which . . . you get the idea. This process is an acceptance of what many in AA call accepting "life on life's

[29] Wallace, *This Is Water*, 89. Kindle Edition.
[30] Ibid., 85.
[31] William James, *Pragmatism* (New York: Barnes and Noble, 2003), 87–8.

terms," and it may have repercussions for our sanity. An earlier defender of AA, psychiatrist Henry Tiebout writes,

> When an individual surrenders, the ability to accept reality functions on the unconscious level, and there is no residual of battle; relaxation with freedom from strain and conflict ensues. In fact, it is perfectly possible to ascertain how much acceptance of reality is on the unconscious level by the degree of relaxation that develops. The greater the relaxation, the greater the inner acceptance of reality.[32]

Email from Wallace: 22 October 2005

I think this is it; I think you've got it. It's not overcoming the in[d]ividual ego's terror of annihilation. It is somehow cathecting enough other people and enough of the world that we identify, less and less, with the individual ego—that we literally care more about the universe than about our own flesh-sac and its needs. Cathxis of and identification with God yiel[d]s "immortality," since the part of us that is or is-in God can clearl[y] not be a[n]nihilated the way the individual ego can.

It's like the old joke: Q: What did the mystic say to the hot dog vendor? A: Make me one with everything.

Very, very hard to actually do, in my experience. Especially because it's not intellectual but rather attitudinal, existential. But each minute bit of progress yields hugely disproportionate gains in terms of less fear, less depression, less loneliness. And minu[t]e bits of progress appear to be what we're in AA to make, once physical sobriety is accomplished.

X, Dave W.

Seeing and the sacred

In *The Brothers Karamazov*, Dostoyevsky writes,

> Love people even in their sin, for that is the semblance of Divine Love and is the highest love on earth. Love all of God's creation, the whole and every grain of sand of it. Love every leaf, every ray of God's light. Love

---

[32] Henry M. Tiebout M. D., "The Act of Surrender in the Therapeutic Process," http://www.thejaywalker.com/pages/tiebout/actofsurrender.html

the animals, love the plants, love everything. If you love everything, you will perceive the divine mystery in things. Once you perceive it, you will begin to comprehend it better every day. And you will come at last to love the whole world with an all-embracing love.[33]

In my previous book *Kneeling at the Altar of Science*, I called this sort of view of religious belief a "religious stance" writing that

The religious stance can be defined as an attitude taken towards the facts of existence whereby the believer interprets these facts as being imbued with grace and love. In a sense this is a way of seeing the world *sub specie aeternitatis*. The religious believer sees the whole of existence as interrelated, not because quantum physics has proven this but because such an interpretation is part and parcel of the fact that this world, with all its foibles, is—for the believer—*God's* world. The direction of seeing is reversed. We do not passively *see* what is there; rather we *interpret* what is there.[34]

These quotations appear to be odds. Dostoevsky is claiming that learning to take a stance of love toward others is a sort of precondition for perceiving the divine mystery in things while I am claiming that we love others *because* we see the world already imbued with divinity. I think both of us are correct, and to see why, let's turn back briefly to Wallace.

In the section above, I mentioned that a Wallacian theology sees that one way we can begin to burrow out of our selfishness is to begin to tell another story about the people we plod around with on this planet. Again, these stories need not be true—who cares about truth when our peace of mind is on the line? The main thing is that such stories should create a sort of "meta-narrative" that justifies other individual's existence and actions. We tell ourselves stories of compassion.

Let's call the attitude we take in these "self-deceptive" stories "faux-love" (or fluv for short). Now fluv is not love but a temporary substitute for love. We tell stories of compassion that involve our fluving others; that is, we tell stories that look and sound as if we care for others' needs and concerns at least as much as we care about our own. What we are really doing is bypassing our default setting. Now here's the rub, if we continue to tell fluving stories about others we may actually be able to transform our fluv

---

[33] Fyodor Dostoyevsky, *The Brothers Karamazov* quoted in Rohr, *Everything Belongs*, 27.
[34] Robert Bolger, *Kneeling at the Altar of Science: The Mistaken Path of Contemporary Religious Scientism* (Eugene, Ore.: Wipf and Stock Publishers, 2012), 131.

into something like real love (or at least true compassion).[35] Here is how this might work.

Pretend you are a hypochondriac who believes every ache, every little pain, and every small twinge that occurs in your body is a sign of a heart attack, terminal cancer, or another horrendous disease that will result in your demise.[36] After years of therapy your doctor convinces you to speak to your pains and body aches as if they were alive, letting them know that you are on to their trick to scare you and declaring that you know their pranks are harmless and ineffective (you are then to let out two hardy chuckles "Ha Ha!"). While you think this makes you look somewhat sicker than you were when you started therapy, you begin to take the Doc's advice.

At first with some trepidation you tell the mild ache in your chest that you are not fooled nor are you scared, "Ha, Ha." As the months go by, you get better and better at this "Ha-Ha-ing." You continue it whenever you feel the crushing anxiety that death is imminent—in the car, at work, at church, in a boat, on a goat, etc. One day you realize you've had a variety of twinges and pangs *without* the debilitating anxiety. No anxiety, no fear! You feel better and you no longer interpret or believe that pain=death/disease. Now of course, your real cure started with a fake story (a lie even, since pains can't hear you talking to them!), a story that got ingrained into your belief system and changed your world.[37]

Couldn't the same type of thing happen with the fluving stories we tell about others? Wallace says, "The really important kind of freedom involves attention, and awareness, and discipline, and effort, and being able truly to care about other people and to sacrifice for them, over and over, in myriad petty little unsexy ways, every day."[38] Earlier he notes that if we learn how to think compassionately "[i]t will actually be within your power to experience a crowded, hot, slow, consumer-hell-type situation as not only meaningful, but sacred, on fire with the same force that lit the stars—compassion, love, the subsurface unity of all things."[39] But these things are instances of real

---

[35] Obviously, this is meant to apply to cases where a loving relation is already presumed to exist. I take it that most of us don't fluv our spouse on our wedding day and hope that after some time of telling fluving stories about them to ourselves we will come to love them.

[36] Alright, since we are being honest here I should admit that this part is autobiographical. For whatever reason I have been afraid of death since I was a child and, due to this fear of death, I have never been a fan of ailments that could bring about my own demise.

[37] Incidentally, something like this sort of "fake it till you make it" philosophy is what Wallace describes as happening to Don Gately when Gately one day realizes he no longer is craving drugs. See Wallace, *Infinite Jest* (New York: Hachette Book Group, 2009), 349.

[38] Wallace, *This is Water*, p. 119. Kindle Edition.

[39] Ibid., p. 93.

love (not fluv); they are instances where we sacrifice for others on a regular basis and where we feel unified with all reality (including other people). These types of feelings, however, can only come if the ego is deflated, if our default setting is short-circuited. If we feel alienated and angry with others, it is going to be very hard to sacrifice for them and nearly impossible to feel we are a part (with them) of something greater. Now let's revisit my dispute with Dostoevsky.

Earlier I said that it seemed that Dostoevsky in *The Brothers Karamazov* encourages us to begin to love other people and in this state of constantly choosing to love we will begin to "perceive the divine mystery in things." In an earlier work, I seemed to insist that if we already believe in a divine presence that imbues reality, we would (as part of this belief) take a religious stance toward all of creation. While these seem incompatible, they really aren't. It may simply be that Dostoevsky is admonishing us to take an attitude of love toward others even if we don't really love them (he is asking us to fluv them), and in that process (over a period of time), the fake love may just be replaced with real love, which leads, ultimately, to seeing others as the divine does. My discussion, on the other hand, begins already with the presumption that someone has taken a religious stance toward reality and then suggests that this stance is partly manifested in our "loving our neighbors as ourselves." Either way what we get is a spiritual point of view that involves an active choice to look on reality in a certain way, and this, I contend, is also what we get in Wallace. This is not a religion of believing certain propositions; it is not doctrinal and not metaphysical. It is an interpretive spirituality, a sort of "seeing-as" (following Wittgenstein).[40]

Before anyone thinks that Wallace is just being cute or pithy presenting a sort of folk-spirituality, they should think again. In her book *Practical Mysticism*, Evelyn Underhill writes, "Mysticism is the art of union with Reality. The mystic is a person who has attained that union in greater or less degree; or who aims at and believes in such attainment."[41] The key is not getting too caught up in what a unified reality amounts to; this is mysticim after all not metaphysics. Later, attempting to explain what the novice mystic is committed to, Underhill writes,

> All that he is asked to consider now is this: that the word "union" represents not so much a rare and unimaginable operation, as something which he is doing, in a vague, imperfect fashion, at every moment of his

---

[40] See Ludwig Wittgenstein, *Philosophical Investigations*, trans. G. E. M. Anscombe, eds. P. M. S. Hacker, and Joachim Schulte, revised 4th edn (Chichester, West Sussex: Wiley-Blackwell, 2009), II.

[41] Evelyn Underhill, *Practical Mysticism*, Loc. 105. Kindle edition.

conscious life; and doing with intensity and thoroughness in all the more valid moments of that life. We know a thing only by uniting with it; by assimilating it; by an interpenetration of it and ourselves.[42]

Finally, Richard Rohr, considered by many a contemporary Catholic Mystic,[43] writes, "In Mature Religion, the secular becomes sacred. There are no longer two worlds. We no longer have to leave the secular world to find sacred space because they've come together."[44] If this sort of unification of reality is part of the historic mystical tradition, then I think it is clear that Wallace is presenting a sort of practical mysticism that places him squarely in a long tradition. To think otherwise is to misread (or misrepresent) what he is saying.[45]

The fish prequel

Wallace's use of the Fish Parable in *This Is Water* is not the story's first appearance. In *Infinite Jest*, the parable is told in a context that may be enlightening for our purposes here.

The telling of the parable in *Infinite Jest* is preceded by Don Gately's appearing at the podium in an AA meeting telling others how difficult of a time he is having finding a "God of his own understanding." Wallace writes, "His [Gately's] sole experience so far is that he takes one of AA's very rare specific suggestions and hits the knees in the A.M. and asks for Help and then hits the knees again at bedtime and says Thank You, whether he believes he's talking to Anything/body or not, *and he somehow gets through that day clean*."[46] He later continues, "when he [Gately] tries to go beyond the very basic rote automatic get-me-through-the-day-please stuff, when he kneels at other times and prays or meditates or tries to achieve a Big-Picture spiritual understanding of a God as he can understand Him, he feels Nothing—not

---

[42] Ibid., Loc. 112, Kindle Edition.
[43] See his book, *The Naked Now: How to See as the Mystics See* (Spring Valley, NY: The Crossroads Publishing Company, 2009).
[44] Rohr, *Everything Belongs*, 134.
[45] I think something like this is what is happening in the chapter on Wallace in *All Things Shining: Reading the Western Classics to Find Meaning in a Secular Age*, by Hubert Dreyfus and Sean Dorrance Kelly (New York: Free Press, 2011). In this book, Wallace's spiritual insights are presented as being out of touch with other historically significant religious thinkers. He is shown as a sort of pop-culture self-help simpleton. I take this as another instance (much like Richard Dawkins, Sam Harris, and the other "new atheists") of intellectuals believing they are experts in fields outside of their own. The authors simply auditing a class in "Introduction to Theology" at Harvard Divinity School would have corrected this error.
[46] Wallace, *Infinite Jest*, 443. Emphasis added.

nothing but *Nothing*."[47] It is in the context of Gately's apparent inability to make intellectual sense of the "God thing" while, oddly enough, experiencing the practical success of sobriety as the result of following rote religious practices, that Wallace inserts the Fish Parable. After the meeting is over, a biker guy thanks Gately for his share[48] and asks if "he's heard the one about the fish."[49] The biker then says, "This wise old whiskery fish[50] swims up to three young fish and goes, 'Morning boys, how's the water?' and swims away; and the three young fish watch him swim away and look at each other and go, 'What the fuck is water?' and swim away."[51] This all seems a bit cryptic and gnostic because Wallace does not further comment on this tale. The biker just shrugs and drives off. But I think, given the context in which the parable is placed, no further comment is necessary. Gately's struggle was to find a Higher Power that existed *outside* of his life; that is, outside of the rote religious actions he performed. He desired a higher power that was more than the simple rote stuff *plus* the benefit of daily sobriety. But he was looking too far away. If Gately had noticed what was right in front of him—that is, the fact that the rote prayers had the pragmatic effect of keeping him sober—he would have seen his higher power in action; Gately didn't have a God-finding problem, he had a God-concept problem.

In the appendix entitled "Spiritual Experience" in the book *Alcoholics Anonymous*, the author writes:

> Most of our experiences are what the psychologist William James calls the 'educational variety' because they develop slowly over a period of time. Quite often friends of the newcomer are aware of the difference long before he is himself. He finally realizes that he has undergone a profound alteration in his reaction to life; that such a change could hardly have been brought about by himself alone. What often takes place in a few months could seldom have been accomplished by years of self-discipline. With few exceptions our members find that they have tapped an unsuspected inner resource which they presently identify with their own conception of a Power greater than themselves.[52]

---

[47] Ibid. Emphasis in the original.

[48] The use of "share" is important since it invokes the personal nature of what Gately had to say from the podium. Gately was not giving a talk, he was sharing his experience.

[49] Wallace, *Infinite Jest*, 445.

[50] Interestingly in *This Is Water*, Wallace clearly states he is not the wise old fish. I take it he knew his audience well enough to know that these kids at Kenyon did not want (or need) to be told what to do by this disheveled, nervousy-type author from Pomona.

[51] Wallace, *This Is Water*, 445.

[52] Anonymous, *Alcoholics Anonymous*, 567.

This is exactly what Wallace presents in Gately, and it is exactly what the biker was trying to get Gately to see by relating to him the Fish Parable. The lesson seems to be that the further we look for the divine, the harder it is to locate. There are times when Wallace equates water with our own innate selfishness or our ability to change our meta-story; we may, however, justifiably begin to see that a spiritual life lived in the presence of God and in union with reality is as close to us as water is to a fish. What we need is to be told just where and how to look. Maybe *This Is Water* is Wallace's secular equivalent of "The Kingdom of God is Within You" or his form of secular mysticism. Whatever it is, I think it is certainly a less "bullshitty" way to live.

4

This Is Water and Religious Self-Deception

Kevin Timpe

Of water and Eskimos

In the spring of 2005, David Foster Wallace offered the commencement speech at Kenyon College, which was soon widely reproduced across the internet.[1] It contains a forceful warning against intellectual arrogance and about the need to "exercise control over *how* and *what* you think" (53, emphasis original). Wallace began his speech with the following parable:

> There are these two young fish swimming along and they happen to meet an older fish swimming the other way, who nods at them and says, "Morning, boys. How's the water?" And the two young fish swim on for a bit, and then eventually one of them looks over at the other and goes, "What the hell is water?"
>
> This is a standard requirement of US commencement speeches, the deployment of didactic little parable-ish stories. The story thing turns out to be one of the better, less bullshitty conventions of the genre[,] . . . but if you're worried that I plan to present myself here as the wise, older fish explaining what water is to you younger fish, please don't be. I am not the wise old fish. The point of the fish story is merely that the most obvious, important realities are often the ones that are hardest to see and talk about. (3–8)

While he's aware that this last sentence expresses "a banal platitude" (9), he also thinks that platitudes such as this can still carry significant importance. While I don't want to suggest that this theme—that "the most obvious,

---

[1] After his death in 2008, this speech was published as *This Is Water: Some Thoughts, Delivered on a Significant Occasion, about Living a Compassionate Life* (New York: Little, Brown, & Co., 2009). All subsequent references to "*This Is Water*" will be made parenthetically and will refer to this printing.

important realities are often the ones that are hardest to see and talk about"—
is the only, or even the most, important part of Wallace's address,[2] in the
following pages I will take this theme as my focus. More specifically, I will
apply this theme to the issue of self-deception and argue that self-deception
is often one of the most important issues we face, even if it's among the
hardest to see. Furthermore, while I think these lessons apply to all kinds
of beliefs, I want to look in particular at religious self-deception. I'm well
aware that Wallace didn't write much explicitly on religion and that it comes
up only peripherally in his commencement address.[3] Nevertheless, I think
that Wallace's plea for intellectual humility has important lessons that many
religious believers (among others) could benefit from.

As Wallace explains the work he wants the fish parable to do, he's interested
in the value of learning how to think. By this, he doesn't mean learning what
to think (that is, learning to think x, y, and z) so much as "the choice of what
to think about" (14). He follows up the fish parable with a related story of two
men talking in a bar in the Alaskan wilderness:

> One of the guys is religious, the other is an atheist, and they're arguing
> about the existence of God with that special intensity that comes after
> about the fourth beer. And the atheist says: "Look, it's not like I don't
> have actual reasons for not believing in God. It's not like I haven't ever
> experimented with the whole God-and-prayer thing. Just last month
> I got caught away from the camp in that terrible blizzard, and I was
> totally lost and I couldn't see a thing, and it was fifty below, and so
> I did, I tried it: I fell to my knees in the snow and cried out 'God, if
> there is a God, I'm lost in this blizzard, and I'm gonna die if you don't
> help me.'"
>
> And now, in the bar, the religious guy looks at the atheist all puzzled:
> "Well then, you must believe now," he says. "After all, here you are, alive."

---

[2] For example, I think that Wallace makes a number of important points regarding the
value of a liberal arts education, particularly when the larger culture continues to see a
university education as increasingly about job prospects.

[3] Despite the fact that religion isn't a central theme in the address, Wallace does give a
passing remark that shows, rightly in my view, that religion isn't as far from his central
theme as one might think: "This, I submit, is the freedom of a real education, of learning
how to be well-adjusted: you get to consciously decide what has meaning and what
doesn't. You get to decide what to worship. . . . Because here's something else that's true.
In the day-to-day trenches of adult life, there is actually no such thing as atheism. There
is no such thing as not worshipping. Everybody worships. The only choice we get is
what to worship" (95–101, emphasis original). Compare Remy Marathe's statement in
Infinite Jest (Cambridge: Cambridge University Press, 1996), 107: "Our attachments are
our temple, what we worship, no? What we give ourselves to, what we invest with faith."

The atheist just rolls his eyes like the religious guy is a total simp: "No, man, all that happened was that a couple Eskimos happened to come wandering by, and they showed me the way back to camp." (18–23)

Wallace challenges his audience to perform a "standard liberal arts analysis" to this this story. As he describes it, the result of this analysis is that "the exact same experience can mean two completely different things to two different people, given those people's two different belief templates and two different ways of constructing meaning from experience" (24). There is a lot in Wallace's speech at this point about how we construct meaning for our lives. But Wallace also notes a second important lesson to take from this story, and this one has to do not with how we come to form our beliefs, but how we hold on to them. We err, Wallace thinks, when we hold too tightly and dogmatically to the beliefs that we do have and refuse to question them and consider that what we take for granted may, in fact, be mistaken:

Plus, there's the matter of arrogance. The nonreligious guy is so totally, obnoxiously certain in his dismissal of the possibility that the Eskimos had anything to do with his prayer for help. True, there are plenty of religious people who seem arrogantly certain of their own interpretations, too. They're probably even more repulsive than atheists, at least to most of us, but the fact is that religious dogmatists' problem is exactly the same as the story's atheist's—arrogance, blind certainty, a closed-mindedness that's like an imprisonment so complete that the prisoner doesn't even know he's locked up. (29–32)

It is here that we begin to see the role that self-deception can play in making us unaware of some of, to use Wallace's phrase, "the most . . . important realities" (8). To perhaps stretch Wallace's earlier parable a bit, one reason we don't see the water that is around us is that we've convinced ourselves that it's not there. As we'll see, there is a strong human disposition to believe what we want to believe. And when we believe something because we want to believe it, and not because we have good reason to believe it, we're engaged in self-deception.

Self-deception

In one particularly noteworthy study of one million American high school seniors in 1976–77, over 70 percent of these students evaluated themselves as above average in leadership ability, while only 2 percent indicated they were below average in this regard. With respect to the ability to get along with others, all of the participants indicated they were above average; 60 percent self-reported in being in the top 10 percent, while a quarter of subjects indicated they were in the top 1 percent.[4] And so you don't think that only students engage in this kind of problematic self-deception; psychologist Thomas Gilovich also recounts that "a survey of university professors found that 94 percent thought they were better at their jobs than their average colleague."[5]

Before examining the mechanisms by which we come to be self-deceived, it will be helpful to first say some words about self-deception in general. One reason for doing so is that the nature—and even possibility—of self-deception is philosophically contentious. Alfred Mele's *Self Deception Unmasked* is perhaps the best recent philosophical work on the subject.[6] Mele rejects the view that self-deception characterizes a single class of phenomenon with a set of necessary and jointly sufficient conditions that always characterize it. In fact, Mele's task in the book is not conceptual analysis of what self-deception is, but rather to develop an explanatory framework that can account for self-deception. But he nevertheless differentiates two kinds of self-deception, which he calls "garden-variety straight self-deception" and "twisted self-deception."[7] Garden-variety straight self-deception (which he also sometimes calls merely "straight self-deception") involves an agent's being self-deceived about some proposition *p*'s being true (or false) when she is motivationally biased in coming to believe that *p* is true (or false).[8] That is, the self-deceived person wants to believe the proposition that she is self-deceived about. Oftentimes, it is our desire that something be the case that causally contributes to our acquiring and retaining unwarranted beliefs that what we want to be the case *really is* the case.

As philosopher Gregg Ten Elshof notes, "the beliefs I have about myself and others need not be *true* to bring me satisfaction. I only need to *believe*

---

[4] Thomas Gilovich, *How We Know What Isn't So: The Fallibility of Human Reason in Everyday Life* (New York: The Free Press, 1991), 77.

[5] Ibid.

[6] Alfred Mele, *Self-Deception Unmasked* (Princeton: Princeton University Press, 2001). For worthwhile responses to Mele's text, see Neil Levy, "Self-Deception Without Thought Experiments" and Martin Davies, "Delusion and Motivationally Biased Belief: Self-Deception in the Two-Factor Framework," both in Tim Bayne and Jordi Fernández (eds), *Delusion and Self-Deception* (New York: Taylor & Francis, 2009).

[7] Mele, *Self-Deception Unmasked*, 25, 94.

[8] Peter Ditto refers to this phenomenon as "motivated cognition" in "Passion, Reason, and Necessity: A Quantity-of-Processing View of Motivated Reasoning," in Bayne and Fernández (eds), *Delusion and Self-Deception*, 24. In their introduction to the same volume, Bayne and Fernández describe self-deception as occurring when "the subject's motivational and affective states have led him or her to flout certain norms of belief formation" (*Delusion and Self-Deception*, 2).

them."[9] And so, in straight self-deception we tend to believe those things that we want to be true precisely because of the satisfaction that such beliefs bring. I feel better about the big game when I believe that the Buckeyes' offense matches up well against the Wolverines' defense. I'm inclined to hold my own political beliefs to a lower evidential standard than my opponent's so that it's "obvious" that my own party's platform is superior. In contrast, twisted self-deception doesn't involve the agent being motivated to believe the proposition in question. Here, Mele gives the following example: "[Twisted self-deception] might be exemplified by an insecure, jealous husband who believes that his wife is having an affair despite his possessing only relatively flimsy evidence for that proposition and despite his wanting it to be false that she is so engaged (and not also wanting it to be true)."[10] Although twisted self-deception warrants attention, given the scope of this essay in what follows I'm going to focus on garden-variety straight self-deception.[11]

Mele doesn't think that cases of garden-variety straight self-deception must involve intentionally bringing it about that you believe a proposition that you didn't used to believe. But this isn't to say that the behaviors or processes involved are unintentional. As Mele puts it, "sometimes we do things that *are* means to certain ends without doing them *as* means to those ends."[12] The same point holds if we restrict ourselves to cases of intentional action. I can intentionally do something that does, as a matter of fact, lead me to engage in self-deception without intentionally doing the action in question as a means of causing myself to be deceived. My desire for *p* to be true can motivate me to do something intentionally that will lead me to believe that *p* is true without it being the case; my desire for *p* to be true motivates me to intentionally engage in self-deception.

Mele differentiates four ways in which the desire for *p* to be true can contribute to an instance of self-deception:

1. *negative misinterpretation*, where the desire for *p* leads us to not properly count some data against *p*;
2. *positive misinterpretation*, where the desire for *p* leads us to count some data for *p* more than we would if we did not have the desire for *p*;

---

[9] Gregg Ten Elshof, *I Told Me So: Self-Deception and the Christian Life* (Grand Rapids: Eerdmans, 2009), 4.

[10] Mele, *Self-Deception Unmasked*, 94.

[11] It's probably worth mentioning at this point that just because a belief is formed via a self-deceptive process doesn't mean that belief is false. Sometimes, we're deceived into believing the truth. My interest in this essay is primarily the epistemic quality of a belief in terms of its justification, not in terms of its truth. All else being equal, a belief formed via self-deception is worse than a belief that isn't formed in this way. But truth is one way that all else isn't always equal.

[12] Mele, *Self-Deception Unmasked*, 44.

3. *selective focusing/attending*, where our desire for *p* leads us to ignore evidence that counts against *p* and focus instead on evidence that supports *p*; and

4. *selective evidence-gathering*, where our desire for *p* leads us to overlook evidence that counts against *p* and to find instead evidence supporting *p* which is less accessible.[13]

These practices based on the desire for *p* to be true are not individually sufficient for self-deception; that is, it's not the case that whenever a person engages in one of these four activities, she's self-deceived. But if she, through one of these four means, were to "acquire relevant false, unwarranted beliefs in the ways described, these are garden-variety instances of self-deception."[14] Note that in these cases it's not that the agent first believes ~*p* and then causes herself to believe *p* instead. Self-deception doesn't have to be explicitly intentional in this way. But Mele thinks, and I agree, that insofar as the behaviors involved in these activities are themselves intentional (e.g., that the agent intentionally seeks for evidence for *p* or intentionally focuses on evidence in favor of *p* rather than undercutting *p*), there is still a sense in which the self-deception comes about as the result of intentional behavior. Gilovich helps unpack this indirect nature of self-deception:

> Our desire to believe comforting things about ourselves and about the world does not mean that we believe willy-nilly what we want to believe. . . . Rather, our motivations have their effects more subtly through the ways in which we cognitively process information relevant to a given belief. What evidence do we consider? How much of it do we consider? What criteria do we use as sufficient evidence for a belief? Cognition and motivation collude to allow our preferences to exert influence over what we believe. . . . Our motivations influence our beliefs through the subtle ways we choose a comforting pattern from the fabric of evidence.[15]

We'll return to the various psychological processes involved in greater detail below. But even at this point, it should be clear that it's often understandable (even if not justified) for agents to engage in such self-deceptive practices. After all, thinking what you want to be the case is actually the case is more pleasant than having to confront the frustration of your desire or admit the falsity of your beliefs. People across a spectrum of behaviors, not just

---

[13] Ibid., 26f.
[14] Ibid., 27.
[15] Gilovich, *How We Know What Isn't So*, 80f.

belief-forming behaviors, often do what is pleasant over what is painful. Furthermore, there are a wide range of documented psychological processes that make this kind of reasoning quite easy.

Problematic psychological processes

In his recent book *Thinking, Fast and Slow*, psychologist and Noble Prize winner Daniel Kahneman explores the biases of human intuitions and judgments. Early in the text, he writes:

> When you are asked what you are thinking about, you can normally answer. You believe you know what goes on in your mind, which often consists of one conscious thought leading in an orderly way to another. But that is not the only way the mind works, nor indeed is that the typical way. Most impressions and thoughts arise in your conscious experience without your knowing how they got there.[16]

Kahneman's book explores the ways in which psychological processes like the endowment effect, loss aversion, anchoring effect, availability bias, and various heuristics affect how we come to form our beliefs. And it's not the only such book. David McRaney's *You Are Not So Smart*, for instance, presents a wealth of social-psychological research on cognitive biases, heuristics, and logical fallacies. He writes that "there is a growing body of work coming out of psychology and cognitive science that says you have no clue why you act the way you do, choose the things you choose, or think the things you think."[17] Simply reading the table of contents—"Confabulation," "Hindsight Bias," "The Availability Heuristic," "Subjective Validation," "Self-Serving Bias"—gives you an idea of just how many ways we can go wrong in forming our beliefs, and most of these ways could contribute to self-deception.

In fact, research into these biases and heuristics has fundamentally changed how social scientists understand human belief formation. Kahneman reports that "social scientists in the 1970s broadly accepted two ideas about human nature. First, people are generally rational, and their thinking is normally sound. Second, emotions such as fear, affection, and hatred explain most of the occasions on which people depart from rationality."[18] But as the research

---

[16] Daniel Kahneman, *Thinking, Fast and Slow* (New York: Farrar, Straus and Giroux, 2011), 4.

[17] David McRaney, *You Are Not So Smart* (New York: Penguin Books, 2011), xi.

[18] Kahneman, *Thinking, Fast and Slow*, 8.

on confirmation bias, hindsight bias, cognitive dissonance, and a host of other processes makes clear, these two assumptions are probably false.[19] Consider, for example, confirmation bias, which Gilovich describes this way:

> when examining evidence relevant to a given belief, people are inclined to see what they expect to see, and conclude what they expect to conclude. Information that is consistent with our pre-existing beliefs is often accepted at face value, whereas evidence that contradicts them is critically scrutinized and discounted. Our beliefs may thus be less responsive than they should be to the implications of new information.[20]

Confirmation bias might involve any of the processes of *positive misinter-pretation*, *selective focusing/attending*, or *selective evidence-gathering* mentioned above; it might also involve more than one. Other research has shown how processing information that confirms one's preexisting views is processed differently by the brain than is information opposing it:

> In a study of people who were being monitored by magnetic resonance imaging (MRI) while they were trying to process dissonant or consonant information about George Bush or John Kerry, Drew Westen and his colleagues found that the reasoning areas of the brain virtually shut down when participants were confronted with dissonant information, and the emotion circuits of the brain lit up happily when consonance was restored.[21]

Even further studies also show that one's preferences affect the amount of evidence that one examines. First, "people exhibit a parallel tendency to focus on positive or confirming instances when they *gather*, rather than simply evaluate, information relevant to a given belief or hypothesis."[22] This can then lead to what Gilovich calls "the problem of hidden or absent data."[23]

---

[19] However, as Gilovich notes, even though these kinds of heuristics often lead us to error, "these strategies are generally effective, but the benefit of simplification is paid for at the cost of *systematic* error" (Gilovich, *How We Know What Isn't So*, 49, emphasis original).

[20] Gilovich, *How We Know What Isn't So*, 50. See also page 81. For an influential psychological study of this effect, see C. G. Lord, L. Ross, and M. R. Lepper, "Biased assimilation and attitude polarization: The effects of prior theories on subsequent considered evidence," *Journal of Personality and Social Psychology* 37 (1979): 2098–109; another influential study illustrating confirmation bias is reported in Gilovich, *How We Know What Isn't So*, 36.

[21] Carol Tavris and Elliot Aronson, *Mistakes Were Made (But Not By Me)* (Orlando: Harcourt Books, 2007), 19. See also Robert Burton, *On Being Certain: Believing You Are Right Even When You're Not* (New York: St. Martin's Press, 2008), 158f.

[22] Gilovich, *How We Know What Isn't So*, 33.

[23] Ibid., 37.

Furthermore, individuals tend to seek further evidence less when the initial evidence confirms their own perspective, thus making them less likely to encounter sufficient counter-evidence to change their minds.[24] Insofar as we are less likely to have evidence that disconfirms our beliefs because we are less likely to seek such data (and we're less likely to take this data seriously even if we do have it), we are often even more resolute in our beliefs than is otherwise justified. Furthermore, the evidence we gather that aligns with our preexisting desires and beliefs also tends to be more memorable than contradictory information, and thus more likely to be recalled later, further exacerbating the problem.

Social psychologist Leon Festinger coined the phrase "cognitive dissonance" to describe the unpleasant mental state in which individuals "find themselves doing things that don't fit with what they know, or having opinions that do not fit with other opinions they hold."[25] In his research, Festinger found that the more committed a person is to a particular belief the more difficult it is for her to give up that belief, even in the face of contradictory evidence. In many cases, in order to reinforce our current beliefs and avoid cognitive dissonance—that is, to not have our "water" challenged—we have reason to engage in self-deception. We might call this "motivational self-deception."

Mele recounts a study by Kunda that illustrates this nicely. One hundred and sixty-one subjects, seventy-five women and eighty-six men, read an article alleging that "women were endangered by caffeine and were strongly advised to avoid caffeine in any form"; that the major danger of caffeine consumption was fibrocystic disease "associated in its advance stages with breast cancer"; and that "caffeine induced the disease by increasing the concentration of a substance called cAMP in the breast."[26] The subjects were then asked a number of questions, including "how convinced they were of the connection between caffeine and fibrocystic disease and of the connection between caffeine [consumption] and cAMP."[27] Among the female subjects, those who self-identified as "heavy consumers" of caffeine were significantly less convinced of the connections detailed in the article than those female subjects who self-identified as "low consumers." The male subjects acted as the control group since the article did not address their health. Among the male subjects, the heavy consumers were slightly more convinced of

---

[24] See, for example, ibid., 82.

[25] Leon Festinger, *A Theory of Cognitive Dissonance* (Stanford: Stanford University Press, 1957), 17.

[26] Ziva Kunda, "Motivated Inference: Self-Serving Generation and Evaluation of Causal Theories," *Journal of Personality and Social Psychology* 53 (1987): 642, as quoted in Mele, *Self-Deception Unmasked*, 12.

[27] Kunda, "Motivated Inference," 643f, as quoted in Mele, *Self-Deception Unmasked*, 12.

the connections than were the low consumers. And both groups of male subjects were considerably more convinced than were the female heavy consumers. Why? Given the motivation that the female heavy consumers have for wanting the claims of the article being false, they have more reason for rejecting the article's claims than were either the female low consumers or the male subjects. Their desire to avoid having to admit that their high caffeine consumption might be damaging to their health provides them with a motivation for rejecting what the other subject groups were much more inclined to accept. But, to pick up on a thread from earlier, it's not as if the female high consumers are aware that they are intentionally disregarding the evidence. That is, if you asked them why they put less credence in the article's claims, the majority of them would not answer: "Because I have a personal stake in the correlations claimed in the article not being factual." The role that their motivations and intentions (if, in fact, they have such intentions) play in their self-deception are hidden from them. But they could nevertheless be quite guilty of self-serving bias.[28]

Not only can these psychological processes contribute to our self-deception, but they can also compound such that one of them is the cause for further kinds of biased belief formation. Consider, for example, a case of confirmation bias involving one's political beliefs. A person inclined toward a certain political position is more likely to read newspapers and watch cable news channels that reinforce the political views he already holds. One study found that subjects spent 36 percent more time reading an essay if that essay aligned with their own opinions.[29] This could then contribute to the availability heuristic, where an individual is more likely to be influenced in her belief-forming processes by easily available information. A person might also evaluate data that confirm his desired belief to be more vivid than are data that oppose the desired belief. Since we tend to recall better and focus on data that are vivid, we have another way in which a cognitive process can increase the likelihood of biased beliefs via another process. This isn't, of course, to say that confirming (or available or vivid or self-serving) data are always false or lacking in evidential force; but the ease with which the formation of our beliefs can be biased in these and other ways give us reason to pause and consider whether we're being epistemically responsible in how we form and hold beliefs that we want to be true.

All of this suggests that there is a kind of "belief endowment effect."[30] Psychologist Richard Thaler coined the phrase "endowment effect" to refer

---

[28] See McRaney, *You Are Not So Smart*, ch. 28.
[29] As quoted in McRaney, *You Are Not So Smart*, 30.
[30] See, for instance, Gilovich, *How We Know What Isn't So*, 86.

to the undervaluing of opportunity costs: "out-of-pocket costs are viewed as losses and opportunity costs are viewed as foregone gains, [and] the former will be more heavily weighted. Furthermore, a certain degree of inertia is introduced into the consumer choice process since goods that are included in the individual's endowment will be more highly valued than those not held in the endowment, *ceteris paribus*."[31] It's not hard to see how the processes with respect to our beliefs could contribute to self-deception.

Religious self-deception

The above discussion should make it evident that self-deception is a threat in all aspects of our cognitive lives. Ten Elshof writes in a book subtitled *Self-Deception in the Christian Life* that "the possibility of self-deception rears its head whenever there is a kind of felt pressure associated with believing something. . . . Arguably, devotion to a cause, even a very good cause, has the potential to blind us to what would otherwise be obvious facts."[32] Insofar as this is correct, I'm not claiming that all self-deception is religious in nature; nor am I claiming that there is more self-deception involved in religious beliefs then, say, political or atheistic beliefs. That would be an empirical question, and one I'm not prepared to address here. But for many people, their religious beliefs are among the most important beliefs they hold. Such beliefs are also often central for an individual's self-identity, both as an individual and as a member of a certain group of like-believing individuals. So it shouldn't be surprising that religious beliefs are among those beliefs that we're most likely to "protect" by engaging in the various psychological processes described above. As Tavris and Aronson note,

> Obviously, certain categories of *us* are more crucial to our identities than the kind of car we drive or the number of dots we can guess on a slide—gender, sexuality, religion, politics, ethnicity, and nationality, for starters. Without feeling attached to groups that give our lives meaning, identity, and purpose, we could suffer the intolerable sensation that we were loose marbles floating in a random universe. Therefore, we will do what it takes to preserve these attachments.[33]

---

[31] Richard Thaler, "Toward A Positive Theory of Consumer Choice," *Journal of Economic Behavior and Organization* 1 (1980): 44. For more on the endowment effect, see Kahneman, *Thinking, Fast and Slow*, ch. 27.

[32] Ten Elshof, *I Told Me So*, 22, 91.

[33] Tavris and Aronson, *Mistakes Were* Made, 59, emphasis original.

A good example of such religious belief's irrationality can be found in Festinger, Riecken, and Schachter's *When Prophecy Fails*, which chronicles social psychologists' infiltration and observation of a religious cult who predicted the end of the world and how the cult's members dealt with the cognitive dissonance that followed from their predictions being shown to be false, even to the point of becoming even more convinced of the truth of their religious views afterwards.[34]

Cognitive dissonance is not the only psychological belief-forming process that can generate self-deception with regard to religious beliefs. Insofar as most religious believers are more inclined to study theology that agrees with their own views, confirmation bias can also feed into an availability heuristic involving religious belief. Given the experiential nature of many religions, individuals who self-identify with a religion are more likely to *feel* that their religious beliefs are correct (e.g., Christians might experience the presence of God in a church service; Muslims might feel closer to Allah while feasting during Ramadan). But psychology has shown us that such feelings are a bad way to evaluate our beliefs. And religious believers may also project their own religious views onto others, a process psychologists refer to as "false consensus effect."[35] So we not only fail to see our own water, but we often project that same water onto others (e.g., we're more likely to think that others in our neighborhood share our religious beliefs, we suspect that others with our religious beliefs will also be inclined toward our political beliefs, etc.). Finally, opportunity costs also matter. In adhering to a particular religion, members of that religion not only commit themselves to things (e.g., extended periods of catechism, religious pilgrimages, regular tithing, etc.) but also commit themselves against things (e.g., dietary and behavioral restrictions, separation from wider culture, etc.). As research has shown, people engage in self-deception to justify their participation in groups that have high entrance or opportunity costs.[36] Psychologists Carol Tavris and Elliot Aronson write that "the more costly a decision, in terms of time, money, effort, or inconvenience, and the more irrevocable its consequences, the greater the dissonance and the greater the need to reduce it by overemphasizing the good things about the choice made."[37] Again, it's not surprising if we experience these consequences with respect to our religious beliefs.

---

[34] Leon Festinger, Henry W. Riecken, and Stanely Schachter, *When Prophecy Fails* (New York: Martino Fine Books, 1956).
[35] Gilovich, *How We Know What Isn't So*, 113ff.
[36] See, for instance, Tavris and Aronson, *Mistakes Were* Made, 15f.
[37] Tavris and Aronson, *Mistakes Were* Made, p. 22.

Nevertheless, looking at one's religious views in such a way that would minimize self-deception is precarious precisely because what one finds when one engages in such a process may well be that one's religious beliefs are importantly and profoundly mistaken. According to Ten Elshof,

> an honest-to-goodness inquiry into the evidence for and against Christian belief is hard—not to mention risky and scary—work. If it turned out that Christianity were irrational, I'd be faced with a tough choice: either settle into a commitment to an irrational religion, or suspend my belief in the truth of Christianity and suffer considerable social consequences.[38]

But as Wallace reminds us in his address, often times "the really important kind of freedom involves attention, and awareness, and discipline, and effort" (120), particularly if we're not simply to fail to notice that the beliefs we take for granted may be mistaken.

What should we do?

Let us return to Mele's work on self-deception. Mele distinguishes three kinds of cognitive activities that contribute to motivationally biased beliefs of the kind involved in garden-variety self-deception:

1. *unintentional* activities (e.g., unintentionally focusing on data of a certain kind),
2. *intentional* activities (e.g., intentionally focusing on data of a certain kind), and
3. intentional activities engaged in as part of an *attempt* to deceive oneself, or to cause oneself to believe something, or to make it easier for oneself to believe something (e.g., intentionally focusing on data of a certain kind as part of an attempt to deceive oneself into believing that *p*).[39]

While an individual may attempt intentionally to engage in self-deception via (3)—that is, one may intentionally try to bring oneself to think that water is air—the most common cause of self-deception will likely involve activities along the lines of (1) and (2). Given this fact, it's not as if we can avoid self-deception simply by either not choosing to engage in self-deception or by

---

[38] Ten Elshof, *I Told Me So*, 35; as consequences, he mentions "loss of my job and alienation from my closest friends and family."

[39] Mele, *Self-Deception Unmasked*, 18.

choosing to avoid it; the phenomenon is too complex for that. As philosopher and theologian Dallas Willard notes:

> One of the worst mistakes we can make in coming to grips with these well-known human failures [involving self-deception] is to think of them solely in terms of will and "will power." Of course the will is involved, but the will is not what immediately governs the "normal" life. Such a life is controlled by inertia, habit, bent of character—stuff we don't really pay much attention to, if any at all, and is some cases "stuff" we don't even recognize or admit is a part of "us." The self that does the deceiving in self-deception is this inertial bulk of habit and bent of character, embedded in our body and its social relations, ready to go without thinking or choice.[40]

That is, this is our water. And because of selective attention and confirmation bias, we often don't change our minds when presented with evidence.[41] We are disposed to not notice the water, to see what we want to see, and this disposition cannot be overcome by mere volitional fiat.

We also need to recognize that the likelihood of self-deception is not simply a function of our desires. The more central a belief is to our self-understanding or the more important the belief is to our fundamental perspective on the world, the more likely we are to engage in self-deception about the belief in question. As a Buckeye fan and parent, I'm more likely—all else being equal—to engage in self-deception about how good of a parent I am than regarding how good the Ohio State University football team is this year, given that the former is more central and important for my belief set. The cognitive costs of me being wrong that I'm a good parent are higher than are the costs for me being wrong that the Buckeyes are a superior football team than, say, the Boise State Broncos. (Mele refers to the kind of cost here as "error cost.")[42] I'm thus more likely—again, all else being equal—to engage in self-deception regarding the former than I am the latter. Given that for many people religion isn't just about *what they do* or *what they believe* but about *who and what they are*, then they're all the more likely to engage in self-deception on such matters than on beliefs that are not so tied to one's self-identity.

In fact, the attempt simply to overcome bias by attention management can sometimes backfire. One might, for example, attempt to overcome confirmation bias and selective focusing by forcing one's self to engage

---

[40] Willard, in Ten Elshof, *I Told Me So*, x.
[41] For a taste of the many experimental studies in this regard, see the studies mentioned in Ten Elshof, *I Told Me So*, 38 note 2.
[42] Mele, *Self-Deception Unmasked*, p. 35 and *passim*.

evidence that disconfirms one's desired beliefs. But, this increased attention can result in one holding the disconfirming evidence to higher evidentiary standards, which then can lead one to think that one's views are less biased than they really are. Daniel Kahneman refers to this as the "illusion of validity."[43] This illusion, to use Wallace's phrase, is often our water.

If willpower isn't enough, what then should we do to take the necessary steps to avoid self-deception? A good first step would be to familiarize ourselves with the above ways that we so easily and naturally are led to self-deception. While we tend to see how others' beliefs are often guided by desire, affect, and emotion, it is harder for us to see that in ourselves. "We prefer to think of ourselves as having conscious reasons for what we believe and what we do,"[44] even if we can see otherwise in others. So we engage in rationalization and confabulation; coming up with a reason why we formed a belief after we've already formed it is not a good guide to why we actually formed that belief.[45] So we cannot simply "read off" from our beliefs where we're engaged in self-deception and avoid it.

The causes, and ease, of self-deception will not simply cease by mental exertion and introspection. But this doesn't mean that we can't take steps to help avoid it. As Gilovich points out,

> These underlying causes of erroneous beliefs will never simply disappear. They must, then, be held in check by compensatory mental habits that promote more sound reasoning. To avoid erroneous beliefs, in other words, it is necessary that we develop certain habits of mind that can shore up various deficiencies in our everyday inferential abilities.[46]

Perhaps the single best habit of mind that we could develop in this respect is intellectual humility, which we can understand in the present context as the disposition to be relatively unconcerned about one's own ideas qua one's own in the pursuit of truth. It is also the capacity to see oneself accurately in light of the real relationships that exist in the world where the prior condition makes the later possible. The more humble we are, the less we're likely to be led astray by our assumptions that we fail to notice. The intellectual virtue of open-mindedness will also be relevant in this context. William Hare writes that "to be open-minded is . . . to be critically receptive to alternate possibilities, to be willing to think again despite having formulated a view, and to be concerned to defuse any factors that constrain one's thinking

43 Kahneman, *Thinking, Fast and Slow*, 39.
44 Ten Elshof, *I Told Me So*, 58.
45 For an introduction to psychological research on confabulation, see, for example, the experiments in McRaney, *You are Not So Smart*, ch. 2.
46 Gilovich, *How We Know What Isn't So*, 186.

in predetermined ways."[47] And as James Spiegel argues in a recent article, "human beings are remarkably vulnerable to the formation of false beliefs due to a variety of factors. . . . Recognizing one's fallibility as a knower turns out to be intellectual humility, or at least one significant form that this trait takes."[48]

Conclusion

David Foster Wallace's *This Is Water* raises a number of worthwhile and important themes. One recurrent theme—and the one that the story of the two men in the bar, reproduced above, focuses on—is intellectual arrogance. A central aim of a liberal-arts education, Wallace thinks, should be to make us a little more intellectually humble. It should help us "to be just a little less arrogant, to have some 'critical awareness' about myself and my certainties . . . because a huge percentage of the stuff that I tend to be automatically certain of is, it turns out, totally wrong and deluded" (33). This is a lesson, I've suggested, we should apply to help avoid self-deception. After exploring how such self-deception comes about, I've focused on religious self-deception in particular. There are steps we can take to minimize self-deception,[49] and I think that religious believers ought to do what they can to minimize the likelihood of self-deception with respect to their religious beliefs.[50] And while, as I've indicated already, I don't think that we need to be more humble only about our religious beliefs, I think we'd all do better if we followed Wallace's advice.[51]

---

[47] William Hare, "The Ideal of Open-Mindedness and its Place in Education," *Journal of Thought* 38, 2 (2003): 4f.

[48] James Spiegel, "Open-mindedness and Intellectual Humility," *Theory and Research in Education* 10, 1 (2012): 33f. For a related article on why open-mindedness is a virtue directly applicable to religious belief, see James Spiegel, "Open-mindedness and Religious Devotion," *Sophia* 10, 1 (2012): 27–38.

[49] See, for instance, Mele, *Self-Deception Unmasked*, 31–42.

[50] How a religious person recognizes self-deception and what specific steps she'll need to take to avoid it will depend on the religious context of her surrounding beliefs. This is, however, an issues deeply entrenched in larger regarding the nature of religious beliefs that I cannot get into here. For two different approaches to this issue, compare Mark Johnston, *Saving God: Religion after Idolatry* (Princeton: Princeton University Press, 2011) and Robert Bolger, *Kneeling at the Altar of Science: The Mistaken Path of Contemporary Religious Scientism* (Eugene, OR: Pickwick Publications, 2012).

[51] I would to thank David Armour, Robert Bolger, Craig Boyd, and Scott Korb for input on the content of this essay. I'm also grateful to Bolger and Korb for the opportunity to contribute to this volume, and David Foster Wallace for a speech that continues to inspire and encourage me after more than a dozen readings.

5

Inside David Foster Wallace's Head: Attention, Loneliness, Suicide, and the Other Side of Boredom

Andrew Bennett

Being alone, loneliness, solitude, and its attendant solipsistic dangers are major themes in David Foster Wallace's novels and short stories. His narratives typically explore what Don DeLillo calls a "spiralling sense of isolation."[1] In interviews and essays, Wallace regularly asserted that the primary function of the novel is to explore what happens inside other people's heads. Old-style realist fiction, he argues in "E Unibus Pluram," his celebrated 1990 essay on America and TV, helps us to "leap over the walls of self and locale and show us unseen or dreamed-of people and cultures and ways to be."[2] Jonathan Franzen has recently argued in an ambivalent if not at times actively hostile article on his "beloved" friend in the *New Yorker*, that Wallace saw fiction as "a solution, the *best* solution, to the problem of existential solitude."[3] "A big part of serious fiction's purpose," Wallace remarked in a 1993 interview, is to "give the reader, who like all of us is sort of marooned in her own skull,

---

[1] Don DeLillo, "Informal Remarks From the David Foster Wallace Memorial Service in New York on October 23, 2008," in Samuel Cohen and Lee Konstantinou (eds), *The Legacy of David Foster Wallace* (Iowa City: University of Iowa Press, 2012), 23.

[2] Wallace, "E Unibus Pluram: Television and U.S. Fiction," in *A Supposedly Fun Thing I'll Never Do Again: Essays and Arguments* (London: Abacus, 1998), 51.

[3] Jonathan Franzen, "Farther Away: *Robinson Crusoe*, David Foster Wallace, and the Island of Solitude," *The New Yorker* (18 April 2011), 92, 93. Franzen speaks eloquently of loneliness and the "near-perfect absence . . . of ordinary love" in Wallace's fiction: according to Franzen, Wallace was "a lifelong prisoner on the island of himself" (90–1). See also James Ryerson, "Introduction: A Head that Throbbed Heart-Like: The Philosophical Mind of David Foster Wallace," in Steven M. Cahn and Maureen Eckert (eds), *Fate, Time, and Language: An Essay on Free Will* (New York: Columbia University Press, 2011), 24–33, on loneliness and philosophical solipsism in Wallace: "There was a palpable strain for Wallace," Ryerson argues, "between engagement with the world, in all its overwhelming fullness, and withdrawal to one's own head, in all its loneliness" (33).

to give her imaginative access to other selves."[4] Reading something "that's good and that's real," he commented in a 2003 interview, using a phrase he favored, allows us to "jump over that wall of self and inhabit somebody else in a way that . . . [we] can't in regular life." But then, he went on, it "gets more complicated" because in reading one also has access to "the mind of the author in a way that we don't have access to each other talking this way."[5] For Wallace, reading fiction can make us seem "less alone inside."[6] But making us seem less alone is not the same as making us not alone, and in Wallace the desire not to be alone is generated precisely by the fact that we are. We are *all* alone, and therefore "terribly terribly lonely."[7] Aloneness is what brings us together, Hal Incandenza comments in Wallace's 1996 novel *Infinite Jest*, in a terrible paradox: that is what "we all have in common."[8]

Being alone, of course, *means* being alone inside one's head, and the iconography of David Foster Wallace itself points up the impenetrability of that important body part. In many of the iconic images of Wallace, the short-story writer and novelist wears a bandana, most often a gray paisley pattern on a white background, which can be understood to perform at least a double function: the bandana draws attention to the writer's head and at the same time conceals it, hides it, denies us access to it. "What a ghastly enterprise to be in, though," Wallace remarked in a 1993 interview of his chosen profession, "and what an odd way to achieve success. I'm an exhibitionist who wants to hide," he went on, "but is unsuccessful at hiding: therefore, somehow I succeed."[9] Writers are "weird hybrids," he said in another interview: "there's a strong streak of egomania coupled with extreme shyness. Writing's kind of like exhibitionism in private."[10] In this sense, writing for Wallace is itself a kind of bandana, both concealing and revealing the inside of his head—indeed that more generally is what fiction does, in its own way, when it both points to and points up the author's head and at the same time conceals that head precisely

---

[4] Larry McCaffery, "An Expanded Interview with David Foster Wallace," in Burn (ed.), *Conversations with David Foster Wallace* (Jackson: University Press of Mississippi, 2012), 21–2; see also 32–3.

[5] "David Foster Wallace Interview 2003 (06/09)" (interview on "Aspekte," German TV channel ZDF, 3 January 2003): accessed on www.youtube.com, 6 February 2014.

[6] McCaffery, "Interview," 22.

[7] Hugh Kennedy and Geoffrey Polk, "Looking for a Garde of Which to be Avant: An Interview with David Foster Wallace," in Burn (ed.), *Conversations with David Foster Wallace*, 16.

[8] David Foster Wallace, *Infinite Jest* (London: Abacus, 1997), 112.

[9] McCaffery, "Interview," 43.

[10] Anne Marie Donahue, "David Foster Wallace Winces at the Suggestion That His Book Is Sloppy in Any Sense," in Burn (ed.), *Conversations with David Foster Wallace*, 70–1: "And there's also a strange loneliness, and a desire to have some kind of conversation with people, but not a real great ability to do it in person," he went on.

by the object (the bandana, so to speak, of writing) that draws it to our attention. Many of Wallace's novels and stories feature depressed individuals and characters who go to considerable lengths to avoid or to otherwise cope with the isolation of their self-involved narcissism, with what Wallace called "terrible self-consciousness," with the searing psychic pain of bipolar disorder or with boredom, addiction, suicide ideation, or even psychosis.[11] Characters engage in inordinate, tortuous, involuted acts of thinking or reasoning, going so far as to involve themselves in exercises in formal logic or in writing fiction or memoirs to avoid or to cope with their mental pain; and they engage in the paradoxical strategies of violence, addiction, serious competitive tennis training, philosophical analysis, and other modes of avoidance and denial. And in some cases they resort to suicide. There is, indubitably, an element of self-reference here, of autobiography, a genre with which Wallace's fiction constantly, playfully, guardedly engages.[12] His own psychological condition is what Wallace may be said both to have revealed in his writing and at the same time to have hidden *by* writing: "I don't think that he ever lost the feeling that there was something shameful about this," his father said after Wallace's death, on his son's depression: "His instinct was to hide it."[13] In representing people as suffering from loneliness and from clinical depression, and as escaping depression by resorting to the uniquely, indeed the metaphysically solitary act of suicide, Wallace continually draws on the special power of literature both to figure the authorial subject and to disguise it, to hide, to depersonalize the self, to eradicate it, in or by articulating it.

And the head is undoubtedly the problem for David Foster Wallace, the writer who once quipped darkly that he wore bandanas because he was "kind of worried that my head's gonna explode."[14] Wallace himself identified a philosophical dimension to violence (at least in a mild or symbolic form) toward his head. During an interview in 1993, Hugh Kennedy and Geoffrey Polk noticed Wallace's habit of "lightly striking the back of his head with an

---

[11] Kennedy and Polk, "Looking for a Garde," 14.

[12] "A lot of The Broom of the System is weirdly autobiographical," Wallace noted, for example, "in ways that no one else knows," (ibid., 12).

[13] Quoted in David Lipsky, "The Lost Years and Last Days of David Foster Wallace," in *The Best American Magazine Writing of 2009*, Compiled by "The American Society of Magazine Editors." Introduction by Chris Anderson (New York: Columbia University Press, 2010), 138.

[14] Lipsky, "The Lost Years," 167; the same comment in a different context is recorded by D. T. Max in *Every Love Story is a Ghost Story: A Life of David Foster Wallace* (London: Granta, 2012), 165. See also Wallace's comment that his *Harper's* journalism pieces "were me peeling back my skull" (ibid., 173), and his remark that what he can do in writing his journalism is to "slice open my head for you, and let you see a cross-section of an averagely bright person's head" (Tom Scocca, "David Foster Wallace," in Burn (ed.), *Conversations with David Foster Wallace*, 86).

open palm, a habit which, Wallace noted, descends in a direct line from his father, a philosopher at the University of Illinois Champagne/Urbana; through his father's teacher, Norman Malcolm, Wittgenstein's last student; back to Wittgenstein himself."[15] But serious pain in, the potential explosiveness of, and extreme violence toward people's heads make up a notable motif in Wallace's fiction. Both his first novel, *The Broom of the System* (1987), and his second, *Infinite Jest*, include exploding heads: in *Broom*, the disappeared great-grandmother leaves behind her a suggestively opaque doodle depicting the exploding head of a barber that, we learn, illustrates a paradox in set theory; while in *Infinite Jest*, the film genius, patriarch, and tennis academy founder, James Incandenza, arranges to kill himself by the technically complicated act of cooking his own head in a microwave oven (his head does indeed explode, almost instantaneously).

This essay is about David Foster Wallace's head, then, and about a small number of the many things—the almost infinite number of things—that may have happened inside it, while at the same time being about the impossibility of knowing any such thing. In particular, I want to try to think about a series of linked ideas—the ideas of philosophy, literature, and reading, as well as of consciousness, attention, loneliness, boredom, and suicide—and I want to think about some of the ways in which these ideas might direct us to important aspects of Wallace's writing as well as to significant questions in literature and philosophy more generally. In order to do so, I will focus on boredom, in particular, the major topic of Wallace's final, incomplete, and posthumously published novel, *The Pale King*.

One of the foundational analyses of boredom in the modern tradition appears in the striking and compelling work of the nineteenth-century philosophical pessimist Arthur Schopenhauer, the first of just five modern philosophers whom Wallace once cited in a list of those writers—otherwise poets and novelists—whose work made him feel that he could have a "deep, significant conversation with another consciousness."[16] Boredom is itself foundational for Schopenhauer. In texts such as *The World as Will and Representation* and his essay "On the Vanity of Human Existence," Schopenhauer identifies boredom as the condition that underlies, indeed underpins, all of human existence. His 1850 essay "On the Suffering of the World" is particularly clear on this question. Schopenhauer starts by proposing that the "purpose" of human life must, logically, be suffering, since if that were *not* the case then "our existence" would be "the most ill-adapted to

---

[15] Kennedy and Polk, "Looking for a Garde," 12.
[16] See Miller, "Interview," 62; the other modern philosophers that Wallace lists are Descartes, Kant, James, and Wittgenstein.

its purpose in the world."[17] Since there *is* suffering, in other words, and since there is in particular endless human suffering, since suffering is particularly, uniquely exacerbated by the condition of being human, there can logically be no purpose or meaning in human life outside of the question of suffering. Suffering is fundamental. If that is the case, Schopenhauer contends, it cannot but follow that suffering is the purpose of human existence.

For Schopenhauer, human suffering is an aspect of the quotidian: suffering for us (whether we know it or not) is pervasive, multiple, diverse, unceasing. His proof of the argument that suffering uniquely underlies *human* existence in particular has to do with boredom. When we are not engaged in "striving after" something—for example, the "continual striving" that is involved in our desire for sensual pleasure—we are "directed back to existence itself," he argues, and in being so directed we are "overtaken" by a sense of the "worthlessness and vanity" of that existence. For Schopenhauer, this experience is itself "the sensation called boredom."[18] Satisfaction, he argues, can be construed as the apparently "painless condition" in which one is in fact "given over" to the existential experience of boredom: boredom, he declares, is "a direct proof that existence is in itself valueless" because it is "nothing other than the sensation of the emptiness of existence."[19] In this sense, boredom is not just a psychological problem but also a philosophical one: it exposes the meaninglessness of life and so brings us directly into contact with that irredeemable metaphysical fact. Schopenhauer argues that one of the "torments" that "plagues our existence" is our specifically and singularly human consciousness of time itself: time, he declares, is a "constant pressure," never letting us "so much as draw our breath" but pursuing us instead "like a taskmaster with a whip." The only time that time stops persecuting us, Schopenhauer says, is when it has "delivered [us] over to boredom."[20] "Work, worry, toil and trouble are indeed the lot of almost all men their whole life long," he declares, but an imaginary utopia in which all such concerns were removed, in which all desires were immediately satisfied, would also in fact be a dystopia: people would either "fight and kill" each other in order to produce for themselves some element of suffering, or they would "die of boredom or hang themselves."[21] Boredom, in other words, is the underlying condition of humanity, its ultimate possibility or promise, and if boredom is not itself the immediate cause of death, it leads

---

[17] Arthur Schopenhauer, "On the Suffering of the World," in R. J. Hollingdale (ed.), *Essays and Aphorisms* (London: Penguin, 1970), 41.
[18] Ibid., 54.
[19] Ibid., 53.
[20] Ibid., 42.
[21] Ibid., 43.

directly, ineluctably to suicide. If you were ever lucky enough to overcome the quotidian frustrations of living, you would die of boredom; but if you didn't simply die of boredom, you would take your own life, thereby dying as an indirect result of boredom anyway.[22] Suicide, then, is never far away in Schopenhauer's analysis of boredom, and our physical existence is "a constantly prevented dying, an ever-deferred death" since we are constantly in danger of being fundamentally, existentially, suicidally bored, bored to death. Unlike animals, for whom boredom is "unknown . . . in the state of nature" and "only very slightly perceptible in the very cleverest domesticated ones," boredom therefore defines the limits of human existence: it determines for us life itself.[23]

I want to suggest that Schopenhauer's analysis of boredom offers a way to begin thinking about David Foster Wallace's fiction and about the inside of his head. The present book is itself testimony to the fact that philosophy— philosophical discourse, philosophical ideas and vocabularies, philosophical values, philosophical thinking—pervades, invades, saturates Wallace's writing.[24] As the son of an academic philosopher, a high-achieving philosophy major at Amherst, the author of a book on the mathematics of infinity, and, at least for a time, a philosophy graduate student at Harvard, Wallace was undoubtedly aware of the foundational role that the question of boredom plays in Schopenhauer's thinking. And while Schopenhauer provides the basis for a thinking of boredom in modern philosophy, Wallace will also have encountered the question in the work of thinkers such as Martin Heidegger, whose *The Fundamental Concepts of Metaphysics* (1929–30) opens with a brilliant one-hundred-page meditation on boredom that itself builds on and moves away from Schopenhauer's analysis.[25] But Wallace was also fascinated by psychology and psychoanalysis, and especially by the para-philosophical discourse of pop-psychology, and his prose owes particular debts to the pervasive and peculiarly American idiom of self-help books.[26] In this respect,

---

[22] Schopenhauer makes a similar point in *The World as Will and Representation*, trans. E. F. J. Payne, 2 vols (New York: Dover, 1969), 311–12.

[23] Arthur Schopenhauer, "On the Suffering of the World," 44–5.

[24] Also see Ryerson, "Introduction," 17–18, for a brief account of Wallace's engagements with philosophy.

[25] On the "affinities" between the two thinkers, see Julian Young, "Schopenhauer, Heidegger, Art, and the Will," in Dale Jacquette (ed.), *Schopenhauer, Philosophy and the Arts* (Cambridge: Cambridge University Press, 1996), 162–80; see also Heidegger's claim that since 1818 Schopenhauer has "most persistently determined the whole tone of all nineteenth- and twentieth-century thought" (*What is Called Thinking*, trans. J. Glenn Gray [New York: Harper and Rowe, 1968], 39).

[26] On Wallace's use of self-help books in his fiction, see Maria Bustillos, "Inside David Foster Wallace's Private Self-Help Library," *The Awl* (5 April 2011) (http://www.theawl.com/2011/04/inside-david-foster-wallaces-private-self-help-library), and her essay included in this collection.

it is worth considering the influence of the Hungarian-American psychologist Mihaly Csikszentmihalyi on Wallace's thinking of boredom. Csikszentmihalyi, whose first book was titled *Beyond Boredom and Anxiety* (1975), is famous for the development of the idea of "flow" as a counter to the default human condition of anxiety and boredom. There is evidence that Wallace was quite profoundly influenced by Csikszentmihalyi, and I want to suggest that it is possible to read *The Pale King*, in particular, as pervasively influenced by Csikszentmihalyi's positive psychology. As it happens, both writers lived in Claremont, California, between 2002 and Wallace's death in 2008—Wallace worked at Pomona College in Claremont, and Csikszentmihalyi taught (and still teaches) at Claremont Graduate University—and *Infinite Jest* refers at least three times to a minor character named Zoltan Csikszentmihalyi in what must surely be a veiled allusion to the Psychology professor.[27] But what is most striking is the use that Wallace made of Csikszentmihalyi's widely read 1990 book *Flow: The Psychology of Optimal Experience*, a book that Wallace owned and carefully annotated. In *Flow*, Csikszentmihalyi defined "flow" as "a state of joy, creativity and total involvement" where "problems seem to disappear" in "an exhilarating feeling of transcendence."[28] Very early in the book, he explains that the problem he is discussing has to do with the fact that despite the inordinate luxury experienced by the inhabitants of modern Western society and the historically unprecedented longevity and physical well-being even of many of its poorest, people "often end up feeling that their lives have been wasted," and that "instead of being filled with happiness" they spend their time on earth experiencing "anxiety and boredom."[29] Directed toward personal fulfillment through the achievement of what he calls "mastery over consciousness itself,"[30] in a sentence underlined by Wallace in his copy of the book, Csikszentmihalyi's critique of modernity and the condition of boredom chimes notably with Schopenhauer's analysis.[31] In another passage that Wallace underlined, Csikszentmihalyi claims that "The

---

27 Wallace, *Infinite Jest*, 98, 965, 1071–2.
28 Mihalyi Csikszentmihalyi, *Flow: The Classic Work on How to Achieve Happiness* (London: Rider, 2002), back-cover blurb. Wallace's copy, at the Harry Ransom Center, in Austin, Texas, is annotated by comments and by side-linings and underlinings, mostly in red pen, on almost every page up to 77, where he seems to have stopped reading. Further references to this book are taken from Wallace's personal copy of *Flow: The Psychology of Optimal Experience* (New York: HarperCollins, 1991) at the Harry Ransom Center.
29 Csikszentmihalyi, *Flow*, 1.
30 Ibid., 9.
31 Although Csikszentmihalyi refers to Schopenhauer in, for example, "Positive Psychology and a Positive World-View: New Hope for the Future of Mankind," in Stewart I. Donaldson, Mihalyi Csikszentmihalyi, and Jeanne Nakamura (eds), *Applied Positive Psychology: Improving Everyday Life, Health, Schools, Work, and Society* (New York: Routledge, 2011), 208, I take the debt to be more implicit and general than specific and direct.

mark of a person who is in control of consciousness is the ability to focus attention at will, to be oblivious to distractions, to concentrate for as long as it takes to achieve a goal." The person who can do this, Csikszentmihalyi goes on, "usually enjoys the normal course of everyday life."[32] Wallace's pithy marginal annotation to these sentences points to a major concern in his own fiction: "Attention = Control of Consciousness." Csikszentmihalyi concludes, in yet another comment underlined by Wallace, that achieving a state of "flow" will "liberate the psychic energy that otherwise would be wasted in boredom or worry."[33]

There is evidence scattered throughout Wallace's work that the question of boredom, its potential value (or the opportunity that it offers in overcoming it), and the existential abyss that it also opens, was an important element in his thinking. His final novel, in particular, investigates the paradoxicality and the intricacy of the structures and strategies of boredom and boredom-evasion generated by the work of the Internal Revenue Service (IRS). I want to suggest that the overlapping but separate ways in which Schopenhauer and Csikszentmihalyi understand boredom might help us to think not only about *The Pale King* but also about Wallace's work more generally. I want to suggest that Wallace's writings can be understood to involve, among other things, a literary-philosophical playing out of a Schopenhauerian conception of boredom, and indeed that the question of boredom in Wallace is itself a site where the complementary and conflicting discourses of philosophy and literature may be seen most clearly to emerge. In his writing, Wallace confronts boredom as one of the fundamental problems in and of human existence, and like the philosophical pessimist Arthur Schopenhauer, he repeatedly links it to death, and specifically to suicide.[34] But as in the work of the optimist psychologist Mihalyi Csikszentmihalyi, Wallace is also interested in the idea of controlling consciousness, controlling what one thinks about, as a way of confronting and finally overcoming boredom.

Few novels play so intricately, so obsessively, on that balancing of boredom with interest, in fact, as Wallace's monumental 1079-page novel *Infinite Jest*—the sheer length and digressive, footnoted intricacy of which has been

---

[32] Csikszentmihalyi, *Flow*, 31.
[33] Ibid., 42. See also 52 (also underlined): "Enjoyment appears at the boundary between boredom and anxiety."
[34] It is significant that Jonathan Franzen has linked Wallace's suicide specifically to boredom: "in one interpretation of his suicide," Franzen speculates, "David had died of boredom and in despair about his future novels"; "If boredom is the soil in which the seeds of addiction sprout, and if the phenomenology and the teleology of suicidality are the same as those of addiction, it seems fair to say that David died of boredom" ("Farther Away," 82, 92).

described by one critic as "at once a challenge, a threat, and an enticement."[35] In this novel, as in *The Pale King*, Wallace is responding to and developing a structural feature of the novel form. The genre of the novel is constitutively digressive and therefore constitutively boring, at least in potential, since digression offers the tedium of the irrelevant: the novel in its simplest form is nothing other than a way of getting from A to B in narrative by the long route. What the novel demands of us is a certain focus of attention, and what it constantly offers us is the possibility of meaning deferred. But in both drawing out and fending off boredom, novels also enact or perform boredom, allow for or threaten boredom at each moment, enticing us to experience the condition or threatening us with it if our attention is lacking or misdirected.[36] *Every* novel can be boring if it is read in a certain way, if it is not attended to or if it is mis-attended to. Boredom constitutes the structural possibility of every novel, of the novel genre itself, and is the structural possibility in particular of *The Pale King*, a novel that may be said to accord with what Roland Barthes calls the "text of bliss," the text that "imposes a state of loss," that "discomforts" perhaps even "to the point of a certain boredom."[37]

Novels, then, fend off boredom, and it is partly for this reason that they concern the question of attention, of consciousness, the question to which boredom is inextricably bound and to which, according to Monroe Beardsley, "literary value" is itself related. In an important 1981 essay, "Aesthetic Value in Literature," Beardsley contends that an appreciation of or attunement with such a quality involves the "fixation of attention on some portion of the sensory or phenomenal field, a sense of liberation from distractions and

---

[35] Marshall Boswell, *Understanding David Foster Wallace* (Columbia: University of South Carolina Press, 2003), 118. The *Broom of the System* "goes on a bit too long," he comments, "as does most of Wallace's output" (64).

[36] On the relationship between the novel as a genre and boredom, see Patricia Meyer Spacks, *Boredom: The Literary History of a State of Mind* (Chicago: University of Chicago Press, 1995): Spacks argues that "the invention of boredom as a concept and of the novel as genre coincided in time and implicated one another" (60). See Elizabeth Goodstein, *Experience Without Qualities: Boredom and Modernity* (Stanford: Stanford University Press, 2005), ch. 3, for a discussion of the prominence of boredom in nineteenth-century European culture. Two more recent studies that have informed the present essay are Peter Toohey, *Boredom: A Lively History* (New Haven: Yale University Press, 2011), and Lars Svendsen, *A Philosophy of Boredom*, trans. John Lyons (London: Reaktion Books, 2005). In *The Pale King* (hereafter cited in the text as *PK*), Wallace points out, through a dense philological passage on the idea of boredom that owes much to Reinhard Kuhn's *The Demon of Noontide: Ennui in Western Literature* (New Jersey: Princeton University Press, 1977) but that seems to have been hallucinated by the character Lane Dean, that the word "bore" only appeared in English "suddenly" in 1766, "just at the time of industry's rise . . . of mass man, the automated turbine and drill bit and bore" (*PK*, 383–4).

[37] Roland Barthes, *The Pleasure of the Text*, trans. Richard Miller (New York: Hill and Wang, 1975), 14.

practical concerns, a notable degree of distance or detachment from emotional oppression, the exhilaration of exercising perceptual and cognitive powers to an unusual degree, a sense of integration and wholeness."[38] In this essay, which is weirdly evocative of Csikszentmihalyi's notion of "flow," Beardsley argues that aesthetic value has to do with the directedness of consciousness, with the control of the subject's or the reader's attention: in this sense, the literary allows one's attention to be "fixed" on something in a way that enables one to avoid being distracted by other, "oppressive" emotions. According to Beardsley, then, the aesthetic in literature has to do with a turn of attention to the literary object and thereby the exclusion of other concerns. Which means, in the first place, that the literary is *about* and is determined by the question of boredom since, as the Norwegian philosopher Lars Svendsen argues, boredom can be conceptualized precisely as the *other* of attention, of attentiveness, as produced either by the saturation and overwhelming of consciousness, or by its starvation or attenuation.[39]

In as much as the novel is founded on some relation with the "real," in as much as our interest in the novel has to do with the promise of a kind of or version of (or representation of) "reality," it is determined, and even defined, by what Roland Barthes calls the "reality effect," which Barthes argues is achieved through the presentation of *unnecessary* details.[40] In other words, the novel offers us unnecessary details in order to produce a sense of "reality" but, just because of that non-negotiable inclusion of such details, threatens to bore us, to turn our attention away. This would constitute a further complication in Beardsley's aesthetics: the literary-aesthetic value of the novel in particular has to do not only with the fixing of one's attention but also with the degree to which that attention is also and at the same time challenged, turned away, risked. The logical end of such an aesthetic would involve not only writing an excessively long, detailed, and complex novel like *Infinite Jest*, which continually and excessively challenges the reader not to be bored, but also writing a novel like *The Pale King*, which takes as its main topic the question of boredom. In other words, the logical consequence of such an aesthetic would include writing a novel that is both about and that plays out the boredom inherent in, for example, the intricacies of the vast bureaucracy—perhaps the ultimate pre-digital bureaucracy—that is the Internal Revenue Service.

[38] Monroe C. Beardsley, "Aesthetic Value in Literature," *Comparative Literature Studies* 18 (1981): 240.
[39] See Lars Svendsen, *A Philosophy of Boredom*, 29–32, on boredom as a function of an overload or lack of meaning or information.
[40] Roland Barthes, "The Reality Effect" (1968), in *The Rustle of Language*, trans. Richard Howard (Oxford: Blackwell, 1986), 141–8.

Supposedly written in 2005 by a certain David Wallace as a memoir of his year working with the IRS in 1985–86 (*PK*, 69–70), *The Pale King* concerns the arrival of new (or newly redeployed) employees of the Internal Revenue Service at its Midwest Regional Examination Center in Peoria, Illinois, in 1985, together with the "backstories" of those individuals. In addition to the newly recruited David Wallace, the "author," who is confused with another, more senior arrival at the Peoria office also called David Wallace, the novel focuses in particular on a small number of characters, including the "fact psychic" Claude Sylvanshine, whose attention is continually interrupted by unwanted information; the interminably digressive Chris Fogle ("Irrelevant" Chris Fogle, as he is known); David Cusk, who suffers from attacks of uncontrollable sweating that he can partly limit by controlling what he pays attention to; the suicidally bored Lane Dean; and the excruciatingly dull Shane Drinion. Drinion is known as "Mr Excitement" because his literalism makes him so dull to talk to, and he also appears somewhere along the autistic spectrum and fails to be bored by the "totally, wrist-bitingly attractive" but also hyper-narcissistic and tedious Meredith Rand. As reviewers of Wallace's book have noted, the major theme or concern of the novel is the question of boredom, the sheer, stifling tedium involved in the low-level processing of income tax data by the employees of the IRS.

One prominent character in *The Pale King* is the anxious, bored IRS employee Claude Sylvanshine, the "fact psychic" who suffers from a condition known as "Random-Fact Intuition," a fictional condition in which the sufferer is bombarded by random, irrelevant, and unwanted information—the precise number of blades of grass on one's front lawn, the date that the underwater explorer William Beebe died (1962, as it happens: Wallace's birth-year), personal or intimate details of people in one's vicinity, and so on and on. The condition, we are told, is a form of extrasensory perception (ESP) that causes "overwhelming" difficulties in concentration and "constant headaches" (*PK*, 121).[41] For Sylvanshine, tedium "is like stress" but is constitutive of "its own Category of Woe" (*PK*, 15). To avoid the madness of this excessive, tedious, unwelcome knowledge, he tries to focus his mind: "It was true," he thinks, "the entire ball game, in terms of both the [IRS] exam and life, was what you gave attention to vs. what you willed yourself to not. . . . The whole ball game was perspective, filtering, the choice of perception's objects. . . . The trick was homing in on which facts were important" (*PK*, 12, 15, 16). He is obsessed, indeed, by attention, by what to pay attention to, in a way that is only an

---

[41] "These subjects' sudden flashes of insight or awareness are structurally similar to but usually far more tedious and quotidian than the dramatically relevant foreknowledge we normally conceive as ESP or precognition" (*PK*, 118).

exaggerated form of an unavoidable human question. For Sylvanshine, thinking itself is the problem—a problem that he thinks might be countered by a Csikszentmihalyi-like "antistress technique" that he calls "Thought Stopping."

As this suggests, Wallace's final novel itself repeatedly, self-reflexively, and perhaps even boringly theorizes boredom. The "Author's Foreword" to the novel, beginning in the published text at page 66, for example, concerns itself with attention and with the relationship between attention and boredom. The author-figure or authorial character David Wallace (a figure that is both the author and not the author) ends the Foreword to what he calls his "memoir," with an extended, page-long meditation on attention and dullness. The "really interesting question," he says, is "why dullness proves to be such a powerful impediment to attention" and why we "recoil from the dull":

> Maybe it's because dullness is intrinsically painful; maybe that's where phrases like "deadly dull" or "excruciatingly dull" come from. But there might be more to it. Maybe dullness is associated with psychic pain because something that's dull or opaque fails to provide enough stimulation to distract people from some other, deeper type of pain that is always there, if only in an ambient low-level way, and which most of us spend nearly all our time and energy trying to distract ourselves from feeling, or at least from feeling directly or with our full attention. (*PK*, 85)

The fundamental condition of existence, this suggests, is some "deeper type of pain." We spend our lives being distracted from such pain by various forms of "stimulation." Boredom *is* a lack of such stimulation and gives us access to the authentic, unavoidable suffering that, as Schopenhauer would have it, constitutes human existence.

Perhaps the most telling of the many commentaries on boredom within *The Pale King*, and what seems to be the point, in the end, of the book, comes in a page-and-a-half section by an unnamed speaker who recalls the two summers in 1984 and 1985 that he spent as a "cart boy" at the IRS in Peoria. The speaker explains that he learned that "the world of men as it exists today is a bureaucracy" and that the "key" to coping with this condition is "the ability to deal with boredom"—which means, in effect, to "function effectively in an environment that precludes everything vital and human. To breathe, so to speak, without air":

> The key is the ability, whether innate or conditioned, to find the other side of the rote, the picayune, the meaningless, the repetitive, the pointlessly complex. To be, in a word, unborable. (*PK*, 437–8)

This, the speaker declares, is "the key to modern life": to be "immune to boredom"—that is, unborable—would mean that there would be "literally nothing you cannot accomplish." The cart boy's comments alert us to the other side of boredom, the possibility of overcoming it, and indeed the potential *redemptiveness* of its transcendence, the sense of "enchantment" that Jane Bennett has recently argued can be generated by the "institutional complexity" of the vast bureaucracies of modernity.[42]

And what this unfinished, impossible, and brilliant novel produces, finally, is the possibility of boredom. Boredom is not only the novel's topic but also what it both enacts and offers its readers. "Irrelevant" Chris Fogle is boring because he fails to discriminate between what is relevant and what is not. It is therefore appropriate that the longest chapter of the book—one hundred pages of it—is devoted to his monologue. But Chris Fogle is nothing other than this fascinating and fascinatingly dull one-hundred page monologue together with other scattered comments by and about him: Chris Fogle is not Chris Fogle but an invention of David Foster Wallace, a novelist who constantly threatens us with, entices us with the dull. Despite his assertion otherwise, the author of *The Pale King* is Chris Fogle.[43] Much of the novel is dedicated to the minutiae of income tax law and lore—than which (so the premise goes) nothing can be more tedious. As if to illustrate the point and force us to encounter such boredom, Wallace devotes one three-page chapter to an account of workers at the IRS repetitively turning pages of the documents on which they are working:

> "Irrelevant" Chris Fogle turns a page. Howard Cardwell turns a page. Ken Wax turns a page. Matt Redgate turns a page. "Groovy" Bruce Channing attaches a form to a file. Ann Williams turns a page. Anand Sing turns two pages at once by mistake and turns one back which makes a slightly different sound. David Cusk turns a page. Sandra Pounder turns a page. Robert Atkins turns two separate pages of two separate files at the same time. Ken Wax turns a page. Lane Dean Jr. turns a page. Olive Borden turns a page. Chris Acquistipace turns a page. (*PK*, 310)

---

[42] See Jane Bennett, *The Enchantment of Modern Life: Attachments, Crossings, and Ethics* (New Jersey: Princeton University Press, 2001): see especially 104–10, on the "ambiguous charm of institutional complexity" in Kafka (surely a precursor, even if a distant one, of Wallace's novel). Like Wallace's, Kafka's stories "perform the anxiety and vertigo of a bureaucratic encounter, but they also enact its strange pleasure," according to Bennett (106). One of the differences between Kafka and Wallace, of course, is that Wallace explores the "strange pleasure" of bureaucracy from the inside, so to speak, from the perspective of the bureaucrat himself.

[43] See *PK*, 259: "I am not Chris Fogle."

And so it goes for three double-column pages. This is compelling in its dullness. There is rich intrigue in the linguistics of naming here and in our sense of the withheld meaningfulness of the employees' personal names (names are or always can be funny, always can signify, this suggests). And both comedy and suspense are generated by the intricate attention to the dull, monotonous, repetitive act of turning pages and the possibility of its intricate variety: this is so dull that we get interested when *two* pages rather than one are turned. "Irrelevant" Chris Fogle, it turns out, is no more boring, no more irrelevant, than anyone else, and the novel implies that there is nothing other than, nothing outside, boredom, tedium, ennui.[44] And yet, and yet.... The paradox of "art," as Wallace asserts, is that it is *not* just representation: "What renders a truth meaningful, worthwhile, &c.," the author of *The Pale King* comments, "is its relevance" (*PK*, 259). Even the boring can be art, by this account, even the boring can be interesting.[45]

Wallace's novel is unfinished, of course, and we can speculate why that is the case—speculate about the nature of novel-writing and boredom, and about the seemingly insuperable feat of writing a novel *about* boredom in order to overcome boredom, to defeat, to transform the experience. In this sense, for all the other ways we may consider it, *The Pale King* is a failed novel, the failure of a novel. But we can glimpse what the novel might have been by reading the notes that Wallace left, on his death, for his unfinished novel— notes that are peculiarly direct and extraordinarily illuminating on the subject of boredom. The first of two "broad arcs" that Wallace posits for his book is that of "paying attention, boredom," while what he calls the "Central Deal" of the novel is "realism, monotony" within a narrative that consists of a "series of set-ups for stuff happening," but where "nothing actually happens" (*PK*, 545–6). One of the characters, the highly literalistic Shane Drinion, we learn, is "*happy*," since he is able to "pay attention":

> It turns out that bliss—a second-by-second joy + gratitude at the gift
> of being alive, conscious—lies on the other side of crushing, crushing
> boredom. Pay close attention to the most tedious thing you can find

---

[44] Ibid., 106, where one unnamed employee's idea for a play is described: an IRS examiner sits working at a table, working longer and longer until everyone in the audience, outraged and bored by the play, has left—at which point the "real action" of the play begins.

[45] See Jonathan Culler, *Structuralist Poetics* (1975; London: Routledge, 2002): "one cannot, finally, be bored in good faith because boredom draws attention to particular aspects of the work (to certain modes of failure) and enables one to make the text interesting by inquiring how and why it bores" (306).

(tax returns, televised golf), and, in waves, a boredom like you've never known will wash over you and just about kill you. Ride these out, and it's like stepping from black and white into color. Like water after days in the desert. Constant bliss in every atom. (*PK*, 546)

There it is, then: a quasi-mystical transcendence, a redemption at work in the novel's exploration of boredom, the possibility of transcendence, of bliss, that may also be said to be at work in the move from Schopenhauer's pessimist analysis of boredom to Csikszentmihalyi's optimistic sense that boredom can be transcended in the experience of "flow," the ability as Wallace puts it in another note, "to be *immersed*" even in the dullest of tasks (*PK*, 547). "Boredom," as Roland Barthes comments in *The Pleasure of the Text*, "is not far from bliss."[46] Boredom *is* even a kind of bliss: in Schopenhauerian terms, if it doesn't kill you it will redeem you, allow you access to a form of quasi-spiritual transcendence, an ecstasy of self-abnegation—a state that might itself be seen as a kind of suicide. The bored IRS employee, the employee (or writer or reader) bored beyond the limits of endurance, the employee (or writer or reader) who passes through such boredom will enter a state in which she will abandon herself, give up her will, forsake her endless, fruitless, intransigent desire for fulfillment, for interest, for attentiveness, and like Schopenhauer's ascetic saint, indeed, will cease striving for something other than boredom.[47] It is this that boredom offers, that boredom threatens: the multiple, endless paradoxicality of everything, infinity. The paradox of the human torment that is the condition of boredom, the *human* condition, in the end, is that it can also and at the same time offer or at least promise the potential of a kind of self-overcoming, a state of quasi-spiritual self-denial, a "shattering" of the self that one might describe as a "constant bliss in every atom."[48]

---

[46] Barthes, *Pleasure*, 26.
[47] On Schopenhauer's concept of the "saint," see, for example, Neil Jordan, *Schopenhauer's Ethics of Patience: Virtue, Salvation, and Value* (Lewiston: Edwin Mellon, 2009), ch. 5.
[48] On "self-shattering," see Leo Bersani, *The Freudian Body: Psychoanalysis and Art* (New York: Columbia University Press, 1990).

6

The Lobster Considered

Robert C. Jones

The day may come, when the rest of the animal creation may acquire those rights which never could have been withholden from them but by the hand of tyranny.

—Jeremy Bentham

Is it not possible that future generations will regard our present agribusiness and eating practices in much the same way we now view Nero's entertainments or Mengele's experiments?

—David Foster Wallace

The arguments to prove man's superiority cannot shatter this hard fact: in suffering the animals are our equals.

—Peter Singer

In 1941 M. F. K. Fisher first asked us to consider the oyster,[1] not as a moral but as a culinary exploration. Sixty-three years later when David Foster Wallace asked us to consider the lobster[2] for ostensibly similar reasons, the investigation quickly abandoned the gustatory and took a turn toward the philosophical and ethical. In that essay, originally published in *Gourmet* magazine, Wallace challenges us to think deeply about the troubling ethical questions raised by the issue of lobster pain and our moral (mis)treatment of these friendly crustaceans. Since the publication of that essay, research on nonhuman animal sentience has exploded. News reports of the findings of research into animal behavior and cognition are common; 2010 saw the publication of a popular book of the title *Do Fish Feel Pain?*[3] In this essay, I accept Wallace's challenge and argue not only that according to our best

---

[1] M. F. K. Fisher, *Consider the Oyster* (New York: Still Point Press, 2001).
[2] David Foster Wallace, "Consider the Lobster," in *Consider the Lobster and Other Essays* (New York: Back Bay Books, 2007), 235–54.
[3] Victoria Braithwaite, *Do Fish Feel Pain?* (Oxford: Oxford University Press, 2010).

science do lobsters feel pain, but also that in light of these findings, the moral status of lobsters—and all crustaceans—is higher than most people imagine and that they are entitled to membership in the moral community.

Moral status explained

When we reflect upon the concept of moral status and contemplate what it means for a being to possess moral status, we imagine a being whose interests must be considered in our moral deliberations. In this sense, the notion of moral status can be thought of as a kind of threshold phenomenon. You either have moral status or you don't; you're either in the club or you're not. Until the last century, philosophers have taken for granted that moral status in this sense is primarily a human affair.[4] (I'll have more to say on this anon.)

But there is another way to make sense of the concept of moral status, one that assumes not an all-or-nothing game but rather *gradations* of moral status. For instance, it makes perfect sense to claim that one being has greater moral status than another, that, for example, a normal adult chimpanzee has greater moral status than an oyster. Used in this sense, "moral status" specifies not only which entities belong to the moral community, but also the degree to which their interests count.

These two senses of moral status reflect a distinction between what philosophers call "moral considerability" and "moral significance."[5] A being is morally considerable just in case she is a bona fide member of the moral community, thus making it possible for her to be wronged in a morally relevant way. In other words, if a being is morally considerable, she is in the moral club. In this sense, the fact that a being is morally considerable places a moral demand on *us*—or more precisely, on anyone who is capable of recognizing his or her moral obligations. Once a being is morally considerable, we may then need to adjudicate questions of relative moral value between kinds of animals, for example, between, say, a chimpanzee and an oyster. Thus, moral significance involves the moral value of the members once admitted to the moral club.

---

[4] The notion of moral status (or moral standing) is modeled on the notion of legal standing. The seminal work on this concept as applied to nonhuman nature is Richard Stone's "Should Trees Have Standing—Toward Legal Rights for Natural Objects," *Southern California Law Review* 45 (1972): 450–502.

[5] To my knowledge, this distinction was first made by Goodpaster in his "On Being Morally Considerable," *The Journal of Philosophy* 75, 6 (1978): 308–25.

Lori Gruen provides us with a nice metaphor here.[6] To establish that a being—any being (a human, a chimpanzee, a lobster, or even a Martian)—is morally considerable (i.e., that it matters morally) is to say that it shows up on our "moral radar screen." But once a being makes it onto our moral radar screen, questions of moral treatment and adjudication of disputes between members become a function the being's moral significance, that is, the strength of the signal and its location on the moral screen. The strength of one's moral signal is determined by those features and capacities deemed valuable by things like one's moral theory (and certain other complex factors).[7]

For utilitarian philosophers such as Peter Singer, all that is required for a being to gain entrance into the moral community is sentience,[8] that is, the capacity for pain and suffering (or pleasure).[9] Beyond sentience, Singer cites capacities such as anticipation, detailed memory, and self-awareness, the possession of which may weight moral significance beyond mere sentience.

Arguing not from a utilitarian stance but from one of inherent rights, Tom Regan argues that the capacity to be the subject of experiences, that is, to be a "subject-of-a-life," is what matters morally.[10] For Regan, individuals are subjects-of-a-life if they possess the ability to experience feelings of pleasure and pain, the capacity for beliefs, desires, perceptions, memory, an emotional life, etc.

Although the two moral theories differ in the role that these criteria play in determining things such as interests, rights, and obligations, what both theories agree on is the moral importance of the possession of the ability to have experiences—a *what it's like* to be that thing—to a being's moral

---

[6] Lori Gruen, "The Moral Status of Animals," *The Stanford Encyclopedia of Philosophy* (Winter 2012 Edition), Edward N. Zalta (ed.), URL=http://plato.stanford.edu/archives/win2012/entries/moral-animal/.

[7] See Bernice Bovenkerk and Franck L. B. Meijboom, "The Moral Status of Fish. The Importance and Limitations of a Fundamental Discussion for Practical Ethical Questions in Fish Farming," *Journal of Agricultural and Environmental Ethics* 25 (2012): 843–60, for a nice discussion of this distinction.

[8] Peter Singer, *Animal Liberation* (New York: HarperCollins, 2009).

[9] 'Sentience' can mean different things to different people including things like the possession of a certain type of subjectivity or self-awareness. However, in the animal ethics literature, *sentience* is a term of art denoting only the capacity for pain and suffering (or pleasure). Some people (e.g., Descartes) argue that suffering requires something beyond mere sentience, something more complex, a kind of second-order awareness of the self. However, (a) that's not what philosophers writing on animal rights mean by the term, and (b) were that the case, newborn human infants would most likely lack the ability to suffer, and that seems implausible. See my paper "Science, Sentience, and Animal Welfare," *Biology & Philosophy* 28, 1 (2013): 1–30, for details.

[10] Tom Regan, *The Case for Animal Rights* (Berkeley and Los Angeles: University of California Press, 2004).

considerability. For example, according to Peter Singer's sentientist view, once a being is determined to be sentient, she just *is* morally considerable.

Given this brief background, we can now get clearer on the focus of this essay. The focus of this essay is not on the moral significance of any one individual lobster, nor of any one species of lobster. Nor even of crustaceans as a whole. This is not an essay whose purpose it is to adjudicate whether a lobster has greater moral significance than a human or a chimpanzee or a snail or a flea. This is not an exploration of moral significance at all.

Given that globally we catch, boil alive, and eat about 200 million lobsters annually,[11] when asked to consider the lobster, the issue is certainly not one of moral significance, but of moral considerability since lobsters currently stand outside the moral community. In considering the lobster, the question is whether these "*Alien*-like" crustaceans of Jurassic origin should join us in the club of beings that are morally considerable. In the remainder of this essay, I argue that lobsters are morally considerable, that they should be "in the club," that they should show up on our moral radar screen, that they are indeed members of the moral community.

A little argument

Here's a little argument:

1. Possession of the capacity for pain and suffering makes the possessor morally considerable.
2. Lobsters possess the capacity for pain and suffering.
3. Therefore, lobsters are morally considerable.

---

[11] Since statistics on lobster "production" (as with figures on the production for food of pigs, cows, chickens, or any land animal) are reported not by the number of actual animals caught (or, in the case of land animals, slaughtered) but by total weight, determining the number (or even an approximation of the number) of lobsters caught globally per year—a figure known as "annual global capture production"—requires a bit of math. According to the folks who keep track of such things, namely the Food and Agriculture Organization of the United Nations, about 280,364 tonnes (known in the US as "metric tons") of lobster are captured each year. Converting tonnes to tons (known in the US as "tons" and in the non-US as "short tons") we get a figure of about 309,000 tons of lobster captured globally every year. That's about 600 million pounds of lobster. Now, according to Encyclopedia.com, the average lobster weighs about 3 pounds. That means that globally, about 200 million lobsters are caught each year. Imagine what would happen if the figures on humans killed annually due to genocide, war atrocities, plane crashes, car wrecks, and the like were reported by total weight instead of number of lives lost. By this measure, Stalin murdered—or perhaps we should say, "produced"—about 1.5 million tons of humanity.

Obviously this argument is valid. The question is whether it is sound. That is, are (1) and (2) true? And how might we answer these questions? (1) is a normative claim, a claim of value; (2), an empirical claim. Personally, I think that (1) is rather uncontroversial and needs little if any argument. Nevertheless, later in the essay, I address an objection to (1). That said, if you buy the truth of (1), then the conclusion rests solely on the truth of (2). And since (2) is an empirical question, in arguing for (2) I will marshal our best science on crustacean pain.

Now I'm sure some may see the conclusion of our little argument as obvious and this task unnecessary. However, although René Descartes famously (or notoriously, depending on who you ask) denied animal sentience way back in the seventeenth century,[12] a number of contemporary philosophers (believe it or not) still maintain that nonhuman animals lack the capacity to feel anything at all, let alone suffer.[13] But it's time to leave behind implausible views and turn to the task at hand.

Animals and the moral landscape

Morality-wise, Western philosophical theory has been constructed on the belief that humans are the proper subjects of moral concern because only humans occupy a moral sphere separate from and superior to that of the nonhuman animals. This view, the accepted view—a view known as *human exceptionalism*—commits us to two theses. The first is the claim that humans are unique in their possession of some capacity (or set of capacities) within the physiological or cognitive domains. The second is the claim that the possession of such capacities makes all and only humans morally superior to beings (such as nonhuman animals) who lack such capacities. Importantly, the first claim is largely empirical, and the second, normative. These two claims constitute the two fronts on which those philosophers seeking to expand the moral status of nonhuman animals mount their attacks in an attempt to dismantle the foundations of human exceptionalism.

Central to the strategy employed by philosophers who seek to undermine human exceptionalism and increase the moral status of animals has been to

---

[12] Though this is the "standard" interpretation of Descartes, recently my colleague Joseph Hwang has come to convince me that perhaps this is too simplistic an interpretation, overstating the case. See also, Peter Harrison, "Descartes on Animals," *The Philosophical Quarterly* 42 (1992): 219–27 and Robert Jones, "The Moral Significance of Animal Cognition" (PhD diss., Stanford University, 2005).

[13] See, for example, Peter Harrison, "Do Animals Feel Pain?," *Philosophy* 66 (1991): 25–40, and Peter Carruthers, *The Animals Issue* (Cambridge: Cambridge University Press, 1992).

attack the empirical aspects of human exceptionalism by presenting evidence that demonstrates the possession by some nonhuman animals of some set of morally relevant physiological or cognitive capacities. When successful, arguments of this kind undermine the first prong of the human exceptionalism thesis. Thus, the strategy for those philosophers like Singer and Regan has been to question the existence of a clear distinction between *all* humans and *all* animals with regard to the possession of morally relevant capacities such as sentience and other what-it's-like experiences. These candidate capacities— sentience, self-awareness, memory, and mindreading[14]—although not the only capacities that might bear on the moral status of individuals, represent a solid starting place. Since as we've seen, the first claim that undergirds human exceptionalism—the claim that humans are unique in their possession of some set of morally relevant capacities—is primarily an empirical one, it is quite useful—and in some cases, indispensable—to see what science has to say about which animals possess which capacities. Thus, the empirical data on this question are central to the question of the moral status, moral considerability, moral significance, and moral treatment of nonhuman animals. For example, with regard to sentience, if no clear distinction can be empirically drawn between humans and animals, then the foundations of human exceptionalism will be substantially weakened and the moral status of nonhuman animals increased.

A cautionary note

Although the possession of the capacity for pain and suffering is crucial in determining which things among the furniture of the universe are the proper objects of moral concern, some caution is in order. Since our epistemic access to the mental lives of animals is even more limited than access to each other's minds, we must be cautious about cognitive attributions, and selective about the kinds of evidence for such attributions we have at our disposal. As Wallace notes, reliance on comparative neuroanatomy as a basis for the moral considerability of animals can be fraught:

> Since pain is a totally subjective mental experience, we do not have direct access to anyone or anything's pain but our own; and even just the principles by which we can infer that others experience pain and have

---

[14] When philosophers talk about mindreading, they're not talking about telepathy, they mean merely the ability to attribute mental states (e.g., beliefs and desires) to others and the understanding that others' beliefs and desires may differ from one's own.

a legitimate interest in not feeling pain involve hard-core philosophy—metaphysics, epistemology, value theory, ethics. The fact that even the most highly evolved nonhuman mammals can't use language to communicate with us about their subjective mental experience is only the first layer of additional complication in trying to extend our reasoning about pain and morality to animals. And everything gets progressively more abstract and convoluted as we move farther and farther out from the higher-type mammals into cattle and swine and dogs and cats and rodents, and then birds and fish, and finally invertebrates like lobsters.[15]

Although Wallace too quickly assumes that pain is a "totally subjective experience,"[16] he makes clear some of the philosophical challenges of attributing pain to beings other than ourselves. (I will return to this issue later in the essay.) A further worry involves numbers. Only a small fraction of the almost 6,000 extant mammalian species, 10,000 avian species, tens of thousands of reptile and amphibian species, a still greater number of fish species, and millions of insects and spiders have been investigated for sentience. Despite these challenges, comparative biological methods remain the most reliable metric in our understanding of the mental lives of nonhuman animals.

Sentience: Pain and suffering[17]

A solid methodological framework for an investigation into whether an animal is sentient includes investigating whether that animal possesses or exhibits

---

[15] Wallace, *Consider the Lobster*, 246.

[16] Surprisingly, Wallace's assumption here, which reflects intuitive, pre-theoretic notions of pain—that access to my own internal pain states is a solely introspective affair involving private, subjective experiences about which my epistemic judgments are immune to error and about which I cannot be wrong—can lead to some strange, unintuitive consequences. For example, if my pain sensation is physical (which seems the case), it follows that it is both located in physical, public space and yet logically private, an odd consequence indeed. Yet, if pain is not physical, what sort of thing could it be? A non-spatial, non-physical, spatiotemporally located event? But what might that be? The philosophical literature on the subjectivity of pain is enormous. If you're interested, you should start with Murat Aydede's entry "Pain" in the *Stanford Encyclopedia of Philosophy* (Aydede, Murat, "Pain," *The Stanford Encyclopedia of Philosophy* (Spring 2013 Edition), Edward N. Zalta (ed.), forthcoming URL=http://plato.stanford.edu/archives/spr2013/entries/pain/.)

[17] See my (2013) for a detailed discussion of animal sentience.

- a central nervous system and other structures and psychoactive chemicals homologous to those known to control pain response in humans (e.g., neuroanatomical (opioid receptors, such as nociceptors) and neurochemical (opioids, such as endorphins and encephalins))[18]
- physiological or behavioral response to noxious[19] (or positive) stimuli, analgesics, and anesthetics.[20]

Although at first glance these properties and capacities may seem to provide a clear framework for investigation, as we've already seen, difficulties quickly arise. Pain is a notoriously difficult phenomenon to understand, not only in ourselves but especially in nonhuman animals.[21] Data on pain present at least two challenges.[22]

The first is that data on the high variability between the physiological mechanisms and the phenomenal aspects of pain are often confounding, raising puzzles about the connection between the two. For example, the very same kind of stimuli can elicit a pain response of widely varying intensity (or none) in different individuals or even in the same individual at different times, making generalizations from humans to animals even more challenging. Although we have a good idea of how the nervous system detects and responds to painful events in humans, exactly how the human brain processes the stimuli and generates the phenomenal aspects of pain induced by injury remains far less clear.

A second challenge presented by the data on the connection between the physiological mechanisms and the phenomenal aspects of pain is abnormalities such as congenital analgesia or, even more puzzling, pain

---

[18] Endorphins and encephalins are two of the more common substances—found in many organisms—known to have morphine-like analgesic effects.

[19] Noxious stimuli used in pain research on nonhumans include "mechanical" (pricking or probing), "thermal" (heating or freezing), "chemical" (exposure to acidic irritants), and "electrical" (shocking).

[20] Marian Dawkins (2006) presents a clear and persuasive analysis of the scientific basis for assessing suffering in animals, highlighting the plurality of mental states that might be properly described as "suffering," and thus somewhat vaguely (and I think, wisely) characterizes suffering as the "experiencing [of] one of a wide range of extremely unpleasant subjective (mental) states," a definition I wholly endorse.

[21] For clear discussions of some of the difficulties peculiar to assessing animal pain, see Collin Allen's, "Animal pain," *Nous* 38, 4 (2004): 617–43 doi:10.1111/j.0029-4624.2004.00486.x, as well as his "Deciphering animal pain," in *Pain: New Essays on Its Nature and the Methodology of Its Study* (Cambridge, MA: Bradford Book/MIT Press, 2005).

[22] For a nice discussion of the difficulties in finding a unified theory of pain, see the Introduction to Aydede's *Pain: New Essays on Its Nature and the Methodology of Its Study* (Cambridge, MA: MIT Press, 2005).

asymbolia, a type of dissociation affect involving pain without painfulness. In these bizarre, almost inconceivable cases, a subject *feels* pain but is not *in* pain.[23] Given these challenges, how might our investigations into the question of animal pain reliably proceed? Common sense suggests that at least mammals and birds are sentient. But what about reptiles? Amphibians? Fish? Invertebrates? Do lobsters feel pain when boiled alive? Scallops, when shucked? Cockroaches, when blasted with insecticide? Here, intuitions begin to break down, and so it seems only science can step in where commonsense intuitions begin to falter.[24]

What exactly is pain?[25]

The International Association for the Study of Pain (IASP) provides what seems at first blush to be a reasonable definition of pain as "an unpleasant sensory and emotional experience associated with actual or potential tissue damage, or described in terms of such damage." The IASP definition is followed by a footnote informing us that "pain is always subjective" and that the IASP definition intentionally "avoids tying pain to the stimulus."[26] However, the IASP definition of pain is both physiologically and philosophically problematic since it (a) emphasizes subjective experience and self-report while supporting conflicting philosophical interpretations of pain (e.g., subjectivist and objectivist views of pain), and (b) remains silent on the question of the relationship of the physiological bases of pain to its phenomenal aspects. Yet, given that pain and suffering are likely very old

[23] In his fascinating 2007 book *Feeling Pain and Being in Pain*, Nikola Grahek presents a quite thorough analysis of the empirical literature on such pain abnormalities and the implications of such data for the "hard problem" of consciousness in the context of pain. Some of these cases are truly bizarre and mind-blowing. For example, Grahek discusses cases of people experiencing pain asymbolia who, after suffering brain trauma (or sometimes just people who have been given a whopping dose of morphine), report that they are experiencing pain but are just not bothered by it. That is, they recognize the sensation of pain but are completely immune to suffering from it.

[24] See the World Society for the Protection of Animals (WSPA) website "Sentience Mosaic" http://www.animalmosaic.org/sentience/ for an exhaustive number of resources on the scientific literature on nonhuman animal sentience and its connection to animal welfare issues.

[25] The focus here is primarily on physical pain, not emotional or psychic pain, though the distinction between the two is not at all clear. Anyone who has suffered severe grief or heartache knows how much they can really *physically* hurt.

[26] H. Merskey and N. Bogduk, *Classification of Chronic Pain: Descriptions of Chronic Pain Syndromes and Definitions of Pain Terms*, 2nd edn (Seattle: IASP Press, 2011).

phenomena, it would be strange were pain not widespread across varied species, did not provide selective advantage, nor serve a similar adaptive function as it does in humans. In other words, it would be very surprising if we were the only animals that experienced pain. Consequently, an understanding of the basic mechanics of pain is imperative to understanding its role in animal sentience.

The mechanics of pain

Pain in humans is at least a two-step process. The first step involves the stimulation of special receptors called *nociceptors* that transmit injury-detecting electrical impulses to the spinal cord, triggering an automatic reflex response. At this first stage, there are no conscious, phenomenal aspects of the experience. In the second stage, the signal then moves from the spinal cord to the neocortex at which point the phenomenal aspects of pain kick in and we experience the unpleasant sensation associated with tissue damage. Although researchers are clear about the mechanisms involved in the first stage, it is the second stage of the process—the conscious experience of pain—that remains somewhat of a mystery.

In addressing the issue of animal pain, we can start with the questions, "Which animal groups possess nociceptors (or exhibit a 'nociceptive response')?" and "Do they (and if so, how do they) respond to noxious stimuli, analgesics, and anesthetics?" We can further explore which organisms possess neural organs more complex than simple neural nets (e.g., organs such as ganglia, brain masses, or brains), and of these, which possess nociceptor-to-brain pathways. It is time now to turn to the evidence.

Do lobsters feel pain?

A lobster, taxonomically speaking, is a marine crustacean of the family Homaridae, characterized by five pairs of jointed legs, the first pair terminating in large pincerish claws used for subduing prey. Moreover, a crustacean is an aquatic arthropod of the class Crustacea, which comprises crabs, shrimp, barnacles, lobsters, and freshwater crayfish. All this is right there on Wikipedia. And an arthropod is an invertebrate member of the phylum Arthropoda, whose phylum covers insects, spiders, crustaceans, and centipedes/millipedes, all of whose main commonality, besides the absence of a centralized brain-spine assembly, is a chitinous exoskeleton composed of segments, to which appendages are articulated in pairs. The point is that lobsters are basically giant sea-insects.[27] Given that, a slight digression involving a review of what our best science has to say about sentience in insects may enhance our understanding of the same in crustaceans.[28]

Insects and spiders

The literature on insect and arachnid pain is astonishingly impoverished. For over 30 years, the established view (made so by one Sir Prof. Vincent Brian Wigglesworth)[29] has been that insects by in large do not feel pain. Yet, Wigglesworth goes on to argue that certain insect behaviors (e.g., escape behavior when presented with noxious stimuli) indicate that some insects must experience some form of pain. Eisemann et al.[30] conclude that the evidence "does not appear to support the occurrence in insects of a pain state."[31] However, Tracey et al.[32] and Tobin and Bargmann have discovered nociception in at least some insects, namely Drosophila.[33] Neely et al. find nociception in response to thermal noxious stimuli as well as what the researchers refer to as a "pain" gene in Drosophila.[34]

---

[27] Factoid: A lobster's blood is colorless but when exposed to oxygen develops a bluish color.

[28] This FN will almost surely not survive the editing process, but here goes:

> The observant reader may notice that this paragraph is taken almost word-for-word from DFW's own lobster essay. Were I to use quotes and then cite as is customary, the somewhat Wallacean subversive intent of this paragraph would be lost entirely (though perhaps the very insertion of this FN might undermine that intent). In any event, I have chosen to drop this FN acknowledging the origin of this paragraph to avoid the conventional the quote-and-cite option. In fact, even the idea of dropping a FN of this kind is borrowed from DFW. Though it is highly doubtful that the lobster is capable of such recursive meta-thinking, fortunately its moral considerability does not depend upon the possession of these kinds of cognitive abilities.

[29] V. Wigglesworth, "Do Insects Feel Pain?" *Antenna* 1 (1980): 8–9.

[30] C. H. Eisemann, W. K. Jorgensen, D. J. Merritt, M. J. Rice, B. W. Cribb, P. D. Webb and M. P. Zalucki, "Do Insects Feel Pain?—A Biological View," *Cellular and Molecular Life Science* 40, 2 (1984): 164–7.

[31] Despite Eisemann et al.'s conclusion that the evidence "does not appear to support the occurrence in insects of a pain state," tellingly, he advises the "experimental biologist . . . to follow, whenever feasible, Wigglesworth's recommendation that insects have their nervous systems inactivated prior to traumatizing manipulation. This procedure not only facilitates handling, but also guards against the remaining possibility of pain infliction and, equally important, helps to preserve in the experimenter an appropriately respectful attitude towards living organisms whose physiology, though different, and perhaps simpler than our own, is as yet far from completely understood."

[32] W. D. Tracey, R. I. Wilson, G. Laurent and S. Benzer, "*painless*, a Drosophila Gene Essential for Nociception," *Cell* 113, 2 (2003): 261–73.

[33] D. M. Tobin and C. I. Bargmann, "Invertebrate Nociception: Behaviors, Neurons and Molecules," *Journal of Neurobiology* 61, 1 (2004): 161–74.

[34] G. G. Neely, A. C. Keene, P. Duchek, E. C. Chang, Q. P. Wang, Y. A. Aksoy, M. Rosenzweig, M. Costigan, C. J. Woolf, P. A. Garrity and J. M. Penninger, "TrpA1&lt Regulates Thermal Nociception in Drosophila," *PLoS ONE* 6, 8 (2011): e24343.

In a fascinating 1999 study carried out by V. E. Dyakonova at the Russian Academy of Sciences, opioid receptors and evidence of pain were discovered in crickets.[35] The experimental setup involved Dyakonova noting the amount of time it took before crickets jumped from a hot plate whose temperature was gradually elevated. Dyakonova then administered morphine to the crickets in three separate and increasing doses. His findings indicate that the morphine elongated the period of the avoidance of the hot surface by the crickets (the length of which increased in correlation with higher doses of morphine).[36] Other evidence of insect pain includes evidence of nociception (or, at least, a nociceptive response) in moth larvae,[37] and in their work on spider pain, Eisner and Camazine find that "[t]he sensing mechanism by which spiders detect injected harmful chemicals such as venoms . . . may be fundamentally similar to the one in humans that is coupled with the perception of pain."[38]

Crustaceans

The evidence for lobster pain is persuasive. At the physiological level, crustaceans possess nociceptors, ganglia, and nociceptor-to-ganglia pathways.[39] Although crustacean pain attribution is not yet widely accepted, findings are beginning to support crustacean sentience.

In a recent study, two researchers from Queen's University, Barry Magee and Robert Elwood, found convincing evidence of crustacean sentience.[40] The study reveals that the European shore crab (*Carcinus maenas*) responds to electric shocks and then attempts to avoid them. To avoid being spotted and eaten by seagulls, European shore crabs take shelter during the day under

---

[35] V. E. Dyakonova, F. Schurmann and D. A. Sakharov, "Effects of Serotonergic and Opioidergic Drugs on Escape Behaviors and Social Status of Male Crickets," *Naturwissenschaften* 86, 9 (1999): 435–37.

[36] Interestingly, the crickets demonstrated a habituation to morphine such that those administered with morphine for just four days did not differ from control crickets in tests on pain sensitivity, and analgesia was achieved only at a higher dose of the morphine for these unfortunate junky crickets.

[37] E. Walters, P. Illich, J. Weeks and M. Lewin, "Defensive Responses of Larval Manduca Sexta and their Sensitization by Noxious Stimuli in the Laboratory and Field," *The Journal of Experimental Biology* 204, 3 (2001): 457–69.

[38] T. Eisner and S. Camazine, "Spider Leg Autotomy Induced by Prey Venom Injection: An Adaptive Response to 'Pain'?" *Proceedings of the National Academy of Sciences* 80, 11 (1983): 3382–5.

[39] L. G. Ross and B. Ross, *Anaesthetic and Sedative Techniques for Aquatic Animals*, 3rd edn (Oxford: Blackwell, 2008).

[40] Barry Magee and Robert W. Elwood. "Shock avoidance by discrimination learning in the shore crab (*Carcinus maenas*) is consistent with a key criterion for pain," *The Journal of Experimental Biology* 216, 3 (2013): 353–8.

dark rocks. In the study, Magee and Elwood placed ninety crabs in a brightly lit area with the option of scuttling to either of two dark shelters. Once the creatures had taken refuge, half were given an electric shock in the first shelter they chose. It took only two iterations of this routine to produce a significant switch in the crabs' behavior such that those shocked in the previous trial were much more likely to switch shelters than those who hadn't been shocked in the previous trial. The crabs would rather sacrifice the value and security of a dark shelter by venturing into the dangerous light environment than face being shocked again. Even after eight iterations without shock, the crustaceans continued to avoid the shelter where they had been shocked. Magee and Elwood conclude that this is more than a simple reflex reaction to pain, and that all decapod crustaceans—*including lobsters*—would exhibit the same response.[41] And in an earlier 2009 study, Robert Elwood and Mirjam Appel found that the more intensely hermit crabs are electrically shocked, the more willing the crustaceans are to abandon their shells for new shells.[42]

In 2008, a team of researchers led by Stuart Barr (a team that included, once again, Robert Elwood) demonstrated that when the antennae of prawns are exposed to noxious chemical stimuli, the crustaceans respond with increased grooming of the antennae, yet when an anesthetic is applied, the grooming behavior subsides. Barr concluded that such findings are "consistent with the idea that these crustaceans can experience pain."[43] And in a 1988 study, a team of researchers from Buenos Aires demonstrated that injections of analgesic and opioid receptor antagonists into male crabs of the species *Chasmagnathus granulatus* reduced response to electric shock.[44]

What is the inference to best explanation of the results of these studies? Clearly, it would appear that crustaceans—including lobsters—possess the capacity for pain and suffering. If this is so, then by premises (1) and (2) of our little argument, lobsters are morally considerable.

Unfortunately there currently exist no regulations regarding the welfare or treatment of crustaceans, allowing practices in some fisheries that involve the cutting off of claws from live crabs before being thrown back into the sea.

---

[41] It's worth noting that in response, a spokesman for the European Food Safety Authority pronounced that despite the results of this research, decapods would not be classified as a sentient species and that the subject of pain in crustaceans remained "controversial" and a matter of data interpretation.

[42] R. W. Elwood and M. Appel, "Pain Experience in Hermit Crabs?" *Animal Behaviour* 77, 5 (2009): 1243–6.

[43] S. Barr, P. R. Laming, J. T. Dick and R. W. Elwood, "Nociception or Pain in a Decapod Crustacean?" *Animal Behavior* 75, 3 (2008): 745–51.

[44] M. Lozada, A. Romano and H. Maldonado, "Effect of Morphine and Naloxone on a Defensive Response of the Crab *Chasmagnathus Granulatus*," *Pharmacology Biochemistry and Behavior* 30, 3 (1988): 635–40.

Even if one remains skeptical of crustacean sentience, when it comes to issues of welfare it would be most prudent to employ the precautionary principle regarding our treatment of these animals, erring on the side of caution.[45]

Objections

A number of objections may be raised against both our little argument and the assumptions that undergird the scientific methodology of looking for evidence of pain in nonhuman animals, particularly crustaceans. Let me address just three.

The "why is pain morally relevant?" objection

One common objection to our little argument is directed against premise (1), which, recall, says that possession of the capacity for pain and suffering makes the possessor morally considerable. I hear this objection quite often and it usually goes something like this:

> Why pick out pain as the criterion for moral considerability? There are so many other abilities and capacities that one could see as being morally relevant. Your view might not be speciesist,[46] but it's certainly sentientist, privileging the capacity for pain and suffering over other capacities that might be more morally relevant (such as the capacity for empathy or reciprocal behavior) and ignoring other domains of moral significance such as non-sentient life (e.g., trees) or entire biotic/ecosystems. Focusing on sentience seems arbitrary and ungrounded.

---

[45] Disturbing factoid: Believe it or not, performing open-heart surgery on neonates without anesthesia was common practice in the US and Europe until the late 1980s. (That's not a misprint!) Surgeons used no anesthesia when operating on infants (since it was "common knowledge" that infants could not feel pain). Instead (and this is the brutal part), doctors would administer paralytic drugs before surgery and no painkiller after surgery. That is, infants would be fully conscious during open-heart surgery but unable to express that they were in pain because they were paralyzed! The reasons that the medical community gave for denying pain in infants included the claims that (a) since babies do not remember pain, pain doesn't matter, and (b) a baby's nervous system is insufficiently developed to experience pain.

[46] Speciesism (analogous to racism and sexism) is the belief that members of one's own species are more valuable than (and morally superior to) members of another species solely in virtue of their being members of the same species as you. Speciesism, it is claimed, often leads to discriminatory prejudice and practices favoring the interests of the members of one's own species and opposing the interests of members of another species. I aspire not to be speciesist.

First, it's important to note what premise (1) does *not* say. It does *not* say that sentience is the *only* morally relevant capacity. Further, it does *not* say that sentience determines moral significance or is the final arbiter in adjudicating between competing interests once we're "in the club." It merely says that the capacity to experience pain and suffering is sufficient for entrance into the sphere of things that are morally considerable. That is, it claims that if you're sentient, you get a ticket into the moral community. Once you're in, then we can weight values by considering various other capacities, properties, and relations to help us determine moral significance and adjudicate moral disputes.

In response to those who see as arbitrary or question the moral importance of the capacity to have experiences (particularly bad experiences), or who cannot clearly find moral relevance wherever there exists a being for whom there is a "what-it's-like" to be that thing (experiences philosophers refer to as *qualia*), I am at a loss. For such folks—those who see the choice of pain as arbitrary—I must ask the reader to reflect on how you would feel about someone who caught stray cats and set them on fire merely because he thought it was fun. Now reflect on *why* you feel that way. If you think that the fact that the cat can suffer isn't sufficient to give you *any* moral reason to refrain from burning her—and that's what you have to say if you reject the sufficiency claim in (1)—then you are a moral monster.

The anthropomorphism objection

Related to the why-is-pain-morally-relevant objection is the anthropomorphism objection directed against premise (2). Recall that premise (2) states that lobsters possess the capacity for pain and suffering. Attributing physiological and mental states like pain and suffering to nonhumans such as lobsters is just so much anthropomorphizing, the objection goes. Pain and suffering are *human* concepts and *human* experiences, and so to attribute these uniquely human characteristics to nonhuman animals is unwarranted, sentimental, and unscientific.

I believe this objection trades on a kind of ambiguity in the term "anthropomorphism." It's helpful here to distinguish *unnecessary anthropomorphism* from *biocentric anthropomorphism*.[47] *Unnecessary anthropomorphism* involves explaining behavior by attributing (what are believed to be uniquely) human traits and characteristics to beings or objects whose behavior can be better explained without such attribution. For example, the explanation of my

---

[47] The term "biocentric anthropomorphism" comes from Mark Bekoff (2000).

computer's not booting up despite my having pressed the power button is not that my computer is angry with me and refuses to power up out of spite for some transgression on my part, but rather that there is some malfunction with the powering-up mechanism. By contrast, *biocentric anthropomorphism* involves the indispensable use of human terms to explain animals' mental lives, emotions, or feelings. It is in this second sense, not the first, that we attribute pain and suffering to nonhuman animals, and thus premise (2) remains resistant to these kinds of objections.

But I think the larger point here is that it is actually advocates of the anthropomorphism objection who beg the question by assuming that pain may be uniquely human whereas on my view, pain is not at all a uniquely human phenomenon, something we have good reason to believe.

The epistemological objection

Related to the anthropomorphism objection is the epistemological objection, an objection that—as I suggested earlier—is directed against a key foundational assumption underlying the very scientific methodology used to investigate questions of the inner lives of animals. Put simply, the objection asks, how can we *know*? How can we *really know* whether lobsters feel pain? Like the anthropomorphism objection, I believe this objection trades on a kind of ambiguity with regard to knowledge and what it means to know.

Again, as Wallace notes, "the principles by which we can infer that others experience pain and have a legitimate interest in not feeling pain involve hard-core philosophy—metaphysics, epistemology, value theory, ethics."[48] The epistemological objection is a species of a more general philosophical worry called the problem of other minds that goes like this: Forget about whether I can ever know if an oyster or lobster or chimpanzee can experience pain and suffering. How can I ever know whether *you* or any other human being experiences pain, suffering, or any mental state? How can we ever *really know* about the mental states of people, let alone animals? Despite your wincing and crying out when you hit your thumb with that hammer, for all I know you could be a philosophical zombie, exhibiting all the behaviors consistent with *my* pain experience when I accidentally hit my thumb with a hammer, yet totally devoid of any what-it's-like experience.[49] Or perhaps you're one of the unfortunate few who suffer from Congenital Insensitivity to

---

[48] Wallace, *Consider the Lobster*, 246.

[49] This is the kind of inner mental life (or should I say lack of inner mental life) that folks like Carruthers and Harrison postulate that animals possess. Though I wholeheartedly believe that a view's being interesting is a virtue of a philosophical theory, this rule of thumb can be trumped in a case where a view is both interesting and implausible.

Pain (CIP), a rare condition in which a person completely lacks the ability to feel physical pain. Perhaps although you suffer from CIP, you are a very good actor, and have learned through careful observation of others' pain behavior to masterfully mimic and exhibit behaviors consistent with pain, although you feel none when the hammer strikes your thumb.

The intuition underlying the problem of other minds is that it appears that I have privileged first-person epistemic access to my own *and only my own* mental states. Thus, to make an inference from my internal mental states to the internal mental states of others is unwarranted given such a limited sample size (namely, one).

To answer the epistemological objection, I don't think it's necessary to solve the mind–body problem or the problem of other minds. As I alluded to, I think the objection trades on a certain kind of ambiguity regarding the meaning of "know." When someone claims that I can never really *know* whether lobsters feel pain, in a sense, they are correct. If what they mean by 'know' requires 100 percent certainty, then they are right; in that sense I do not *know* whether lobsters (or oysters or chimpanzees or other humans) feel pain since I lack epistemic access to their internal mental states. But that's not at all what I or anybody else means when they claim that crustaceans have the capacity to experience pain. What we mean when we say this is something like: given what we know about things like human and animal anatomy, neurophysiology, brain function, biomechanics, etc., it looks from here like lobsters feel pain and bricks don't. That's all we mean.

That's why the findings of science on these issues are indispensible; since science is the best (but not perfect) method we have so far devised to gain insight, understanding, and knowledge of the inner lives of other animals. Construed broadly, the way I know whether you have a mind or whether lobsters feel pain is this: inference from behavior. That's just about the only (reliable) game in town. And the closer the creature in question is to us physiologically, the more reliable our inferences will be in general. Until and unless we develop some kind of Vulcan mind-meld, we're basically S.O.L. on absolute certainty when it comes to other minds; but fortunately we can get by just fine while requiring that our evidence be merely reasonable.

A more sophisticated version of the epistemological objection might go something like this: Look, I'm not trying to be a skeptic and I don't care about absolute certainty. And it's obvious to me that dogs feel pain. But lobsters are a different story. The fact that crustaceans don't groom their antennae when we give them morphine is definitely some evidence, but it's not clear that it's knockdown evidence. Maybe the morphine is merely blocking neural pathways but that the crustaceans don't feel pain.

To this more sophisticated version of the epistemological objection I reply that I agree, the scientific evidence is not knockdown, but it is solid. The ability to experience pain confers selective advantage on the pain-bearer. As we have seen, humans and other vertebrates possess not only pain-firing nerve cells (nociceptors) but also endogenous pain killers (opioids) and opioid receptors. There is a good chance that the reason why arthropods possess things like nociceptors and opioid receptors (and why crickets get hooked on morphine) is the same reason that we do: because they experience pain.[50] All of this is certainly enough to warrant invoking the precautionary principle, calling us to err on the side of lobster pain. And that's all I need and have been arguing for in this essay, a rather biological weak yet morally profound conclusion indeed.

Conclusion

At the close of his essay, Wallace ruminates on whether his unease with the Maine Lobster Festival and, more generally, our treatment of the lobster is warranted or only so much sentimentalism. He further calls into question the foundations for his belief that animals are less morally important than human beings. If my argument here has been successful, it should be clear that Wallace's unease was, in fact, well grounded. If in considering the lobster I have persuaded you that lobsters are at least morally considerable, then I will have at least helped advance the status of lobsters—and crustaceans in general—from that of "things" to "whos." However—to be clear—even if my arguments are successful, nothing I have said here would discourage Wallace's belief that animals are less morally important that human beings. That's an argument for another day.

Acknowledgments: I'd like to thank Mark Balaguer, Troy Jollimore, and editors Robert Bolger and Scott Korb for their super-helpful and extensive comments on an early draft of this chapter, and Dr. Julius Heyman for letting me pick his brain about the mechanics of pain, analgesics, and anesthesia.

---

[50] This is not to say that all similarly functioning characteristics must have evolved through adaptation. It could be the case that nociceptors and opioid receptors originally evolved for some function other than pain perception, but were then co-opted for that function in vertebrates much later, a process biologists call "exaptation." For example, feathers, which initially evolved for heat regulation, were later co-opted for use in flight. However, there is little evidence that vertebrate pain mechanisms are the result of exaptation and not adaptation.

7

The Terrible Master: David Foster Wallace and the Suffering of Consciousness (with guest Arthur Schopenhauer)

Blakey Vermeule

The guest

Here is a dream. At summer's high noon we throw a party. We rent a rambling farmhouse somewhere—perhaps in upstate New York or the hills above Florence. We cook. We invite friends—the fun ones, the nice ones, the kind mellow, jolly ones, the friends who won't be too picky or make a scene. Let's keep away the bores, the bullies, the egomaniacs, the fussy protocol mongers who pull a sour face if our chat gets too raucous, the smooth and subtle boasters, the culture vultures who will school us for hours about the finer points of Alsatian wines.

We can be casual, everyone in bare feet and shorts. The kids can play games, the grownups can read, nap, chat, and drink wine. Someone will keep a cold pitcher of margaritas going. Someone else will put up a badminton net. We will meet at the long rough wooden table in the main room to talk, eat, and laugh. If you have a crush on someone, bring that person along too—the heart needs a bit of mysterious electricity to run.

This is my dream. The warm sun, the light mood, the jokes, the food lovingly prepared, the life lived easily among other people. To navigate these waters, we do not steer, we float. Imagine a day—your own perfect day—freed entirely from the sorts of "irksome little downers" that might afflict a group of people eating together in a common space.

Such downers might, but in our case will not, include those David Foster Wallace made so memorable when, in 2004, *Gourmet* magazine ("The Magazine of Good Living") sent him to cover the Maine Lobster Festival. Wallace's downers included:

— "A Main Eating Tent, for which there is a constant Disneyland-grade queue, and which turns out to be a square quarter mile of awning-shaded

cafeteria lines and rows of long institutional tables at which friend and
stranger alike sit cheek by jowl, cracking and chewing and dribbling."
    —"smells, which . . . are strong and only partly food-related"
    —"suppers . . . in Styrofoam trays, . . . soft drinks . . . iceless and
flat, . . . convenience-store coffee in more Styrofoam"
    —being "squeezed onto benches alongside children of various ages
and vastly different levels of fine-motor development—not to mention
the people who've somehow smuggled in their own beer in enormous
aisle-blocking coolers, or who all of a sudden produce their own plastic
tablecloths and spread them over large portions of tables to try to reserve
them (the tables) for their own little groups."
    —"And so on."[1]

Nor will our day involve any cruelty to lobsters, those tasty arthropods whose
low ganglion count makes their suffering a matter of much (human) debate.
Nobody seems to know for sure whether lobsters suffer when they are kept
alive inside a small slimy tank of sea water "from which you"—the diner—"can
pick out your supper while [they watch] you point"[2] or when they are placed,
madly scrabbling, into a pot of boiling water.[3] Nobody is sure because lobsters
lack a cerebral cortex, the outermost layer of brain tissue that is "involved
in what's variously called suffering, distress, or the emotional experience
of pain—i.e., experiencing painful stimuli as unpleasant, very unpleasant,
unbearable, and so on."[4] Actually, Wallace gets this partly wrong. Lobsters
have pain receptors. What they lack is the outermost brain tissue that, at
least in humans, prompts awareness and interpretation. Wallace means that
lobsters do not suffer in a specific human sense: they have no representation
of themselves as suffering. Yet cerebral cortices or not, male lobsters lead
lives of noisy desperation in a brutally competitive stew of winner-take-all
status hierarchy. Their fights are so vicious that a lobster may end up shorn
of his antennae, his legs, his claws—still alive, but barely, a lump of shell
lying on the ocean floor, dragging himself around by his mouthparts.[5] But
I digress.
    To take all of these considerations off the table—after all, our friends are
likely to be inquisitive talkative types and we don't want to give them too much

[1]   David Foster Wallace, *Consider the Lobster and Other Essays* (New York: Little, Brown
      and Co., 2005), 239.
[2]   David Foster Wallace, *Oblivion: Stories* (New York: Little, Brown and Company, 2004),
      246.
[3]   Wallace, *Consider the Lobster*, 242.
[4]   Ibid., 246.
[5]   Trevor Corson, *The Secret Life of Lobsters: How Fishermen and Scientists Are Unraveling
      the Mysteries of Our Favorite Crustacean* (New York: Harper Perennial, 2005), 76.

food for thought—we will not serve lobsters, or for that matter intelligent octopi, veal, lamb, foie gras, animals with faces who suckle their young, or the magisterial fowl of the air. Please don't ask me what we will serve—cheese pizza, perhaps, or in a pinch we can resort to flounder—but not anything caught by giant trawlers or raised in chemically fetid aquaculture pools. For we will be very mindful of all nervous systems, but especially human. Human nervous systems are sensitive, excitable, and once goaded, not easily soothed back to placidity.

I hope I will not ruin (what is left of) the mood by admitting I'm planning to invite someone you may not much like. Nobody much likes him, but he is an expert on what human nervous systems endure. Despite being funny, urbane, highly intelligent, and extremely cultivated, he has what might be called a difficult personality, a penchant for howling at the dark side of the moon, a gift for plucking defeat from the jaws of victory. Truth be told, he is a bit of a buzz kill. His own mother, a woman of great personal force, wrote as much in a letter to him:

> . . . I am acquainted with your disposition . . . you are irritating and unbearable and I consider it most difficult to live with you. All your good qualities are darkened by your super-cleverness and thus rendered useless to the world . . . you find fault everywhere except in yourself . . . thereby you embitter the people around you—no one wishes to be improved or illuminated in such a forcible manner, least of all by such an insignificant individual as you still are.[6]

My guest is Arthur Schopenhauer, who, super-cleverness and faultfinding aside, is one of the funniest philosophers ever to pick up a pen. He is also one of the bleakest, darkest, and most depressing—a true connoisseur of human misery. His views are hair-raising. Here are a few of his zingier aphorisms:

"Life swings like a pendulum to and fro between pain and boredom."[7]

"The fruits of Christianity were religious wars, butcheries, crusades, inquisitions, extermination of the natives of America and the introduction of African slaves in their place."[8]

---

6   The translation is Yalom's.

7   Arthur Schopenhauer, *The World as Will and Representation* (New York: Dover Publications, 1969), 312.

8   Arthur Schopenhauer, *Parerga and Paralipomena: A Collection of Philosophical Essays* (New York: Cosimo, Inc., 2007), 50.

"Towards the end of life, much the same happens as at the end of a masked ball when the masks are removed. We now see who those really were with whom we had come in contact during the course of our life."[9]

"The development of the genital system begins latest, and only at the age of manhood are irritability, reproduction, and the genital function in full force; then, as a rule, they have the ascendency over the brain function. From this it can be explained why children, in general, are so sensible, reasonable, eager to learn and easy to teach, in fact are on the whole are more disposed to and suitable for all theoretical occupation than grown-up people."[10]

"A man can be himself only so long as he is alone."[11]

"Almost all of our sorrows spring out of our relations with other people." (. . . *fast alle unsere Leiden aus der Gesellschaft entspringen . . .*).[12]

"Hatred comes from the heart; contempt from the head; and neither feeling is quite within our control."[13]

"In our monogamous part of the world, to marry means to halve one's rights and double one's duties."[14]

He wrote essays with titles like "On the Suffering of the World," in which he argued that we would be better off if we could just accept that the world is a giant penal colony. This thought is meant to be consoling.

As a reliable compass for orientating yourself in life nothing is more useful than to accustom yourself to regarding this world as a place of atonement, a sort of penal colony. When you have done this you will order your expectations of life according to the nature of things and no longer regard the calamities, sufferings, torments and miseries of life as something irregular and not to be expected but will find them entirely in order, well knowing that each of us is here being punished for his existence and each in his own particular way. This outlook will enable us to view the so-called imperfections of the majority of men, i.e. their moral and intellectual shortcomings and the facial appearance resulting

---

[9] Arthur Schopenhauer, *Parerga and Paralipomena: Six Long Philosophical Essays* (Oxford: Oxford University Press, 1974), 492.

[10] Arthur Schopenhauer, *The World as Will and Representation, Vol. 2*, trans. Payne, E. F. (New York: Dover Publications, 1966), 394.

[11] Schopenhauer, *Parerga and Paralipomena*, 2007, 24.

[12] Arthur Schopenhauer, *Aphorismen* (Alten münster: Jazzybee Verlag, n.d.), § 8.

[13] Arthur Schopenhauer, *Studies in Pessimism, On Human Nature, and Religion: A Dialogue, Etc.* (New York: Digireads.com Publishing, 2008), 22.

[14] Arthur Schopenhauer and R. J. Hollingdale, *Essays and Aphorisms (Classics)*, New edition (New York: Penguin, 2004), 87.

therefrom, without surprise and certainly without indignation: for we shall always bear in mind where we are and consequently regard every man first and foremost as a being who exists only as a consequence of his culpability and whose life is an expiation of the crime of being born. The conviction that the world, and therefore man too, is something which really ought not to exist is in fact calculated to instill in us indulgence towards one another: for what can be expected of beings placed in such a situation as we are? From this point of view one might indeed consider that the appropriate form of address between man and man ought to be, not *monsieur, sir*, but *fellow sufferer, Compagnon de Miseres*. However strange this may sound it corresponds to the nature of the case, makes us see other men in a true light and reminds us of what are the most necessary of all things: tolerance, patience, forbearance and charity, which each of us needs and which each of us therefore owes.[15]

Though secular, Schopenhauer's penal colony borrows freely from the doctrine of original sin—we suffer for the sin of being born. I will admit that I do find the idea consoling, even therapeutic—just as I have found the Darwinian vision of humans as close cousins to chimpanzees and gorillas consoling. Far from undermining human dignity, evolutionary materialism makes human grace and aesthetic ecstasy (when they appear) seem even more magical, fragile, thrilling—like finding a bright pink coral blooming on the edge of a reef tucked inside a rough and pounding surge. In fact, I like this passage so much that I once read it out loud to a graduating senior. I wanted to warn him about the cauldron he was about to plunge into. Maybe I also wanted ever so slightly to nick his calm and worldly self-assurance. To his credit, he nicked my pompousness-posing-as-wisdom right back. As I talked Schopenhauer, the student looked around my office, its books piled haphazardly high, papers strewn hither and yon. The bright northern California sun was splashing in; the mismatched furniture and prints flashed the eccentric grooves of my taste. He shot me a sly look and deadpanned, "This looks like a pretty nice quote unquote penal colony to me, professor."

Where did Schopenhauer acquire his views? From a very early age he wanted to be a scholar. His father hated the idea and tried to dissuade him. When Arthur was fifteen, his father offered him a deal. If Arthur agreed to pursue a life of business, his father would take him on a grand tour through Europe. Arthur agonized but finally agreed. The trip lasted for 18 months. For part of the time he was miserably stuck in a boarding school in Wimbledon. He kept a journal in which he recorded his impressions of the trip. What he

---

15 Ibid., 49–50.

saw horrified him, especially the six thousand prisoners in Toulon condemned to hard labor and put on display for tourists (his biographer thinks this may have been the germ of his world as penal colony idea).

> In my seventeenth year, without any learned school education, I was affected by the wretchedness of life, as was the Buddha when in his youth he caught sight of sickness, old age, pain, and death.... [T]he result for me was that this world could not be the work of an all-good being, but rather that of a devil who had summoned into existence creatures, in order to gloat of the sight of their agony.[16]

Several years later, as Schopenhauer was struggling to adapt to life as a businessman, his father jumped out of the window of his office building and into a canal below. For the rest of his life, Schopenhauer tried to make sense of the suicide question for himself. "For it is quite certainly a universal rule that a human actually resorts to suicide as soon as the immensely strong, inborn drive to the preservation of life is definitely overpowered by great suffering; daily experience shows this."[17]

Then there was the encounter with his neighbor Caroline Marquet, a small moment of passion that changed his life forever. Herr Schopenhauer, Arthur's father, threw himself out of the window of his firm when Arthur was eighteen. Arthur inherited money—enough so that he didn't have to work but not enough to live lavishly. He was unable to secure academic employment. His one attempt at teaching failed when he purposely scheduled his lectures at the same time as his arch-nemesis Hegel, whom he regarded as a bloated fraud. Predictably, the students flocked to Hegel's lectures and Schopenhauer was left to lecture to an empty room. Schopenhauer retreated to Frankfurt and settled into a life as a writer.

One morning as he was working, he heard his neighbor talking loudly to a friend in the vestibule outside his door. He went out and asked them to be quiet. They kept talking. Voices were raised. Schopenhauer picked her up and forcibly removed her from his vestibule. She stumbled and fell down one or two stairs. The police were called. She accused him of assault. She sued him in court. She won a small amount of money. Then she went back to court claiming that she was permanently disabled from the fall. He vigorously defended himself. The case dragged on and on for six long years. Eventually she won. Arthur was ordered to pay his neighbor an annual stipend for as long as her injury continued, which rather unsurprisingly turned out to be

---

[16] David E. Cartwright, *Schopenhauer: A Biography* (Cambridge; New York: Cambridge University Press, 2010), 78.
[17] Ibid., 92.

for the rest of her life. She lived for another 20 years. When she died, he wrote in his journal: *"anus obit, abit onus."* The asshole is dead, the burden is lifted.[18]

So why invite him? If we wanted to spend the weekend with an arch-pessimist with legal troubles and mother issues, why not invite, say, Woody Allen? Here is Woody Allen sounding a great deal like Schopenhauer:

Q: What drives you nuts?

A: The human predicament: the fact that we're living in a nightmare that everyone is making excuses for and having to find ways to sugarcoat. And the fact that life, at its best, is a pretty horrible proposition. But people's behavior makes it much, much worse than it has to be.[19]

I invite him because I'm an academic and I have ambitions. (And, no, academic ambitions are not like military music, jumbo shrimp, Norwegian Solar, or its partner company, Dutch Calvinist Party Planning.) I see David Foster Wallace as a writer worthy of Schopenhauer, perhaps even his intellectual heir (along with Samuel Beckett and J. M. Coetzee). Wallace—"a hilarious guy, a quirky, generous spirit, who happened to be a genius and suffer from depression" (according to his sister Amy)[20]—has issued us all a set of Schopenhauerian challenges, started a Schopenhauer-style pick-up game, thrown the gauntlet our way, and practically begged us to take it up.

Despite his having put Schopenhauer only in the middle of the list of books that have "sort of rung my cherries" in an interview he gave to Laura Miller at *Salon*, Wallace is Schopenhauer's partner in the highlight-reel-worthy double plays of philosophical-poetical interpreters of suffering.[21] (Schopenhauer backhands the ball at shortstop and flicks it to DFW at second, who pivots off his back foot and fires a spark-filled missile to first.) Wallace wrote endlessly, passionately, clinically, exhaustively about suffering (as I am hardly the first to notice). Here is Lee Konstantinou: "Taken as a whole, Wallace's oeuvre might be seen as a single long survey of the different forms individual human suffering can take in a postindustrial or postmodern society. Characters in Wallace's fiction constantly confront the paradoxes

---

[18] Ibid., 411. Cartwright translates the epigram "the old woman is dead, the burden is lifted," but old woman seems to be a secondary meaning; the primary meaning is "ring" or anus.

[19] "Woody Allen on Inspiration," *The Browser*, accessed 25 July 2013, http://www.old.thebrowser.com/interviews/woody-allen-on-memory.

[20] David Lipsky, *Although of Course You End up Becoming Yourself: A Road Trip with David Foster Wallace* (New York: Broadway Books, 2010), xxiv.

[21] "David Foster Wallace," accessed 2 July 2013, http://www.salon.com/1996/03/09/wallace_5/.

inherent in their suffering, and—tellingly—usually find psychological and pharmaceutical approaches to their problems unsatisfying or ineffective, unable to attack the foundation of their discontents, which come to seem intractable."[22] Wallace quite evidently suffered. His mental acuity, sharpness of eye, suffocating addictions to drugs and alcohol—also his depression, pathological sensitivity to the kinds of details most of us are able to ignore, and finally his fatal withdrawal from Nardil and his suicide—all of these are merely traces of a life that was washed in the wide river of suffering. And suffering of a particularly Schopenhauerian kind: the suffering of an acutely sensitive consciousness trapped and thrashing in a hostile world like, dare I say it, a highly intelligent lobster in a pot—a creature so sensitive that it was morbidly able to scrutinize its own predicament. David died of boredom, his friend Jonathan Franzen famously wrote.[23] "Want and boredom are indeed the twin poles of human life," wrote Schopenhauer.[24] "David Wallace," the so-called author of the so-called memoir *The Pale King*, announces rather directly the theme of his (last, great, unfinished) work. The theme is the tax code:

> If you know the position a person takes on taxes, you can determine [his] whole philosophy. The tax code, once you get to know it, embodies all the essence of [human] life: greed, politics, power, goodness, charity. To these qualities. . . . I would respectfully add one more: boredom. Opacity. User-unfriendliness.[25]

The will

Here is a teaching tip. If you ever need to explain Schopenhauer's philosophy in a hurry, just assign the cruise ship piece. In 1996 Wallace was paid by *Harper's* to take a cruise to the Caribbean. His article on the experience became instantly famous, passed around from hand to hand, its funniest bits read breathlessly over the phone.[26] This was in the period just before the internet not only set information free but turned it, Circe-like, into a swarm of angry irradiated chiggers each wanting just one tiny little nibble of your time and attention. Back before all that, Wallace had "done a thing

[22] Lee Konstantinou, "No Bull: David Foster Wallace and Postironic Belief," in *The Legacy of David Foster Wallace* (Iowa City, Iowa: University of Iowa Press), 104–5.

[23] Jonathan Franzen, "Farther Away," *The New Yorker*, 18 April 2011, http://www.newyorker. com/reporting/2011/04/18/110418fa_fact_franzen?currentPage=all.

[24] Schopenhauer and Hollingdale, *Essays and Aphorisms (Classics)*, 45.

[25] David Foster Wallace, *The Pale King* (London: Hamish Hamilton, 2012), p. 83.

[26] Lipsky, *Although of Course You End up Becoming Yourself*, xxviii.

that was gigantic, he'd captured everybody's brain voice."[27] If that's true, then everybody's brain voice must have had a great deal of Schopenhauer inside of it. I do not mean Schopenhauer's complicated dualist metaphysics where the will stands in the same relation to representation as the forms stand in relation to matter (Plato) or the thing-in-itself stands in relation to appearances (Kant). Nor do I mean the somewhat mysterious process by which the will objectifies itself in grades, moving from ideas in the first stage of the will's objectification to particulars in the second stage. Rather I mean the will itself, the malign ceaselessly roiling force that subtends all matter, organic and inorganic.[28] If you want to know what the will is like, in its total destructive power, look no further than how Wallace describes the ocean—the "primordial nada, bottomless, depths inhabited by cackling tooth-studded things rising toward you at the rate a feather falls." Far from being a soothing warm "uterine" "baby-blanket blue," the ocean "turns out to be basically one enormous engine of decay. Seawater corrodes vessels with amazing speed—rusts them, exfoliates paint, strips varnish, dulls shine, coats ships' hulls with barnacles and kelp-clumps and a vague ubiquitous nautical snot that seems like death incarnate. We saw some real horrors in port, local boats that looked dipped in a mixture of acid and shit, scabbed with rust and goo, ravaged by what they float in."[29] Well then. No skinny-dipping for us.

All that liquefied shit is like the sweetest nectar dripping from an ethereal honeysuckle branch, however, compared to what the will does to our psyches. Here is Schopenhauer:

> All willing springs from lack, from deficiency, and thus from suffering. Fulfillment brings this to an end; yet for one wish that is fulfilled there remain at least ten that are denied. Further, desiring lasts a long time,

[27] Ibid., xxviii.

[28] When the will does objectify itself and coalesce into particular things, the results are grotesque: "Teeth, gullet, and intestinal canal are objectified hunger; the genitals are objectified sexual impulse; grasping hands and nimble feet correspond to the more indirect strivings of the will which they represent." These bodily extrusions clinch into place at the highest levels of the will's individuation. The lower levels are equally grotesque. The will is in deepest conflict with itself: "the most glaring example of this kind is afforded by the bulldog-ant of Australia, for when it is cut in two, a battle begins between the head and the tail. The head attacks the tail with its teeth, and the tail defends itself bravely by stinging the head. The contest usually lasts for half an hour, until they die or are dragged away by other ants. This takes place every time. . . . On the banks of the Missouri one sometimes sees a mighty oak with its trunk and all its branches so entwined, fettered, and interlaced by a gigantic wild vine, that it must wither as if choked." Schopenhauer, *The World as Will and Representation,* 1969, 107.

[29] Wallace, *A Supposedly Fun Thing I'll Never Do Again: Essays and Arguments* (Boston: Little, Brown and Co., 1997), 263.

demands and requests go on to infinity; fulfillment is short and meted out sparingly. But even the final satisfaction itself is only apparent; the wish fulfilled at once makes way for a new one; the former is a known delusion, the latter a delusion not as yet known. No attained object of willing can give a satisfaction that lasts and no longer declines; but it is always like the alms thrown to a beggar, which reprieves him today so that his misery may be prolonged till tomorrow. Therefore, so long as our consciousness is filled by our will, so long as we are given up to the throng of desires with its constant hopes and fears, so long as we are the subject of willing, we never obtain lasting happiness or peace. Essentially, it is all the same whether we pursue or flee, fear harm or aspire to enjoyment; care for the constantly demanding will, no matter in what form, continually fills and moves consciousness; but without peace and calm, true well-being is absolutely impossible. Thus the subject of willing is constantly lying on the revolving wheel of Ixion, is always drawing water in the sieve of the Danaids, and is the eternally thirsting Tantalus.[30]

In the cruise ship piece, Wallace makes himself Schopenhauer's spokesman. He stretches himself on the wheel of Ixion, hydrates himself with the sieve of the Danaids, and stands knee deep in the muck with the constantly thirsting Tantalus. While his fellow passengers sip their slippery nipples and basically just chill out, Wallace sits alone in his room and broods. He orders room service in bed and worries about his state of mind: "I have felt as bleak as I've felt since puberty, and have filled almost three Mead notebooks trying to figure out whether it was Them or Just Me." Later he decides that what ails him is not mere malaise but something much worse:

> On board the *Nadir*—especially at night, when all the ship's structured fun and reassurances and gaiety-noise ceased—I felt despair. The word's overused and banalified now, *despair*, but it's a serious word, and I'm using it seriously. For me it denotes a simple admixture—a weird yearning for death combined with a crushing sense of my own smallness and futility that presents as a fear of death. It's maybe close to what people call dread or angst. But it's not these things, quite. It's more like wanting to die in order to escape the unbearable feeling of becoming aware that I'm small and weak and selfish and going without any doubt at all to die. It's wanting to jump overboard.[31]

---

[30] Schopenhauer, *The World as Will and Representation*, 1969, 195.
[31] Wallace, *A Supposedly Fun Thing I'll Never Do Again*, 261.

A few weeks earlier, a sixteen-year-old boy had "done a half-Brody" off a high cruise ship deck; Wallace says he knows how the kid felt.

But then, just when we think things can't get any worse for our humble correspondent, the will tips its evil hand, ripping off its play mask of Caribbean bonhomie and revealing itself in all its monstrous insatiability. One morning Wallace is standing on the deck of the *Nadir* while the ship is docked in some balmy but tatty tropical port. What should pull up into the very next berth but a cruise ship of such astonishing length, girth, and megawatt brightness that his own luxury cruise liner starts to seem worn, shabby, and ordinary by contrast. And so begins a series of thoughts, judgments, comparisons, doubts, anxieties, suspicions, worries of the sort familiar to anybody who has ever had a sibling. Their cruise ship is better than our cruise ship. They get more of the good stuff. They have nicer cabins, better food, fluffier towels. Waaah.

> I am suffering here from a delusion, and I know it's a delusion, this envy of another ship, and still it's painful. It's also representative of a psychological syndrome that I notice has gotten steadily worse as the Cruise wears on, a mental list of dissatisfactions and grievances that started picayune but has quickly become nearly despair-grade. I know that the syndrome's cause is not simply the contempt bred of a week's familiarity with the poor old *Nadir*, and that the source of all the dissatisfactions isn't the *Nadir* at all but rather plain old humanly conscious me, or, more precisely, that ur-American part of me that craves and responds to pampering and passive pleasure: the Dissatisfied Infant part of me, the part that always and indiscriminately WANTS. Hence this syndrome by which, for example, just four days ago I experienced such embarrassment over the perceived self-indulgence of ordering even more gratis food from Cabin Service that I littered the bed with fake evidence of hard work and missed meals, whereas by last night I find myself looking at my watch in real annoyance after fifteen minutes and wondering where the fuck is that Cabin Service guy with the tray already. And by now I notice how the tray's sandwiches are kind of small, and how the wedge of dill pickle 86 always soaks into the starboard crust of the bread, and how the damn Port hallway is too narrow to really let me put the used Cabin Service tray outside 1009's door at night when I'm done eating, so that the tray sits in the cabin all night and in the A.M. adulterates the olfactory sterility of 1009 with a smell of rancid horseradish, and how this seems, by the Luxury Cruise's fifth day, deeply dissatisfying.[32]

---

[32] Ibid., 315–16.

All of us have this deeply infantile, wanting, wailing part—funny that it comes out when things are great rather than when they are bleak. A few years back, I was press-ganged into vacationing with my family at a French "all-inclusive" package resort. Food and drink are available all day. One never has to set foot outside the property (compound?) to get meals. This particular resort featured a kids' camp, where children were entertained, stimulated, challenged, and basted with joy for hours on end. Yet despite this paradise of abundance, I saw no evidence that anybody's will had been slaked or even mildly calmed—just the opposite. I had some work to do, so I sat with my laptop in the main lounge, watching the hotel staff field one petty aggrieved complaint after another. When guests approached, the eyes of the staff members shrank in fear and hostility. I heard one woman accost a bartender—a person who was even then mixing her a margarita—and shriek: "there's no hand towels! Or toilet paper" in a voice that sounded like a raven's caw. Meanwhile over in the kids' camp, Franco-American cultural agita was running high. The French kids made caveman noises to imitate the sound of English speakers. The American kids grumbled about how the French kids were horribly pushy and rude and snobby. And I was put in mind of this lovely passage from Schopenhauer:

> Work, worry, toil and trouble are indeed the lot of almost all men their whole life long. And yet if every desire were satisfied as soon as it arose how would men occupy their lives, how would they pass the time? Imagine this race transported to a Utopia where everything grows of its own accord and turkeys fly around ready-roasted, where lovers find one another without any delay and keep one another without any difficulty: in such a place some men would die of boredom or hang themselves, some would fight and kill one another, and thus they would create for themselves more suffering than nature inflicts on them as it is. Thus for a race such as this no stage, no form of existence is suitable other than the one it already possesses.[33]

Wallace has courage to address this infantile wanting part of all of us (you'll notice that in the foregoing scene, I position myself on the couch with my laptop, rather than, say, banging on the desk and demanding clean towels). We all know the infantile part is there. All of us sweat on what psychologists call the hedonic treadmill, running ever more quickly to maintain a constant

---

[33] Schopenhauer, *Essays and Aphorisms (Classics)*, 43.

level of happiness. There may even be, some philosophers have suggested, a powerful evolutionary logic to the treadmill:

> But let's not evade the deeper question. Is there a case for phenomenological pessimism? The concept may be defined as the thesis that the variety of phenomenal experience generated by the human brain is not a treasure but a burden: Averaged over a lifetime, the balance between joy and suffering is weighted toward the latter in almost all of its bearers. From Buddha to Schopenhauer, there is a long philosophical tradition positing, essentially, that life is not worth living. I will not repeat the arguments of the pessimists here, but let me point out that one new way of looking at the physical universe and the evolution of consciousness is as an expanding ocean of suffering and confusion where previously there was none. Yes, it is true that conscious self-models first brought the experience of pleasure and joy into the physical universe—a universe where no such phenomena existed before. But it is also becoming evident that psychological evolution never optimized us for lasting happiness; on the contrary, it placed us on the hedonic treadmill. We are driven to seek pleasure and joy, to avoid pain and depression. The hedonic treadmill is the motor that nature invented to keep the organism running. We can recognize this structure in ourselves, but we will never be able to escape it. We are this structure.[34]

Let me see if I can sharpen one of Wallace's Schopenhauerian challenges to us, to make it pointed and specific. The challenge is not something large and insoluble like the problem of suffering, nor indeed something that can be put into propositional form and debated, like the question of whether pessimism is a coherent or warranted intellectual stance. Rather the challenge springs from the view, expressed over and over again in Wallace's work, that human-style consciousness tortures the bearer of it. "Consciousness is nature's nightmare," runs the slogan of the O Verily Corporation, the faceless media conglomerate in Wallace's late story "The Suffering Channel." And the O Verily Corporation should know, since it profits handsomely from dumping toxic sludge into people's psychic waterways. O Verily launches a television channel devoted to the most hideous images of human and animal suffering—just in time, as it will later turn out, for 9/11.

---

[34] Thomas Metzinger, *The Ego Tunnel the Science of the Mind and the Myth of the Self* (New York: Basic Books, 2009), 199.

Schopenhauer saw it this way too: consciousness is a special curse. Since the most developed form of consciousness is to be found in humans, humans are specially cursed. The essence of human consciousness is egoism, the "principle of individuation" by which the world renders itself intelligible to us at all:

> every individual, completely vanishing and reduced to nothing in a boundless world, nevertheless makes himself the centre of the world, and considers his own existence and well-being before everything else. In fact, from the natural standpoint, he is ready for this to sacrifice everything else; he is ready to annihilate the world, in order to maintain his own self, that drop in the ocean, a little longer.[35]

How close this passage sounds to the haunting and lyrical words spoken by Wallace in his Kenyon College graduation speech about our "default-setting, which is to be deeply and literally self-centered, and to see and interpret everything through this lens of self":

> everything in my own immediate experience supports my deep belief that I am the absolute center of the universe, the realest, most vivid and important person in existence. We rarely talk about this sort of natural, basic self-centeredness, because it's so socially repulsive, but it's pretty much the same for all of us, deep down. It is our default-setting, hardwired into our boards at birth. Think about it: There is no experience you've had that you were not at the absolute center of. The world as you experience it is right there in front of you, or behind you, to the left or right of you, on your TV, or your monitor, or whatever. Other people's thoughts and feelings have to be communicated to you somehow, but your own are so immediate, urgent, real—you get the idea.[36]

Comparing these passages, you can see two highly intelligent writers trying to tack close to the same basic psychological fact—call it the most powerful cognitive illusion of all, the illusion that we are the protagonists of a unique and personal drama in which everyone else is a secondary player. To ourselves we are round, complex, and infinitely variable—we possess "a huge and totally unorganizable set of inner thoughts, feelings, memories and impressions."[37] Other people are a little bit flatter. Sometimes other people get in our way. Unless of course their dramas can interest us enough to get "through our keyhole."

---

[35] Schopenhauer, *The World as Will and Representation*, 311.
[36] "David Foster Wallace on Life and Work," *Wall Street Journal*, 19 September 2008, sec. Books, http://online.wsj.com/article/SB122178211966454607.html.
[37] Wallace, *Oblivion: Stories* (New York: Little, Brown and Co., 2004), 180.

Of course the two writers have different tones, at least in the passages I have chosen here. Schopenhauer is sharp and hateful toward the self-centered bipeds he is forced to live among. He is full of bitterness toward the egoism of other people. Egoism ruins our peace of mind, and worse. We see its vile effects "in the lives of great tyrants and evildoers, and in world-devastating wars":

> We see not only how everyone tries to snatch from another what he himself wants, but how one often even destroys another's whole happiness or life, in order to increase by an insignificant amount his own well-being. This is the highest expression of egoism, the phenomena of which in this respect are surpassed only by those of real wickedness that seeks, quite disinterestedly, the pain and injury of others without any advantage to itself.[38]

Wallace did not go that far, at least not in the Kenyon College speech. He is full of empathy for his "*compagnon de misères,*" his fellow-sufferers trapped in "crowded, loud, slow, consumer-hell-type situation(s)"—the "fat, dead-eyed, over-made-lady who just screamed at her little child in the checkout line," the people imprisoned each in his own SUV in a traffic jam. These people each deserve compassion because each is suffering his or her own little private hell, the hell of "day in, day out" "boredom, routine, and petty frustration." He offers a totally chilling-in-retrospect observation about why people commit suicide by shooting themselves in the head—so that they can kill the "terrible master," the mind.

> It is not the least bit coincidental that adults who commit suicide with firearms almost always shoot themselves in the head. And the truth is that most of these suicides are actually dead long before they pull the trigger. And I submit that this is what the real, no-bull- value of your liberal-arts education is supposed to be about: How to keep from going through your comfortable, prosperous, respectable adult life dead, unconscious, a slave to your head and to your natural default-setting of being uniquely, completely, imperially alone, day in and day out.

The solution he offers—since this is a college graduation speech, he cannot simply send out a terrible diagnosis and not offer a solution—is "attention, and awareness, and discipline, and effort, and being able truly to care about other people and to sacrifice for them, over and over, in myriad petty little unsexy ways, every day. That is real freedom. The alternative is unconsciousness, the

---

[38] Ibid., 180–1.

default-setting, the 'rat race'—the constant gnawing sense of having had and lost some infinite thing."[39]

But here is a problem or a question or a caveat or what have you. If you are Schopenhauer, or David Foster Wallace, or even Professor Vermeule in her office on the eve of a young person's graduation day, and if you think that consciousness might open you up to a distinctive kind of pain, or even worse if you intuit that consciousness might *cause* a distinctive kind of pain, why spread the news? If consciousness is nature's nightmare, why ask people to confront the hideous fact, to, as it were, consider how the lobster suffers too? Wallace developed a niche as an essayist. He wrote about "supposedly fun" things—a cruise, a lobster festival, a college graduation. And he agonized about them. He wrote incredibly funny, wise, intelligent things about his agony. I don't want to step all over this kind of joke by analyzing it to death. I love the joke. I love it when Schopenhauer does it and I love it when Wallace does it—and yet. Part of Wallace's dare I call it shtick involves inserting his own suffering consciousness into the middle of other people's fun times and watching as the fun slowly circles the drain—in this light, the Maine Lobster Fest "begins to take on the aspect of something like a Roman circus or medieval torture-fest."

The recovery movement has a saying: I am the piece of shit the world revolves around. Robert Bolger tells me of another common phrase: "I am an egomaniac with an inferiority complex." Both sayings capture the mix of self-loathing, abjection, and yet paradoxically utter narcissistic self-involvement of the person emerging from the maelstrom of addiction. The idea is that you believe that you are uniquely responsible for the chaos in your life and you feel guilty about it, but are still so attached to the thought of your own special badness as a person that you can't step outside of it or let go of it. You remain stuck in a state of self-punishing abjection. The sayings also capture something about how egoism looks when it is hung up on a boulder in the midst of a rushing stream.

I can't help but think sayings like this get at the heart of Wallace's Schopenhauerian ethos.[40] The mind is divided against itself and that

---

[39] "David Foster Wallace on Life and Work."

[40] Granada House, the halfway house in Cambridge where Wallace did much of his recovery work, has on its website "an ex-resident's story"—the style and details make it seem very likely that Wallace wrote it. The ex-resident tells how the residents of Granada House listened to him:

> They also recognized bullshit, and manipulation, and meaningless intellectualization as a way of evading terrible truths—and on many days the most helpful thing they did was to laugh at me and make fun of my dodges (which were, I realize now, pathetically easy for a fellow addict to spot), and to advise me just not to use chemicals today because tomorrow might very well look different.
> http://www.granadahouse.org/people/letters_from_our_alum.html

there's no real way out of the trap of division—despite the Kenyon college graduate speech offer of compassion or empathy or insight or the liberal arts or whatever. That's the force of the pessimism. And in truth I think that David Foster Wallace had it worse in this regard even than Schopenhauer. After all, Schopenhauer's whole philosophical system had an UBA (in "The Suffering Channel" that's glossy magazine "industry shorthand for an upbeat angle. . . . The triumph of creative achievement in even the unlikeliest places.")[41] Schopenhauer's UBA was art, or more specifically the "aesthetic method of consideration," which puts us in touch with the Platonic essence of things and also turns us into will-less subjects of contemplation. By putting ourselves into a state of aesthetic contemplation, we can turn down the ceaseless pressure of the will and achieve "the painless state, prized by Epicurus as the highest good and as the state of the gods; for that moment we are delivered from the miserable pressure of the will. We celebrate the Sabbath of the penal servitude of willing; the wheel of Ixion stands still."[42]

So why do I think that Wallace ultimately trumped Schopenhauer in the pessimism stakes? Wallace's late story "The Suffering Channel" has all kinds of Schopenhauerian resonances. It is a parable of an artist who seems to be an avatar for Wallace. (Artists are obviously especially vulnerable to torture-by-consciousness, being highly sensitive, acute, self-aware and self-monitoring beings whose stock in trade it is to try to express their vision.) Actually let me back up a little. The story is about a style magazine editor in New York whose beat is a feature called "What in the World"—zany doings in the wide world, shock titillation for the Prada set. The editor gets a lead on a story about a man in Indiana who shits out exquisite works of art—although as we later find out (everyone is speechless when confronted with the artworks, so nobody describes them) they are not originals but rather incredibly lifelike copies of familiar masterpieces. That artist, Brint Moltke, is practically mute—his agent in both a financial and personal sense is his obese wife Amber who, when the editor pays the couple a visit, sexually smothers him in her folds and her girth. Amber, views her mute and defecating husband (a man whose "lack of personal verve . . . almost approached death in life") as her ticket to the New York art world big time. As the circus rolls into town, Brint Moltke speaks up—he shits out the words "Help me" (including the quotation marks) in front of the editor's hotel door. The editor doesn't help him—instead Brint Moltke ends up on the Suffering Channel—defecating off screen while his wife talks about the artist's "abusive childhood and the terrific shame, ambivalence, and sheer human suffering involved in his unchosen art. Edited portions of this

[41] Wallace, *Oblivion*, 245.
[42] Schopenhauer, *The World as Will and Representation*, 1969, 195.

interview will compose the voiceover as TSC viewers watch the artist's face in the act of creation, its every wince and grimace captured by the special camera hidden within the chassis of the commode's monitor."[43] Brint Moltke (er, BM), like DFW, is the piece of shit the world revolves around. But rather than solacing his suffering in an aesthetic method of contemplation, he ends up as prime Suffering Channel real estate, his own will not so much turned down as simply pushed aside by the gargantuan desires of his Brobdignagian wife and the pushy, manic New York art world to make him shit it out. I feel as though Wallace was plowing the same terrain as Schopenhauer but on the whole came to infinitely bleaker conclusions about how art can never cure the unrelieved suffering of consciousness. Maybe if we invite them both to a party, Schopenhauer could have talked to DFW and told him what all that exquisite art he made was good for.

[43] Wallace, *Oblivion*, 327.

8

Philosophy, Self-Help, and the Death of David Wallace[1]

Maria Bustillos

*"I absolutely ran out of rope last winter, and I simply have got to find
a different way to live."*
—David Foster Wallace, from a letter to Dale Peterson written
ca. 1988–89, quoted in D. T. Max's *Every Love Story is a Ghost Story*

"A troubled little soldier"

David Foster Wallace was introduced to the study of philosophy at an early
age, as James Ryerson describes in his preface to *Fate, Time, and Language,*
Wallace's recently published undergraduate thesis:

> When [Wallace] was about 14 years old, he asked his father, the University
> of Illinois philosophy professor James D. Wallace, to explain to him what
> philosophy is, so that when people would ask him exactly what it was
> that his father did, he could give them an answer. James had the two of
> them read Plato's *Phaedo* dialogue together, an experience that turned
> out to be pivotal in his understanding of his son. "I had never had an
> undergraduate student who caught on so quickly or who responded with
> such maturity and sophistication," James recalls. "This was this first time
> I realized what a phenomenal mind David had."[2]

Ryerson notes that when Wallace became an undergraduate himself, his
intention was to follow in his father's footsteps and pursue philosophy as a
profession. It's significant that his decision to write fiction instead was based

---

[1] Ideas for this essay originally appeared as "Inside David Foster Wallace's Private Self-Help Library," *The Awl* (5 April 2011).

[2] James Ryerson, "Preface" to Wallace, *Fate, Time, and Language: An Essay on Free* Will, eds. Steven M. Cahn and Maureen Eckert (New York: Columbia University Press, 2011), 3.

on a sense of intellectual challenge; he was very competitive. He wrote two theses in his senior year at Amherst, one the novel *The Broom of the System*, and the other, *Fate, Time, and Language*; years later, he would explain his decision to *Rolling Stone* journalist David Lipsky this way: "writing *Broom of the System* felt like it was using 97 percent of me, whereas the philosophy thesis was using 50 percent of me."[3]

But during those undergraduate years, a period of triumph in which he'd been held in something near awe by his professors and fellow-students alike, Wallace had been enduring, in secret, the torments of the damned. He'd become addicted to alcohol and drugs, and suffered episodes of depression, anxiety, and suicidal ideation so fierce and so terrifying that he had to take a year off from school.

Like many "gifted" kids, Wallace valued his own intelligence for the attention and praise it won him—a quality intensified in his childhood home by the sky-high regard his parents had for scholarship and intellect—but he was also deeply in love on his own account with the pleasures of study. He described his situation as an undergraduate to Larry McCaffrey in 1993.

> Return with us now to Deare Olde Amherst. For most of my college career I was a hard-core syntax wienie, a philosophy major with a specialization in math and logic. I was, to put it modestly, quite good at the stuff, mostly because I spent all my free time doing it. Wienieish or not, I was actually chasing a special sort of buzz, a special moment that comes sometimes. One teacher called these moments "mathematical experiences." What I didn't know then was that a mathematical experience was aesthetic in nature, an epiphany in Joyce's original sense. These moments appeared in proof-completions, or maybe algorithms. Or like a gorgeously simple solution to a problem you suddenly see after half a notebook with gnarly attempted solutions. It was really an experience of what I think Yeats called "the click of a well-made box." Something like that.[4] The word I always think of it as is "click."
>
> Anyway, I was just awfully good at technical philosophy, and it was the first thing I'd ever really been good at, and so everybody, including me, anticipated I'd make it a career. But it sort of emptied out for me somewhere around age twenty. I just got tired of it, and panicked

[3] David Lipsky, *Although Of Course You End Up Becoming Yourself: A Road Trip With David Foster* Wallace (New York: Broadway Books, 2010), 261.
[4] Yeats, from a 1936 letter to Dorothy Wellesley: "The correction of prose, because it has no fixed laws, is endless, a poem comes right with a click like a closing box." William Butler Yeats, Dorothy Wellesley, *Letters on Poetry: From Yeats to Dorothy Wellesley* (Oxford: Oxford University Press, 1964), 22.

because I was suddenly not getting any joy from the one thing I was
clearly supposed to do because I was good at it and people liked me for
being good at it. Not a fun time. . . .

So what I did, I went back home for a term, planning to play solitaire
and stare out the window, whatever you do in a crisis. And all of a
sudden I found myself writing fiction. . . . It was real lucky that just when
I stopped being able to get the click from math logic I started to be able
to get it from fiction.[5]

There is a great deal left out of this account; the "crisis" of 1983 is described
so coolly here, 10 years after the fact, as an intellectual and professional
one, but the least observant student of Wallace's life and work can readily
see that there was something far worse and bone-deep at the core of his
troubles, although it's likely to remain impossible to identify their ultimate
origins. Whence came the psychological strain that drove him to seek
relief in drugs? Or did his addiction proceed from some other source?
Was his depression responsible for his drug problems, or was it the other
way around? Was he genetically predisposed to substance abuse and/or
emotional instability?

Whatever the cause, there can be no doubt that Wallace was just barely
scotch-taped together during the whole of his early adulthood, compulsively
drinking and drugging and experiencing serious intermittent breakdowns.
He was desperately troubled. Wallace's sister Amy told biographer D. T. Max
that in this period, his "potential as an autonomous adult was pretty much
vaporizing."[6] Though there was never a moment during all his years in school
when Wallace didn't do brilliantly well, his studies were utterly performative,
somehow kept separate from the afflictions of his inner life.

The short story Wallace wrote during his year off from school, "The Planet
Trillaphon as It Stands in Relation to the Bad Thing"—a piece, presumably,
that gave him the "click"—speaks very clearly to the huge schism in his psyche,
his ability to do a beautiful job in every class while falling apart inside.

It wasn't as if I thought I was two people who could have a dialogue,
or as if I heard voices from Venus or anything, I knew I was just one
person, but this one person, here, was a troubled little soldier who
could withstand neither the substance nor the implications of the noise
produced by the inside of his own head.

5   Wallace, "An Interview with David Foster Wallace," by Larry McCaffery, *Review of
    Contemporary Fiction* 13 (2 Summer 1993): 127–51.
6   D. T. Max, *Every Story Is a Love Story: A Life of David Foster Wallace* (New York: Viking,
    2012), 34.

Anyway, all this extremely delightful stuff was going on while I was doing well and making my otherwise quite worried and less-than-pleased parents happy school-wise during the year . . .

So I went off to Brown University in the fall, and . . . it was supposed to be all hard but it really wasn't, so I had plenty of time to do well in classes and have people say "Outstanding" and still be neurotic and weird as hell. . . . I didn't ever go to see anyone at Brown, mainly because I was afraid that if I ever opened my mouth in that context stuff would come out that would ensure that I'd be put in a place like the place I was put after the hilariously stupid business in the bathroom.

"The Planet Trillaphon" is a terrifyingly immediate account of suicidal depression. But the troubled little soldier soldiered on, made it into graduate school, and performed like a superstar there, too, though he was still a severely disturbed, drug-addicted wreck.

And then in 1989, at the age of 27, Wallace gained a respite from his sufferings that would last nearly 20 years. He gave up drugs and alcohol and was able to write his great novel, *Infinite Jest*, and to see it through to publication, in just 7 years' time. But he didn't find his salvation in academic work, nor in the satisfactions of a career, nor in any author, philosopher, or professor; instead it arrived in the form of the determinedly populist, unintellectual, mass-market practice of AA.

If it isn't surprising that one of the best philosophy students at one of the best American universities should have been able to maintain the highest academic standards, to succeed at such a stratospheric level, and yet to be in such brutal pain and in such terrible danger, maybe it should be. We've grown to accept in some way that genius comes with a burden of suffering, or even that "brilliant" and "abnormal" are somehow synonymous. Wallace's untimely death shows that we must reevaluate those assumptions.

There is a temptation to suppose that a talent as exceptional as Wallace's makes him an outlier in every other respect, but I don't believe that to be so. What I want to illuminate in beginning an analysis of Wallace's relationship to self-help literature is the deficiency of modern academic disciplines in encouraging students, and particularly young people, to build a whole, healthy psyche, and to situate their efforts in the context of a greater world in which they have both rights and responsibilities; a world more complex, more fragile, more interconnected, and more in need of their help and engagement than the kind of work required to gain a high SAT score and a pile of A's from a fancy college might suggest.

If the Enlightenment tradition in which many of us were reared requires a strong, seeking and inventive mind operating freely in a condition of eternal doubt, it's worth noting that our pedagogical methods, including those employed in the teaching of philosophy, seldom favor the development of such minds. The student who wishes to excel as Wallace did isn't taught to seek or to ask new questions, but rather to produce what is required or expected within increasingly challenging fixed parameters. A particularly gifted student like Wallace performs like an Olympic athlete in a dazzling routine. It's a competitive sport, in fact—one where the "best" will "win." But the student is rarely invited to reflect on the connection between what he is learning and his own life, his own experiences. In the case of philosophy, this seems especially and ironically absurd.

An increasing number of "civilian" writers have been calling persuasively, if biliously, for a reassessment of the value of The Humanities, typically in the context of disastrous budget cuts to education that are occurring all over the developed world in the wake of the 2008 fiscal crisis. It's often an incoherent message, vaguely bemoaning the "decline" of "culture," or of books, or of "reading." The general wailing and gnashing of teeth is well illustrated by Alain de Botton's 2011 *BBC News* essay, "Justifying Culture."

> Don't get me wrong, I care deeply for the humanities and believe they have a vital role to play in a healthy society. I just think that the way culture is currently taught in universities is a travesty of its real potential, and that the government cuts are an understandable, if not at all nice, consequence of the failure of current teaching methods and goals. . . .
> My personal view of what the humanities are for is simple—they should help us to live.[7]

de Botton goes on to quote John Stuart Mill: "The object of universities is not to make skillful lawyers, physicians or engineers. It is to make capable and cultivated human beings."

The exact means by which the study of humanities is to make us more capable or cultivated are usually left unclear in these diatribes. But de Botton has a stab at it.

> How should universities be rearranged? In my view, departments should be required to identify the problematic areas in people's lives and to design courses that address them head on. . . . There should be classes in, among other topics, being alone, reconsidering work, improving

---

7   Alain de Botton, "A Point of View: Justifying Culture," *BBC News*, 7 January 2011. http://www.bbc.co.uk/news/magazine-12136511 [accessed 3 July 2013].

relationships with children, reconnecting with nature and facing illness. A university alive to the true responsibilities of cultural artefacts within a secular age would establish a Department for Relationships, an Institute of Dying and a Centre for Self-Knowledge.

Universities may well be teaching the right books but they too often fail to ask direct questions of them, declining to advance sufficiently vulgar, neo-religious enquiries because they are embarrassed to admit the true nature of our inner needs. They are fatefully in love with ambiguity, they trust in the absurd modernist doctrine that great art should have no moral content or desire to change its audience.

In colloquial parlance, "philosophy" is often used in the sense of a fixed system of beliefs, rather than in the sense of an intellectual discipline. In its everyday use, the word means not searching for answers but having already found them, and the common phrase, "my philosophy," indicates a set of personal precepts, like a guide to behavior. Though it addresses de Botton's call for "direct questions," this homely understanding is antithetical to the intellectual discipline of philosophy, one of the very few we have that stretches back into the time of the Greeks in a state very little altered, a discipline that concerns itself with seeking rather than finding, and the taproot, perhaps, of our "modernist love of ambiguity."

Does the formal study of philosophy ask more of us than it gives back? Can it answer the needs of a person who's "run out of rope"? Must it? Should it? Does the flourishing of self-help literature, at a time when philosophy has receded from the mainstream of public discourse, speak to the possibility of a real deficiency?

In its post-Enlightenment inflection especially, philosophy is a pluralistic discipline that asks a great deal of us; it asks that we keep the jury out forever on the great questions, and that all our conclusions remain chastely provisional; it demands that we hold many approaches in our minds simultaneously, and that we work to attain and then remain forever suspended at a lofty remove from the world, in a state of pure intellection. In these circumstances, "supposing oneself to have found" must seem like something worse than hubris, something vulgar almost. Yet no amount of study will absolve even the most brilliant of us from his creaturely imperatives, from fear or panic or the threat of trouble, from illness, depression, sadness, despair, or death.

None of this is to say that moral philosophy is dead, or that academic philosophers have turned their backs on pragmatic concerns. For over fifty years, since G. E. M. Anscombe jump-started virtue ethics in the 1958 essay "Modern Moral Philosophy," neo-Aristotelian questions of how we should live have engendered a dynamic and significant philosophical literature; virtue ethics has been examined and recast in Christian terms, in Thomist terms, in terms of the later Wittgenstein's theories of language, etc. But it can't be denied that formal philosophical works, which consist largely in making the finest of distinctions in the most precise manner possible, are essentially esoteric. Necessarily, they offer little in the way of immediate assistance to the suicidal drug addict or the victim of an anxiety disorder.

The work of latter-day virtue ethicists such as Hursthouse, Annas, MacIntyre, et al. may well come to yield better ways of addressing practical problems in people's lives. It is to be hoped, fervently hoped, that it will. Because it can escape nobody that neither AA nor psychiatry nor a profound dedication to "culture" and the life of the mind were enough to save David Foster Wallace, or to save or heal countless unhappy people in our world. If we should come closer to real answers to the oldest questions regarding virtue and happiness, there can be little doubt that they will eventually translate into a better understanding of how real people might best seek the good life.

That said, it's worth examining how a fine though troubled man who found some years' grace through the literature of self-help came to do so, and how his relationship to that literature shaped his work and studies in the brief time that remained to him.

Though Wallace was a born pointy-head who remained deeply committed to the academy and to academic work throughout his adult life, holding various teaching jobs and ending as the first Roy E. Disney Professor of Creative Writing at Pomona College, he was very much alive to the contradiction between the humble philosophy of his recovery and the hubris inherent in having once believed himself to be "above" such stuff. Indeed he came to see his former "intellectual superiority" as having been dangerous to him. He discussed the matter explicitly with David Lipsky (Lipsky in italics):

> *There's still something basically false about your approach here. To some degree. Which is this: that I think you still feel you're smarter than other people. And you're acting like someone—you're acting like someone who's about thirty-one or thirty-two, who's playing in the kid's softball game, and is trying to hold back his power hitting, to check his swing at the plate, more or less.*
>
> You mean in the book?
>
> *No, I mean in your social persona. And you're someone who's really trying—*
>
> You're a tough room.
>
> *You make a point of holding back—there's a point, there's something obvious about you somehow in a gentle way holding back what you're aware of as your intelligence to be with people who are somehow younger or . . .*
>
> Boy, that would make me a real asshole, wouldn't it?

No it wouldn't: It would make you a reformed person . . .

The parts of me that used to think I was different or smarter or whatever, almost made me die.

I understand that.

And I think it's also like, I think one of the true ways that I've gotten smarter is, I've realized that I'm not that much smarter than other people.[8]

Though there has been no formal acknowledgement from Granada House, the recovery facility where he spent 6 months in 1989–90, Wallace is widely believed to have been the author of the anonymous testimonial "An Ex-Resident's Story" posted on their website. (I, at least, have neither met nor heard of any scholar who doesn't believe Wallace to have been its author.) It contains a plain assessment of the author's ambivalence with respect to the principles of AA.

> Six months in Granada House helped me immeasurably. I still wince at some of the hyperbole and melodrama that are used in recovery-speak, but the fact of the matter is that my experience at Granada House helped me, starting with the fact that the staff admitted me despite the obnoxious condescension with which I spoke of them, the House, and the 12-Step programs of recovery they tried to enable. They were patient, but they were not pushovers. They enforced a structure and discipline about recovery that I was not capable of on my own: mandatory counseling, mandatory AA or NA meetings, mandatory employment, curfew, chores, etc. Not to mention required reading of AA/NA literature whether I found it literarily distinguished or not. . . .
>
> I resented the radical simplicity of 12-Step programs' advice to newcomers: go to a 12-Step meeting every day, make one such meeting your home group, get a sponsor and tell him the truth, get active with some kind of job in your home group, pray for help whether you believe in God or not, etc. The whole thing seemed uncomfortable and undignified and dumb. Now, from the perspective of almost fourteen years sober, it looks like precisely what I needed.[9]

But by far the most complete and persuasive account of Wallace's ideas about AA appears in *Infinite Jest* itself, in the character of Don Gately. On the surface, the character "closest" to Wallace in the novel is the tennis-playing

---

[8]   Lipsky, 216.
[9]   Anonymous, "An Ex-Resident's Story," Granada House (2004). http://www.granadahouse. org/people/letters_from_our_alum.html [accessed 3 July 2013].

intellectual prodigy Hal Incandenza, but there are equally deep parallels between Wallace and Gately; I think of Hal as representing the pre-recovery Wallace, and of Gately as the flawed but healed, heroic, and mighty figure whom Wallace was trying to become. Though Gately's instincts (post-recovery) are uniformly humane and good, it's no accident that Wallace chose a drug addict, thief, and murderer, a profoundly uneducated man, to be the hero of his book. As if to say that wisdom and heroism exist in places we might not imagine or expect.

Unintellectual he may be, but Gately's reactions to the maudlin embarrassingness and awfulness of AA's precepts sound very much like Wallace's in "An Ex-Resident's Story," and for this reader they provide the realest and most beautiful and exact account of the author's own experiences.

And then this goofy slapdash anarchic system of low-rent gatherings and corny slogans and saccharin grins and hideous coffee is so lame you just know there's no way it could ever possibly work except for the utterest morons . . . and then Gately seems to find out AA turns out to be the very loyal friend he thought he'd had and then lost, when you Came In. And so you Hang In and stay sober and straight, and out of sheer hand-burned-on-hot-stove-terror you heed the improbable-sounding warnings not to stop pounding out the nightly meetings even after the Substance-cravings have left and you feel like you've got a grip on the thing at last and can now go it alone, you still don't try to go it alone, you need the improbable warnings because by now you have no faith in your own sense of what's really improbable and what isn't, since AA seems, improbably enough, to be working, and with no faith in your own senses you're confused, flummoxed, and when people with AA time strongly advise you to keep coming you nod robotically and keep coming, and you sweep floors and scrub out ashtrays and fill stained steel urns with hideous coffee, and you keep getting ritually down on your big knees every morning and night asking for help from a sky that still seems a burnished shield against all who would ask aid of it—how can you pray to a "God" you believe only morons believe in, still?—but the old guys say it doesn't yet matter what you believe or don't believe, Just Do It they say, and like a shock-trained organism, without any kind of independent human will you do exactly what you are told, you keep coming and coming, nightly, and now you take pains not to get booted out of the squalid halfway house you'd at first tried so hard to get discharged from, you Hang In and Hang In, meeting after meeting, warm day after cold day . . .; and not only does the urge to get high stay more or less away, but more general life-quality-type-things—just as improbably promised, at first, when you'd Come In—things seem to get progressively somehow better, inside, for a while, then worse, then even better, then for a while worse in a way that's still somehow better, realer, you feel weirdly unblinded, which is good, even though a lot of the things you now see about yourself and how you've lived are horrible to have to see—and by this time the whole thing is so improbable and unparsable that you're so flummoxed you've convinced you're maybe brain-damaged, still, at this point, from all the years of Substances, and you figure you'd better Hang In in this Boston AA where older guys who seem to be less damaged—or at least less flummoxed by their damage—will tell you in terse simple imperative clauses exactly what to do, and where and when to do it (though never How or Why); and at this point you've started to have an almost classic sort of Blind Faith in the older guys, a Blind Faith in them born not of zealotry or even belief but just of a chilled conviction that you have no faith whatsoever left in yourself; [footnote 135] and now if the older guys say Jump you ask them to hold their hand at the desired height, and now they've got you, and you're free.

Footnote 135: A conviction common to all who Hang In with AA, after a while, and abstracted in the slogan "My Best Thinking Got Me Here."[10]

Lifeline

The story of self-help literature in English is intimately entwined with the history of Christianity in the Anglophone world, specifically to that anti-authoritarian spirit that sought to put men in charge of their own salvation, removing the mediation of ecclesiastical authorities in Rome or anywhere else. In the fourteenth century, many decades before the invention of the printing press, the English philosopher, theologian, and lay preacher John Wycliffe undertook to translate the Bible from the Latin Vulgate into English, in order that ordinary people might study it for themselves. This was a revolutionary notion; portions of the Bible had been translated into English earlier, but as theologian Gotthard Victor Lechler observed in his 1878 *John Wycliffe and his English precursors*, "[I]n none of these [earlier] translations was it designed to make the Word of God accessible to the mass of the people, and to spread scriptural knowledge among them. . . . [Eventually] a translation of the whole Bible had been executed, and that, too, with the design of becoming the common property of the nation."[11]

---

[10] Wallace, *Infinite Jest* (Boston: Little, Brown, 1996), 350, 1026.
[11] Gotthard Victor Lechler, *John Wycliffe and his English Precursors*, trans. Perter Lorimer (London: The Religious Tract Society, 1904), 229.

Wycliffe and his followers distributed sermons, tracts, and portions of their English translation of the Bible with a view comparable to that of today's self-help authors: the delivery of responsibility for bettering his own life straight into the reader's hands. Wycliffe was charged with heresy and thrown out of Oxford in his own time, but by the mid-nineteenth century, the Christian press was praising him openly, as the Dublin *Catholic Layman* did in 1856: "It was John Wycliffe—a name for ever memorable as that of the first teacher who shook with any lasting effect the dominion of the Romish hierarchy,—who sowed deep in the popular mind thoughts, opinions, and convictions, which eventually led to the emancipation of a good part of the Christian world from the usurped authority of the Roman Pontiff. Nay, more, it was the name of the man who first conferred upon the English people the priceless treasure of the Word of God, translated into their own mother tongue."[12]

The same spirit animated the American Evangelicals of the early colonial period, from the birth of the movement in First Great Awakening through the early years of the nineteenth century and into our own day: a church on its feet, personal, emotional, missionary, active. The system of distributing pamphlets in order to convert the heathen and provide encouragement to those in need is alive and well in the form of *Watchtower* pamphlets, the productions of the American Tract Society, etc. Self-help meant "Christian salvation" in its earliest form; soon it came to mean other kinds of "success" as well.

In 1845, the Scottish editor, suffragist, and reformer Samuel Smiles self-published a book called *Self-Help*. It sold over a quarter million copies, and made its author rich. It consists mostly of capsule biographies of great men, inventors, captains of industry and so on, and strongly advises hard work and frugality as the way to follow in their footsteps, a kind of Get Rich Slow message. Here began the conflation of virtue with material success that would find its apotheosis in such fads as EST, the Prosperity Gospel, and *The Seven Habits of Highly Effective People*.

Over subsequent decades, the self-help genre developed along four distinct paths:

- the classic form as exemplified by the earliest Christian tracts, which purport to teach us how to be good Christians;
- the Smiles variants, which encourage us to believe that personal virtue will lead to other kinds of success, including happiness and/or material success;

12 "John Wycliffe," *The Catholic Layman* 5, 59 (15 November 1856): 121–3.

- systems which leave aside all pretensions to moral philosophy or ethics, and promise material rather than spiritual success through following some specific formula of work, exercise, diet, prayer, networking, etc.;
- the occult version of self-help, offering incantations, spells, astrological formulas and so on in order to achieve a specific result; these rely on magical thinking for achieving either grace or success that specifically require no thought or discipline.

The latter categories in particular have given the genre a bad name, because so many of their formulas are sheer hucksterism, obvious tissues of lies confected to part the credulous from their money. Jim Bakker used to advise his Prosperity Gospel congregants to pray for a specific color of Cadillac, for example. It's hard to imagine what Jesus would have made of that.

Popular self-help books in our own times have tended to offer some combination of these attributes. Dr Norman Vincent Peale's *The Power of Positive Thinking* (1952) is a Christian book advising almost incantatory prayers in order to overcome our fears, but its true value and charm lie in the comradeliness of the author's irresistibly sunny voice, and in his enormously practical suggestions for achieving self-acceptance. Dr Peale's guidance is warm, funny, and, I daresay, could be very helpful and cheering to many a nonbeliever. *How I Made $1,000,000 In Mail Order* by E. Joseph Cossman sounds like the work of a charlatan, but is actually very like Dr Peale's book in its sunshiny, encouraging tone and its confidence-inspiring optimism in the values of hard work and faith. Both, too, are full of splendid anecdotes and just plain fun to read. Who can resist the advice of a man who made a fortune selling Spud Guns?

That Wallace came to approach self-help literature with the same clear-eyed, absolutely undeceived seriousness with which he read everything else is evident in the markings of the books from his personal library collected at the Harry Ransom Center in Austin. Though most of the 300-odd books in the collection are novels and short-story collections, the rest of them are all over the map: there are books about narcissism, the teaching of philosophy, the limits of consciousness, changing your life with the aid of Christ, "money and the meaning of life," and "ways to self-reliance and maturity," together with how-to writing guides and works of literary theory. Books and authors from the most arcane to the humblest are represented here.

Because of his history with AA, Wallace had been conditioned to accept certain premises of self-help literature that ordinary readers might balk at. As we saw in the Gately passage from *Infinite Jest*, by Wallace's lights AA relies for its legitimate success, to some degree, on a series of mindless, incantatory formulas that you must repeat, though you do not believe in them. "One Day

At A Time." "Fake It Till You Make It." Maybe these formulas lack elegance, they may make you cringe, but they *work*, according to his own experience. Wallace was a phobic and a highly superstitious guy, the kind who hung onto his lucky pens and lucky leather jacket. Faith, even blind faith, meant something very real to him. In this way, having habituated himself to the deepest skepticism regarding his own assumptions, Wallace's initial feelings about best-selling pop psychology books were liable to have been pitched in a very different key from those of an ordinary reader. He took their ideas on board in exactly the same manner as those of any other author.

This question of blind faith—faith in the mysterious workings of AA, faith in the lucky pen—brings us in a roundabout way to the role of Christianity in Wallace's life. The question is unsettled; the only biographer we have so far, D. T. Max, failed to shed much light on it, either in his book or in subsequent interviews. John Williams at the *New York Times* asked Max about this omission directly:

> John Williams: You write that Wallace "never lost his hope that he could find faith," but religion isn't a big part of this biography. You say some of his writing about fellow churchgoers was actually code for AA members, but did he consistently attend church? How much of his thinking (and searching) about religion do you see reflected in his work?
>
> D.T. Max: Oh, I think religion is a *huge* part of the story I tell. One big reason I wanted to spend all these years with Wallace was to help me with my own questions of faith by examining his. But faith is different from worship in houses with pointy roofs. David did go to church sometimes, but as a sipper. He liked one's pageantry, the other's earnestness, the Danishes at a third. Yet God was central to his thoughts. He had no natural predisposition for belief in a divine being, but I think he forced himself to overcome it mostly to remind himself he wasn't He. It helped him to relax to know not everything was under his control.[13]

Having examined Wallace's markings in the books touching on Christian themes in the Ransom Center collection, I couldn't disagree more with Max; it is nothing but evident that he read these books with the utmost care, and not in a detached or clinical way. Furthermore, I'm not sure Wallace ever did much relaxing; but if he did, I'd venture to guess that what he would have

---

[13] D. T. Max, "God, Mary Karr and Ronald Reagan: D. T. Max on David Foster Wallace," *New York Times*, 12 September 2012. http://artsbeat.blogs.nytimes.com/2012/09/12/god-mary-karr-and-ronald-reagan-d-t-max-on-david-foster-wallace/ [accessed 3 July 2013].

liked was *more* control, or even *any* control, rather than the complete absence of control that he seems to have felt himself to have, in general, in his life. Nor can I agree that "he had no natural predisposition for belief in a divine being." The part of Wallace that had submitted to a Higher Power through AA was real, though full of contradictions. Wallace doesn't seem to have belonged to a specific church, but he had an authentic affinity for Christianity and, at least from what we can learn through his reading, that affinity seems to have been both intellectual and intimately personal.

One of the lists of favorite books he gave a magazine had C. S. Lewis's *The Screwtape Letters* at the top of it; Max also reports that he gave a copy of the book to a lover. It's not the least bit surprising that Wallace loved *The Screwtape Letters*, a Christian book about human susceptibility to demonic interference. Inner demons, devils, whatever! Lewis, a scholarly man himself, has a whole passage about how intellectuals aren't immune to malign influence, and chapter after chapter about how demons can exploit human vulnerabilities to bring down their prey.

It is striking how the ingrained secularist character of modern literary analysis has skewed readings of Wallace; there's almost a deliberate refusal to see what is right before us. Whereas it's very difficult for this reader, at least, to avoid the impression that Wallace was a doubter, but not a scoffer. Andrew Sullivan is one of very few writers to accord Wallace's views on Christianity any kind of serious consideration:

> [Wallace] once admitted how difficult it was to discuss such questions, in an almost eerie preview of the hesitation we now find among those scrutinizing his life:
>
>> . . . it's very hard to talk about people's relationship with any kind of God, in any book later than like Dostoyevsky. I mean the culture, it's all wrong for it now. You know? No, no. Plausibly realistic characters don't sit around talking about this stuff. You know?

I always come back to this comment of Wallace's during his interview with Lipsky:

> It's more like, if you can think of times in your life that you've treated people with extraordinary decency and love, and pure uninterested concern, just because they were valuable as human beings. The ability to do that with ourselves. To treat ourselves the way we would treat a really good, precious friend. Or a tiny child of ours that we absolutely loved more than life itself. And I think it's probably possible to achieve that. I think part of the job we're here for is to learn how to do it. [Spits with mouthful voice into cup.] I know that sounds a little pious.

The term for what he's describing, in Christian theology, is *grace*.

Wallace's life, it seems to me, was a search for it.[14]

Indeed there are many references to grace in the marginal notes of Wallace's books. I can't imagine spending any time in the archive and coming away with any other impression than this: it's not so much that Wallace wished to become a believer, or not. It's more that all the books he read gave only partial or unsatisfactory answers to his questions. Seemingly, he loved Borges, and Markson, and Dostoevsky so much exactly because they went further toward addressing his personal concerns than other books had been able to do.

There are many indications that Wallace wasn't—as Max often implies— just using church as a smokescreen for AA. For just one example, there's a handwritten note from 1997 in the Ransom Center archive, written when he was in very low spirits, in the middle of a dry patch in his writing. He was almost always full of anxiety about losing his ability to write; you'd have thought that having written *Infinite Jest* would have finally persuaded him that he had the real thing and he could stop worrying about it but no, not a bit. "The thing is I get scared it won't come. I'm back to thinking that [*Infinite Jest*] was a fluke." He frets, he quotes Goethe (on the subject of "commitment"); he wonders, incredibly, how to "schedule things so that a certain portion of each day is devoted to writing." On the reverse side of these gloomy observations, there is a program suggesting how the problem might be addressed, in which AA appears quite distinct from Church:

What Balance Would Look Like.

2–3 hours a day on writing.

Up at 8–9

Only a couple late nights a week

Daily exercise

Minimum time spent teaching

2 nights/week spent w/other friends

5 AA/week

Church

Nor can I see why, if he wasn't truly interested in Christianity, if he didn't believe there was such a thing as a serious-minded Christian, Wallace would have owned and read and marked up as many books on Christian themes as he did.

Let's take *Inside Out* by Dr Larry Crabb as an example. Wallace's copious markings (underlinings, notes, circled page numbers, asterisks) indicate

---

[14] Sullivan, Andrew, "Everybody Worships," *The Daily Beast* (9 August 2012). http:// andrewsullivan.thedailybeast.com/2012/08/everybody-worships.html [accessed 3 July 2013].

clearly that he read the book closely, and that he related its message to precepts from AA and to his own life. He appears to have read the book at some point after 2002. And in the margin beside this paragraph—

> Very few Christians feel their disappointment with life deeply enough to fix their hope on what is yet to come. Even fewer face their sin so thoroughly that forgiveness becomes their most valued blessing. But most Christians vaguely sense that they long for so much more than what they experience on a daily basis, and they suppress a terror that no one could know them fully and still want to be their friend.

—he wrote: "Ulp."

"The pressure to model for others what maturity looks like can lead to breakdown or pride," Crabb writes. "You realize that others think of you as better than you know yourself to be." (This is all underlined; alongside is the note, "AA long-timer.")

Crabb's message about maintaining faith and strength of character in the face of the pressures of leadership didn't only apply to Wallace as an AA long-timer; they applied to him as a public intellectual, too.

> The awful distance from people that the aura of leadership creates, can be bridged. . . . Vulnerability, humility, intimacy, power—qualities of character that the pressures of leadership often weaken—can be developed.

In January of 2006, I attended a reading Wallace gave at the Hammer Museum in Los Angeles; there's an audio file available online.[15] He read "The View From Mrs. Thompson's," an account of his experiences on 9/11 among friends from "church" (Max writes that he really spent that day among his "recovery group circle.") He took questions after, the most memorable of which came from a young man in his twenties.

> Q: I'm just wondering if you could say a little bit about the role religion plays in your life, and work. Cause you mentioned going to church: do you still go to church?
>
> DFW: Why don't you give a quick statement of what role religion plays in your life and work so I'll know how to do this? [laughter] I . . . you know, like on tests, here's the problem, "Sample:" Right? Cause it's the

15 Armand Hammer Museum, "Hammer Readings: David Foster Wallace," 15 January 2006. <http://hammer.ucla.edu/watchlisten/watchlisten/show_id/25789/show_type/audio?browse=none&category=0&search=> [accessed 3 July 2013].

sort of thing that you either don't say anything, or you talk for three hours about. The latter of which would not be good.

Q: Um. Well. . . . I do actually go to church every week and my own view is, religion is, needs to be "redeemed," so to speak. Um, although I'm not a, not a, I'm very skeptical about religion and I think that all religions have potential for—for peace, and justice, but um, so that's my own . . .

DFW: That's good! The big . . . so—you—we can, we can more or less pretend that that is the answer I gave, although I have to say that since I moved to California I don't go to church every week, but the que— but, suppose I said I did? Then the question would be nididid no no no nonono the question would be, why if you feel the way you do, do you go to church every week. If you're skeptical about it, if you feel that it needs to be redeemed, what gets you to show up every week?

Q: I very much identified with your discussion of your church community, because I think it's a really important way to connect with people who are very different from me. I mean, you know most of my friends are liberal lefty types, and it's a great diversity of people who are very different and I think it's important to try to find some other type of community, I guess.

DFW: I am *not* being sarcastic when I say more or less Ditto. Usually the more important or circumambient a subject is to us, the more difficult it is to talk about straight out. And one of the neat things about a lot of literary forms—at least, one of the reasons I like to read them—is sometimes they're one of the very few verbal ways can talk about stuff obliquely. So um, yeah. We could have a long argument about whether in fact I write about it or not. Sometimes I feel like it's sort of the only thing that's interesting and it's all I write about. The problem is the minute you start using the G-word or terms out of religion, at least for me it becomes very hard to be clear, and it becomes very hard to talk to anybody other than me without stopping to explain, or reach some kind of consensus on what we mean by various words, and then you know everybody whips out guns, and it just gets, I don't know.

What I gathered from this, then and now, is a highly inclusive, pro-Enlightenment, post-secularist, post-postmodern approach—something like the one Jürgen Habermas has been articulating for many years, as, for example, in a 1999 interview:

> Christianity has functioned for the normative understanding of modernity as more than a mere precursor or catalyst. Egalitarian universalism,

from which sprang the ideas of freedom and social solidarity, of an autonomous conduct of life and emancipation, the individual morality of conscience, human rights and democracy, is the direct heir to the Judaic ethic of justice and the Christian ethic of love. This legacy, substantially unchanged, has been the object of continual critical appropriation and reinterpretation. To this day, there is no alternative to it. And in light of current challenges of a postnational constellation, we continue to draw on the substance of this heritage. Everything else is idle postmodern talk.[16]

There's a highly relevant account of Wallace's mistrust of conventional styles of reading in a review of Joseph Frank's supersized four-volume *Dostoevsky*, published in the *Voice Literary Supplement* in April 1996.

It is the loss of an ability to countenance and discuss the *particularity* of works of literary genius that is maybe most to be loathed about the theory industry's rise to power in contemporary fiction-criticism. A lot of poststructural theory is fascinating in its own right, but when it comes to actually reading some piece of fiction, most theoretical readings consist in just running it through a kind of powerful philosophical machine. This is in all meaningful ways equivalent to dissecting a flower instead of looking at it or smelling it. Dissection has its place, as do systems and general applications of method; but so does appreciation, and so does countenancing the singularity of something beautiful.

On the face of it this is about the analysis of Dostoevsky or other "works of literary genius," but I submit that Wallace was a skeptic through and through, with an ineradicable suspicion of prevailing intellectual conventions. Appreciation of the author as described above is evident in every book Wallace ever marked, from DeLillo to Larry Crabb to Malcolm Gladwell. He'd had more occasion than most to realize that all human curiosity is interconnected in a profound and vital way, and it all has a shot at revealing to us what we want to learn in this life.

In his copy of Jacob Needleman's *Money and the Meaning of Life*, Wallace marked the following passage:

In our time and culture, the battlefield of life is money. Instead of horses and chariots, guns and fortresses, there are banks, checkbooks, credit

---

[16] Jürgen Habermas, "A Conversation about God and the World," in *Time of Translations*, trans. of an interview from 1999 with Eduardo Mendieta (Polity Press, 2006), 150–1.

cards, mortgages, salaries, the IRS. But the inner enemies remain the same now as they were in ancient India or feudal Japan: fear, self-deception, vanity, egoism, wishful thinking, tension, and violence.

And next to it he wrote: "I have them all (so does everyone else.)"

It's so simple, really. Here is the bit of rope, the lifeline that a self-help book, or really any book written for a popular audience, can throw out to a reader in distress: *so does everyone else.*

9

Untrendy Problems: *The Pale King's* Philosophical Inspirations

Jon Baskin

It is not all books that are as dull as their readers. There are probably words addressed to our condition, which, if we could really hear and understand, would be more salutary than the morning or the spring to our lives, and possibly put a new aspect on the face of things for us.

—Thoreau, *Walden*

Early in his career, David Foster Wallace was often chided for his "pretentious" postmodern difficulty,[1] but in recent years a new and more enlightening criticism of his writing has emerged. The criticism has been expressed in different ways, by different kinds of critics. One symptom of it is apparent in Hubert Dreyfus and Sean Dorrance Kelly's chapter on Wallace, in their book on modern ethics, *All Things Shining* (2011). Dreyfus and Kelly begin by calling Wallace "the greatest writer of his generation; perhaps the greatest mind altogether," yet in what follows they suggest that his ethical outlook was juvenile and hubristic, and can usefully be compared to that of the sentimental memoirist Elizabeth Gilbert. A second version, or variety, of the kind of criticism I am thinking of, can be found in Jonathan Franzen's 2011 *New Yorker* essay, "Farther Away." Wallace, Franzen suggests, was a gifted writer with a rare talent for describing Midwestern weather, yet his fiction was marred by his penchant for "moralism and theologizing," bad habits at least partially attributable (Franzen implies) to

---

[1] Small examples of this kind of thing can be found almost at random; a big one came in A. O. Scott's mid-career assessment for the *New York Review of Books*, in which Scott described aspects of *Infinite Jest* as "impressive in the manner of a precocious child's performance at a dinner party, and, in the same way, ultimately irritating." ("The Panic of Influence," *New York Review of Books*, 10 February 2000). A similar kind of exhaustion with what was considered to be Wallace's over-clever bag of tricks can be sensed behind James Wood's influential characterization of *Jest* as a work of "hysterical realism" (James Wood, "Human, All Too Inhuman," *The New Republic*, 24 July 2000).

his lifelong battle with mental illness.[2] A third instance appears in an article by the critic Gerald Howard, posted on *Salon* late in 2012. In the article, Howard, who helped edit Wallace's first novel, expresses disappointment with Wallace's late fiction and essays and especially with Wallace's famous Kenyon commencement speech, which struck him as "uncomfortably close to those books of affirmations, no doubt inspiring but of questionable use when the hard stuff arrives."[3]

What the three commentaries share in common, despite vast differences in tone and intention, is the identification of Wallace with a directness about personal moral matters that's held to be excessive and possibly jejune. All three authors express an anxiety, even an embarrassment, about the fact that Wallace, especially in his later fiction and essays, really did commit himself to "untrendy human problems and emotions," just as he had promised he would in an oft-quoted early essay.[4] A way they express their condescension toward this commitment is by implying, each in their own way, that it stems from fundamentally "personal" concerns, rather than, say, literary or philosophical ones.[5]

I am less interested in defending Wallace against the charge that his later fiction or essays resemble "books of affirmations" than I am in questioning (or showing how Wallace questions) the assumption that motivates it—namely that the genre to which such books belong, call it "self-help," operates in a region distinct from and irrelevant to what we take to be more serious forms of culture. One way of crediting the "insights" above, without crediting their implication of reproach, would be to say that they indicate, far better than the charge that Wallace was an over-clever postmodernist, the field Wallace was playing on. To take Wallace seriously as a thinker is to take seriously his fervent, perhaps even sometimes his embarrassing, commitment to the problems of the self. But that does not mean that that commitment need be conceived of as grossly personal, or emotional, or that it should consign Wallace's writing to the same kind of (in)attention we give to (what we normally call) self-help. Indeed, one of the things Wallace's fiction consistently demonstrates is how problems customarily cordoned off into self-help, or (in their high form) "psychology," are also philosophical problems, or have components that can be best treated philosophically.

---

[2]   Jonathan Franzen, "Farther Away," *The New Yorker*, 18 April 2011.

[3]   Gerald Howard, "I Know Why Brett Easton Ellis Hates David Foster Wallace," *Salon*, 7 September 2012. http://www.salon.com/2012/09/07/i_know_why_bret_easton_ellis_hates_david_foster_wallace/

[4]   Wallace, *A Supposedly Fun Thing I'll Never Do Again: Essays and Arguments* (Boston: Little, Brown & Co., 1997), 81.

[5]   Dreyfus and Kelly, for instance, intersperse their chapter with paragraph-length descriptions of the depression that led to Wallace's suicide.

If *The Pale King*, long portions of which take their cue from the Kenyon commencement, is the book critics have been most apt to associate with Wallace's supposed deviation into sentimentality or moralism or self-help, it is no coincidence that we can also find in Wallace's late, unfinished novel some of the most vivid examples of the methods Wallace employed in the hopes of returning literature, or philosophy, from the high ledge of abstraction and theory to what he conceived of as the concrete difficulties of individual experience. The two longest portions of *The Pale King*—one dealing with the "legendarily attractive" IRS agent Meredith Rand, and the other with the former "wastoid" auditor Chris Fogle—offer unusually transparent object lessons in the strategies that were most prominent in Wallace's late fiction, and specifically in his late fiction's attempt to *philosophically* address what might at first glance appear to be merely "personal" problems. Below, I will connect the first of them with Wittgenstein's notion of philosophy as therapy, and the second with the literary-philosophical tradition that Stanley Cavell calls "Perfectionism."[6]

***

Although professional philosophers who have taken up Wallace's fiction have tended to focus on the explicit references, especially in his early writing, to Wittgensteinian arguments and themes, it is possible to conceive of Wallace's project as a whole as a continuation of Wittgensteinian philosophy by other means. In a previous article, I described Wallace's fiction as "therapeutic in the Wittgensteinian sense."[7] The key passage in Wittgenstein, for understanding what this sense is, comes in the *Investigations*:

> The real discovery is the one that makes me capable of stopping doing philosophy when I want to.—The one that gives philosophy peace,

---

[6] For a summary and discussion of Wallace's public comments and statements on Wittgenstein, see James Ryerson's excellent introduction to Wallace's undergraduate thesis, *Fate, Time, and Language*. Nothing comparable has been written about Wallace's relationship with Cavell, although the critic Paul Giles connects them briefly in his essay "All Swallowed Up: David Foster Wallace and American Literature" (in *The Legacy of David Foster Wallace*). In his biography of Wallace, D. T. Max describes Cavell as "a philosopher who held a special place in Wallace's esteem. . . . Indeed Cavell may have been one of [Wallace's] literary models." Max also details Wallace's disappointment at finding Cavell to be a poor teacher during his year of postgraduate work at Harvard. (Wallace stopped going to Cavell's class after finding the first few meetings indulgent and virtually unintelligible.) (D. T. Max, *Every Love Story is a Ghost Story* [New York: Viking, 2013], 132.) For more on Wallace's engagement with actual self-help, the best resource is Maria Bustillos's article "Inside David Foster Wallace's Private Self-Help Library" (*The Awl*, 5 April 2011), which has been adapted and collected in this volume.

[7] Jon Baskin, "Death is not the End: David Foster Wallace: His Legacy and his Critics," *The Point* 1 (Spring 2009).

so that it is no longer tormented by questions which bring *itself* in question.—Instead, we now demonstrate a method, by examples; and the series of examples can be broken off.—Problems are solved (difficulties eliminated), not a *single* problem.

There is not *a* philosophical method, though there are indeed methods, like different therapies.[8]

Much of Wallace's mature fiction can fruitfully be viewed, I believe, as a "series of examples" (Wallace called them "conversations"), meant to treat not only a set of problems but also a point of view, or what Wittgenstein would have called a "picture." The picture Wallace was most concerned with was the one he felt had captivated his generation's "postmodern" intellectuals and artists—a picture according to which the *authentic* contemporary individual sacrificed sincerity and fellow feeling for the deeper truths of abstraction, alienation, and cynicism. But, for Wallace, intellectuals and artists only represented the leading edge of a more pervasive problem. Like Wittgenstein, Wallace believed that philosophical pictures manifested themselves not only in arguments and artworks but also in "forms of life." This means that postmodernism could not be a philosophical problem without also being a cultural and therefore a personal one.

The story Meredith Rand tells, in the second longest chapter in *The Pale King*, revolves around a series of sessions with a sickly nighttime attendant at a recovery center where, as a teenager, she had been sent for "cutting." The attendant was not a doctor, Rand says, but rather a "natural therapist" who spoke to Rand as if he were "talking to a child"—that is, "to somebody so locked into the problem that she can't even see that it's her problem and not just the way the world is" (499). Really the attendant was a philosophical therapist. His dialogues with Rand resemble those "scenes of instruction" in Wittgenstein's *Investigations*, in which a "central character is the child."[9] The late-night attendant explained to Rand that she had set herself a "neat little trap [to] ensure that I never really had to grow up and so I could stay immature and waiting forever for somebody to save me" (498). The trap was common to girls in Rand's extremely juvenile or adolescent generation, the attendant said. Rand's real wish was to be able to "go around thinking that my real problem was that no one could see or love the real me the way I needed so I'd always have my problem to sit and hold and stroke on and make believe was the real problem" (498).

---

[8] Ludwig Wittgenstein, *Philosophical Investigations*, 3rd edn, trans. G. E. M. Anscombe (Englewood Cliffs, NJ: Prentice-Hall, 1958), 51.

[9] Stanley Cavell, *The Claim of Reason: Wittgenstein, Skepticism, Morality, and Tragedy* (New York: Oxford University Press, 1979), 124.

We might be tempted to call the trap the attendant describes "psychological," rather than "philosophical"—for Wallace, it does not matter what we call the trap; what matters is how we treat it. What we commonly call psychology has a way of treating it, and this way of treating it, as Wallace goes on about *ad nauseum* in his fiction,[10] is not likely to help Rand with her "core problem," and possibly not even with its symptoms (e.g., the cutting). The biggest difference between the attendant's therapy and the therapy practiced by the conventionally trained doctors at the facility is that the attendant informs Rand "it doesn't ultimately matter why I do it or what it, like, represents . . . all that matters is that I was doing it and to stop doing it." The doctors, however, "thought that diagnosis was the same as cure. That if you knew why, you would stop" (*PK*, 486). Rand calls this latter thought "bullshit," which is a succinct summary of Wallace's own judgment, in an early essay, of the "frankly idealistic" contemporary (postmodern, but also modern) belief that "etiology and diagnosis pointed toward cure, that a revelation of imprisonment led to freedom."[11] Wallace's therapy is anti-Freudian and even antimodern in the sense that he attempts to break rather than to encourage his reader's addiction to introspection; more precisely, to get her to see introspection as nothing more than an addiction—with its pleasures and excesses like any other. The sickly late-night attendant teaches Rand that "it doesn't matter why I cut or what the psychological machinery is behind the cutting, like if it's projecting self-hatred or whatever. Because whatever the institutional reason, it's hurting myself, it's me being mean to myself, which was childish" (*PK*, 506).

Evidently, since it is repeated several times, this is a conclusion Wallace senses his reader will be apt to doubt or to misinterpret. The attendant's point is not that institutions have nothing to do with Rand's problem (how could he know what they have to do with it?; how could she?); it is that, at the pass she has come to, it will not be of any help to Rand to better understand herself as a product of her upbringing or of her society, and that it is precisely such structures of thinking that keep her "going around and around inside" of her problem as opposed to "really looking" at it (496). The visual metaphors re-enforce the Wittgensteinian tenor of the attendant's therapy, the deepest target of which is the younger Rand's adolescent—one might say "romantic"—philosophical picture of herself. "I wanted people to look past the prettiness thing and the sexual thing and see who I was,

---

[10] Probably no writer has ever presented more scenes of *failed* talk therapy than David Foster Wallace. The most memorable examples revolve around Hal Incandenza, who makes a complete mockery of the "grief counselor" meant to help him overcome his father's death in *Infinite Jest*.

[11] Wallace, *A Supposedly Fun Thing I'll Never Do Again*, 66.

like as a person," Rand says, "and I felt really mad and sorry for myself that people didn't." But "in reality," the attendant gets her to see, "everything was the surface . . . because under the surface were just all these feelings and conflicts about the surface; about how I looked and the effect on people I had" (499). As in Wallace's earlier short story, "The Depressed Person," the dialogue here reproduces almost verbatim certain moments from the section on private language in the *Investigations*; more than probably any writer since Wittgenstein, Wallace obsessed himself with the *personal* (i.e., the emotional and psychological) consequences of believing in a private language and therefore in a private self (as Rand calls it, a "real me"). The attendant might have told Rand, "The human body is the best picture of the human soul."[12]

As with so many of Wallace's therapeutic subjects, the extent to which the sickly late-night attendant's message has really sunk in for Rand—the extent to which she now lives what she claims to have learned from him—is unclear, and not just (I don't think) because Wallace never finished *The Pale King*. Rand tells the entire story about her time at the rehabilitation center to an IRS co-worker, Shane Drinion, during an after-work happy hour. The conversation is laced with Rand's anxiety that what she is saying is "boring" or "banal" (say that her story is no more interesting, or deserving of respect, than self-help); moreover, as she gets deeper into the story, she begins to imitate aspects of her younger, less mature self (489). Drinion, described by co-workers as "possibly the dullest human being currently alive" (448), is nevertheless capable of exceptional feats of attention, so much so that he is later said to participate in an auditing competition with a computer. Toward the end of the story, having paid exceedingly close attention to what Rand is telling him (not only is Drinion never bored, he doesn't seem to know what the word means), Drinion wonders matter-of-factly at the paradox that, though the sickly attendant had seemed to teach Rand a valuable lesson about her childish and self-destructive need to be "saved," the story would seem to cast the attendant himself—who later became Rand's husband—as precisely the savior she had (so childishly) been looking for. Rand admits this paradox, and cannot resolve it.

Insofar as Wallace's therapy is always aimed ultimately at his reader, rather than at the characters inside the book, it is fitting that the novel's most explicitly therapeutic section would include a kind of warning about the inherent dangers, in therapy (philosophical or otherwise), of transference. But a second, harder point of the scene—or of the indeterminacy of Rand's

---

[12] *Investigations*, 178.

therapeutic outcome—might be described like this: there is no once-and-for-all way to escape, to put behind us for good, the human dimension of adolescence. A way of summarizing Rand's problem as a teenager is that she was narcissistic—that is, she thought her difficulties were special, rather than common or natural. This is an adolescent thought, but it is also a human one. The Wittgensteinian point would be that the problem was not with Rand's narcissism, but with her perspective on her narcissism—namely the perspective that made her narcissism into a much bigger and different kind of problem ("just the way the world is") than it was.[13] But Wallace also wants to show how seductive and even natural that perspective is, to the adult Rand as surely as to the adolescent one. Rand's conversations at the recovery center helped her to see her problem from a new vantage, but they did not offer (as most self-anointed self-help would) a permanent solution to it. If we equate such conversations with the kind Wallace attempted to carry on with his readers, then this would be one way of underscoring the interminability (and also the inexhaustibility) of Wallace's literary-philosophical project. The "series of examples" can go on and on; our need for "reminders" will come to an end only when life does.

There is one concluding note about the conversation between Rand and Drinion, which may appear tangential here but will bear on our next section. At a climactic moment in the conversation, much remarked upon by perplexed reviewers of *The Pale King*, Drinion is said to "levitate slightly"[14] as he becomes so "completely immersed" in Rand's story that he loses consciousness of himself. This appears to be Wallace's way of dramatizing Drinion's complete innocence and impartiality—a kind of fantasy of unselfconsciousness that held no small appeal for many in Wallace's television-obsessed generation.[15] Yet Wallace seems to suggest, precisely with such notes as the levitation, that Drinion has not overcome narcissism; he has never felt it; hence he is not

---

[13] I am thinking of Wittgenstein's claim, which comes right above the already-quoted portion of § 133 in the *Investigations*, that, using his method of philosophy, "philosophical problems should completely disappear." The line can look very different depending on whether you emphasize the word "problems" or (as has been customary in English translations) the word "completely."

[14] Incidentally, the same feeling Wallace described having had while writing fiction in college (Max, *Every Love Story is a Ghost Story*, 167).

[15] In "E Unibus Pluram," Wallace writes of television actors who carry the "Emersonian holiday" in their eye, that is, "the promise of a vacation from human self-consciousness. Not worrying about how you come across. A total unallergy to gazes. It is contemporarily heroic. It is frightening and strong. It is also, of course, an act" (*A Supposedly Fun Thing I'll Never Do Again*, 25). This "self-conscious appearance of unself-consciousnes," Wallace said, was the "the real door" to TV's "hall of mirrors" appeal. The connection of Emerson to acting is itself borrowed from Cavell's *Pursuits of Happiness*, according to Paul Giles ("All Swallowed Up," 9).

properly human, rather in- or sub- or superhuman. This means that nothing in the therapy Rand (or Wallace's reader) receives would put her on a path toward becoming Drinion, for Drinion has not mastered the problem of narcissism so much as he has been spared from it (a similar point could be made with regard to the relationship between Hal and his deformed brother Mario in *Infinite Jest*). At the same time, one can sense the appeal of such a figure for Wallace; and there are long portions of *The Pale King* devoted to exploring how a more normally self-conscious being might approximate Drinion's seemingly mystical equanimity and focus. The most prominent of these sections is the one recounting the story of Chris Fogle, to which we turn next.

***

Like Wallace, Stanley Cavell spent much of his intellectual life considering how to inherit the late Wittgenstein. The term "Moral Perfectionism" combined for Cavell the instructive or therapeutic elements he admired in the *Investigations* with more traditional modes of literary-philosophical "inspiration," evident in works as diverse as Augustine's *Confessions*, Kierkegaard's *Either/Or* and Emerson's "Experience." In the introduction to his Carus Lectures, Cavell describes Perfectionism as an (oft-neglected) tradition in Western thought concerned with "what used to be called the state of one's soul," and which imagines philosophy less as a search for better facts than as a "journey of ascent" toward a better self.[16] In lieu of further definition, he advances a list of texts containing Perfectionist elements, beginning with Plato's *Republic* and Shakespeare's *Hamlet* and carrying on to Cavell's "doorstep" with works by Freud, Thoreau, Beckett, and Wittgenstein.

Even more than Rand, Chris Fogle is imagined, in the longest continuous portion of *The Pale King*, as the product of an extended and debilitating adolescence. But the pivotal sequence in Fogle's life involves, not a set of therapeutic conversations but a lecture, almost a sermon, which presents as inspirational precisely what Fogle, in his conformity with his culture, had previously viewed as banal or pathetic. This is what marks the section, for me, as being more Perfectionist than (philosophically) therapeutic. In tone and method, it resembles less the Wittgenstein of the *Investigations* than it does the Kierkegaard of *Fear and Trembling* or the Thoreau of *Walden*.

The great philosophical enemy of the Perfectionist text is skepticism or nihilism (they are intimately related in Cavell's hands), but with these words

---

[16] Cavell, *Conditions Handsome and Unhandsome: The Constitution of Emersonian Perfectionism* (Chicago: University of Chicago Press, 1991), 2, 7.

being understood, as Wallace always understood them, to describe less a self-conscious philosophical position than a perspective or a way of life. In the course of his narration, Fogle refers to his younger self as a nihilist no less than four times. Like many in his generation, Fogle says, he "was not raised as anything" and as a teenager he romanticized what he now recognizes as a "narcissistic despair." (He might have said that he and his friends lived lives of "quiet desperation," or that they felt a "stereotyped but unconscious despair.")[17] In a sense, Fogle's journey began when he learned the definition of the word "nihilism" (appropriately, in the "sixth week of theater class in high school") (163), and culminated with his realization that he had in fact become "a real nihilist," that it "wasn't just a hip pose. That I drifted and quit because nothing meant anything, no one choice was really better" (223). In this, he was much like his peers. "Everyone I knew and hung out with was a wastoid," he remembers. "It was hip to be ashamed of it, in a strange way . . . or just to feel directionless and lost" (165).

Several events prompted or "primed" Fogle for what he describes as his "change in direction," but he did not finally manage to "put away childish things" (172) until he wandered, mistakenly, into an Advanced Accounting class at the Catholic DePaul University. The class was being taught by a "substitute Jesuit" (in a Freudian slip, Fogle later calls him a "substitute father" [176]), capable of summarizing extant property tax law with a dry yet apparently undeniable dignity. At the end of the class, in what is alternately a parody and a paraphrase of Kierkegaard, the Jesuit delivers a peroration on the necessity of the "leap outward" into adulthood. The leap is into "reality," where there is "no audience," but from the perspective of which all other kinds of heroism appear as mere "theater" (229). The students in the class had so far lived a "crude approximation of a human life," the Jesuit says. Real heroism or courage was not what they thought it was. To work day after day at a thankless job, giving oneself to "the care of other people's money"—this was "effacement, perdurance, sacrifice, valor" (231).

For all its hyperbole, the speech works a change in Fogle. The change begins with his recognition that he really had been living a "*crude approximation of a human life*" (237, italics in original). The recognition is inseparable from his realization that there might be something else he could be living—say (what Thoreau called) a "whole human life." As Cavell points out, Perfectionist thinkers do not take sides in the various Kantian problematics that occupy much of professional moral philosophy; their concern is not with what *should* compel us to change our behavior, but with what *does*. By showing us

---

[17] Thoreau, "Walden," (1854) in Brooks Atkinson (ed.), *Walden and Other Writings* (New York: Random House, 1992), 8.

visions of our rejected selves, of selves that look better than our current ones, such texts hope to trigger in us "that aversion to ourselves in our conformity that will constitute our becoming as it were, ashamed of our shame."[18] For Fogle, the Jesuit functions something like a substitute self, manifesting exactly the qualities that Fogle believed he had rejected in himself: the Jesuit "was 'indifferent'—not in a meaningless, drifting, nihilistic way, but rather in a secure, self-confident way"; he had "a kind of zealous integrity that manifested not as style but as the lack of it"; he didn't feel the need to "joke or try to slightly undercut what he was about to say" (226).

Here is virtually a catalogue of the qualities Wallace himself said he admired in certain literary "authorities" (such as Dostoevsky), but which he confessed it was not easy to reproduce, either for himself personally or for any contemporary writer, in a literary climate where the undermining of authority was valued more highly than the expression of it. This is one reason for taking the Fogle section, despite its own undercutting gestures (in a certain mood, the substitute Jesuit can seem merely hilarious, and it is hinted that Fogle's "transformation" was at least in part abetted by a prescription drug), as the moral and philosophical center of *The Pale King*—the place where we, the readers, may become averse to our own conformity, our own penchant for "hip nihilism," and our own romanticization of despair. Fogle, for his part, now sees that all his own "non-conformist" behavior was little more than theater ("I remember once shaving off just one sideburn and going around like that for a period of time, believing the one sideburn made me a nonconformist—I'm not kidding" [161]). Later he announces the discovery of a better, deeper self:

> There were depths in me that were not bullshit or childish but profound, and were not abstract but much realer than my clothes or self-image, and that blazed in an almost sacred way—I'm being serious; I'm not just trying to make it more dramatic than it was.

That this is one of the places Fogle stops to insist ("I'm being *serious . . .*") hints at what Wallace takes to be the radicality of the claim, for his audience, that there might be something "much realer" than one's personality. But the truly radical, or challenging, aspect of the story is that Fogle believes that his decision to work as an accountant for the IRS has anything to do with his access to such inner "depths." American fiction has generally preferred characters who have preferred not to assent to the deadening daily grind of office work—and contemporary culture boasts no shortage of books and TV

---

[18] *Conditions*, 58.

shows whose comedy is predicated on the widespread consensus that the white collar office is as absurd and soul-destroying as it is inescapable. Yet the effectiveness of *The Pale King*, or of its philosophical instruction, depends upon the reader coming to see that the renunciation of conformism may take many forms, and that the forms of rebellion we learned about as children will turn out, almost by definition, to have been childish. Kierkegaard knew that even the tax collector could escape conformism, because conformism was a matter of inner freedom and not, as we may be tempted to believe in our eternal adolescence, a matter of "self-image." The important thing about Fogle's decision to become an IRS agent is that it was a decision; that is, that he had chosen something over nothing. The choice, which had looked to the childish Fogle like a narrowing of his freedom, led instead to the discovery of a "much realer" self than the one that had "chosen to have nothing matter." The point is not that working a desk job at the IRS is required for such a discovery, but that, for the one who has truly made a *choice*, even the "tedious and dronelike" will be powerless to distract him from it.

***

A difference between Rand's and Fogle's philosophical journeys might be described as follows: Whereas Rand is brought, via a series of interactive dialogues, to see the contingency of what she had been convinced was her "real self" ("the real me"), Fogle is inspired, primarily by the Jesuit's peroration, to trade a false or a shallow for a real or a deep self. In a sense, then, Fogle ends up where Rand begins. In another sense, Fogle progresses to a state that is unimagined by (the teenage *or* the adult) Rand—call it authenticity, or wholeness, or happiness, or grace.

Cavell implies that Perfectionism is an outgrowth of Wittgenstein's notion of philosophy as therapy,[19] but the difference between Rand's and Fogle's stories in *The Pale King* demonstrates what I consider to be a consequential distinction between their methods of instruction, or inspiration. Famously, Wittgenstein maintained that the philosopher should not speak directly about ethics. Accordingly, and in contrast to many Perfectionist authors, Wittgenstein does not offer his reader a vision of some better, more authentic or more awake way of living; he does not speak at all (as Thoreau does) of a "*whole* human life," or of an ethically or spiritually fulfilling life (as Kierkegaard or Augustine might), or of an authentic or a natural one (as do Heidegger and Rousseau). Wittgenstein speaks strictly of a human life, and of the human being's all-too-human desire to go beyond the human, and thus

---

[19] Cf. *Conditions*, 2.

of her need constantly to be called back, as to herself, her humanity (he calls this condition "peace," and it is always temporary).[20]

Rand's therapeutic progress in *The Pale King* remains provisional; and, for his part, the "sickly" late night attendant is not presented as leading a spiritually superior life to Rand's, only a less tortured one. In Fogle's section, however, there is a suggestion that certain lives are not just more "peaceful" than others, but that they may be lived at a higher, or deeper, or more profound pitch. In the notes arranged after the culmination of *The Pale King's* narrative, probably the most quoted passage in reviews of the book, there lies a vision of a life lived in what might be called the sacramental key:

> It turns out that bliss—a second-by-second joy + gratitude at the gift of being alive, conscious—lies on the other side of crushing, crushing boredom. Pay close attention to the most tedious thing you can find (tax returns, televised golf), and, in waves, a boredom like you've never known will wash over you and just about kill you. Ride these out, and it's like stepping from black and white into color. Like water after days in the desert.

We do not know how Wallace would have incorporated these words into his novel (they appear in the notes next to other notations regarding Drinion), had he finished it; at the same time, the gravitation of early critics to the passage would seem to support the suspicion that it encapsulates something that was new, or newly direct, about *The Pale King*. For all his desire to be a "morally passionate, passionately moral" writer in the Dostoevskian mode,[21] Wallace would seem to have accepted, in the majority of his mature fiction (possibly for different reasons, possibly not),[22] Wittgenstein's prohibition

---

[20] This is a description of Wittgenstein's ambitions that I virtually steal from Cavell. My favorite of Cavell's many evocative descriptions of Wittgenstein's project comes in his autobiography, where he calls "the subject sketched in Wittgenstein's *Philosophical Investigations* the subject perpetually seeking peace, therefore endlessly homeless" (Cavell, *Little Did I Know: Excerpts from Memory* [Stanford, CA: Stanford University Press, 2010], 100).

[21] Wallace, *Consider the Lobster and Other Essays* (New York: Back Bay Books, 2007), 274.

[22] Commentators have often described Wallace's trepidation about writing fiction that was too morally or spiritually direct as stemming from his fear of appearing sentimental or moralistic, or of disappointing the sophisticated audience he had built up with his early fiction. Wallace sometimes described the struggle that way himself. But it can also be conceived of as a struggle between conflicting intellectual commitments—on the one hand, Wallace's commitment to the idea that literature should be morally edifying for a large audience; on the other, his commitment to Wittgenstein's eloquent argument (made especially at the end of the *Tractatus* and in his "Lecture on Ethics") that ethical and spiritual matters should be approached in language only indirectly, if at all.

against direct ethical appeals. *The Pale King* marked a new stage in Wallace's development insofar as it aimed not merely to free his reader from philosophical confusions but also to galvanize her with a quasi-ascetic vision of a life ecstatically lived. If Rand's section reprises Wallace's attempt to give his readers some temporary "peace" from their torments, in Fogle's portion, and elsewhere in the book, there emerges a (tentative) vision of a mode of experience that would seem to transcend the therapeutic, together with the "untrendy human troubles" it is meant to address, altogether.

If these can be described as the most Perfectionist moments in the book, they are also connected intimately to *The Pale King's* expression of the counterpart to Perfectionism's lofty idealism—namely its intense despair about our *present* condition. Cavell begins his lectures on Perfectionism with the question of whether Moral Perfectionism is "inherently elitist" with regard to society, granting that "some idea of being true to oneself—or to the humanity in oneself, or of the soul as on a journey (upward or onward) . . . requires a refusal of society, perhaps above all of democratic, leveling society." Cavell argues that Perfectionism in fact "happily consents to democracy" and is even inextricable from the "democratic aspiration." I do not mean here to judge Cavell's case for Perfectionism as a democratic option, or necessity, only to raise the possibility that the consequences of Perfectionism's elitism may manifest themselves personally (as elitism toward the unimproved self) before they do so socially, or politically (as elitism toward society as it stands). The sense that is voiced repeatedly by Thoreau at the beginning of *Walden*, that the mass of American men are living impoverished or desperate lives, that they "labor under a mistake," that they are "doing penance in a thousand remarkable ways,"[23] finds its counterpart in the portions of *The Pale King* that regard its characters' self-consciousness and narcissism as symptoms of spiritual deficiency and cultural decline. When the critic Jonathan Raban described a "fundamentalist streak" in Wallace's final novel, it was likely these elements of the book's tone and subject matter that he had in mind.[24]

Doubtless, Cavell would describe any "fundamentalism" in the book as marking a deviation from Perfectionism, not an expression of it. Yet for the man who accepts Fogle's picture of the sacred within the human (which is also often Perfectionism's picture), it may be hard to resist the suspicion that he is falling short of his highest, most authentic potential, failing to measure up to his "genius" (in Emerson's version) or to be who he is (in Nietzsche's). His sense of failure, or of falling short of authenticity, or sincerity, is the

---

[23] Cf. *Walden*, 4–6, 8.
[24] Jonathan Raban, "Divine Drudgery," *New York Review of Books*, 12 May 2011.

engine that gets Perfectionism going; the danger is just that, *therapeutically* speaking, that same sense of failure is also one of Perfectionism's likely outcomes.

***

But I want to end by emphasizing two things that unite Rand's and Fogle's stories, and thus draw attention to what I think Wallace's project shares with both Perfectionism and philosophical therapy. The first is a preoccupation, especially compared to other conceptions of philosophy today, with self-knowledge, and the modes and methods by which it might be achieved. A second is the conjoining of states of philosophical confusion with stages of personal development—with childhood, or adolescence—as if these are not simply biological moments we will grow out of but permanent human possibilities and temptations.

In regard to this second point, I would emphasize the language that Rand and Fogle use, looking back on their former selves, to describe their conditions. Rand was not just confused and self-indulgent, she was "going around and around inside the problem instead of really looking at the problem" (496). Fogle was not only dejected and aimless, he was "the worst kind of nihilist— the kind who didn't even know he was a nihilist" (154). In both cases, the subject had assumed a philosophical position, but without meaning to and without (until much later) recognizing that she/he had assumed one. Rand and Fogle thus both demonstrate how one can "go around and around" in a philosophical problem while all the time thinking that one is addressing it, or (even more troubling) that there is nothing to be addressed. (It is precisely this ignorance that is "worst" about being a nihilist without knowing it.) This is why they furnish good examples of Wallace's attempt to dramatize how philosophical problems manifest themselves in personal lives—even and especially in the personal lives of *non*-philosophers.

A critic may still maintain, perhaps condescendingly, that adolescence is a trivial and banal subject, surely a serious obstacle for certain damaged Americans (like Rand and Fogle), and even something that may once have occupied a class of serious philosophers and poets (call them romantics), but, for all that, not particularly worthy of serious investigation today, when we have so many other more pressing problems to attend to. A task worthy of Wallace criticism might then be to show, or to demonstrate how Wallace shows, adolescence to be not only *a* philosophical problem but to be *our* philosophical problem. This would be at the same time to show that there could be *no* words "addressed to our condition" which were not addressed to our—extended and debilitating—adolescence.

For as does *Walden*, *The Pale King* posits that a whole culture can persist in a state of immaturity and blindness to itself. Possibly this culture fetishizes the notion of choice at the same time that it "chooses [like Chris Fogle] to have nothing matter" (223). This, Wallace might have said, was one way of describing the consequences of intellectual postmodernism, or of intellectual postmodernism's unwitting collusion with commercial capitalism, for American society. In *The Pale King's* various "civics" chapters, there hums an argument about the truly awe-inspiring childishness of the American people, a people so sheltered and self-deluding that they could demand less taxes and more public services at the same time, and not even acknowledge the contradiction. "[Not] infantile so much as adolescent," one of the accountants says of this benighted people, "that is, ambivalent about its twin desire for both authoritarian structure and the end of parental hegemony" (147).

In such an America, the pervasiveness of self-help, not to mention books of affirmations, yoga, evangelical preaching, and television makeover shows, might be seen as evidence not of the insignificance or shallowness of the problem of adolescence, but of its depth and urgency. A benefit of Cavell's coining of the term "Perfectionism" is to remind us of, and to give us a vocabulary for talking about, philosophy's perennial commitment to such a problem. The Perfectionist, says Cavell, treats "what we call adolescence" less as a "phase of individual development [than as] a dimension of human existence as such."[25] It is simultaneously the dimension in us that desires to be helped and yet does not know what help it needs, that wants to change but is stuck within a perspective from which there appears to be no path forward, or (more likely in what Wallace once called our national "confusion of permissions") so many paths that it seems impossible to ever choose one.

The ability of this self to transform itself is for the Perfectionist hardly peripheral to philosophy; it is rather something like philosophy's highest ambition, though one from which it is easily and almost systematically distracted. To remain faithful to it may demand, among other things, an embrace of formal experimentation, as well as the courage to cross disciplinary boundaries into areas more usually reserved for literature, or religion, or therapy, even if that means risking one's thought being confused with what Cavell calls "debased perfectionisms"[26]—those omnipresent lists of instructions attempting to tell the self, as from the outside, and dogmatically, how it ought to improve. And perhaps this is the real problem with most self-proclaimed self-help: not that it is so often unhelpful (what would be

---

[25] *Conditions*, 51–2.
[26] Ibid., 16.

the harm in that?), but that it can so easily become programmatic, even dangerous in its self-certainty.

The virtue of philosophy as Perfectionism, or as therapy, would then lie in its ability to answer the question of how reading (or culture) may benefit the self without tyrannizing or sentimentalizing it. At their best, the works in this tradition do not offer answers so much as prompting or "priming"[27] their readers to ask themselves certain kinds of questions.

Are these *philosophical* questions? That depends on whether you accept Perfectionism's argument that the development of the soul is a philosophical (as opposed to a merely personal or, say, a religious) problem. Perfectionist texts, as well as philosophically therapeutic ones, will tend to frame things that way. For its part, *The Pale King*'s narrative threads almost all coalesce into stories of conversion or transformation, with its various narrators recounting their paths from a self-incurred immaturity to something resembling enlightenment, maturity, or wisdom. That maturity *requires* wisdom, or enlightenment—rather than just natural growth, or experience—may be described as the discovery that unites Rand's and Fogle's narratives, just as it constitutes a recurring motif in philosophy from Plato to Kierkegaard to Wittgenstein to Cavell. The reader may ignore or condescend to such a discovery but, if the Wallace of *The Pale King* is to be believed, such tactics will only postpone her from having to contend with it.

---

[27] The word surfaces several times in *The Pale King*, usually in the context of a character about to make a major change in her life. "Primed" is also "one of the IRS words for putting Examiners in a state where they pay maximum attention to returns" (*PK*, 540).

10

The Formative Years: David Foster Wallace's Philosophical Influences and *The Broom of the System*

Thomas Tracey

This chapter hopes to demonstrate a number of important points to enrich our understanding of the uses to which David Foster Wallace puts philosophy in the service of his fiction: first and foremost, that Wallace's extensive philosophical training equipped him with the tools to negotiate the concerns of Pragmatist ethics alongside Wittgenstein's philosophy of language within the framework of the novel; second, that Wallace's philosopher-father was a supplementary influence on the author's personal and intellectual development beyond the halls of academe. Both encounters positioned the author effectively to manipulate and reconfigure philosophical concepts in concrete terms, by way of a narrative exploration of the social ironies of contemporary life. Wallace's work thus came to engage in an evaluative dialogue between the history of morality and a native intellectual tradition presented within a deliberately American context.

The family background

To understand the sources of philosophical inspiration for Wallace's writing, we must take into account a number of key facts. It is essential to keep in mind that Wallace majored in Philosophy (with a focus on technical philosophy, especially logic and the philosophy of mathematics) at Amherst College, Massachusetts, from 1980 to 1985, winning the Gail Kennedy Memorial

Prize for his senior thesis.[1] In reading Philosophy at his father's alma mater, Wallace had been following in family footsteps.[2] James Donald Wallace himself went on to pursue a career as a professional philosopher at the University of Illinois at Urbana-Champaign, following a PhD at Cornell, and is now author of four books of moral philosophy: *Virtues and Vices* (1978), *Moral Relevance and Moral Conflict* (1988), *Ethical Norms, Particular Cases* (1996), and *Norms and Practices* (2008).[3] These monographs evince how James Wallace's own philosophy has drawn deeply on American Pragmatism, especially the work of John Dewey, and serve as one avenue into looking at what intellectual influence the father's writings may have exerted on his son. Notably, David Foster Wallace is credited as a proof-reader in the Preface to the 1988 publication, so he is likely to have been reading his father's drafts around the same time he was completing his own first novel, *The Broom of the System* (1987).

In the earliest years of Amherst Philosophy's Departmental History, Charles Edward Garman was well known to the wider philosophical community, not least to William James and John Dewey[4]—so there has always been a connection between Amherst Philosophy and American Pragmatist thought. Gail Kennedy was an internationally known authority on American philosophy, especially that of John Dewey. Between 1952 and 1987, Joseph Epstein taught a seminar on Pragmatism.[5] This covers the timeframe within which both James Donald *and* David Foster Wallace were students at Amherst; therefore, both would have been in a position to attend these seminars. William E. Kennick also taught a seminar on Wittgenstein up until 1993, thus overlapping with Wallace's period of study with the department.

The influence of Wittgenstein has already been widely accepted by Wallace scholars. This chapter argues that the other major influence is the more native tradition of American Pragmatism. This aspect has been little explored in Wallace scholarship, yet it is imperative to a proper comprehension of the

---

[1] "Richard Taylor's 'Fatalism' and the Semantics of Physical Modality." [Thesis, Amherst College Archives and Special Collections, by permission of the author.] Its title is echoed during the opening interview scene of *Infinite Jest*, where one of several papers written by the prodigious Hal Incandenza is mentioned: "Montague Grammar and the Semantics of Physical Modality" (*IJ*, 7). Montague's work features in Wallace's original thesis, which has been posthumously published under the title *Fate, Time and Language: An Essay on Free Will* (New York: Columbia University Press, 2011).

[2] James Donald Wallace's 1959 Thesis was on "Bradley's sceptical arguments."

[3] James Donald Wallace is a Professor Emeritus at Illinois, with stated interests in Ethics, Biomedical Ethics, and Philosophy of Art [see U.I.U.C. website].

[4] "A Brief History of the Department of Philosophy at Amherst College," 3: http://www.amherst.edu/~philo/dept/history/index.html.

[5] Ibid., 5.

oeuvre.[6] The claim is that this tradition was transmitted to Wallace through both his formal education and the habitual influence of his father, not least through the latter's writings—whose viewpoints, I suggest, would also have translated into criteria for practical instances of the moral upbringing of his son. The simple fact remains, that the parent is the primary influence on the ethical development of the child.[7] Added to this, we must acknowledge the stylized socialization of formal education. This formative educational context cannot be underestimated when considering, as we shall do here, the influence of American Pragmatism upon Wallace's work.

Common factors exist between Wittgenstein's philosophy of language, as well as his philosophical psychology, and certain elements of American Pragmatism. This point is important because it synthesizes a common ground upon which the vying influencers under discussion are reasonably reconciled. As David H. Evans has pointed out in relation to the influence of William James upon David Wallace, "Pragmatism anticipates some of the central themes of the *Philosophical Investigations*."[8] While Marshall Boswell, among others, has already pointed to the Wittgensteinian portion of this ancestry, and while it is culturally sensitive to highlight the American flavor of Wallace's philosophical origins, it is more fundamental to an understanding of the genesis of Wallace's moral and ethical concerns to glean knowledge of the commonalities shared with certain aspects of the Anglo-American tradition. The main difficulty in reconciling Wallace and Pragmatism is that the latter is not a unified school in any facile sense, but rather a medley of inflections upon certain mutual preoccupations. There is also a historical progression within the Pragmatist tradition that can be said to mirror social, scientific, and religious attitudes at different times. For reasons of space, I am forced to concentrate on American Pragmatism here.[9]

---

[6] Clare Hayes-Brady's essay on *Broom* devotes two pages to Rorty's influence in David Hering (ed.), *Consider David Foster Wallace: Critical Essays* (Los Angeles/Austin: SSMG Press, 2010), 31–3. More recently, David H. Evans has explored the influence of William James in Marshall Boswell and Stephen Burn (eds), *A Companion to David Foster Wallace Studies* (New York: Palgrave Macmillan, 2013).

[7] In keeping with this spirit, James Donald Wallace remarks: "'Growth,' according to Dewey, 'is the only moral "end".'" *Ethical Norms, Particular Cases* (Ithaca & London: Cornell University Press, 1996), 42.

[8] Marshall Boswell and Stephen Burn (eds), *A Companion to David Foster Wallace Studies* (New York: Palgrave Macmillan, 2013), 172.

[9] James Donald Wallace concurs: "Our notion of a human being living well is bound up with a multiplicity of complicated moral and social values. There is an obvious conventional aspect to these matters, and therefore conceptions of good human life have varied so from time to time and from community to community." *Virtues and Vices* (Ithaca and London: Cornell University Press, 1978), 33.

We can view moral philosophical lineage much like a family tree, foregrounding resemblances between various members of the Anglo-American tradition. "Family resemblances" is *not* meant to imply that there is some absolute lowest denominator intrinsic to *all* instances, but rather general likenesses or formal similarities shared among diverse varieties. As Wittgenstein put it: "the strength of the thread does not reside in the fact that some one fibre runs through its whole length, but in the overlapping of many fibres."[10] The undertaking, then, is both expository and comparative; it is meant as a dipartite overview incorporating firstly the American Pragmatists and secondly the ethical writings of James Donald Wallace.

It must be noted that this chapter is not about Philosophy or Pragmatism per se. It is only so in regard to their relation to Wallace's work. The analysis of influence will emerge by integrating an expository treatment of Pragmatist philosophies with Wallace's most clearly Wittgensteinian text, *The Broom of the System*. *Broom* foregrounds a number of distinct and significant ways in which Wallace lays suitable philosophical foundations for the maturation of his artistic project.

The American Way

Let us now examine the native influence of American Pragmatism as Wallace exploits it in relation to the Wittgensteinian threads running through *Broom*. The discussion is channeled through four proponents of Pragmatism: C. S. Peirce, William James, John Dewey, and Richard Rorty.

In *The Two Pragmatisms: From Peirce to Rorty*, H. O. Mounce indicates how Peirce "replaced an absolute with a relative conception of knowledge" by initiating a shift toward a perspectival approach to epistemology.[11] This approach takes account of the fact that human beings are implicated in and therefore affect the study of Nature. Peirce's Objective Idealism held that "the world is constituted by an order which is mental in character but which is quite independent of the human mind."[12] This mirrors Wittgenstein's idea that the limits of language map out the limits of the world; at the same time, that world transcends language. "Whereof one cannot speak, thereof one must be silent."[13] When such an approach is applied to the act of sense perception,

---

[10] Ludwig Wittgenstein, *Philosophical Investigations*, trans. by G. E. M. Anscombe (Oxford: Blackwell, 1978), 67.

[11] H. O. Mounce, *The Two Pragmatisms: From Peirce to Rorty* (London & New York: Routledge, 1997), 14.

[12] Ibid., 9.

[13] Ludwig Wittgenstein, *Tractatus Logico-Philosophicus* (London & New York: Routledge, 1990), § 7.

it results in the fact that "sensations call attention not to themselves but to what they signify.... Their function may be likened to that of signs or symbols.... Peirce became convinced that it is through signs or symbols that all our knowledge of the world is mediated."[14] Perception entails an active rather than passive intellect: "We notice not just what is there, but what we look for."[15] This dictum may be applicable to the intrinsic momentum of all quest narratives, including *Broom*. Lenore's world is a semiotic jungle where she seeks clues to the whereabouts of her Gramma, often to the detriment of the most obvious yet important observations concerning the life around her, such as tensions in her personal relationships.

Peirce's conviction concerning the nature of signs is crucial to the claim that knowledge is only ever paradigmatic and conditional. Our epistemic apprehension of the world is bound to the semantic multiplicity of our language systems, which evolve within the history of their usage, prone to fluctuation and modification, not to mention uncertainty (and this is consistent with the *Philosophical Investigations*). But this uncertainty is of the theoretical kind. Peirce distinguishes *theoretical* inquiry from *practical* certainty. Meaning, for human beings, is initiated in terms of the *practical*: "One grasps the meaning of a concept, not by contemplating an entity, but by acquiring a *capacity* or *habit* in handling it."[16] *Habit* is fundamentally related to the acquisition of human meaning, something Wallace thematically develops most thoroughly in *Infinite Jest*. In the context of ethics, compare James Donald Wallace on morality's relation to habit, citing Aristotle's *Nichomachean Ethics*: "Intellectual virtue in the main owes both its birth and its growth to teaching (for which reason it requires experience and time), while moral virtue comes about as a result of habit."[17] The need for the cultivation of forms of virtue through personal habit will come to be seen as a pressing concern in David Foster Wallace's work. It is by a step-by-step approach, taking successive cases, that one acquires practical knowledge and its attendant meaning.

Likewise, doubt proceeds through a stepping-stone-like displacement of our epistemic terra firma, rather than an all-out undermining of our conceptual terrain. To appropriate Wittgenstein's man/slope image, it is rather more a part-sliding, part-climbing, than a helpless sinking in the sand. As Mounce explains, "One cannot simultaneously revise all one's beliefs, for then one would have no way of distinguishing which beliefs are true and which false."[18] Inquiry is initiated by some presupposed belief's frustrated

---

[14] Mounce, 8.
[15] Ibid., 15.
[16] Ibid., 13.
[17] J. D. Wallace, *Virtues and Vices*, 44, citing *NE*, II, 1, 1103a15–17.
[18] Mounce, *The Two Pragmatisms*, 15.

expectation. In Lenore's case, it is a sudden undermining of the presumption that Gramma will always be there for her that leads to the vicissitudes of her personal quest. "Pragmatism," Mounce notes, "elucidates doubt of belief by relating it to the one who inquires. . . . how the world appears will depend partly on how it is but partly also on the position from which one observes it."[19] It is from Lenore's perspective that we view the hermeneutic horizon that circumscribes the quest narrative in which she is implicated.

Peirce's theory of signs relates the linguistic character of mental activity to our personal relationship with the world as it is, in such a way as to make it "implicitly metaphysical."[20] But an oft-overlooked corollary of the pragmatist message is that the disciplinary disjunction between epistemology and metaphysics in the Western philosophical tradition is at odds with the actual nature of linguistically-mediated experience: "Language flows out of the relations between creatures and the world and these relations already have the characteristic of meaning."[21] A patent example is the sharing of the name "Lenore" between Gramma Beadsman and her great-granddaughter. Multivalent function is intended to suggest alterity and individuation, rather than the banality of sameness. Peirce's theory elucidates the role language plays in the establishment of knowledge and meaning in the world through the notion of habit or disposition. Insofar as language is about habitual use and disposition to logical continuity in usage, then our world is understood in terms of generality and continuity. Any hard and fast distinction between the behavior of an object and its nature cannot be readily made. This connection between law, habit, and disposition is the key feature of Peirce's mature philosophical Realism, without which Pragmatism would be unintelligible.

Where C. S. Peirce and William James differ is the way in which James pushes Peirce's Pragmatic Maxim beyond its claim about conceptual meaning, toward a like claim for truth.[22] In "What Pragmatism Means", James presents an instrumental view of truth: "*ideas (which themselves are but parts of our experience) become true just in so far as they help us get into satisfactory relation with other parts of our experience.*"[23] The ideal of getting into a satisfactory relation with truth by understanding experience as essentially *functional* is

---

[19] Ibid., 16.

[20] Ibid., 23.

[21] Ibid., 26.

[22] Peirce's Pragmatic Maxim: "a conception can have no logical effect or import differing from that of a second conception except so far as, taken in connection with other conceptions and intentions, it might *conceivably modify our practical conduct differently from that second exception*" [*emphasis mine*]. Ibid., 33.

[23] William James, *Pragmatism* (New York: Dover, 1995), 23. Italics original.

incorporated into the realm of human relations by Reverend Sykes near the end of *Broom*: "Tonight we must attempt to see together that to be *satisfied in a spiritual sense is to be used*."[24] James claims that the Pragmatist view of epistemology is actually a conservative one, because it does not demand the complete overturning of our "previous mass of opinions" to be replaced by a whole set of new ones. It is rather a preservation of the old stock "with a minimum of modification."[25] James submits that "[t]he most violent revolutions in an individual's belief leave most of his old order standing."[26] Wallace's use of Pragmatism is aptly "non-revolutionary" in a similar sense. Wallace has described the next real literary rebels as "*anti-rebels*" for their turning away from the self-reflexive ironies of postmodernist aesthetics toward a reinstatement and unabashed championing of "plain old untrendy human troubles and emotions," favoring rounded character development over formalist pyrotechnics.[27] The carrying of old beliefs over the threshold of new information marries tradition and innovation: "New truth is always a go-between, a smoother-over of transitions."[28]

The offshoot from James's claim is that truth becomes merely expedient. Theories serve not as answers to enigmas but as tools for thinking. James connects truth with moral value and moral action in the following passage: "'*The true,' to put it briefly, is only the expedient in the way of our thinking, just as 'the right' is only the expedient in the way of our behaving*."[29] This expediency is echoed by James Donald Wallace's Aristotelian view that ethics, the study of the good life, is a practical subject: "In solving unprecedented practical problems, we change our store of practical knowledge, we to a degree alter our aims, standards, and ways. Efforts to solve moral relevance and conflict problems inevitably change morality."[30] Since the "true" and the "good" are conflated for the benefit of human life, it is not too great a leap to entertain the expediency of "faith" or religious belief: "*If theological ideas prove to have a value for concrete life, they will be true, for pragmatism, in the sense of being good for so much. For how much more they are true, will depend entirely on their relations to other truths that also have to be acknowledged*."[31] The theological idea of a Higher Power beyond the Self will gather greater significance in *Infinite Jest*, where Wallace prescribes a socio-moral application of AA's treatment of

---

[24] Wallace, *Broom*, 464.
[25] James, *Pragmatism*, 24.
[26] Ibid.
[27] Wallace, *A Supposedly Fun Thing I'll Never Do Again* (London: Abacus, 2004), 81.
[28] James, *Pragmatism*, 24.
[29] Ibid., 86. Italics original.
[30] J. D. Wallace, *Moral Relevance and Moral Conflict*, 4.
[31] James, *Pragmatism*, 29. Italics original.

addiction, in an attempt to diagnose and remedy postmodern anomie. Many of AA's ideas on a Higher Power were taken by Bill Wilson from James's *The Varieties of Religious Experience*. James's suppositions also materialize in denatured form as *Broom's* quasi-theological construct, the G.O.D., and take abstract psychological form in Blentner's Hygiene Theory. The second part of James's assertion corresponds to the idea that truth theories have become functional modes of an advantageous "*adaptation* to reality."[32] This may be read as a psychological response to environment in terms of a sociobiological re-conception of the human being's epistemic relation to its habitat.

Concepts, for James, are things with which to come back into experience. James's philosophy is primarily concerned with the life lived, *ipso facto* an ethical life.[33] Ideas act as cicerones in our dealings with environmental reality, in much the same way as LaVache slips into the role of Lenore's philosophical guide. As James asserts:

> The essential thing is the process of being guided. Any idea that helps us to *deal*, whether practically or intellectually, with either the reality or its belongings, that doesn't entangle our progress in frustrations, that *fits*, in fact, and adapts our life to the reality's whole setting, will agree sufficiently to meet the requirement. It will hold true of that reality.[34]

The moral aspect to this approach is put in relief when one understands reality as social reality and man as a social animal operating within a community environment. James Donald Wallace supports this claim: "The notion that our attitudes toward . . . actions can be explained without reference to a social context is implausible."[35] For the individual, then, the key is "to be a decent social unit."[36] Central to this is an economy of exchange, rather than one of self-preservation. Exchange of ideas becomes a medium for social change. James's employment of the crudely fiscal term *cash-value* to his valuation of the experiential should not deter us from noting how his conception of human truth is expressed in terms of an economy of vital interests within lived experience. It is noteworthy that LaVache, a mediating presence for Lenore, has a name which translates from French as "The Cow."

---

[32] Ibid., 74–5. Italics original.

[33] Similarly, David H. Evans has noted that "The most important parallel between [Wallace's] religious attitudes and those of James . . . is [Wallace's] focus on the consequences of faith in the life of the individual rather than on the nature of the divine" (Boswell and Burn, *A Companion*, 183).

[34] James, *Pragmatism*, 82. Italics original.

[35] J. D. Wallace, *Virtues and Vices*, 117. (Of course, this is also Wittgenstein's point in the *Investigations*.)

[36] James, *Pragmatism*, 89.

Wittgenstein has described language's relation to philosophy metaphorically as "the money we use to buy the cow," our medium of exchange in the realm of wisdom.[37]

Moral choice is liberated in a responsibility to the future that Pragmatism's destabilization of the conceptual bridge between truth and reality initiates. As James concludes: "The essential contrast is that *for rationalism reality is ready-made and complete from all eternity, while for pragmatism it is still in the making, and awaits part of its complexion from the future.*"[38] Moral reality is likewise prone to mutational evolution and complexional variety. This can be extended to the moral realm of a narrative world, with its particular social complexion. Dr Jay echoes this sentiment regarding the storied nature of that world: "The truth is that there's no difference between a life and a story? But a life pretends to be something more? But it really isn't more?"[39] It is in face of the future that the moral life awaits us.

John Dewey had conceived of contending philosophies "as arising not out of intellectual but out of social and emotional material": "Instead of the disputes of rivals about the nature of reality, we have the scene of human clash of social purpose and aspirations."[40] Dewey's refusal to admit "facts" into his metaphysic was just a refusal to concede that facts could not be *manipulated*. Dewey's position is presented in *The Need for a Recovery of Philosophy* (1917). "Anthropomorphic Naturalism" is the term Morris Cohen applies to this position, where the standard reality/appearance distinction is challenged and ordinary human experience is made the measure of reality.[41] Postmodern quest narratives and parodies thereof, like Wallace's *Broom*, are often about shifting paradigms of self-understanding. Bertrand Russell's sketching out of Dewey's stance on "good" and "bad" beliefs reflects their latently moral-developmental flavor: "Whether a belief is good or bad depends upon whether the activities which it inspires in the organism entertaining the belief have consequences which are satisfactory or unsatisfactory to it."[42] Dewey's philosophical psychology proposes that it is only *after* we pursue whatever activities constitute our business with the world, and witness their consequences, that we gain a clear insight into the true purpose of our intentions, motives, and desires.[43] This collapses any strict hierarchy between

---

[37] Wittgenstein, *Philosophical Investigations*, § 120.
[38] James, *Pragmatism*, 99. Italics original. Wallace's novels are hued with a certain (moral) complexion by fact of their being set in the near-future.
[39] Wallace, *Broom*, 120.
[40] Mounce, 148.
[41] Ibid., 155.
[42] Bertrand Russell, *History of Western Philosophy* (London & New York: Routledge, 2005), 735.
[43] Mounce, *The Two Pragmatisms*, 131.

ends and means (by extension, between teleology and the pragmatics of ethical life in its native social realm). Lenore's search for Gramma is really an inverted search to "find herself." This is the fundamental purpose of quest narrative—a mode in which the hero/heroine learns their lesson retrospectively and via the quest itself, which evolves its own kind of moral. "Morals breed stories, stories morals" might be a proverb we could coin to evoke this sentiment. In such a vein, Rick Vigorous laments: "Whatever happened to happy stories, Lenore? Or at least morals? I'd fall ravenously on one of the sort of didactic Salingerian solace-found-in-the-unlikeliest-places pieces I was getting by the gross at Hunt and Peck."[44] Such an ordering is constitutive of a formidable hermeneutic task, witnessed for instance in the games of perpetual banter over semantics that preoccupy Lenore and her interlocutors.

The socially contextualized exemplars of *an* experience precipitate as species of game, rounded activities in the world which, by adherence to their rules and to their empirical nature, are circumscribed with a beginning, a ludic middle, and a definite end, much like the conventional story arc. Wallace's well-known passion for tennis is particularly indicative as a sport of choice. While the game can theoretically go on forever—it has infinite potential—tennis must have an end in real time, in human terms. In the same way that a game or story must inevitably have its termination, so must an experience, so must a life. As Dewey asserts in *Art as Experience*: "we have *an* experience when the material experienced runs its course to fulfilment. Then and then only is it integrated within and demarcated in the general stream of experience from other experiences. A piece of work is finished in a way that satisfies; a problem receives its solution."[45] While art may be the apotheosis of the singularity of an experience, Dewey credits with aesthetic qualities any activity where randomness and routine are mastered by imagination and intellect. Sport, gourmandizing, mental gymnastics, social intercourse, literary endeavor, political canvassing, all fit the bill: "a game is played through; a situation, whether that of eating a meal, playing a game of chess, carrying on a conversation, writing a book, or taking part in a political campaign, is so rounded out that its close is a consummation and not a cessation."[46] Many of these activities occur over the course of Wallace's writings: from tennis in *Infinite Jest*, to mathematics in *Everything & More*, to the ethics of lobster-boiling and the media circus of Presidential candidacy in *Consider the Lobster*.

---

[44] Wallace, *Broom*, 125.
[45] John Dewey, *Art as Experience* (New York: Minton, Balch & Company, 1934), quoted in H. O. Mounce, *The Two Pragmatisms: From Peirce to Rorty* (London & New York: Routledge, 1997), 170–2.
[46] Ibid.

The "game" element of the cited activities takes on a more complex social significance consequent to our discussion of Wittgenstein. Games, conversation, and of course writing are three concerns embodied in Wallace's work. It is not solely in certain works of art that we see unity amidst difference and discover the cultivation of meaning, but also in the music of everyday discourse. Conversation exemplifies quotidian aesthetic experience. The melodic line latent in conversation follows implicit rules its inner logic elaborates over time. James Donald Wallace points out how our mode of dealing with particular ethical issues recalls the typically improvisational quality of conversation and melodic creation:

> The procedure here is improvisational, and ingenuity is an important virtue. Even if the positive morality is relatively harmonious and adequate at one particular time, the next problems a changing world presents are apt to be ones people are not prepared for. If they are intelligent and resourceful enough to adapt their ways to solve novel problems and to deal with the conflicts that such adaptations may engender, then they grow, they progress. This, I take it, is the sort of growth that Dewey called the "only moral end."[47]

The substance of this should be kept in mind for when we come to examine the organic maturation of Wallace's moral aesthetic. The sense of shared community that such an aesthetic moment can foster is what's felt by Dewey to be most powerful and valuable.

Richard Rorty's *Contingency, Irony and Solidarity* picks up on the theme of community through his vision of a utopia in which human solidarity would be achieved by "the imaginative ability to see strange people as fellow sufferers."[48] Rorty pointedly moves away from theory as the medium for achieving his utopian goal, instead advocating genres such as "ethnography, the journalist's report, the docudrama." But primarily: the novel.[49] Rorty proceeds from a recognition of linguistic contingency to "a recognition of the contingency of conscience." The upshot is that "both recognitions lead to a picture of intellectual and moral progress as a history of increasingly useful metaphors rather than of increasing understanding of how things really

---

[47] J. D. Wallace, *Ethical Norms*, 45.

[48] Richard Rorty, *Contingency, Irony and Solidarity* (Cambridge: C.U.P., 1989), Introduction, xvi. (It would be hard to doubt that Wallace was acquainted with Rorty's work, the most overt indication being the short story "Philosophy and the Mirror of Nature," a clear allusion to Rorty's eponymous study.)

[49] James Donald Wallace concurs: "history, biography, and fiction are the research protocols of human ethnology." *Virtues and Vices*, 18–19.

are."[50] An example of such moral historical development's relation to our epistemological reality is outlined by LaVache, speaking on evolution as a cultural phenomenon, where he remarks upon a change in worldview from the religious of antiquity to the modern scientific. This has repercussions for the significance of moral fiction in the life of a society: "After the *Origin*, the Bible has to retreat. . . . The Bible ceases to be a historical record of actual events and instead becomes a piece of moral fiction, useful only as a guide for making decisions about how to live. No longer purporting to tell what was and is, but only what ought to be."[51] John, Lenore's brother, offers a critique of Christian Morality that also possesses Pragmatist strains revealed in the critical language in which LaVache summarizes his argument: "that Christianity is the universe's way of punishing itself, that what Christianity is, really, is the offer of an irresistible reward in exchange for an unperformable service."[52] The point is that morality should be performable (*this is the very spirit of ethics*) and thereby have a functional role in the life of the moral agent.

Implicit here is the claim that the social function of fiction in a secular world is that of moral guidance and spiritual nourishment. We will continue to uncover this notion as a substratum in Wallace's work. Rorty's assertion concerning useful metaphors shifts his discussion into a markedly moral register. Conscience guides us morally through life in a way similar to how ideas help us navigate the tides of experience. Experience becomes mapped, via the contingency of language, within the realm of moral meaning. If we accept that selfhood is born of consciousness, and consciousness takes expression in language, and language is inherently a social tool, it's clear that our inheritance of language at a certain historical moment will effectively shape our sense of self, of identity. Rorty sees moral consciousness "as historically conditioned, a product as much of time and chance as of political or aesthetic consciousness."[53] (This tenet is much-emphasized in the work of James Donald Wallace.) Human beings engage with one another through the contingencies of language in the social sphere as a means of communication and interaction, ultimately of fostering communion, and thereby, morally speaking, of "tying oneself up with other human beings."[54] It is poignant that Rick Vigorous, in a last desperate attempt to bond with Lenore, or at least not to have their existent bond inevitably rent asunder, literally ties himself

---

[50] Rorty, *Contingency*, 9.
[51] Wallace, *Broom*, 217–18.
[52] Ibid., 281.
[53] Rorty, *Contingency*, 30.
[54] Ibid., 41.

up to her using handcuffs.[55] (This scene, set in the Great Ohio Desert, echoes the Death Valley finale that concludes Frank Norris's *McTeague*—a novel we know Wallace studied and admired[56]—in which the dying Marcus handcuffs himself to McTeague in order to ensure their joint demise.)[57] By means of this narrative turn, then, Wallace takes what is originally a philosophical theorem and embodies it in human terms, to darkly humorous effect; he takes an initially abstract philosophical concept and reconfigures it for novelistic ends. Wallace's appropriation of philosophy for narrative and thematic purposes is a technique that recurs throughout his work. Another clear example of this is the reference to Rorty in the title of the story "Philosophy and the Mirror of Nature," which traces the ironies of embodiment and disfigurement in social contexts. Indeed, an array of references to Pragmatist philosophers are peppered throughout Wallace's other books, such as the solace the character Randy Lenz takes from William James in the novel *Infinite Jest*. We learn that Lenz has been in possession of "Bill James's gargantuan Large Print *Principles of Psychology and The Gifford Lectures on Natural Religion*."[58] Lenz, it turns out, has absorbed some of William James's psychological wisdom, but has turned them to dire misuse:

> it was discovered that resolving [the cat-baiting issues] inside the yards and porches of people that owned them provided more adrenal excitation and thus more sense of what Bill James one time called a *Catharsis* of resolving, [with] which Lenz felt he could agree.... [S]ome line in the book had arrested Lenz's attention: something about the more basically Powerless an individual feels, the more the likelihood for the propensity for violent acting out—and Lenz found the observation to be sound.[59]

In this passage, as elsewhere, we are shown how Wallace deploys Jamesian principles in unconventional fictional scenarios to humorous but poignant ends.

The sense of a bond of conscience and consciousness is vital to the flourishing of human life. Rorty avers that new vocabularies are often needed to re-describe our changing environment so as to cope with its challenges

[55] Regarding the *double entendre* on bondage, compare B.I. #48 in Wallace's *Brief Interviews with Hideous Men* (London: Abacus, 2002), 85–97.
[56] Cf. Wallace, *Broom*, 430.
[57] Frank Norris, *McTeague: A Story of San Francisco* (London: Penguin, 1994), 442. Likewise, Lenore's parrot may be an oblique echo of McTeague's canary.
[58] David Foster Wallace, *Infinite Jest* (London: Abacus, 2002), 543.
[59] Wallace, *Infinite Jest*, 544–5.

effectively. The same can be said of moral challenges posed by novel ethical dilemmas which, described in the old vocabulary, might be irresolvable.[60] Why is such lexical innovation necessary? Rorty's answer is that, because of our relationship to the contingent world, in which we experience "brute power and naked pain," and faced with these "nonhuman, non-linguistic" elements in Nature, language is our only way to recognize in each other a like contingency and pain.[61] It is a form of human solidarity. Therefore language, especially the language of morality, must work as a vernacular that is developed unflaggingly in a spirit of complexity yet perspicuity. Rorty quotes Michael Oakshott's *Of Human Conduct* in this regard:

> A morality is neither a system of general principles nor a code of rules, but a vernacular language. . . . What has to be learned in a moral education is not a theorem such as that good conduct is acting fairly or being charitable, nor is it a rule such as "always tell the truth," but how to speak the language intelligently . . . a practice in terms of which to think, to choose, to act, and to utter.[62]

The utility of a regulated vernacular is given considerable attention in Wallace's 2001 essay, "Authority and American Usage." Suffice it to say here that Wallace's essay is prefaced by a proclamation from St Augustine, *Dilige et quod vis fac* ("Love, and do as thou wilt"), whose maxim here is arguably an apology for ethical pragmatism based upon moral diligence and human compassion. In a world where fiction bears moral weight, a habitually diligent vernacular becomes a performative tool that can be plied for ethical purposes. The clearest apology for such utility in *Broom* is Rick Vigorous's harangue on the performative element to language usage. It is arguably the core theme of the novel in toto: "Some words have to be explicitly uttered, Lenore. Only by actually uttering certain words does one really *do* what one *says*. 'Love' is one of those words, performative words. Some words can literally make things real."[63]

This transmogrification from word into action is exemplified by Lenore's take on the transformative power of love: "But then if you get to where you,

---

[60] As James Donald Wallace puts it: "New, unprecedented problems will require changes in old ways. Respect for morality must coexist with the realization that intelligent adaptation of old ways to new problems is required so that the morality can continue to deserve that respect" (*Moral Relevance and Moral Conflict*, 62). This ethos will gain importance when considering Wallace's critique of, and challenge to, the moral status of the ironic stance ascribed to the "postmodern condition."

[61] Rorty, *Contingency*, 40.

[62] Ibid., 58.

[63] Wallace, *Broom*, 285.

you know, love a person, everything sort of reverses. It's not that you love the person because of certain things about the person anymore; it's that you love the things about the person because you love the person. It kind of radiates out, instead of in."[64] The passage recalls Plato's paradoxical moral question in the *Republic*: of whether something is good *because* God decrees it, or whether it is *because* it is good that God decrees it so. In the case of expressing one's love, action takes its embodiment in a performative idiom. As Reverend Sykes fervently declaims at the novel's close: "everyone has desire in their lives, that's part of the *experience* of what it is to be human in God's world."[65]

Rorty's thought makes an extraordinary turn in view of the traditional outlook on the relationship between language and morality in human life. Rorty emphasizes that pain, which all animals suffer, is nonlinguistic, and that this is what ties us not only to each other but also to the "nonlanguage-using beasts."[66] He posits that "all we share with other human beings is the same thing we share with all other animals—the ability to feel pain."[67] This necessitates a redescription of the moral status of the human.

Rorty's approach to redescription takes its cue from John Dewey. Rorty, like Dewey, finds in Art the medium for this task, providing a creative realm in which the imagination performs its magic upon our descriptive sensibilities. Rorty cites Dewey's *Art as Experience* to advance his purpose: "imagination is the chief instrument of the good . . . *art is more moral than moralities*. For the latter either are, or tend to become, consecrations of the status quo. . . . The moral prophets of humanity have always been poets even though they spoke in free verse or by parable" [my emphasis].[68] What is so extraordinary about authors is their ability to undermine our lazy acquiescence to the metaphysical ideology of a "final vocabulary." To reach an instrumental good, we need some vehicle to transport us there. Art, through imagination, provides this transport. It steers us toward the moral life. Integral to this is the vexed question of the conception of the self in its relation to existential hermeneutics:

> The traditional picture of the self as divided into the cognitive quest for true belief, the moral quest for right action, and the aesthetic quest for beauty (or for the "adequate expression of feeling") leaves little room either for irony or for the pursuit of autonomy.

[64] Ibid., 287.
[65] Ibid., 461.
[66] Rorty, *Contingency*, 94.
[67] Ibid., 177.
[68] Ibid., 69.

If we abandon the traditional picture, we shall stop asking questions like "Does this book aim at truth or at beauty? At promoting right conduct or at pleasure?" and instead ask, "What purposes does this book serve?"[69]

A definitive answer, set in stone, would be contrary to the spirit of the novel's own Pragmatist sensibilities, which favor re-description over a monolithic final vocabulary. The question will extend in complexity and implication when examining whether and to what extent Wallace's work employs irony in any straightforward or uncritical way—not to mention what useful artistic and social purpose he may thereby imply contemporary fiction ought to serve.

Like father like son

The influence of James Donald Wallace's moral philosophy upon his son would be presumed to have a certain generality. For the moment, I would like to focus on the first two of James Donald's three monographs, as they are the works which antedate and coincide with *Broom*, respectively. It is clear from the above sections on Pragmatism how its broader epistemological outlook infused David Foster Wallace's distinct philosophical sensibility and therefore informed his writing. In this section, I would like to point out a few key ways that Pragmatist thought links with James Donald Wallace's philosophy, in order to trace the transmission of Pragmatism's intellectual legacy from James the father to David the son. The intention is to underscore for the benefit of summation some of the main strands we have discussed heretofore.

James Donald Wallace published *Virtues and Vices* in 1978, when David Foster Wallace was about 16 years old. The main context for James Donald's early viewpoint is expressed by the Wittgensteinian concept of the "form of life":

> If the form of life is valued as social—as human life seems by nature to be—then people's attitude to other members of their community will be of critical importance. To value community life, one must see the other members of the community as worthy partners in the enterprise—one must to some extent value other members of the community. Members of a human community will need to have for one another, then, the

---

.[69] Ibid., 143.

sort of direct concern that one has for someone or something one values. . . . Such traits, if prevalent in a community, can bind together the members, promoting both individual and community morale.[70]

It is worth comparing the closing section of *Broom*, where we find a summary vignette of some central thematic strands. We witness a literary rendering of these in the form of the Reverend Sykes' Partners With God Club. It is at once a parody of TV evangelism, a comment on contemporary frames of reference for Middle America's moral instruction, and a partly sympathetic gleaning of what possible valuable message might be extracted from the trite rhetoric of that medium. Thus Reverend Sykes: "I stand here before you tonight to say that a partner is a worker . . . an individual who *recognizes* that individuals working together are stronger in the service of the Lord than individuals going their own *separate*, individual ways."[71] The Aristotelian idea of a human *ergon*, or work characteristic of "social life informed by convention," is locatable here.[72] Partnership, a moral bond to another individual and a basic recognition of the viability of greater community, lays the ground for society: "Is not an individual who is a *partner* with God simply an individual who *recognizes*, and finds within his own soul the strength to perform, the *function* God has *assigned* to him? We must ask how can we be *useful* to God."[73] The Reverend is adopting a Pragmatist idiom to express his theological credo, but we might imagine Wallace asking us to transpose its religious terminology into a morality of secular social life. As readers, we are asked to play a game of rule-adaptation and creative substitution. Reverend Sykes concludes thus: "So there is the game, friends, and now here are the stakes tonight. . . . *Every* player . . . who can feel the individual imprisoned inside these secular shells of impotent pain and desire. . . . Use me, friends. Let us play the game together. I promise that no player will feel alone."[74] The image of the "shell of impotent pain" is a forceful one, anticipatory of Wallace's young Hamlet-like antihero, Hal Incandenza, bound in a nutshell of incapacitating self-absorption, and suffering the "bad dreams" of a marijuana-induced paranoia in *Infinite Jest*.

But there is also present the promise of Wallace the author. Perhaps Wallace's most preoccupying theme is the debilitating loneliness imposed upon the individual by the socially alienating infrastructures of post-industrial

[70] J. D. Wallace, *Virtues and Vices*, 160.
[71] Wallace, *Broom*, 458.
[72] J. D. Wallace, *Virtues and Vices*, 37.
[73] Wallace, *Broom*, 465.
[74] Ibid., 465–6.

life.[75] For Wallace, writing is a game played between writer and reader, but a fair game and a rite of intimate union, whereby the author faithfully follows those parametric rules of transmission and reception he has laid down, and that are tacitly agreed upon in an implicit social contract between participants. Wallace exhorts actively involving the reader, inviting her to adapt her practical skills of habituated linguistic interpretation and attendant moral reasoning to unprecedented or, we might say, *novel* scenarios. James Donald Wallace reminds us that the "contextualist" stance of pragmatist thought does not present us with a pre-packaged "decision-procedure" or algorithm for dealing with issues of morality, citing Dewey to further his point.[76] The mechanics of David Foster Wallace's fictional worlds would equally discourage a passive consumerist (encourage an actively engaged) attitude to our reception of innovative works of literary art. From this grows a solidarity that recognizes such loneliness as a common human plight. Wallace's father reframes the ideal in terms of a habituated praxis:

> The upshot of our practical education, including its moral aspect, is that we acquire certain habits of action—including habits of thought. Many of these habits are the loci in individuals of the ways of the community, developed over time, of solving problems of living together. By acquiring similar habits, individuals are able to share a way of life. Community is thus possible.[77]

In *Moral Relevance and Moral Conflict*, James Donald Wallace understands moral considerations as "items of practical knowledge which, in individuals, take the form of character—complex learned dispositions consisting of knowledge, skills, concerns, values, and commitments."[78] The idea of morality is directly bound up with the nature of character, and their maturation is coterminous. Thinking of character not just in the everyday sense of a person's intrinsic qualities, but in the literary sense of a created fictional personality, we see that the above point augments in significance when applied to our understanding of novelistic character development in relation to the moral tenor of a work. Referencing Alasdair MacIntyre, James Donald Wallace reminds us of an etymological basis for preserving these connections: "the Greek 'ethikos', meaning 'pertaining to character', was translated by the Latin 'moralis', a word invented by the Romans to translate 'ethikos'. The early uses of the English 'moral' were to translate 'moralis', although 'moral' also came

---

[75] See "A Radically Condensed History of Postindustrial Life," in Wallace, *Brief Interviews*.
[76] J. D. Wallace, *Moral Relevance and Moral Conflict*, 93–4.
[77] Ibid., 70.
[78] Ibid., 54–5.

to be used as a noun meaning the practical lesson taught by a story."[79] It is this decidedly anti-rebellious conception of the "moral" that asks what useful service character can perform to teach us how to respond pragmatically to the ethics of everyday life. It is a perspective that must be countenanced in order to understand the use to which Wallace puts character in *The Broom of the System*. It would likewise prove instructive to follow this line of inquiry when examining the broader growth and progression of Wallace's narrative art.

In conclusion, this chapter hopes to have outlined the significant influence of the Pragmatist legacy upon David Foster Wallace's philosophical and literary development, clearly exemplified by the nascent intellectual preoccupations of his first novel, *The Broom of the System*. This legacy was inherited from two distinct but closely related sources: first, via Wallace's formal philosophical education at Amherst College; and second, via Wallace's upbringing and intellectual association with his philosopher-father, James Donald, whose own ethical philosophy was firmly rooted within a vibrant American Pragmatist tradition. Both of these formative intellectual influences furnished Wallace with useful conceptual tools with which to address the ethical challenges of postmodernity and the ironies of contemporary social relations within a domain of richly imagined narrative worlds.

---

[79] Ibid., 59. And compare: "MacIntyre maintains that the unity of a self or person and whatever unity a person's life has are the sort of unity we find in narratives—stories or histories. . . . In *Art as Experience*, John Dewey develops the idea that aesthetic qualities, which artists strive to embody in their works, are heightened and intensified instances of certain of the most basic and important qualities of our ordinary experience" (152).

11

Beyond Philosophy: David Foster Wallace on Literature, Wittgenstein, and the Dangers of Theorizing*

Randy Ramal

On Wallace and narrative philosophy

In his introduction to the posthumous publication of Wallace's undergraduate thesis in philosophy,[1] James Ryerson draws attention to the role that philosophy played in Wallace's fiction and other writings. He claims that Wallace's thesis "offers a point of entry into an overlooked aspect of his intellectual life: a serious early engagement with philosophy that would play a lasting role in his work and thought, including his ideas about the purpose and possibilities of fiction."[2] Ryerson takes *The Broom of the System* and *Infinite Jest* as examples of the kind of fiction that shows the influence of philosophy on Wallace, calling them "big, brainy novels," and adds that Wallace also tackled a wide range of intellectual topics in his other writings—for example, the morality of consuming sentient beings in "Consider the Lobster," the question of beauty in athletics in "Federer as Religious Experience," the illusion of freedom in "A Supposedly Fun Thing I'll Never Do Again," and the nature of language in "Authority and American Usage."[3]

I am very appreciative of Ryerson's exposition of where philosophical thinking surfaces in Wallace's fiction and other writings, but he leaves out significant issues related to the points he makes. For example, Ryerson does

---

* I want to thank the editors for their very helpful comments on an earlier draft of my chapter that resulted in several stylistic and content-based revisions.
[1] James Ryerson, "Introduction: A Head that Throbbed Heartlike—the Philosophical Mind of David Foster Wallace," in Steven M. Cahn and Maureen Eckert (eds), *Fate, Time, and Language: An Essay on Free Will* (New York: Columbia University Press, 2011), 1–33. Wallace's honors thesis in philosophy was completed at Amherst College, together with another honors thesis in English, in 1985.
[2] Ibid., 1.
[3] Ibid., 1ff.

not explain how and where Wallace's overall engagement with philosophy affected his specific understanding of the aims of fiction. He indicates that Wallace wanted to unite literature and philosophy in the same way David Markson did in *Wittgenstein's Mistress*,[4] but he does not explore Wallace's views on the nature of philosophy and its relation to literature. Ryerson's focus rests mainly on Wallace's insistence that the task of fiction is to make heads throb heartlike, which is to draw out the emotional implications of the literary work without getting lost in its abstract and intellectual details.[5]

My chapter takes off from where Ryerson leaves the topic. I discuss Wallace's views on the nature of philosophy and the implications thereof for his writing fiction and "creative non-fiction"— the latter term used by Wallace to mean "a broad category of prose works such as personal essays and memoirs, profiles, nature and travel writings of a certain quality, essays of ideas, new journalism, and so on."[6] I argue that, in all areas of writing, philosophic and otherwise, Wallace opposed the tendency to offer generalized accounts of human nature and existence as such while still finding in literature, rather than philosophy, a means of expressing and dealing with existential matters. I use the term "literature" here to refer to both fiction and creative non-fiction, and, in comparing it with philosophy, I mean by the latter the kind of philosophy the later Wittgenstein advocated—which is really the philosophy Wallace came eventually to admire. Those familiar with Wittgenstein's work will recognize this philosophy as the activity of describing and clarifying everyday concepts without interfering with, or attempting to change, what is described. I show that Wallace wanted to do in literature what he thought could not be done, as a rule, in this kind of philosophy.

I do not think that Wallace always understood Wittgenstein correctly, but this fact is irrelevant to my chapter's main topic and I shall not pursue it here except where relevant—for example, when Wallace describes Wittgenstein as an artist, which I think is a problematic description.[7] Regarding the nature of philosophy, the issue for Wallace is logical, it seems to me—is philosophy such that it can be used to make the same points Wallace wanted to make in a narrative form? Wallace was impressed, at first, by the prescriptive and

---

[4] Ryerson writes: "Wallace felt that Markson's novel had succeeded in uniting literature and philosophy in the way that he, in *Broom*, tried but failed to do" ("Introduction," 27). See David Markson, *Wittgenstein's Mistress* (Champaign, IL: Dalkey Archive Press, 1988).

[5] Ibid., 14, 21.

[6] See D. T. Max, *Every Love Story is a Ghost Story: A Life of David Foster Wallace* (New York: Viking, 2012), 237.

[7] I discuss this topic in the last section of the chapter.

theoretical beauty of the *Tractatus* over the less structured and anti-systematic *Philosophical Investigations*, even calling the latter "silly."[8] But, as I show later, even as he was writing *The Broom of the System*, a novel inspired initially by his reading of the *Tractatus*, Wallace gradually came to find greater value in the antitheoretical and anti-systematic philosophy of the later Wittgenstein. Furthermore, although Wallace was not always consistent about the role of fiction in life, he gradually reached the conclusion that philosophy as such is unsuitable for the thinker, the artist, or the creative writer who wants to not only describe and analyze concepts but also offer therapeutic alternatives to existential problems.[9] Literature seems to have been the natural alternative, especially if someone had the talent for it, as Wallace did.

I am convinced that Wallace's views on the natures of philosophy and literature warrant situating him in the tradition of narrative philosophy. By narrative philosophy here I mean the kind of narrative that incorporates existential-philosophical themes and reflections in its content, without being restricted to the task of analyzing concepts for the sheer purpose of understanding them. Analysis and understanding are of utmost importance considering the complexity and ambiguity of the concepts we use in our daily lives, and there is merit in the claim that philosophy ought to restrict its task to that of clarifying concepts rather than prescribing values. But we also need other intelligent ways of reflecting on human lives that are not restricted to the task of clarification and that do not claim to be neutral in their critique of certain aspects of people's lives. This is one reason as to why narrative philosophy is important.

Narrative philosophy does not have exact boundaries and, in my use of the term, it includes existential thinkers such as Camus, Sartre, and Dostoevsky, all of whom were admired by Wallace, as well as philosophically-oriented

---

[8] See Ryerson, "Introduction," 4.

[9] In his 1993 interview with Larry McCaffery, Wallace says: "I just think that fiction that isn't exploring what it means to be human today isn't art" (Larry McCaffery, "A Conversation with David Foster Wallace," in Stephen J. Burn (ed.), *Conversations with David Foster Wallace* [Jackson, MS: University Press of Mississippi, 2012], 26). At this point in his literary life, Wallace seems to have taken a descriptive view of literature. Thus, in the same interview with McCaffery, he states: it "isn't that it's fiction's duty to edify or teach, or to make us good little Christians or Republicans; I'm not trying to line up behind Tolstoy or Gardner" (Ibid.). I show later that he changed his mind on this issue, but Wallace also struggled to write after completing his MFA program at the University of Arizona and thought that returning to philosophy might be the answer to his writer's block. He enrolled in the philosophy program at Harvard University only to find out that the "click" he found earlier in writing fiction could not be had in philosophy (See David Lipsky, "The Lost Years and the Last Days of David Foster Wallace," in Stephen J. Burn (ed.), *Conversations with David Foster Wallace* [Jackson, MS: University Press of Mississippi, 2012], 172).

writers such as J. M. Coetzee, Virginia Woolf, and Ursula K. Le Guin.[10] Wallace mentions that he was attracted to Dostoevsky because of the latter's spiritual conversion from literary self-glory to moral progress and, in a letter to Tom Bissell, he states that Camus is "very clear, as a thinker, and tough— completely intolerant of bullshit. It makes my soul feel clean to read him."[11] I think Camus's *Stranger* can be read as expressing and containing existential points of the kind Wallace felt admirable—for example, the attitude of Meursault, its main character, toward God and the people in his life (his mother, girlfriend, the person he kills without regret), which can be seen as a way of tackling the Socratic question of how to examine one's life, proposing that as long as one is genuine to one's feelings and conscience then no moral harm could come to that person.[12] Perhaps Wallace would have also liked Roquentin, the young existentialist writer in Sartre's *Nausea*, because of the existential purity he shows while reflecting on life and human existence— for example, Roquentin's view that, since life does not carry a preconceived essential meaning to be appropriated and followed, existence can only gain sense as we create it.[13]

Of course, Wallace admired other writers not in the existential-philosophical tradition, as Ryerson and others rightly state, but even these writers are "brainy," to use Ryerson's word, and mostly concerned with human nature.[14] It is important to stress here that, in the 1990s, Wallace believed that American fiction was in both aesthetic and moral crises, and that he wanted to write a new kind of fiction to tackle these crises, as well other existential issues he deeply cared about—for example, nihilism, depression, boredom, dullness, the effects of entertainment on people's lives. With his friend, the novelist Jonathan Franzen, Wallace spoke frequently of the need to reinvent literature, and both considered Wallace's *Girl with Curious Hair* to be an example of literature reinvented.[15]

In the next three sections, I illustrate how Wallace's background in Wittgenstein's philosophy helped him develop the views he did on the natures

---

[10] I am thinking of the following works as entailing elements of narrative philosophy: Coetzee's *Waiting for the Barbarians* and *The Lives of Animals*, Woolf's short story "Solid Objects," and Le Guin's "The Ones Who Walk Away from Omelas," the last of which I analyze in significant detail later in the chapter.

[11] D. T. Max, *Every Love Story is a Ghost Story*, 209; 298–9.

[12] See Albert Camus, *The Stranger* (New York: Vintage, 1989).

[13] This is not necessarily the central issue in *Nausea*, but the novella seems to suggest it as a nuanced argument with directed clues from Roquentin. See J. P. Sartre, *Nausea* (New York: New Directions Publishing, 1964).

[14] Ryerson places Wallace, for example, in the tradition of intellectual novelists such as Thomas Pynchon and William Gaddis, both of whom were admired by Wallace in his early days of writing fiction (See Ryerson, "Introduction," 1).

[15] D. T. Max, *Every Love Story is a Ghost Story*, 130–1.

of philosophy and literature, and how he found incorporating philosophical narratives in his literature to be a creative way of reinventing literature and using it to fight aesthetic and existential crises. I proceed by discussing Wallace's journalistic assignment, "Consider the Lobster," in relation to Le Guin's "The Ones Who Walk Away from Omelas," then by analyzing the existential themes of boredom and dullness in Wallace's unfinished novel, *The Pale King*, and finally by linking his *The Broom of the System* and his graduation speech at Kenyon College, *This Is Water*, with Wittgenstein's ideas about theorizing and not knowing one's way about language.

On Lobsters, Omelas, and battling boredom

In "Consider the Lobster," Wallace raises an ethical question about the practice of boiling lobsters alive for human consumption: "So then here is a question that's all but unavoidable at the World's Largest Lobster Cooker, and may arise in kitchens across the U.S.: Is it all right to boil a sentient creature alive just for our gustatory pleasure?"[16] Wallace raises this question after providing a good deal of factual information about the economy behind the annual lobster festival in Maine and the science behind whether or not lobsters actually feel pain. But Wallace's main interest, it seems to me, is in telling a story about human nature.

He states, for example, that it is socially awkward, even uncomfortable, to talk about moral issues that might prove people selfish, and people often opt to avoid this type of conversation. Wallace assumes, obviously, that boiling lobsters alive for consumption is a selfish act and, since he believes that there is "no honest way to avoid certain moral questions" in life,[17] as he puts it, he opts to write about the morality of eating lobsters in a "creative," journalistic account. He addresses the relevance of traditional philosophy here as follows: "the questions of whether and how different kinds of animals feel pain, and of whether and why it might be justifiable to inflict pain on them in order to eat them, turn out to be extremely complex and difficult"— scientifically speaking, it is difficult to establish how lobsters exactly feel pain but, more importantly, "the principles by which we can infer that others experience pain and have a legitimate interest in not feeling pain involve hard-core philosophy—metaphysics, epistemology, value theory, ethics."[18]

---

[16] David F. Wallace, "Consider the Lobster," in *Consider the Lobster and Other Essays* (New York: Little, Brown & Co., 2005), 243.

[17] Ibid., 247.

[18] Ibid., 246.

The question is, what would the involvement of hard-core philosophy be like and how would creative nonfiction such as "Consider the Lobster" make it any different, if at all?

An associative reference to Thomas Nagel and Peter Singer, two philosophers who have written extensively on topics relevant to Wallace's concerns here, might be helpful. Nagel famously argued in "What's It Like to Be a Bat?"[19] that although we might know what it is like for a human being to be a bat, we cannot really know what it is like for a bat to be a bat. The reason for this epistemic restriction, according to Nagel, is that conscious experience, which is also available to mammals such as bats, is introspective and subjective, and therefore cannot be fully experienced and known from a phenomenological, externalist perspective such as the perspective of human beings. In "Consider the Lobster," Wallace rejects the kind of argument Nagel provides from a behavioristic viewpoint: "Since pain is a totally subjective mental experience, we do not have direct access to anyone or anything's pain but our own," he states, but does this mean we cannot know whether or not others, including lobsters, could experience pain?[20] In response, Wallace writes:

> The lobster . . . behaves very much as you or I would behave if we were plunged into boiling water (with the obvious exception of screaming). A blunter way to say this is that the lobster acts as if it's in terrible pain, causing some cooks to leave the kitchen altogether and to take one of those little lightweight plastic oven timers with them into another room and wait until the whole process is over.[21]

Wallace appeals to the reader's commonsense, and emotions, it seems to me, in order to substantiate the idea that we can know for sure the kind of pain lobsters feel, and to reject any Nagel-like philosophical justification to the contrary. This in itself does not settle the question, for Wallace, as to whether or not lobsters are of equal moral importance to humans. In fact, on a personal level, he did not seem to think so, although he could not find any *philosophical* justification for his view—he states, for example, that he had not succeeded up to that point "in working out any sort of personal ethical system in which the belief [that lobsters are morally less important than humans] is truly defensible instead of just selfishly convenient."[22]

---

[19] T. Nagel, "What's It Like to Be a Bat?," *The Philosophical Review* 83, 4 (October 1974): 435–50.

[20] Wallace, "Consider the Lobster," 246.

[21] Ibid., 248.

[22] Ibid., 253.

This is where Peter Singer comes into play. Singer is a utilitarian philosopher who has consistently argued against inflicting suffering on animals due to the fact that they are sentient beings that feel pain. The utilitarian argument he makes is that people have a moral obligation to do what is good, and prevent any harm from happening, unless something of comparable moral importance is being simultaneously sacrificed. In the case of giving up eating sentient beings such as lobsters, this kind of sacrifice, if we are to call it a sacrifice at all, is of less moral importance for Singer than preventing the harm of inflicting suffering on them.[23]

Singer is different from Nagel and other traditional philosophers who debate the question of animal treatment solely on the basis of whether or not animals have consciousness, and on how to go about establishing our ability to know their conscious experience. I am suggesting that Wallace is more of a behaviorist than a philosopher of mind, although keep in mind that he also appeals to human emotions when making the behavioristic point about the pain lobsters feel when boiled alive. He is obviously not a traditional philosopher in the way, say, the behaviorist philosopher Gilbert Ryle is.

On a personal level, Wallace seems to approve of Singer's non-neutral attitude toward animal suffering, and he does not really consider the actual philosophical arguments Singer makes when referring to him in a footnote.[24] But he is generally critical of the utilitarian tradition in which Singer sits, declaring its pleasure- or happiness-based consideration to be a distraction, a way of addressing the symptoms of pain and not the pain itself.[25] In essence, he blames utilitarianism for having turned pleasure into a value and an end in itself.

The above reference to Nagel and Singer is meant to demonstrate a certain distaste that Wallace felt toward traditional, or classical, utilitarianism and

---

[23] See, for example, Singer's well-known *Animal Liberation* (New York: Harper Collins, 1975).

[24] Wallace, "Consider the Lobster," footnote 16.

[25] "Look at utilitarianism," he tells McCaffery with an accusative tone of voice, "and you see a whole teleology predicated on the idea that the best human life is one that maximizes the pleasure-to-pain ratio" (Larry McCaffery, "A Conversation with David Foster Wallace," 23). In its traditional form, utilitarianism states that we must weigh the difference between the pleasure and pain that issues, or could issue, from a certain act, decision, or idea so that *if* we can determine that, in certain situations, more pleasure/happiness and less pain/harm could come to everyone relevant to that situation—that act/decision/ idea would be the right one to make or have (see, e.g., John Stuart Mill, *Utilitarianism* [London: Parker, Son, and Bourn, 1863]). As with Wallace's reading of Wittgenstein, I am less concerned as to whether or not Wallace represents utilitarianism fully correctly or faithfully. I am interested, rather, in how his critique of utilitarianism demonstrates his wanting to move away from traditional philosophy as a way of discussing moral and existential issues that he found to be important.

philosophy of mind. It seems to me that Wallace uses "Consider the Lobster" as a literary medium, a form of creative nonfiction, to articulate a moral perspective on human nature beyond the confines of traditional philosophy. Perhaps he could have written his narrative about lobsters in a similar fashion to how Singer writes philosophy, but I think he found himself unable to do so. Singer sees himself as a philosopher who need not be neutral about the issue of suffering, whereas Wallace, under Wittgenstein's influence, seems to have thought otherwise. I cannot prove this claim with absolute definiteness but, considering Wallace's esteem for Wittgenstein's philosophy, and the latter's view that philosophers should not promote personal agendas when doing philosophy (a topic I discuss in the next section), the claim I am making about Wallace's views about philosophy is very plausible. Here is a comparison with Le Guin's "The Ones Who Walk Away from Omelas,"[26] a work of similar literary agenda to "Consider the Lobster," that gives further support to my claims.

Le Guin raises a moral question regarding utilitarianism similar to Wallace's question about boiling lobsters. Could the happiness of a whole town (Omelas) be justified when it comes at the expense of one child who needs to be locked up in order for that happiness to be sustained? In the story, the child has to be confined to a small and smelly cellar room, with no windows at all, and with one door that is always locked except for when Omelas's citizens—children and adults—come to peer at the child. The visitors "come in and kick the child to make it stand up" or they simply look at it "with frightened, disgusted eyes" while food and water are hastily provided before the door is locked again behind them.[27] The child is feeble in both body and mind, we are told, perhaps because it was born defective but most probably because of malnutrition and isolation: "It is so thin there are no calves to its legs; its belly protrudes; it lives on a half-bowl of corn meal and grease a day. It is naked. Its buttocks and thighs are a mass of festered sores, as it sits in its own excrement continually."[28]

As with Wallace's description of the lobster's behavior during its boiling process, Le Guin's description of the child's behavior and conditions of existence makes it difficult not to feel sympathy toward it. At first, the child "used to scream for help at night, and cry a good deal," we are told, "but now it only makes a kind of whining, 'eh-haa, eh-haa,' and it speaks less and less often"; when it finally speaks during the time it has visitors, it sometimes

---

[26] Ursula K. Le Guin, "The Ones Who Walk Away from Omelas," in *The Wind's Twelve Quarters* (New York: Harper Collins, 1987), 275–84.

[27] Ibid., 281.

[28] Ibid.

cries out: "I will be good. . . . Please let me out. I will be good!"[29] But this cannot happen, since any violation of the stipulated condition that the child remain locked up will bring about the end of happiness to the city—even if it were simply talking kindly to the child, let alone taking it out of the cellar.[30]

Le Guin was apparently inspired by William James's call in "The Moral Philosopher and the Moral Life" to live life according to more penetrating ideals rather than at the expense of others' suffering.[31] So, the issue for her is as personal as Wallace's moral reflections on his own feelings about eating lobsters. But she and Wallace differ in how they offer a solution to the moral difficulty they discuss: in her story, some people make a decision to leave Omelas forever, leaving their homes and old lives behind—"Each one goes alone, youth or girl, man or woman. . . . They leave Omelas, they walk ahead into the darkness, and they do not come back."[32] Le Guin leaves no room for uncertainty regarding what needs to be done about the situation. Everyone in Omelas should feel and do what these few individuals felt and did. This kind of absolute certainty is not evident in "Consider the Lobster," although Wallace presents the same level of certainty regarding human nature: it is selfish and pitiless when it comes to animal consumption.

The main reason for bringing Le Guin into the discussion is that, like Wallace, she engages in a highbrow topic that has been thoroughly discussed by philosophers (ethicists), and yet both she and Wallace find the philosophical discussions somewhat inadequate. I am not aware that Wallace read or made references to Le Guin's story, but I am certain that, in spite of the differences in the level of certainty each has regarding free choice and decision-making, he would have considered Le Guin's story worthy of the narrative philosophy he admired. Furthermore, there is an element of suggestive self-reflection in both of their narratives that seems to be aimed at the reader—one that demonstrates awareness on both of their parts that there are significant advantages to writing literature rather than philosophy.

By suggestive self-reflection, I mean that Wallace and Le Guin make an attempt to direct the reader to think about the moral issue at hand—in this case, how to treat defenseless creatures—and also about the justificatory basis of raising the question itself about the moral issue. Thus, at one point, Wallace compares how people treat lobsters to medieval torture fests, wondering

---

[29] Ibid.

[30] "If the child were brought up into the sunlight out of that vile place, if it were cleaned and fed and comforted, that would be a good thing indeed," the narrator writes, "but if it were done, in that day and hour all the prosperity and beauty and delight of Omelas would wither and be destroyed. Those are the terms" (Ibid., 282).

[31] Ibid., 275–6.

[32] Ibid.

whether "future generations will regard our own present agribusiness and eating practices in much the same way we now view Nero's entertainments or Aztec sacrifices?"[33] But, then, he wonders whether the comparison goes too far: "A related set of concerns: Is the previous question [about eating lobsters] irksomely PC or sentimental? What does 'all right' even mean in this context [namely whether it is 'all right' to inflict suffering on lobsters]? Is it all just a matter of individual choice?"[34] Similarly, Le Guin has suggestive questions about the aim of fiction and the justificatory criteria for writing about pleasure and happiness. Her narrator notes that other writers and artists might object to her focusing on the theme of happiness in fiction because happiness is not as interesting as pain or evil: "The trouble is that we have a bad habit, encouraged by pedants and sophisticates, of considering happiness as something rather stupid."[35] But the narrator quickly rebuffs these charges, insisting that artists commit treason when they consider only pain and evil to be interesting. In reality, she states, evil could be banal and pain terribly boring and, furthermore, "to praise despair is to condemn delight [and] to embrace violence is to lose hold of everything else."[36] In both cases, Le Guin's and Wallace's, the reader is invited to join them in critiquing traditional philosophy, in this case utilitarianism, while reflecting on the role of literature in life. In Wallace's case, as I show next, *The Pale King*[37] demonstrates this move beyond traditional philosophy even more dramatically.

The Pale King continues the interest Wallace had in existential themes, in this case with a main emphasis on the questions of dullness and boredom. The novel, set in an IRS center in Peoria, Illinois, raises central questions about the nature of these two interrelated phenomena—for example, why are boredom and dullness such powerful impediments to attention, and what is it about them that leads people to recoil from them? Are they intrinsically painful or do they hide a deeper type of pain that is always there and that could lead to nihilistic tendencies in humans? These questions are difficult to elucidate and write about. Wallace told his editor Michael Pietsch that working on the novel was akin to getting a tornadic feeling one gets as a result of "wrestling sheets of balsa wood in a high wind."[38] I am led to believe that in trying to face the difficulty of elucidating the nature of boredom and dullness, as well as their consequences, Wallace made a methodological effort to write *The Pale King* in mostly a dull way. I think he intended the

---

[33] Wallace, "Consider the Lobster," 253.
[34] Ibid., 243.
[35] Le Guin, "The Ones Who Walk Away from Omelas," 278.
[36] Ibid.
[37] Wallace, *The Pale King: An Unfinished Novel* (New York: Little, Brown & Co., 2011).
[38] Michael Pietsch, "Editor's Note," in D. F. Wallace, *The Pale King*, v–viii.

dullness to be part of the reading experience so that the reader might come to an appreciation of what Wallace wanted to say about both boredom and dullness, and the struggles of writing about them.

But what elucidations does *The Pale King* provide regarding these two phenomena, as well as related existential themes, that would have been impossible to produce philosophically? Although there are many examples to choose from, I focus on one story in the novel that I think best characterizes what Wallace wanted to do in narrative philosophy—the story of Lane Dean Jr. we are told, hates his job but does it as a necessity in order to support his family. He needs to go through one tax return after another, searching for signs to audit any one of them, and he cannot escape the boredom inherent in this kind of job. Comically but sadly, one way Lane handles his boredom is by flexing his buttocks every few completed tax returns and holding to a count of ten while imagining a warm beach with mellow surf. He does this continually every three or more tax returns, realizing all along that this is "boredom beyond any boredom he's ever felt."[39]

Wallace portrays Lane as someone who is receptive of certain etymological connotations associated with the word "boring"—for example, he gets the unbidden thought "that *boring* also meant something that drilled in and made a hole."[40] As a result, he feels "a great type of hole or emptiness falling through him and continuing to fall and never hitting the floor," and he realizes that "Never before in his life up to now had he once thought of suicide."[41] These thoughts and feelings leave Lane exhausted and, by then, his buttocks ache from flexing and he cannot envision the desolate beach he is supposed to invoke to distract himself from boredom. He struggles to complete a few more returns and begins to imagine "different high places to jump off of," and he then feels he is "in a position to say he knew now that hell had nothing to do with fires or frozen troops."[42] The hell that Lane realizes he lives in leads him to imagine himself "running around on the break waving his arms and shouting gibberish and holding ten cigarettes at once in his mouth like a panpipe."[43] Prayer does not help him, and, as he contemplates the etymology of the word "boredom," Wallace makes us aware of a sardonic dream that Lane had the night after his first day of work at the IRS: a stick that breaks over and over without getting smaller, and a Frenchman who pushes a stone uphill throughout eternity.[44]

---

[39] Wallace, *The Pale King*, 377.
[40] Ibid., 378.
[41] Ibid.
[42] Ibid., 379.
[43] Ibid.
[44] Ibid., 384.

Obviously, Lane's existential circumstances cannot be alleviated through intellectual analysis. Philosophy is, or ought to be, disinterested, but even the portrayal of Lane's frame of mind could not be had in traditional ways of analysis. When Lane attempts different ways of distracting himself from the tasks at hand, for instance—relocating his infant son's photo on the desk, using the adding machine with his left hand rather than right hand, pretending he has had a stroke—he suddenly feels that the image of the beach that ordinarily helps him get through the day becomes one of solid cement instead of sand, and the water becomes gray and barely moving "like Jell-O that's almost set," and then: "Unbidden came ways to kill himself with Jell-O."[45] These are powerful illustrations of suicidal thoughts. One imagines Wallace saying that even a good philosopher who embarks on logical analysis of the concepts of suicide and boredom will ultimately rely more on discussing the concepts than elucidating them with commanding examples such as the above. His depictions of Lane's suicidal thoughts are undeniably raw and gut-wrenching.

Furthermore, Wallace is interested in exploring therapeutic options for Lane's frame of mind, or at least of investigating possible ways of overcoming boredom. He ultimately ties the issue of overcoming boredom with the question of how to succeed in life. If we are able to deal with boredom by being unborable, Lane thinks to himself, then we can "function effectively in an environment that precludes everything vital and human: . . . If you are immune to boredom, there is literally nothing you cannot accomplish."[46] But how does one become unborable? The answer is obviously individualistic, not collective, and Wallace seems to have believed that people need to negotiate their way through it. In the last section of the chapter, I touch on the question of the inevitability of dullness in people's lives, which Wallace addresses in a different part of *The Pale King*, and how specifically he thought that such dullness could be negotiated.

Here, another worry linked to the nature of philosophy arises: Wallace thought that philosophers and other intellectuals offered theories, psychological and otherwise, to explain the existence of boredom and ways of overcoming it, which he thought was problematic. He believed that theorizing about human nature, in both fiction and philosophy, entails certain dangers from which the narrative philosopher ought to steer away. Wallace must have encountered the references to the danger of theorizing in Wittgenstein, as I show next.

---

[45] Ibid., 380.
[46] Ibid., 437–8.

On Wittgenstein and the danger of theorizing

In the chapter's first section, I discussed Ryerson's view that Wallace admired Markson's ability to unite literature and philosophy in *Wittgenstein's Mistress*, and I complicated the issue by showing the place that narrative philosophy has in Wallace's thinking. But there is something about Markson's novel—that "erudite, breathtakingly cerebral novel whose prose is crystal & whose voice rivets & whose conclusion defies you not to cry"[47]—that made Wallace even more intrigued by it. On the one hand, he saw the novel as a realistic portrait of the negative consequences of living in the kind of world that Wittgenstein depicted in the *Tractatus*, but, on the other hand, he also found that it suffers from the same fate as many narratives that promote metaphysical, or generalized, theories—namely the temptation to offer an explanation for the radically diverse and complex existence we have. The problem, as I show in this section, is not merely the offering of a simplified explanation for a complex situation; it is also the idea itself of offering an explanation in the first place. As with Wittgenstein, Wallace understood theoretical explanations to be too generalized and distorting of the phenomena they seek to explain.

The *Tractatus* is notoriously difficult to understand, and this is not the place to analyze its complexity or to gauge Wallace's understanding of it. In *The Broom of the System*, Wallace addresses various issues he found intriguing in the *Tractatus*, focusing on two interrelated topics: (1) Wittgenstein's depiction of the relation between language and the world, and, more importantly, (2) the imposition of a theorized system of interpretation to make sense of this relation. Wallace read the *Tractatus* to suggest that language sets limits to our understanding of the world, in such a way that we might not be able to know the world as it is in itself—or even lose the world, as he puts it in one interview.[48] Gradually, he came to see the mathematical beauty of the *Tractatus* as something that comes at the expense of giving a pragmatic depiction of what it means to be actually trapped in language. His main characters in *Broom*, especially Lenore Stonecipher Beadsman, express existential worries about the possibility that they might be trapped in words—angst, dread, uncertainty, etc.—and, therefore, that they are divorced from the world in which they live. As I show next, Wallace complicates the issue by limning how the attempt to systematize language and the world into a coherent account ultimately fails.

---

[47] Wallace, "The Empty Plenum: David Markson's *Wittgenstein's Mistress*," in David Markson, *Wittgenstein's Mistress* (Champaign, IL: Dalkey Archive Press, 1988), 269.
[48] See D. T. Max, *Every Love Story is a Ghost Story*, 44.

Apparently, Wallace believed that Markson was able to express the same existential worry he wanted to depict, as well as other negative consequences of living in the kind of world Wittgenstein depicted in the *Tractatus*, better than he did in *Broom*. He praises Markson's novel as "an imaginative portrait of what it would be like actually to *live* in the sort of world the logic & metaphysics of Wittgenstein's *Tractatus* posits," stating that it "transforms metaphysics into angst" while revealing that "philosophy is first and last about spirit."[49] He finds in Kate, Markson's protagonist, a vividly existential example, albeit fictional, of the supposedly solipsistic world Wittgenstein depicts in the *Tractatus*.

Kate believes she has been the only person alive for several years by the time she begins writing down her thoughts and feelings. Her physical solitariness is accompanied by a mentally disjointed, atomized, forgetful, and solipsistic life, one that exemplifies for Wallace the metaphysically atomized facts of the *Tractatus*.[50] Markson depicts Kate as being trapped in a cycle of associative words and ambiguous language that she can barely escape. She reminds herself repeatedly of the proper context that gives words their true meaning in order to make sense of her existence. Here is one example where this happens: "Even in late spring, there was snow on the mountain. Somebody went there to die, I believe, in one of the old stories. Paris, perhaps.

[49] Wallace, "The Empty Plenum," 247. I am not certain what Wallace means by the idea that Wittgenstein's philosophy is about spirit, but he seems to link it with another view he has of Wittgenstein—namely that Wittgenstein's ability to solve the problem of solipsism in the *Tractatus*, which he does in the *Investigations* by showing the impossibility of a private language, warrants describing him as an artist. Wallace states: "One of the things that makes Wittgenstein a real artist to me is that he realized that no conclusion could be more horrible than solipsism. And so he trashed everything he'd been lauded for in the 'Tractatus' and wrote the 'Investigations', which is the single most comprehensive and beautiful argument against solipsism that's ever been made" (McCaffery, "A Conversation with David Foster Wallace," 44). The idea that philosophy is about spirit or that the later Wittgenstein is an artist is very problematic. Wallace may have wanted to extol Wittgenstein's ability to provide a powerful solution to an existential problem, which he associated with the task of the artist (as I show in the next and final section of the chapter), but if the commendation is meant descriptively, then I think Wallace is mistaken about it. The later Wittgenstein conceived philosophy to always be a descriptive activity whereas being an artist would require treating his philosophy as something normative, which Wittgenstein would have found to be very problematic, and which, ironically, is one significant reason that Wallace himself chose to write narrative, rather than traditional, philosophy. See my discussion of this topic in the final section of the chapter.

[50] In the *Tractatus*, Wittgenstein introduces his picture theory of language, which postulates a harmonious relation between empirical propositions and the facts of the world. When he theorized what the ultimate, atomized facts of the world were, Wittgenstein described them as "logical objects" and did not have actual examples to illustrate what they were (See Ludwig Wittgenstein, *Tractatus Logico-Philosophical* [London: Routledge & Kegan Paul, Ltd., 1922], 5.6.)

I mean the Paris who had been Helen's lover, naturally."[51] It is as if Kate had to remind herself that Paris was a "somebody" rather than a city. In another reference to the writer Guy de Maupassant, whose habit of eating at the Eiffel tower in order to avoid seeing it is picked up by Kate, she feels the need to be careful about the words she uses: "When I said that Guy de Maupassant ate his lunch every day at the Eiffel Tower, so that he did not have to look at it, I meant that it was the Eiffel Tower he did not wish to look at, naturally, and not his lunch."[52]

As Kate reminds us that ordinary language is frequently imprecise, we also realize that language controls her rather than the other way round. This is also a reminder by Markson that we are lost in the world if we accept the Tractarian hypothesis about the connection between language and the world. All the associative connections Kate makes—for example, between Rembrandt and Spinoza, Brahms and Wittgenstein, and Sor Juan Ínés de la Cruz and John of the Cross—are treated by her as theoretical and tentative: "Again, however, I am by no means implying that there is any significance in such connections."[53] In that kind of theoretical world, she is really Wittgenstein's mistress, Wallace states, "the linguistic beloved of a man who could not, in emotional practice, confer identity on a woman via 'love.'"[54]

Connecting the above with the task of the philosopher versus the task of the creative narrativist, Wallace states that *Wittgenstein's Mistress* "in a deep-nonsensical way that's much more effective than argument or allegory'd be, speaks to why I'm starting to think most people who somehow must write must write."[55] His philosophical hero in this case is the later Wittgenstein whose critique of the tendency to theorize and explain extends over a good chunk of Part II of the *Investigations*.[56] The later Wittgenstein objects to

---

[51] Markson, *Wittgenstein's Mistress*, 8.

[52] Ibid., 42.

[53] Ibid., 102.

[54] Wallace, "The Empty Plenum," 251, footnote 10.

[55] Whether or not the reference is intentional, the designation "deep-nonsensical way" pertains to the ending of the *Tractatus* where Wittgenstein writes: "My propositions are elucidatory in this way: he who understands me finally recognizes them as senseless/nonsensical (*unsinnig*), when he has climbed out through them, on them, over them" (*Tractatus*, 6.54). Some philosophers make a distinction between deep nonsense and ordinary nonsense, suggesting that Wittgenstein could not have possibly meant ordinary nonsense when referring to his entire work. (Briefly on this controversial issue, see D. Z. Phillips, "Introduction: On Reading Wittgenstein on Religion," in D. Z. Phillips and Mario von der Ruhr (eds), *Religion and Wittgenstein's Legacy* [Burlington, VT: Ashgate, 2005)], 1–2). Wallace seems to be either agreeing with this point or simply using the term to say something obviously positive about Markson's novel.

[56] Ludwig Wittgenstein, *Philosophical Investigations*, 3rd edn, eds. G. E. M. Anscombe and Rush Rhees, trans. G. E. M. Anscombe (Englewood Cliffs, NJ: Prentice Hall, 1958).

stipulating explanations—psychological, emotional, or causal—as always the needed factors behind a proper understanding of what is real and meaningful. For example, he attacks the idea that psychological theorizing necessarily explains the inner life of people and, in Section xii of Part II, he is particularly adamant about rejecting the attempt to trace a causal connection between concepts and the natural world.

We can rely on theories in the hard sciences, one imagines Wallace saying, as he himself partially does when trying to determine whether or not the physiology of lobsters indicates the presence of pain in them. But when it comes to existential issues relating to boredom, death, making responsible choices, etc., it is doubtful that theories could perform the job they are supposed to do, whether in philosophy or literature. Wallace seems to have been aware of this point, as his critiques of utilitarianism and Markson's novel suggest.

Wallace praises Markson for going beyond the limitations of a purely philosophical work such as the *Tractatus*, but he is also critical of one aspect of his novel, and for the same reasons he is critical of the theoretical underpinnings of the *Tractatus*. The novel contains suspicious attempts to offer psychological explanations of Kate's emotional condition. For example, Wallace notices that Markson identifies Kate's character with both Helen of Troy and biblical Eve, shifting from one to the other throughout the novel. The norm in fiction has been to identify troubled women with Eve, Wallace claims, explaining their psychological conditions on the basis of one sexual neurosis or another. In Markson's case, he sometimes leans toward identifying Kate with Eve rather than the stronger Helen of Troy, thus inevitably offering a psychological explanation of her madness: she could only be a mistress of a homosexual man—Wittgenstein—because she cheated on her husband and lost both him and her son.[57] Wallace writes:

> It seems very interesting to me that Markson has created a Kate who dwells so convincingly in a hell of utter subjectivity, yet cannot, finally, himself help but objectify her—ie by "explaining" her metaphysical condition as emotional/psychical, reducing her bottled missive to a mad monologue by a smart woman driven mad by the consequences of culpable sexual agency, Markson is basically subsuming Kate under one of the comparatively stock rubrics via which we guys apparently must organize & process fey mystery, feminine pathos, Strengthless & Female fruit.[58]

[57] Markson, *Wittgenstein's Mistress*, 262.
[58] Ibid., 266-7.

What is disappointing about the novel and what makes it weaker than it could otherwise be, Wallace states, is not so much that it fails as an explanation but rather "*because* it's an explanation."[59] Wallace's worry here, which was also the later Wittgenstein's worry, is that whereas theories are oftentimes promoted as the explanation of where meaning and sense reside, the latter could easily escape the scope of theorizing. For this reason, I do not think Wallace gives himself enough credit when he compares his creativity to that of Markson unfavorably. *The Broom of the System* illustrates the problem of theorizing remarkably, whether in regard to how language functions in our lives, the futility of systems that purport to explain the world's structures, or other important existential themes. I believe the title of the novel is a clever way of saying that systems can be brushed into dust if they do not heed their relevance to how things function in everyday life.

In *The Broom of the System*, Lenore has a great-grandmother who is said to have been a former student of the later Wittgenstein. She tries to teach Lenore that life is nothing but words, supposedly echoing the views of one of Wittgenstein's students, Alice Ambrose,[60] and Lenore worries throughout the novel that she might be nothing but a linguistic construct. Yet Lenore is the one to take up the challenge of finding her great grandmother when the latter escapes the home she was at after deliberately leaving a copy of the *Investigations* behind.[61] The clues Lenore gathers lead her to investigate her great-grandmother's claim that the meaning of the broom lies in its use, not in something it essentially has independently of that use.[62] This is a standard theme in the later Wittgenstein's philosophy and Wallace vividly illustrates it through various episodes related to the switchboard where Lenore works as an operator.

In the novel, the switchboard begins to collapse when its intended use is disordered. For example, people who dial a sex-line end up at the switchboard with Lenore answering their calls. When the experts are called in to fix the underground telephone system, the task proves impossible, and the entire switchboard system comes tumbling down. So, what is the lesson to be learned? In brief, Wallace echoes Wittgenstein's point, suggested in the *Investigations*, that system-building and explanatory theorizing are hopeless endeavors in the attempt to understand existential, psychological, moral, or aesthetic issues in people's lives. We lose our way about language, Wallace states, again echoing Wittgenstein, if we get ourselves trapped

---

[59] Ibid., 268.
[60] See Ryerson, "Introduction," 19.
[61] Wallace, *The Broom of the System* (New York: Penguin, 1987), 119–21.
[62] Ibid., 149–50.

in theorizing rather than paying attention to what people mean by what they say.[63] I explore this idea in the next and final section of the chapter, bringing into discussion Wallace's graduation speech at Kenyon College and his treatment of the themes of making choices and giving advice in *The Pale King.*

On preaching, choosing, and knowing one's way about language

For a novelist with aims toward the kind of narrative philosophy I depicted in this chapter, the ability to use language in a suggestive but clear way is of utmost importance. Wallace appreciated Wittgenstein's insistence that language sets up traps for us because of its inherent ambiguity. He worried that he did not always know his way about language, even in fiction: "Wittgenstein's conclusions [regarding our loss in language] seem completely sound to me, always have," Wallace states in his interview with McCaffery. "And if there's one thing that consistently bugs me writing-wise, it's that I don't feel I really 'do' know my way around inside language—I never seem to get the kind of clarity and concision I want."[64]

It is fair to say that Wallace worked hard on trying to know his way about language so that he could produce the existentially meaningful narratives he desired. He is at his best, I think, when he distinguishes the task of the artist from that of the philosopher. "In dark times," he tells McCaffery, "good art . . . locates and applies CPR to those elements of what's human and magical that still live and glow despite the times' darkness . . . it'd find a way both to depict this world and to illuminate the possibilities for being alive and human in it."[65] Whereas the philosopher clarifies the ambiguities of language in order to arrive at the true meaning of concepts, one imagines Wallace thinking, the artist aims to bring the reader's attention to the particular values he or she wants to promote.[66]

Thus, in wanting to warn readers about excessive television watching and accepting a materialistic world, which Wallace thought were detrimental to happiness, his hands would have been tied had he acted as a philosopher.

---

[63] Wittgenstein makes this point as follows: "A philosophical problem has the form: 'I don't know my way about'" (*Philosophical Investigations*, § 123).

[64] McCaffery, "A Conversation with David Foster Wallace," 45.

[65] Ibid., 26.

[66] This is the reason I argued earlier in the chapter that Wallace is mistaken to call Wittgenstein an artist if he meant the remark descriptively.

He would not have been able to provide a moral judgment against the negative role of television in society and offer art as the medium through which such role could be minimized. But that is precisely what he does in his interview with McCaffery. In dark times, he asserts, it is art's job to raise the question of "how is it that we as human beings still have the capacity for joy, charity, genuine connections, for stuff that doesn't have a price? And can these capacities be made to thrive? And if so, how, and if not why not?"[67] If loneliness is the issue to address, then in Wallace's view fictive narratives help us address rather than avoid that issue by intensifying it. As he puts it,

> The interesting thing is why we're so desperate for this anesthetic against loneliness. You don't have to think very hard to realize that our dread of both relationships and loneliness . . . has to do with angst about death, the recognition that I'm going to die, and die very much alone, and the rest of the world is going to go merrily on without me. I'm not sure I could give you a steeple-fingered theoretical justification, but I strongly suspect a big part of real art fiction's job is to aggravate this sense of entrapment and loneliness and death in people, to move people to countenance it, since any possible human redemption requires us first to face what's dreadful, what we want to deny.[68]

Notice the explicit hesitation about, near rejection of, the possibility of giving "a steeple-fingered theoretical justification" for an anesthetic against loneliness and the dread of mortality. As a successful philosopher, Wallace would have been either a theorist akin to how he read the author of the *Tractatus*, or a descriptive philosopher, akin to the later Wittgenstein, who does not prescribe how people should live their lives. But as a fiction and creative nonfiction writer who is trying to tackle existential-philosophical concerns, Wallace becomes a critic of theories and abstractions, and an advocate of therapeutic art. The idea that people would flock to philosophy to avoid the boredom in their lives, or the dullness associated with bad television, bad movies, and bad literature, etc., is hard to imagine. But narrative philosophy might be able to do the trick if people actively participate in negotiating their lives around boredom and nihilism, reading narratives and considering existential views that remind them of their responsibilities toward other human beings, animals, and the world at large.

Wallace might come across as less preachy, or prescriptive, and more cautiously philosophical in some of his writings, but I do not think this

---

[67] McCaffery, "A Conversation with David Foster Wallace," 27.
[68] Ibid., 32.

aspect of his writing is overriding at all. For example, in "Consider the Lobster" he expresses his worry that his critique of utilitarianism might be taken as an apologetic sermon of some sort, which, he states, is something he wanted to avoid: "I am also concerned not to come off as shrill or preachy when what I really am is confused."[69] His confusion here, it is important to point out, is philosophical, not personal—it pertains to his struggle between knowing that his enjoyment of consuming lobsters is selfish while not being able to justify this selfishness in any established ethical theory. We should not forget that the statement itself that we do things out of selfishness is a personal justification, not a philosophical one. Any philosophical attempt to justify moral egoism, as James Rachels rightly claims, is self-defeating since the theory dictates that you must promote egoism for everyone, which is contrary to how your interests are served.[70]

Similarly, in his graduation speech, later published as *This Is Water*, Wallace begins by telling the funny story of how two young fish come across an older fish who asks them how the water is, and briefly afterwards, one of them asks "What the hell is water"?[71] The point of the story, Wallace proceeds to tell us, is "that the most obvious, ubiquitous, important realities are often the ones that are the hardest to see and talk about."[72] One of these obvious realities is the hard-wired self-centeredness of our existence, he insists, although he emphasizes, simultaneously, that he is not trying to be the wise fish who tells others what is objectively right and wrong. In line with the emphasis on responsible choosing that we find in Sartre, Wallace explains his position as follows: "it's a matter of my choosing to do the work of somehow altering or getting free of my natural, hard-wired default setting, which is to be deeply and literally self-centered, and to see and interpret everything through this lens of self."[73] Well, this could be read as a nonphilosophical form of preaching nonetheless, as I think the rest of the speech demonstrates.

A philosopher, as Wittgenstein held, is not a preacher, and in saying that he is not the wise fish, Wallace is indirectly saying he is not a philosopher who could justify why people ought to be good and unselfish in life except for these values themselves. It is as if we cannot be logically asked to justify what we take to be the justification itself for why we are who we are. Rachels makes the same argument when he reminds moral skeptics who require of us to explain why we ought not to hurt others, that they

[69] Wallace, "Consider the Lobster," 253.
[70] James Rachels, "Egoism and Moral Skepticism," in James E. White (ed.), *Contemporary Moral Problems*, 8th edn (Belmont, CA: Thomson Wadsworth, 2006), 16.
[71] David Foster Wallace, *This Is Water* (New York: Little, Brown and Company, 2009), 4.
[72] Ibid., 8.
[73] Ibid., 44.

had forgotten this is already the explanation and that we cannot give the explanation a further explanation. We ought not to hurt others, he states, because it hurts them![74]

We also encounter a positive treatment of a good preacher in *The Pale King* where a substitute teacher, who is also a priest, emphasizes that there are certain things in life that need to be done in order for us to have a community of some sort—for example, working at the IRS. He speaks of the commitment to do what is needed in life as a form of heroism, describing it as "the loss of options, a type of death, the death of childhood's limitless possibility, of the flattery of choice without duress."[75] The teacher *informs* the students that although the accounting profession in which they might end up is often tedious, it is nonetheless brave and worthy:

> Gentlemen . . . here is the truth: Enduring tedium over real time in a confined space is what real courage is. Such endurance is, as it happens, the distillate of what is, today, in this world neither I nor you have made, heroism. Heroism. . . . By which I mean true heroism, not heroism as you might know it from films or the tales of childhood. . . . Gentlemen, welcome to the world of reality – there is no audience. No one to applaud, to admire. No one to see you. Do you understand? Here is the truth— actual heroism receives no ovation, entertains no one. No one queues up to see it. No one is interested.[76]

Clearly, the teacher/priest is preaching to the class about heroism and dullness. When he links these two topics with service to others and self-effacement, which, as we shall see, is what Wallace himself does in his graduation speech, the teacher suggests that this may be the first time they have heard the truth about this matter. "To give oneself to the care of others' money—this is effacement, perdurance, sacrifice, honor, doughtiness, valor," he tells them, and "Routine, repetition, tedium, monotony, ephemeracy, inconsequence, abstraction, disorder, boredom, angst, ennui—these are the true hero's enemies, and make no mistake, they are fearsome indeed. For they are real."[77]

In this, the teacher is proposing what he takes to be the true meanings of heroism, yet it is obviously a one-sided perspective. It is not true, of course, that the only legitimate form of heroism is limited to the self-effacing, self-sacrificial form the priest portrays. But, in fiction, one is entitled to promote

---

[74] Rachels, "Egoism and Moral Skepticism," 17.
[75] Wallace, *The Pale King*, 228.
[76] Ibid., 229.
[77] Ibid., 231.

one moral perspective over others with the hope of persuading readers of his or her perspective. What needs to be realized, however, is that when a preacher, or Wallace in his graduation speech, or anyone else for that matter, promotes a single meaning of a concept as its sole sense, that person is not acting as a philosopher. The philosopher needs to account for all perspectives possible without taking a position as to what counts as the only true meaning of one concept or another—"heroism," "dullness," "boredom," etc. This is what Wallace might have realized as he wavered between the temptation of being a traditional philosopher and that of practicing narrative philosophy.

The idea of responsible choosing is important here, as Wallace realized. Choosing, he states in his graduation speech, is required to counter the default setting of thinking that the world is in our way of achieving comfort, satisfaction, or happiness—for example, the boringly crowded streets and supermarkets and parking lots. The easy and default option, Wallace states, is to be disgusted and frustrated with the behavior of other human beings who, we tell ourselves, are wasteful and inconsiderate and selfish—for example, driving SUVs that pollute the environment. But this state of mind is not really choosing, states Wallace. Who knows whether or not there are more urgent needs on the minds of other drivers or shoppers whom we tend to think are in our way—for example, maybe some were in accidents before and feel safer driving SUVs or maybe some are rushing in order to get their children to a hospital.[78] Existential choosing is different.

Like Sartre, Wallace does not think that existential choice is necessarily tied up with what is true objectively but rather with what holds meaning in people's lives. It is a matter of perspective, one might say—"You get to decide what to worship," he tells the students in his graduation speech.[79] If they do not decide, Wallace states, then they might unintentionally worship the wrong things—money, power, their bodies, beauty, etc. It is better to make a choice, spiritually, religiously, ethically, Wallace remarks. Real freedom, the important freedom, "involves attention, and awareness, and discipline, and effort, and being able truly to care about other people and to sacrifice for them, over and over, in myriad petty little unsexy ways, every day," he suggests.[80]

Wallace ends his graduation speech by saying that adhering to some of what he said in real life might be the clue as to how people make it to 30 or 50 years old without shooting ourselves in the head. I cannot think of a better way to end this chapter than let Wallace have the last word.

---

[78] Wallace, *This Is Water*, 85.
[79] Ibid., 96.
[80] Ibid., 120.

12

Good Faith and Sincerity: Sartrean Virtues of Self-Becoming in David Foster Wallace's *Infinite Jest*[1]

Allard den Dulk

Introduction

Sincerity is widely regarded as an important theme in the work of David Foster Wallace. However, most publications that discuss the importance of sincerity in Wallace's writing take up this theme—perhaps precisely because it has become such a commonplace characterization—without defining exactly what that notion of sincerity means, and without adequately mapping out where in Wallace's work it can be found.[2] In this chapter, I hope to contribute to furthering our understanding of this theme in Wallace's work by offering a philosophical analysis of *Infinite Jest*'s portrayal of the characters Mario Incandenza, Don Gately, and Hal Incandenza, as individuals who

---

[1] This chapter offers a condensed version of the chapter on sincerity from my upcoming book, *Existentialist Engagement in Wallace, Eggers, and Foer: A Philosophical Analysis of Contemporary American Literature* (New York: Bloomsbury, 2014).

[2] E.g. Adam Kirsch, "The Importance of Being Earnest," *The New Republic*, 18 August 2011; A. O. Scott, "The Panic of Influence—Review of *Brief Interviews with Hideous Men*," *The New York Review of Books* 47, 2 (2000): 39–43. An exception is, for example: Adam Kelly, "David Foster Wallace and the New Sincerity in American Fiction," in David Hering (ed.), *Consider David Foster Wallace. Critical Essays* (Los Angeles/Austin: SSMG Press, 2010), 131–46. However, Kelly's broad approach is different from the more specific one employed in this chapter, which offers a philosophical analysis of the portrayal of sincerity in *Infinite Jest*. For my own, more general exploration, see: Allard den Dulk, "American Literature: A New Aesthetic of Sincerity, Reality and Community," in Thomas Vaessens and Yra van Dijk (eds), *Reconsidering the Postmodern. European Literature Beyond Relativism* (Amsterdam: Amsterdam University Press, 2011), 225–41.

embody what can be regarded as a contemporary version of the "virtue" of sincerity.[3]

To this end, I will employ relevant aspects of Jean-Paul Sartre's early, phenomenological-existentialist philosophy as a heuristic perspective. Although Wallace does not make explicit reference to Sartre in either his fiction or in interviews and essays, Zadie Smith describes Sartre as a "great favourite" of Wallace, and Smith also suggests that Sartre's dicta of being "condemned to be free" and "responsible for that freedom" characterize the predicament of Wallace's characters. The connection between Sartre and Wallace follows from the way each describes consciousness in his various works: namely that consciousness should always be directed outward. To formulate this in Sartrean terms, consciousness should "transcend" itself toward the world. As Smith writes: "If Wallace insists on awareness, his particular creed is—to use a Wallacerian word—*extrorse*," which means "facing outward," "awareness must move always in an outward direction."[4] Let me explore this idea a bit more below.

Existentialist philosophy in general offers one of the most illuminating perspectives on Wallace's fiction.[5] The view of consciousness outlined above ties in with the general existentialist conception of the self, which can be recognized throughout Wallace's work. According to this conception, an individual is not automatically a self, but has to *become* one. In the existentialist view, there is no true core that an individual always already is or has, and which underlies selfhood.[6] Becoming a self is the task of

---

[3] Throughout this chapter, the term "virtue" refers to what is needed to "be" human, a self; cf. "In the general sense, virtue is capacity; in the particular sense, it is human capacity, the power to be human" (André Comte-Sponville, *A Short Treatise on the Great Virtues. The Uses of Philosophy in Everyday Life*, trans. Catherine Temerson [London: Vintage, 2003], 3). Cf. Wallace's remark about the task of fiction: "Fiction's about what it is to be a fucking *human being*" (Wallace, "An Interview with David Foster Wallace," by Larry McCaffery, *Review of Contemporary Fiction* 13 [2 Summer 1993]: 131).

[4] Zadie Smith, "Brief Interviews with Hideous Men: The Difficult Gifts of David Foster Wallace," in *Changing My Mind: Occasional Essays* (London: Hamish Hamilton, 2009), 264, 268.

[5] Cf. Allard den Dulk, "Beyond Endless 'Aesthetic' Irony: A Comparison of the Irony Critique of Søren Kierkegaard and David Foster Wallace's *Infinite Jest*," *Studies in the Novel* 44, 3 (2012): 325–45. With the term "existentialism," I am referring mainly to the philosophical and/or literary work of Kierkegaard, Sartre, and Camus, but also Dostoevsky and Kafka.

[6] Cf. Wallace's remark, in a talk on Kafka, that it is a common mistake to think "that a self is something you just *have*." According to Wallace, we should acknowledge "that the horrific struggle to establish a human self results in a self whose humanity is inseparable from that horrific struggle. That our endless and impossible journey toward home is in fact our home" (David Foster Wallace, "Some Remarks on Kafka's Funniness from Which Probably Not Enough Has Been Removed," in *Consider the Lobster and Other Essays* [New York: Little, Brown and Co., 2005], 64–5).

human life: a human being has to integrate his individual limitations and possibilities into a unified existence that he regards as his responsibility— this is the process of developing a self. We can recognize this view of the self underlying *Infinite Jest*'s portrayal of its characters; for example, in a negative way (that is, through what happens when the self is not so developed), when the characters suffering from addiction are described as having no self, as being "empty" inside; conversely, Don Gately is described as "returned to himself" after his life has become informed by values and principles through his participation in AA.[7] Throughout this chapter, I will argue that sincerity is the "self-ideal" or virtue that follows from this view of the self and that is portrayed in *Infinite Jest*.

What might seem problematic about such an assertion is that several influential theorists have argued that sincerity is an outdated (pre-Enlightenment) ideal and that, in fact, authenticity represents the self-ideal appropriate to contemporary Western life.[8] One objection raised against sincerity is that it seems to be an ideal pursued not for oneself but for the sake of others; that sincerity is actually a social obligation, namely not to deceive others.[9] A second objection is that sincerity, as a supposed "congruence between avowal and actual feeling," seems to imply a fixed, static self with certain essential qualities that can be sincerely communicated through an utterance or action.[10]

It remains to be seen, however, whether these objections against sincerity are necessarily justified. It is true that sincerity, as a striving for a connection between the self and its actions in the world, has an undeniably public character. But the fact that sincerity reveals itself through action, and, consequently, is always public and (partly) aimed at the other, does not mean that it amounts to merely fulfilling a public role and therefore cannot be undertaken for the self.[11] Also, this connection between self and action

[7] David Foster Wallace, *Infinite Jest: A Novel* (Boston: Little, Brown and Co., 1996), 694–5, 204, 860.
[8] E.g. Lionel Trilling, *Sincerity and Authenticity* (Cambridge: Harvard University Press, 1973), p. 6; Charles Guignon, *On Being Authentic* (London: Routledge, 2008), 26–7; Jacob Golomb, *In Search of Authenticity. From Kierkegaard to Camus* (New York: Routledge, 1995), 9.
[9] Cf. Guignon, *On Being Authentic*, 27; Trilling, *Sincerity and Authenticity*, 9.
[10] Trilling, *Sincerity and Authenticity*, 2; Golomb speaks of an individual "whose inner convictions and commitments are congruent with that individual's behaviour," and "[such] correspondence presumes a static subject" (Golomb, *In Search of Authenticity*, 9).
[11] I agree with Mariëtte Willemsen's observation that it is, by definition, impossible to be sincere toward others and at the same time insincere, untruthful to oneself; and that sincerity, truthfulness toward oneself seems to be a condition of sincerity toward others (Mariëtte Willemsen, "Friedrich Nietzsches getuigenis: de waarachtigheid van een immoralist," in Atie Th. Brüggemann-Kruijff, Henk G. Geertsema and Mariëtte F. Willemsen (eds), *"Levensecht en bescheiden": essays over authenticiteit* [Kampen: Kok Agora, 1998], 148).

does not necessarily imply a static, essential self: it means, above all, that the self *is* its actions (that the self comes into being in the world). This does not equal a naïve theory of the correspondence of inner and outer. When we speak of a sincere promise, the sincerity of that promise is judged by what I undertake to fulfill that promise, not by some internal state of being.[12] I will argue that this—the opening-up of the self, the connection of the self and its actions—is portrayed in *Infinite Jest* as what the contemporary individual stands in need of.

Conversely, the ideal of authenticity *does* seem to imply a fixed self-essence, and also a constant self-reflection that isolates the individual from the world (and its actions in that world)—which, in turn, is what is criticized in *Infinite Jest*.[13] The authentic individual lives purely according to his own self-acquired laws and insights, free from corrupting outside constraints. First, this ideal (over against the outer-directed ideal of sincerity) seems to depend on the implicit assumption of a profound, internal purity of the self that differs fundamentally from the impurity that lies outside it. Although most theorists speak of authenticity as the supposed product of continuous self-creation and development, if there is nothing inherent about the authentic self, the question arises as to whether we can even speak meaningfully about something—a self—that is at risk of being corrupted from the outside, in the first place. If authenticity requires the self to be autonomous—that is, not subject to any external influences, being completely self-defining—then that self-definition (if it is even possible) has to consist, by definition, of influences that are inherently present in that self. Secondly, this ideal requires constant self-reflection from the individual, analyzing and securing his own autonomy, and distancing himself from the outside world, which is after all the source of inauthentic, corrupting influences.[14]

So, both authenticity and sincerity *can* be seen to imply the erroneous conception of the self as something essential and fixed. But only the notion of sincerity, with its emphasis on the importance of the other and on the connection between the self and its actions, can also be regarded as expressive of a concept of the self as *external*, as shaped through choice and action, and through community and dialogue with others. And this, as I will argue, is the virtue that arises from Wallace's *Infinite Jest*.

---

[12] Choosing, taking responsibility for my actions, is also what existentialist thinkers like Sartre desire from the individual who has to become a self.
[13] This ties in with, among other things, the problem of irony, and the critique of that formulated in *Infinite Jest*; cf. Den Dulk, "Beyond Endless 'Aesthetic' Irony," 325–45.
[14] Cf. Guignon, *On Being Authentic*, 92.

What might seem to be a problematic aspect of my existentialist analysis of the virtue of sincerity is that Sartre speaks of *authenticity* when labeling the self-ideal of his existentialist philosophy, and he explicitly *criticizes* what he calls sincerity.[15] However, I will show that Sartre's use of the term authenticity and his critique of sincerity are in fact inconsistent with his own descriptions of consciousness.

A bigger problem than terminology is the fact that existentialism is often seen as emphasizing the importance of the autonomy of the individual. This aspect of existentialism accounts for its alleged social pessimism: that the individual, in his attempts to be a self, is in constant struggle with the outside world and with other people. Another important aspect of existentialism, however, casts a completely different light on its call to become a self; namely, existentialism emphasizes the importance of choice and action as well as the importance of others in self-becoming, expressed by the notion of sincerity. Furthermore, as we have already noted, existentialism is opposed to the notion of an inner self, implied in the ideal of authenticity.

Through its contemporary portrayal of existentialist self-becoming, *Infinite Jest* involves itself in the discussion about the virtue that the existentialist tradition can be seen to pursue, and, in my opinion, contributes a much-needed corrective to the tradition. *Infinite Jest* corrects the above-described, recurring fascination with autonomy that represents the major inconsistency of existentialism. My analysis of *Infinite Jest* will rehabilitate a redefined notion of sincerity as the basic existentialist virtue of the contemporary individual.

Here is how I will proceed in what follows. First, I will outline a corrected and reconstructed version of Sartre's view of self-becoming, one consistent with his general view of consciousness and that can serve as a framework for understanding *Infinite Jest*. It is important to note that the conceptual demarcations of this reconstruction of the Sartrean concept of sincerity are partly prompted by what I have found in Wallace's work. Second, I will analyze the characters Mario, Gately, and Hal in order to show how we can recognize the redefined concept of sincerity in *Infinite Jest*.

---

[15] Authenticity is often used as the term for the self-ideal that existentialist philosophy *in general* can be seen to promote, but, in fact, only Sartre explicitly employs the term. Kierkegaard does not use it, although he is sometimes translated as doing so—rather he speaks of "passion," "purity of will," etc. Camus uses the term sporadically, but in a general sense, not as embodying a clear notion of the self (e.g. Albert Camus, *The Rebel: An Essay on Man in Revolt*, trans. Anthony Bower [New York: Vintage Books, 1991], 285). For the rest, Camus can actually be seen as championing the importance of other-directedness for the meaningful existence of the self (especially in *The Rebel*).

Sincerity: A Sartrean, existentialist ideal

One of the most famous notions of Sartre's early philosophy is the notion of bad faith, a form of self-deceit in which the individual tries to escape the tension that characterizes self-becoming. Sartre's writings contain multiple notions that might appear to be an alternative to bad faith, for example: good faith, sincerity, and authenticity. However, he employs these terms inconsistently; as a result, it is unclear what the alternative to bad faith looks like, and what it is called. Therefore, with the portrayals offered by Wallace's work in mind, and with the help of critical reconstructions of Sartre's philosophy (most importantly, those of Ronald Santoni and Joseph Catalano), I will try to sketch out a consistent terminology, one that is in line with Sartre's general view of consciousness but, above all, serves as a fruitful heuristic perspective for the analysis of *Infinite Jest* offered further on in this chapter.[16]

Good faith and bad faith

Sartre formulates the distinction between good and bad faith as follows: "Bad faith does not hold the norms and criteria of truth as they are accepted by the critical thought of good faith. What it decides first, in fact, is the nature of truth."[17] Bad faith is a form of self-deceit.[18] According to Sartre, "the double property of the human being" is that he "*is* at once a *facticity* and a *transcendence*": a human being always finds himself in a certain factual situation, but at the same time is always already beyond that situation, in the sense that he is always free to relate to it in a new way. The individual in bad faith tries to mask for himself this tension that characterizes his existence. To that end, he formulates "two-faced concepts" and decides to be convinced by these concepts, while "[i]n truth, [he has] not persuaded [him]self."[19] This is what Sartre means by bad faith not holding the norms and criteria of critical thought.

---

[16] Seeing that this interpretation is my final goal, and not a reading of Sartre per se, I am not concerned with taking into consideration all of Sartre's work and adhering to his contrasting, inconsistent use of the terms good faith, sincerity, and authenticity therein. As stated above, the goal of this section is a critical reconstruction of Sartre's terminology that offers a consistent perspective for the analysis of *Infinite Jest*.

[17] Jean-Paul Sartre, *Being and Nothingness. An Essay on Phenomenological Ontology*, trans. Hazel E. Barnes (London: Routledge, 2010), 91.

[18] Cf. "in bad faith it is from myself that I am hiding the truth" (Sartre, *Being and Nothingness*, 72); cf. the addicted characters in *Infinite Jest*, who offer countless textbook examples of bad faith behavior (see the next section).

[19] Ibid., 79, 91.

Sartre's description implies that, conversely, good faith *does* hold the norms and criteria of critical thought. It demands persuasive evidence, while with bad faith "a peculiar type of evidence appears; non-persuasive evidence," says Sartre.[20] Santoni writes: "[whereas bad faith] is a closed, uncritical attitude toward available evidence, the fundamental attitude or original determination of being in good faith is an open, critical attitude toward evidence."[21]

Unfortunately, Sartre elaborates very little on the spontaneous-critical character of good faith. Further on in *Being and Nothingness*, it even seems as if Sartre qualifies good faith as a form of bad faith. However, we have to distinguish between normal good faith, and good faith that turns itself into an ideal, that is, that wants to coincide with its own belief. That there is nothing wrong with the former is shown by Sartre's own example: "I believe [*in good faith*] that my friend Pierre feels friendship for me." I believe it, even though "I do not have for it any self-evident intuition, for the nature of the object does not lend itself to intuition."[22] Friendship is not something that can be known with complete certainty, as for example a mathematical sum can: "past and present actions seem to indicate this friendship, but this evidence can never present itself to me as apodictic, as proving his friendship in the sense that two and two is four," writes Catalano.[23] The friendship is something that I have to "trust," says Sartre, "I decide to believe in it, and to maintain myself in this decision," in good faith.[24] There is nothing wrong with believing in good faith that someone is your friend based on certain signals and indicators, because, according to Sartre, friendship is something than can *never* be known to be there with complete certainty. You can only believe that someone is your friend.

Good faith becomes problematic for Sartre *only* when it turns its own belief into an ideal; that is, when faith in one's friendship with Pierre is not prompted by signs of that friendship, but by the wish to "believe what one believes," the wish to fully "*coincide*" with one's belief.[25] According to Sartre, the characteristic of believing is that "every belief involves not quite believing." "Is Pierre my friend? I do not know; I believe so." Believing is

---

[20] Ibid., 91.
[21] Ronald E. Santoni, *Bad Faith, Good Faith, and Authenticity in Sartre's Early Philosophy* (Philadelphia: Temple University Press, 1995), 71; cf. Joseph S. Catalano, *A Commentary on Jean-Paul Sartre's* Being and Nothingness (Chicago: University of Chicago Press, 1985), 87.
[22] Sartre, *Being and Nothingness*, 92.
[23] Catalano, *A Commentary on Jean-Paul Sartre's* Being and Nothingness, 87.
[24] Sartre, *Being and Nothingness*, 92.
[25] cf. Joseph S. Catalano, *Good Faith and Other Essays. Perspectives on a Sartrean Ethics* (Lanham: Rowman & Littlefield Publishers, 1996), 80–1; Santoni, *Bad Faith, Good Faith, and Authenticity in Sartre's Early Philosophy,* 73–4.

not knowing something for sure; when you would know for sure, it would cease to be belief, writes Sartre. Therefore, the desire "to believe what one believes"[26]—that is, striving to coincide with one's belief—implies an attempt to disguise and deny the uncertainty of belief, the norms and criteria of critical thought, and is thus a form of bad faith.

But this does not apply to normal good faith. Catalano explains: "good faith would seem to be a project of being spontaneously willing to be critical and open."[27] That is, as an immediate attitude, good faith implies a pre-reflective acceptance of the tension in human existence. Contrary to bad faith, good faith implies a truthful recognition of freedom, of our constant not coinciding with ourselves: "Sartre repeatedly states that bad faith is an attempt to flee from our freedom, whereas good faith is an attempt to face our freedom," writes Catalano.[28]

So, bad faith is not the one "fundamental ontological condition of freedom," not man's original relation to his freedom, even though this is—partly due to Sartre's own inconsistencies and obscurities—quite a common reading of *Being and Nothingness*.[29] Human being is characterized by a "lack of being" (it always transcends what it is at any moment), and, as a result of that lack, is driven by an unfulfillable "*desire to be*"[30] (consciousness casting itself toward the world, but never being able to coincide with it, to "be" as the world "is"). That desire cannot be suppressed, because it is what consciousness is—"there would be nothing else," writes Sartre.[31] But at the same time, this lack of being and desire to be, constitutes a consciousness of not being able to "be," of not being able to fully coincide with anything; in other words, it is consciousness of the freedom of consciousness and, thus, of the unfulfillability of its desire to be. Bad faith consciousness would imply trying to hide this impossibility for itself. Good faith, even though it shares the "desire to be" that characterizes all consciousness, is an open, critical attitude that does not try to conceal the truth, but recognizes its own freedom, including its "unhappy" character (being driven by a desire that never lets itself be fulfilled).[32]

Are good and bad faith then two equally fundamental, spontaneous options that man has in relation to his freedom? In spite of his concise and

[26] Sartre, *Being and Nothingness*, 93, 92.
[27] Catalano, *A Commentary on Jean-Paul Sartre's Being and Nothingness*, 81.
[28] Ibid., 89.
[29] Catalano, *Good Faith and Other Essays*, 77.
[30] Sartre, *Being and Nothingness*, 586.
[31] Jean-Paul Sartre, *Notebooks for an Ethics*, trans. David Pellauer (Chicago: The University of Chicago Press, 1992), 37; cf. Santoni, *Bad Faith, Good Faith, and Authenticity in Sartre's Early Philosophy*, 83–4.
[32] Sartre, *Being and Nothingness*, p. 114; cf. Catalano, *A Commentary on Jean-Paul Sartre's Being and Nothingness*, p. 90.

sometimes inconsistent treatment of good faith, this seems to be Sartre's conclusion. He speaks of "the two immediate attitudes which we can take in the face of our being." However, Sartre's own view of consciousness and of the realization of bad faith makes it impossible for bad faith to be a fully spontaneous and pre-reflective attitude. For Sartre claims that: "Since the unreflective consciousness is a spontaneous self-projection toward its possibilities, it can never be deceived about itself."[33] Pre-reflective consciousness is sheer intentionality: it does not reflect on itself, so it cannot decide anything about itself, and thus cannot deceive itself about itself. Santoni concludes: "if, in fact bad faith is a pre-reflective consciousness, then it would appear to follow that, insofar as bad faith is self-deception, bad faith is not possible."[34]

Moreover, looking at the descriptions of bad faith itself, it seems impossible to maintain that it is a phenomenon of spontaneous, pre-reflective consciousness. Bad faith is based on a "firm resolution," forcing itself to believe things that, intuitively, it does not believe. Bad faith does so by means of "two-faced concepts" which, according to Sartre, "we forge expressly to persuade ourselves," when we are not really persuaded.[35] These steps that consciousness undertakes to put itself in bad faith, require a reflective operation: consciousness has to turn its attention toward itself, at least in part, if it is to resolve anything about itself and "forge expressly" the concepts for its own deception.[36] Within Sartre's view of consciousness, bad faith as a form of self-deceit simply cannot be characterized as a pre-reflective, basic attitude of being (even though Sartre—erroneously—describes it as such).

Sartre repeatedly emphasizes that consciousness pre-reflectively knows that it is freedom.[37] Although Sartre is not consistent in some of his descriptions of this aspect of consciousness, bad faith is undeniably to be regarded as the flight of consciousness from its own freedom. In that case, "there remains the question of how consciousness is aware that it is totally free, which is the necessary condition for flight behavior. One possible explanation is to push the issue on to the pre-reflective consciousness," suggests Thomas Busch. "Against all attempts to reduce consciousness to

[33] Sartre, *Being and Nothingness*, pp. 93, 493.
[34] Santoni, *Bad Faith, Good Faith, and Authenticity*, 125.
[35] Sartre, *Being and Nothingness*, 91.
[36] Cf. Santoni, *Bad Faith, Good Faith, and Authenticity*, 125–6.
[37] E.g. "And this impossibility is not hidden from consciousness; on the contrary, it is the very stuff of consciousness"; "at the very moment when I struggle to attain it, I have a vague prejudicative comprehension that I shall not attain it" (Sartre, *Being and Nothingness*, 85–6, 89). These passages are related to the "desire to be" in what Sartre calls "sincerity"; further on in this chapter, I will show that Sartre, erroneously, describes sincerity as wanting to be what one is and therefore as a form of bad faith.

a thing there persists 'the contestation of non-thetic self-consciousness'. In these cases pre-reflective self-consciousness is treated as an inescapable lucidity of freedom to itself."[38]

This pre-reflective consciousness, which embodies a truthful awareness and acceptance of "human-reality,"[39] clearly matches the heart of the attitude of good faith. Indeed, I contend that good faith *is* this pre-reflective awareness that cannot be deceived about itself. In other words, good faith is the imperative, pre-reflective (immediate) basic attitude of man, and bad faith the nonimperative but widespread reflective attitude of flight from, and thus ensuing, the pre-reflective insights of good faith.

Pure reflection and sincerity

As mentioned above, consciousness is driven by a "desire to be," which it, at the same time, pre-reflectively knows is unfulfillable. According to Sartre, reflection initially appears in service of, as accessory to, this "desire to be," to found itself.[40] In reflection, consciousness is made into an object: the individual tries to determine herself as an object, which is in bad faith. Sartre calls this "impure reflection."[41]

The emergence of impure reflection, however, also carries with it the possibility of a conversion, of the emergence of a pure (or: purifying) reflection that realizes the deceit of bad faith and impure reflection.[42] Sartre writes: "What is given first in daily life is impure or constituent reflection." As such, it can form the occasion for "a modification which it effects on itself and which is in the form of a katharsis."[43] That katharsis is pure reflection: it represents a reflective resumption of the pre-reflective awareness and acceptation of human-reality in good faith.[44]

---

[38] Thomas W. Busch, *The Power of Consciousness and the Force of Circumstances in Sartre's Philosophy* (Bloomington: Indiana University Press, 1990), 37–8.

[39] This is Sartre's term for human existence as characterized by consciousness of being facticity and transcendence.

[40] Cf. Sartre, *Notebooks for an Ethics*, 11; "By reflection the for-itself, which has lost itself outside itself, attempts to put itself inside its own being," and "This effort to be to itself its own foundation, . . . inevitably results in failure; and it is precisely this failure which is reflection" (Sartre, *Being and Nothingness*, 176–7).

[41] Sartre, *Being and Nothingness*, 184.

[42] Cf. "Impure reflection is motivation for pure reflection" (Sartre, *Notebooks for an Ethics*, 12).

[43] Sartre, *Being and Nothingness*, 182.

[44] Cf. "Pure reflection can effect upon itself a 'catharsis' and as a result, in its thematization of the pre-reflective, take cognizance of the 'break in being,' of the non-positional presence to self. . . . in pure reflection the self is grasped as 'break in being' . . . and as 'having to be'" (Busch, *The Power of Consciousness*, 32).

Therefore, Sartre concludes: "Pure reflection is good faith."[45] Pure reflection does not involve a new awareness—because it was there all along, masked by bad faith—but an internal modification that again reveals the pre-reflective insight of good faith. The realization that one has lived in bad faith "implies a kind of ontological precomprehension of good faith," writes Santoni, who adds: "[the reflective conversion] adopts, or perhaps returns to, good faith's non-thetic, 'joyful' affirmation of freedom."[46] Pure reflection means that we are "both inside and outside at the same time," and "place spontaneity between parentheses," "without depriving it of its affirmative force," Sartre writes.[47] Catalano describes pure reflection as "a momentary grasp of ourselves while not ceasing in the activity and not turning the activity into an object of study."[48]

Still, even though pure reflection and good faith entail the same awareness, they are not identical, because the relation of both attitudes to that awareness differs. Good faith is pre-reflective, immediate, not effected by volition; for, as Sartre writes, "[the voluntary act] requires the appearance of a reflective consciousness."[49] Good faith is like an intuition, an immediate belief in what is important and what is not, occurring without what could be properly called a *choice*. One can only speak of choice when there is the possibility of conscious consideration of doing something different. That possibility arises with reflection, which emerges as the bad faith attempt to mask the insight of good faith, and subsequently with the possibility of reflectively acknowledging that self-deceit and (again: reflectively) *choosing* the insights of good faith. This reflective resumption of good faith is an act of volition, a choice to live in the awareness and acceptance of that insight, and give shape to the self.

It is this reflective attitude, resuming the awareness of good faith, that I would like to call sincerity, even though Sartre himself calls this attitude authenticity[50] and describes sincerity as a form of bad faith. However: first of all, with authenticity Sartre chooses a misleading term that implies the opposite of what he wants to recommend. As Catalano explains:

> It is clear that Sartre would be opposed to a use of the term "authenticity" that referred either to being true to oneself or to a privileged reflection. . . .

[45] Sartre, *Notebooks for an Ethics*, 12.
[46] Santoni, *Bad Faith, Good Faith, and Authenticity in Sartre's Early Philosophy*, 124; cf. Hazel E. Barnes, "Sartre's Concept of the Self," in Harold Bloom (ed.), *Jean-Paul Sartre* (New York: Chelsea House, 2001), 75.
[47] Sartre, *Notebooks for an Ethics*, 4, 5; cf. Busch, *The Power of Consciousness*, 34.
[48] Catalano, *Good Faith and Other Essays*, 156.
[49] Sartre, *Being and Nothingness*, 473.
[50] In a famous, concise footnote, Sartre writes: "this supposes a self-recovery of being which was previously corrupted. This self-recovery we shall call authenticity, the description of which has no place here" (Ibid., 94).

In all these senses, the term "authenticity" implies that we have had an original bond either with our own true self or with Nature or Being, and that we have been led astray by the demands of the world.[51]

Most Sartre scholars choose to maintain the term authenticity nonetheless, and construe the concept in an idiosyncratic, Sartrean way. I will, however, replace Sartre's term of authenticity with sincerity.

Secondly, Sartre's own conception of sincerity is very limited (almost caricatural), and therefore does not do justice to the possibilities of that attitude.[52] Sartre describes sincerity as a "confession" that we employ so as to no longer be responsible for what we have confessed to.[53] Of course, Sartre, as the acute psychologist of bad faith, is right in holding that the individual could use expressions of seeming sincerity in such a way.[54] However, this description does not do justice to what we generally take sincerity to mean. Generally, we regard someone as sincere when he is honest about himself, toward himself and toward the world; by that we mean exactly the acknowledgment of the multiplicities, the inconsistencies, and the possibilities that every individual consists of at any moment. He is (in a more Sartrean formulation) someone who acknowledges and accepts that he is freedom, who "exists" (in the literal sense of "standing out," actively maintaining, abiding)[55] the tension between transcendence and facticity. Such a conception of sincerity fits smoothly into Sartre's general philosophy and terminology.[56]

Therefore, and considering the objections to the term authenticity discussed earlier, it seems to me that sincerity, as it was defined above, embodies the existential attitude of the individual who is conscious of his free being, and who, in the reflective resumption of good faith, realizes that he is responsible for the shaping and meaning of his own existence.

---

[51] Catalano, *Good Faith and Other Essays*, 153–4.

[52] Cf. Santoni, *Bad Faith, Good Faith, and Authenticity in Sartre's Early Philosophy*, 10–11.

[53] Cf. "the sincere man constitutes himself as what he is *in order not to be it*. . . . Total, constant sincerity as a constant effort to adhere to oneself is by nature a constant effort to dissociate oneself from oneself. A person frees himself from himself by the very act by which he makes himself an object for himself. To draw up a perpetual inventory of what one is means constantly to redeny oneself and to take refuge in a sphere where one is no longer anything but a pure, free regard" (Sartre, *Being and Nothingness*, 88–9).

[54] Although, a confession for which an individual does not feel accountable to others, would rather seem to be an expression of the "self-ideal" of authenticity.

[55] There is a clear connection between this conception of existence and the central role of "abiding" in Don Gately's AA recovery in *Infinite Jest* (e.g. Wallace, *Infinite Jest*, 860–1). Cf. Allard den Dulk, "The Transcendence of a Meaningful Life: The Portrayal of the Contemporary Self in David Foster Wallace's *Infinite Jest*," in Wessel Stoker and W. L. van der Merwe (eds), *Looking Beyond? Shifting Views of Transcendence in Philosophy, Theology, Art, and Politics* (Amsterdam/New York: Rodopi, 2012), 413–29.

[56] Cf. Santoni, *Bad Faith, Good Faith, and Authenticity in Sartre's Early Philosophy*, 16–17.

Good faith and sincerity in *Infinite Jest*

As mentioned, the understanding of sincerity outlined in the previous section was partly prompted by considerations derived from *Infinite Jest*. Now that we have clearly outlined the concepts of good faith and sincerity, below we will examine their portrayal in the novel, through analyses of its most important characters—Mario, Gately, and Hal.

Good faith: Mario Incandenza

When we read that Mario Incandenza "doesn't seem to resemble much of anyone," this might at first seem to refer solely to his physical appearance. But Mario's not resembling anyone quickly turns out to refer to something deeper than his physique. Whereas everybody else "finds stuff that's really real uncomfortable and they get embarrassed," Mario is different and likes to visit Ennet House, the nearby halfway facility, because "it's very real." "People are crying and making noise and getting less unhappy, and once he heard somebody say *God* with a straight face and nobody looked at them . . . in any sort of way where you could tell they were worried inside."[57] It is not Mario's physical appearance but his utter lack of cynicism, his focus on "outside"— expressed through many passages like the above—that distinguishes him from everybody else in the novel.

Mario provides an alternative to the novel's many cynical, depressed characters. Mentally, Mario is "slow," "but *not*, verifiably *not*, retarded or cognitively damaged or bradyphrenic, more like refracted, almost, ever so slightly epistemically bent, a pole poked into mental water and just a little off and just taking a little bit longer." Words like "bent" and "off" stress a deviation from the norm. Mario *is* a deviation, an abnormality: he stands for a different way of thinking about the self and its relation to the world, symbolizing the much-needed change that the rest of the novel illustrates. His younger brother Hal regards Mario as a "miracle" and his mother Avril sees him as the family's "real prodigy."[58] Mario's role is in many ways akin to that of an "angel" or a "holy fool."[59]

That Mario—like angels and fools—is perhaps neurologically incapable of irony and cynicism, does not mean that his character cannot teach us

---

[57] Wallace, *Infinite Jest*, 101, 591, 592.

[58] Ibid., 314, 316, 317.

[59] Cf. Timothy Jacobs, "The Brothers Incandenza: Translating Ideology in Fyodor Dostoevsky's *The Brothers Karamazov* and David Foster Wallace's *Infinite Jest*," *Texas Studies in Literature and Language: A Journal of the Humanities* 49 (2007): 272.

anything valuable for overcoming the problems under consideration. His importance lies not in the (congenital) causes of his other way of thinking, but in its results, its consequences: he shows the structures of an alternative attitude, which regards the self as always already public and involved with others, and shows us that this life-view works. Mario functions as an exemplary character, demonstrating the immediate, intuitive adaptation of a life-view that other characters—most importantly, Gately and Hal—will only arrive at through a great deal of effort, through a route that requires reflection.

Another of Mario's characteristics that should arouse our interest, is that, despite being the novel's most empathetic character, always perceptive of other people's pain and suffering, Mario himself does not feel pain. He suffers from "Familial Dysautonomia, a neurological deficit whereby he can't feel physical pain very well."[60] We could disregard this as simply another addition to the long list of Mario's physical ailments. This neurological deficit, however, seems an unmistakable reference to Wittgenstein's so-called "private language arguments," which focus repeatedly on the misguided conviction that the meaning of the utterance "I am in pain" is determined by an individual's private sample (a memory, a mental image) of pain.[61] Mario simply *cannot* base his conception of what pain is on a private sample of pain, because he feels no pain and thus cannot gaze inside and say "this is pain." Because of his neurological deficiency, Mario is immune to the self-reflective mistake of regarding inner processes as objects that an individual possesses and that only that individual can access as part of an immanent, inner process. Most other characters in *Infinite Jest* are subject to this illusion.[62]

Mario's existence seems to be based on the intuitive awareness that the self is something that comes into being outside himself, not in some

---

[60] Wallace, *Infinite Jest*, 590.
[61] Cf. Allard den Dulk, "Wallace and Wittgenstein: Literature as Dialogue Concerning the Real World," in Sébastian Hüsch (ed.), *Philosophy and Literature and the Crisis of Metaphysics* (Würzburg: Verlag Königshausen & Neumann, 2011), 343–58. There are significant parallels between Sartre's and Wittgenstein's views of self-consciousness and self-knowledge. For Sartre, too, the tendency to regard thoughts, feelings, and "character" as objects that we somehow possess inside ourselves, is a crucial mistake in how we view ourselves. For both, self-knowledge is not a result of consciousness looking at itself, as if it is an object, but of consciousness looking at its own relations to the world. Both Sartre and Wittgenstein regard self-consciousness as inextricably tied in with the world outside consciousness, a view that undermines the threat of solipsism. Cf. Kathleen Wider, "Hell and the Private Language Argument: Sartre and Wittgenstein on Self-Consciousness, the Body, and Others," *Journal of the British Society for Phenomenology* 18, 2 (1987): 120–32; Béatrice Longuenesse, "Self-Consciousness and Self-Reference: Sartre and Wittgenstein," *European Journal of Philosophy* 16, 1 (2008): 1–21.
[62] Cf. Wallace, *Infinite Jest*, 692–3.

immanent, private sphere, but in what transcends his consciousness: in the world and through his actions. This seems to form an important aspect of his life-view. Mario is repeatedly described as "inclined ever forward."[63] Again, at first this simply seems to be a reference to Mario's physical abnormalities. However, as a result of this repeated emphasis, Mario's "forward-inclination" becomes more and more a characterization not just of his posture but also of his life-view. As Greg Carlisle observes: "[Mario is] able to choose, to contribute, not caught in a cycle of stasis and passivity."[64] Other characters, such as the novel's many drug addicts, *are* caught in such a cycle: they are empty shells, without real selves. Conversely, Mario is committed to the world outside, capable of acting and, therefore, of becoming a self.

As discussed earlier, Mario displays this behavior intuitively: he does not have to make any (reflective) effort to stay immune to the problems that affect other characters. In other words, his virtue is completely pre-reflective. In Mario, therefore, we encounter an embodiment of *good faith*, which contrasts sharply with the reflection-induced bad faith of most of the other characters. The fact that Mario does not feel pain symbolizes his innate immunity to the temptation of seeking all meaning inside himself, which would lead to bad faith; he does not find his self inside, but in his relations to the world and others. As a result, Mario is focused on what is "really real," that is, he intuitively and honestly acknowledges what is really important. Instead of fleeing from the task of self-becoming, Mario takes on the reality of his existence. He succeeds in becoming a stable self because he is aware that the self is connected to the world outside consciousness and takes shape through actions. As such, Mario is the paragon of what it means to be human. He shows the reality and desirability of the virtue that he embodies, thereby functioning as an example to other characters who will strive for a similar attitude, who will reflectively grasp the insight of good faith. As such, Mario *is* good faith: he *is* the life-view that is resumed by others through reflection.

Sincerity: Don Gately and Hal Incandenza

Unlike Mario, Gately and Hal *do* struggle with excessive self-reflection, irony, and cynicism, which can be regarded as examples of bad faith behavior. It is my contention that both characters undergo a development from these

---

[63] Ibid., 313, 315.
[64] Greg Carlisle, *Elegant Complexity: A Study of David Foster Wallace's* Infinite Jest (Los Angeles/Austin: SSMG Press, 2007), 199.

problems toward an attitude of sincerity. Below, I will first give a broad outline of Gately's relatively clear-cut development. Then, I will analyze Hal's more puzzling situation in further detail. Although Hal and Gately do not meet during the intervals of the story that the novel explicitly narrates, a meeting between the two characters in the missing intermediate year is suggested by a memory Hal has during the opening scene ("Donald Gately and I dig up my father's head") and a vision Gately has toward the end of the novel ("He dreams he's with a very sad kid and they're in a graveyard digging some dead guy's head up").[65]

The most important aspect of Gately's development toward sincerity is the role AA plays in it. We have already seen that *Infinite Jest* portrays a society in which "stuff that's really real," real emotions, grief, and meaning, are regarded as outdated, as clichés that are to be ignored. AA forms an exception, as a community in which the importance of such clichés, of real things, *is* pointed out.[66] What AA does is bring fellow-sufferers together, see to it that they open themselves up, that they are honest with others—if only through that one sentence, "I am an addict"—and, in the course of doing that, learn to be honest with themselves, and thus become selves.

Openness, sincerity, and a stable self are not established instantly; they are gradually realized. These are things that AA members are encouraged to *do*, in the presence of each other. Initially the hyperreflexive, ironic mind of the addict regards AA's insights and guidelines as clichés (just like the "real stuff" of existence, that the addicts have neglected for years and that has to be brought back into sight again by these guidelines), for as Gately observes: "every one of the seminal little mini-epiphanies you have in early AA is always polyesterishly banal." But, he continues: "the thing is that the clichéd directives are a lot more deep and hard to actually *do*. To try and live by instead of just say."[67] The attitude, and the resulting self, that AA strives toward, can only emerge from acts in the world, even though the start of such actions can only be dutiful, at best.[68]

---

[65] Wallace, *Infinite Jest*, 18, 934.
[66] Ibid., 369.
[67] Ibid., 358, 273.
[68] Cf. "It's called 'Fake It Till You Make It'" (Ibid., 369). We can connect this to Sartre's assertion that we can never "believe what we believe": good faith means that we have to place trust in phenomena about which we cannot possibly acquire absolute certainty, such as friendship or the fact that AA works, but have to do so, based on signals that convince us that these things are in fact the case. In AA this means that a new member can recognize that this program might help him, as it seems to help others, but this does not yet take away his desperation concerning his own fate.

According to Gately, each AA insight or guideline initially incites aversion in the addict, because it seems such a "quilted-sampler-type cliché."[69] "Just Do It" and "Keep Coming" are two of those clichéd guidelines, but everybody is encouraged to keep doing them, to keep coming, and ultimately see the real stuff behind the supposed clichés. This leads to Gately's katharsis, one might say.[70] Gately is, as Bell and Dowling formulate it, the evident "hero" of *Infinite Jest*, because of his "transformation of character in the months he has been free of his addiction and doing his best to aid other battered souls in their struggle with their own demons."[71] Gately is the "knight" (one of his nicknames is "Sir Osis") who, from a situation of addiction, develops into a stable self, an honest man who tries to form a meaningful life as a live-in staff member of Ennet House by helping others, counseling new residents during their recovery.

Whereas Gately's situation during the novel is quite clear, interpreting Hal's development is anything but simple. In *Infinite Jest*'s opening scene (and, chronologically, the last episode of the story line), Hal, at that moment seen from his own first-person perspective, seems quite normal. However, the admission committee of the University of Arizona perceives him as animal-like, primitive, and damaged. This contradiction leaves it up to the reader to decide what kind of state Hal is in, here, at the end of the story line. Judging by the reactions from the people around him, there is something wrong with Hal; several possible causes are alluded to in the novel. However, what these tentative suggestions can make us lose sight of is the possibility that Hal, compared with how he is in the rest of the novel, is actually getting better. Interpreting this will depend partly on how one judges Hal's surroundings, the cultural context described in the novel; for it is this context that determines the perception of Hal as suffering from some sort of fundamental defect.

In some ways, Hal is an extraordinary, abnormal character—a prodigy in both sport and academic study—but in many respects Hal is also utterly normal: his addiction, and accompanying hyperreflexivity and endless irony, are typical of the society portrayed in *Infinite Jest*. The first part of Hal's

[69] Ibid., 446.

[70] Cf. "after maybe five months Gately . . . all of a sudden realized that quite a few days had gone by since he'd even thought of Demerol or Talwin or even weed. . . . He was, in a way, Free. It was the first time he'd been out of this kind of mental cage since he was maybe ten" (Ibid., 467–8).

[71] Robert H. Bell and William Dowling, *A Reader's Companion to* Infinite Jest (Bloomington: Xlibris, 2005), 95–6.

story line contains many descriptions of the gravity of his addiction, and the accompanying state of "Analysis-Paralysis."[72]

When Hal decides to quit marijuana, he confesses his former drug use and his fear of the impendent withdrawal symptoms to his brother Mario, and asks him for help:

> "I feel a hole. It's going to be a huge hole, in a month. . . . And the hole's going to get a little bigger every day until I fly apart in different directions. . . . I do not know what to do."
>
> "Hal, if I tell you the truth, will you get mad and tell me be a fucking?"
>
> "I trust you. You're smart, Boo."
>
> "Then Hal?"
>
> "Tell me what I should do."
>
> "I think you just did it. What you should do. I think you just did."
>
> ". . ."
>
> "Do you see what I mean?"[73]

This confession and call for help indicate an unprecedented open-heartedness on Hal's part.[74] This might be part of what is described as the "whole new Hal, a Hal who does not get high, or hide, a Hal who in 29 days is going to hand his own personal urine over to authority figures with a wide smile and exemplary posture and not a secretive thought in his head."[75]

Shortly after his confession to Mario, Hal starts to narrate from a first-person perspective and, chronologically speaking, keeps on doing so.[76] Up to that moment, Hal's perspective has always been rendered in the third-person, or Hal has been described from the third-person perspective of other characters. We can regard the fact that Hal starts narrating in the first-person as a sign of the fact that Hal starts to develop a self.

However, at the same moment that Hal starts to narrate in first-person, other characters start asking him whether there is something wrong, and Hal has no idea what they are talking about. The others perceive Hal as having a constant "hilarity face," and either ask why he is crying or why he is laughing, while he thinks he is doing neither.[77] This discrepancy in (self)perception is

---

[72] E.g. Wallace, *Infinite Jest*, 334.

[73] Ibid., 785.

[74] E.g. Ibid., 852.

[75] Ibid., 635.

[76] Starting at: Ibid., 851.

[77] E.g. Ibid., 865, 875–6. Cf. the "whole new Hal['s]" "wide smile" noted above; also see below for a comparison with Mario and his "involuntarily constant smile."

at its most extreme in the opening scene. Hal, via his first-person perspective, seems normal and thinks: "I believe I appear neutral, maybe even pleasant." But when he tries to express what he thinks and feels, the admission committee perceives his facial expression as "animal-like" and "contorted," and his voice as a hysterical, terrifying scream.[78] The novel then describes the buildup to this opening scene. The question "What happened to/is wrong with Hal?" is one of *Infinite Jest*'s main narrative threads, but the novel offers no explicit answer. Two possible explanations— use of the drug DMZ or having watched the film *"Infinite Jest"*—imply that such an event has taken place in the intervening year that the novel does not describe; these explanations are therefore the most mysterious, as well as the most sensationalist (potent drug! fatal film!). As such they are very much in line with the techniques of the commercial, addictive entertainment culture that the novel criticizes, and should therefore perhaps not be taken too seriously. Moreover, the supposed symptoms of what is potentially wrong with Hal have started before this time, before he might have seen the film or used the drug.

Another possibility is that Hal, who is repeatedly described as suffering from anhedonia (characterized as a mild form of depression), has sunk into a deeper, clinical form of depression. Hal displays several striking similarities to Kate Gompert, a character described as suffering from clinical depression. Several descriptions of her facial expression call to mind those of Hal's "hilarity-face."[79] Another similarity is that both Kate and Hal are not just addicted to marijuana, but also to the secrecy surrounding their use of it.[80] However, there are also unmistakable and crucial differences between Kate's depression and Hal's situation. The uncomprehendedness that Kate describes as connected to depression—"Classic unipolars were usually tormented by the conviction that no one else could hear or understand them when they tried to communicate"—perhaps calls to mind Hal's uncomprehendedness (for instance, vis-à-vis the admission committee). But Hal's situation, here, is opposite to Kate's. Kate is completely absorbed by the psychic pain she experiences, and consequently is incapable of the empathy that is needed to explain herself to other people. Hal, however, makes frantic efforts to explain who he is, what he feels and what he deems important. For example, when before the admission committee, he says: "I am not just a boy who plays tennis. I have an intricate history. Experiences and feelings. I'm complex."[81]

[78] Ibid., 3, 12.
[79] Cf. Ibid., 76.
[80] Ibid., 49, 77, 695.
[81] Ibid., 11, 12, 75, 696.

These statements fit the development, discussed above, in which Hal becomes increasingly aware of his own feelings, starts to open up and become a self. Instead of assuming that something is wrong with Hal, we could turn the diagnosis around: *Infinite Jest* describes a society in which a lot is clearly amiss, and it is in this society that Hal has grown up: "We are shown how to fashion masks of ennui and jaded irony at a young age. . . . And then it's stuck there, the weary cynicism that saves us from gooey sentiment and unsophisticated naïveté." In his cynical contempt for a self that gives sincere expression to its thoughts and emotions, the old Hal complies perfectly with what is normal within the described culture: "One of the really American things about Hal, probably, is the way he despises what he is really lonely for: this hideous internal self, incontinent of sentiment and need, that pules and writhes under the hip empty mask, anhedonia."[82] Hal's disgust is described as a "fear of being really human, since to be really human (at least as he conceptualizes it) is probably to be unavoidably sentimental and naïve and goo-prone and generally pathetic." He regards it as being childlike and underdeveloped (the self is "incontinent," it "pules" and "writhes," looking deformed and hideous): "[to be really human] is to be in some basic interior way forever infantile, some sort of not-quite-right-looking infant dragging itself anaclitically around the map, with big wet eyes and froggy-soft skin, huge skull, gooey drool."[83]

These descriptions call to mind Mario, who is described as "at 18+ in a range somewhere between elf and jockey," dragging himself along "in the sort of lurchy stumble of a vaudeville inebriate," and having a "[large but] withered-looking head," "khaki-colored skin, an odd dead gray-green that . . . [gave him] an almost uncannily reptilian/dinosaurian look." Additionally, Mario has an "involuntarily constant smile"; compare this to Hal's hilarity-face and the description of the "whole new Hal" who does not do drugs anymore and submits his own urine "with a wide smile." Mario's sincerity is regarded by the rest of society as a lack of development and sophistication, as some sort of awful handicap. Primitive and hideous is also how Hal is perceived in the opening scene of the book: he fills the members of the admission committee with horror.[84]

Accordingly, we can perhaps conclude that there is nothing wrong with Hal, but that a change has taken place, from self-reflective irony and cynicism to an openness, to the formation of a self—a change the rest of the novel

[82] Ibid., 694, 695.
[83] Ibid., 694–5.
[84] Ibid., 12, 14, 154, 216, 313, 314; also, in this scene Hal calls himself an "infantophile," a term capturing the negative perception the desire for sincerity and spontaneity, as felt by the outside world, but at that point not by Hal himself anymore (Ibid., 16).

illustrates the desirability of—and conclude that there is something wrong with the society that is horrified by him.[85]

Catherine Nichols writes the following about Hal and Gately: "the trajectory of their transformation is one of restoring personal agency by turning the self inside-out rather than suppressing it beneath deliberate artifice."[86] Gately and Hal gradually open themselves up to the world around them, instead of remaining confined in themselves. In Gately's case, we can see that AA makes him open up and be honest, to others and to himself. This does not happen automatically: it requires a (reflective) decision from the addict to act according to the guidelines, which can be regarded as a reminder of good faith insights. AA brings about a *pure reflection* in Gately: its guidelines, constituting the formation of the self, are taken on by Gately in his actions in AA and in Ennet House; his transformation is based on adopting these insights through a process of reflection.

Hal undergoes a similar development, although it seems crucial that whereas Gately is part of a community of fellow-sufferers, Hal is alone, facing the ironic community from which he has detached himself. This can also explain the contrast between the clarity of Hal's internal monologue and the complete lack of understanding of his words by the people around him. Hal's development to the attitude of sincerity is connected to a change in language-games, in communities of language and meaning, into which he has become initiated at the time of the opening scene (perhaps via Gately and Mario). And as a result, he seems more at ease with his new self than a year earlier, in the scenes at the end of the book. However, most people around him are not familiar with the language-game of sincerity, and therefore do not understand him, and get the impression that he is uttering primitive drivel. Therefore, it might seem as if Hal, in the end, is still (or even more deeply) confined in himself; but this could be explained by the fact that he has no support network, that other people are still missing from what we get to see of Hal's life—that he may, in fact, be on the right path.

From the moment of his confession and call for help to Mario, Hal opens up and acknowledges the importance of the other in judging and becoming who you are. Hal's transition is prompted by the reflective realization (*pure reflection*) that Mario's good faith gives him a better understanding of himself, reality, and other people. The encounter with Gately, who has after all gained a similar understanding, may also have contributed to that. Hal decides (that

---

[85] In Hal's self-explanation to the committee we can read a rejection of the ironic, postmodernist conception of the self, when Hal says: "I'm not just a creātus, manufactured, conditioned, bred for a function" (Ibid., 12).

[86] Catherine Nichols, "Dialogizing Postmodern Carnival: David Foster Wallace's *Infinite Jest*," *Critique: Studies in Contemporary Fiction* 43, 1 (2001): 13.

is, through a voluntary act) that the intuition he has about what it means to be, as he formulates it himself, "really human" (open, vulnerable, etc.) is true and desirable, and he chooses to live according to this insight. And as such he becomes a *sincere* self.

Conclusion

In this chapter, the Sartrean view of consciousness served to clarify the role of sincerity in *Infinite Jest*, while at the same time Wallace's novel served to point out and correct both Sartre's own, as well as the more general, philosophical misconception of the phenomenon of sincerity. We have seen that *good faith* is the pre-reflective awareness and acceptance of human-reality, as the need to become a self in connection to the world outside consciousness, by "existing" the tension between transcendence and facticity. *Sincerity* consists of resuming this awareness reflectively, through a "pure reflection," which implies grasping oneself without depriving consciousness of its spontaneity and directedness at the world. Mario Incandenza has been analyzed as a paragon of good faith, who, through his intuitive awareness of the task of self-becoming, functions as an exemplary character demonstrating a life-view that other characters are subsequently shown to arrive at through a more difficult, reflected route. The attitude of sincerity was analyzed through the cases of Don Gately and Hal Incandenza. *Infinite Jest* shows these characters overcoming their reflexive-ironic attitude, by realizing the transcendent character of the self; they show that, to achieve a meaningful existence, consciousness has to be connected to the world outside itself.

13

Theories of Everything and More: Infinity is Not the End

Ryan David Mullins

Not empiricism and yet realism in philosophy, that is the hardest thing.
—Ludwig Wittgenstein

A human is that being which prefers to represent itself within finitude, whose sign is death, rather than knowing itself to be entirely traversed and encircled by the omnipresence of infinity.

— Alain Badiou

One very important interpretive key that can help readers understand and appreciate the complexity of *Infinite Jest* lies in the analysis of its recursive structures. Most of the novel's constitutive narrative and sub-narratives pivot around precisely this mechanism. *Infinite Jest* is about a film "Infinite Jest," a film so entertaining that viewers cannot escape its paralysis-inducing pleasures. Viewers are sucked into an infinite loop of views until the regress concludes in the death of the viewer. One literally watches the film to death. The recursive nature of the title is just the start of the endless jest of infinities!

This chapter will make explicit the *implicit* metaphysical position underlying David Foster Wallace's infinitely complex second novel *Infinite Jest*. First, I will explore the fundamental dichotomy operative in contemporary philosophical debates in the wake of Kant's "Critical" philosophy: the *linguistic turn* and the *metaphysical turn*. It's quite common that readers of Wallace's work place him within a certain Wittgenstein-inspired meta-philosophy, that is, *the linguistic turn*. I find this exclusivity mistaken and will provide a much-needed correction. In fact, *Infinite Jest* provides the seeds for the development of a quite radical *metaphysical* position that I'll make explicit below. The section will conclude with what I'll call a Doomsday Argument: *the* world does not exist. I'll investigate the extent to which Wallace's use of a Sierpinski Triangle as the "structural synecdoche" underlying *Infinite Jest* contributes to such a *prima facie* absurd thesis as the nonexistence of *the* world. Second, I will explore what I take to be Wallace's preferred methodology, what I'll call a *phenomenology of worlds*. I'll distinguish Wallace's objective phenomenology, which peers into the logical structure of worlds, from orthodox phenomenological investigation, which peers into the logical and transcendental structure of intentionality. Last, I will illustrate two types of infinities operative within *Infinite Jest*, namely bad and good infinity. I will argue that Wallace's theory of freedom evolves out of his notion of what constitutes the internal mechanisms of infinite sets. "Bad Infinity" comprises an incessant recursion in virtue of the activation of an algorithm, that is, an inconclusive, mechanical repetition. "Good Infinity," on the contrary, consists in the higher-order reflection on the mechanisms or algorithms governing a particular set. By focusing on this higher-order reflection, we can illuminate Wallace's view of human freedom.

Metaphysics is dead. Long live metaphysics!

"Grand Metaphysics is dead!" is the slogan which applies to the majority of contemporary philosophers, whether continentals or of analytic profession. They all treat metaphysics as a dead dog.
—Francis Volpi

La Métaphysique n'est pas morte.
—Frederic Nef

The *metaphysical turn* represents a fundamental change of attitude in relation to the methodological power of the *linguistic turn*. It became *au courant* in philosophical circles, in the wake of Kant's "Critical" philosophy, to restrict philosophical investigation to *limning the structure of language, thought, and access-conditions to the world.* The old Zen proverb captures this logic quite nicely: "when the finger points to the moon, the fool looks at the finger." Most of philosophy (or *fool*osophy?!), then, since Kant was indeed mainly because claims about reality were unwittingly taken as claims about our claims about the reality! In the introduction to *The Linguistic Turn*, Richard Rorty explains,

> The purpose of the present volume is to provide materials for reflection on the most recent philosophical revolution, that of linguistic philosophy. I shall mean by "linguistic philosophy" the view that philosophical

problems are problems which may be solved (or dissolved) either by reforming language, or by understanding more about the language we presently use.[1]

Instead of investigating the fundamental nature of the world, such a conception regards the proper task of philosophical reflection as the analysis of *our thought or talk about the world*.[2] Whether the philosopher investigates language, concepts, representations, or access-conditions to the world, she remains on the *res cogitans* side and implicitly *presumably* puts the world "over there," *ipso facto* engendering the infamous gap between mind and world. The natural sciences, more specifically theoretical and experimental physics, investigate the fundamental nature of *res extensa*. If philosophy mingles at all with the latter, it is only indirectly in its proper custodial duties of cleaning up the conceptual and linguistic mess. This is an *idealism about philosophy*, that is, philosophy's proper domain of activity consists in the investigation into the fundamental nature of *res cogitans*. At the very least, "linguisticism" fails to thematize "the world" to render perspicuous its—the world's—precise meaning.

However, let's not be misled by this meta-philosophical sleight-of-hand. Linguisticism operates according to its own ontology. It would be appropriate therefore to inquire into the ontology of language. Presumably, since the proper domain of philosophical investigation consists in the analysis of thought, concepts, and the logical structure of representation, that which is analyzed and investigated must exist! Thus, there's an implicit ontology at play and focusing on language doesn't get one off the hook ontologically or metaphysically.

So that we don't lose track, let me add again that the secondary literature on Wallace focuses almost exclusively on his inclusion and participation within the *linguistic turn*. Indeed, Wallace presents profound insights and explorations of representational solipsism, linguistic idealism, descriptivist accounts of language with strong parallels to ordinary language philosophy, strong interest in mathematical logic and arithmetical systems all of which seem to indicate that Wallace's S.O.P. (standard operating procedure) consists in staging within the domain of fiction various problems within philosophy of

---

[1]   Richard Rorty (ed.), *The Linguistic Turn: Recent Essays in Philosophical Method* (Chicago: University of Chicago Press, 1967), 3.

[2]   A. J. Ayer had the following to say in his 1936 classic *Language, Truth and Logic*, "The Philosopher, as an analyst, is not directly concerned with the physical properties of things. He is concerned only with the way in which speak about them. In other words, the propositions of philosophy are not factual, but linguistic in character—that is, they do not describe the behaviour of physical, or even mental, objects; they express definitions, or the formal consequences of definitions" (61–2). A. J. Ayer, *Language, Truth and Logic* (London: Victor Gollancz, 1936).

language that have been a staple of philosophical thought since its inception. It's difficult to give a succinct and fair overview of the linguistic turn here, but I think the preceding will suffice for my purposes.

Metaphysicians now generally storm the gates of the world right past the epistemological and linguistic protestors. They operate "from the gut," as John Heil calls it. That is, they seek "head-on confrontations with the universe."[3] Metaphysics has generally been defined as the investigation into the fundamental nature of reality. So, instead of bothering with our access-conditions to the world, metaphysicians find it perfectly within their rights to take literally their claims about the nature of the world. When someone says something about the nature of the moon, metaphysicians don't take too seriously the idea that the claim about the nature of the moon was *really* a claim about the claim about the nature of the moon. Metaphysics, then, by making certain claims about the nature of the world already operates with an implicit ontology. Ontology, as far as this paper is concerned, consists in the higher-order explication of existence criteria. It—ontology—is not concerned directly with *what there is*, nor is it simply an investigation into the *meaning* of the concept "existence." It's concerned, rather, with making explicit the existence criteria with which we are always already operating. We make explicit our ontology *après-coup* insofar as, in order to make *something* explicit, it must already be operative in some implicit fashion. For example, when I claim, "there is a prime number between 2 and 9," and furthermore this claim is true, then I'm committed to the existence of numbers. Our everyday acts—whether non-propositional or propositional—perform these ontological commitments. It would be strange indeed were we to live and move in the world without being at least implicitly committed to the existence of *something!*

I've referred to Wallace's implicit position as a "metaphysical pluralism." Metaphysical pluralism should be understood in contrast to its opposite, namely metaphysical monism. Pluralism liberates our concept of existence from the strictures of monism. Metaphysical monism is the view that there is only one world/domain—henceforth I will use "world" and "domain" interchangeably—made of one kind of stuff. Metaphysical pluralism, on the contrary, advocates domain plurality, that is, reality comprises a transfinite proliferation of domains. Monism conflates "the world" and "reality" and defines existence in terms of law-governed, space–time coordinates. The ontology of metaphysical monism defines existence in terms of appearance within the domain "the world," where the latter denotes the physical universe.

---

[3] John Heil, *The Universe as We Find It* (Oxford: Oxford University Press, 2012), 1.

I suggest we think differently. The physical universe is *a* world, not *the* world. A world or a domain is a set of objects the collection of which is governed by the inclusion criteria of one's ontology. Alexius Meinong's "ghetto" notion of existence offended Bertrand Russell's *parsimonious* sense of reality. However, Russell's parsimonious sense of reality offends what I take to be Wallace's *promiscuous* sense of reality. As we'll see below, existence is always relative to a domain. To be real is to be *actual* in the physical world. On this account, "Ghosts exist," is meaningless until one provides the proper domain in which ghosts exist. Ghosts do not exist, I'm sorry to say, in the actual world of the physical universe. So, "Ghosts do not exist in physical reality" is true. However, "Ghosts exist in *Infinite Jest*" is true. "Ghosts exist in the original television series *Scooby Doo, Where are You!*" is false given that the show's fundamental premise is concerned with debunking supernatural ontologies. It's very important not to confuse *reality* with *existence* or *materially* existence with *existence*. Ghosts exist despite not being real. Given that existence is relative to inclusion within a domain, ghosts exist in the domain of fictional characters without being real. To be real, then, is to exist in the actual, physical world. So, ontology is the investigation into the implicit existence criteria according to which we're always already operating, while metaphysics refers to the attempt to investigate the fundamental nature of that which appears in *a* domain.

If existence is relative to a domain, then we can go in two directions: we reduce the world to one domain, namely the domain of physical reality, or we proliferate our domains and advocate a flat ontology,[4] that is, a metaphysical pluralism in which an infinite number of domains exist. A flat ontology is committed to the idea that *all things equally exist, but all things do not exist equally.*[5] The notion of a domain will be important below. To repeat, a domain denotes a set of objects collected according to a certain rule. What's included within a domain is established by the operative inclusion or existence criteria. So, when I say that "existence is relative to a domain" think of the inclusion of a particular object within a set the inclusion of which is set by inclusion or existence criteria. It follows, on such an account, that it is not always contradictory to claim that *there are* nonexistent things. To assert, "there is no coffee" is not to employ an unrestricted quantifier that quantifies over everything in the world. One could assert "there is no coffee" while coffee nonetheless exists in the other room. I will not argue for this thesis here, even though it's relevant to the discussion below, but this is why one can't

---

[4] Of course, these two positions certainly don't exhaust the options. However, for my purpose in this chapter, I will focus on these two positions.
[5] I credit Ian Bogost with this formulation.

quantify over everything. That is, there are no unrestricted quantifiers. This is important because we'll see below that Wallace implicitly defends what I've been calling a metaphysical pluralism in *Infinite Jest*. In fact, his fiction is fundamentally concerned with the plurality of domains in which we find ourselves moving and existing.

In virtue of the fact that domains can have sub-domains—that is, domains can exist in domains—it's important to recognize that *domains themselves exist*. This is the fundamental point of the above critique of the linguistic turn. To restrict existence questions to the domain of language is a mistake insofar as one remains committed to the existence of language in order to analyze it. The linguistic turn operates with an implicit ontology and an implicit metaphysics. However, it places these beyond the proper domain of philosophical investigation. Quine, for example, was concerned with something he called "ontological commitment." What exists is always relative to what quantifies over our true theories of the world. That is, for Quine, to exist is "to be the value of a variable."[6] This formulation seeks to capture the ontological commitments of a theory already regimented in first-order, quantificational logic. I find Quine's formulation persuasive on the condition that we modify his intentions. Instead of speaking about ontological commitments, it's more fruitful to interpret Quine's position as proffering a theory of existence *überhaupt*. And, as we said above, existence is relative to a domain and, in the words of David Lewis, domains "come and go with the pragmatic wind"![7] Existence, on my account, is not a first-order property of individual objects. Rather, it's a higher-order relation.

To summarize where we are. I've explored what I take to be the two dominate strands in contemporary philosophical discussion: the linguistic approach and the metaphysical approach. The linguistic turn advocates epistemology as first philosophy insofar as philosophy's proper domain of investigation consists in the analysis of language, while the metaphysical turn bypasses the restrictions on talk about the world by doing just that, making claims about the nature of fundamental reality. I've suggested, moreover, that we modify the orthodox conception of metaphysics by avoiding its domain-reductionism and enable the proliferation of domains. Metaphysics, then, would receive a promiscuous makeover: metaphysics investigates

---

[6] W. V. Quine, *From a Logical Point of View: Nine Logico-Philosophical Essays* (Harvard: Harvard University Press, 1980), 13.

[7] David Lewis, *On the Plurality of Worlds* (Oxford: Blackwell Publishers, 2001), 164.

the fundamental nature of those elements appearing in their respective domains.

Doomsday argument: *The* world doesn't exist

A symphony must be like the world. It must embrace everything!

—Gustav Mahler

Imagine a work so grand that it mirrors the entire world.

—Gustav Mahler

Wallace's metaphysical pluralism indirectly positions itself against any and all metaphysical positions that seek to reduce the complexity and multilayered reality to one particular world. For Wallace, *the* world doesn't exist. Instead of a bird's-eye view of totality, we must remain mummified within our flesh. However, higher-order contemplation enables us to hop from skin to skin, domain to domain, world to world, thinking and tinkering with their constitutive laws. While the bird's-eye view is jettisoned, Wallace permits what Max Tegmark calls a "frog's view".[8] We're not caged within one world but rather simultaneous occupants of many worlds the number of which seem to extend to the infinitesimally small to the transfinitely large. This foreshadows Wallace's notion of freedom, which we'll address in section 3 below.

How could one possibly argue for the nonexistence of *the* world? Of course the world exists, one might object. Where else do we live than in the world? Fair enough. But, where is this world? We can't have a possible experience of the world. One can't point to the world. Indeed, one can point to various objects that appear within a world; however, *the* world itself can never be a possible object of experience.

The physical universe, moreover, is not *the* world. If one posits that the world is the domain in which everything exists, this definition begs the question in virtue of the fact that the physical universe, in order to exist, would have to appear within itself. Consider the List of all Lists. If one presents a list of everything, then the list would be incomplete unless of course the list itself, which presumably exists, appears in the list. However, once the list

---

[8] Max Tegmark, "The Mathematical Universe": http://arxiv.org/pdf/0704.0646.pdf, (accessed 24 September 2013).

itself appears in the list, we then need another, more encompassing list that contains everything and so on *ad infinitum*. This infinite regress illustrates the meaning behind the claim that only worlds/domains (or lists) exist. There is no domain of all domains, set of all sets, list of all lists, or world of all worlds.[9]

Wallace has admitted in various contexts that he employed a Sierpinski Triangle as a structural model of *Infinite Jest*. The most informative elaboration of his employment of a Sierpinski Triangle can be found in his 1996 interview on KCRW's show *Bookworm*. Wallace makes the following claim in response to host Michael Silverblatt's intuition that Wallace employed a fractal geometry to structure the novel:

> That's one of the things that's structurally going on. It's actually structured like something called a Sierpinski Gasket, which is a very primitive, kind of pyramidical fractal; although what was structured like a Sierpinski Gasket was the first draft that I delivered to Michael [Pietsch, Wallace's Editor] in 1994 and it went through some mercy cuts. So, it's probably kind of a lopsided Sierpinski Gasket now. But, it's interesting, that's one of the structural ways that it's supposed to kind of come together'. And later: 'It seems to me that so much of pre-millennial life in America consists of enormous amounts of what seem like discrete bits of information coming and that the real kind of intellectual adventure is finding ways to relate them into each other and to find larger patterns and meanings, which of course is essentially narrative but that structurally it's a bit different.[10]

Let's pause to say a few words about fractals. To interpret *Infinite Jest* and Wallace's intentions ontologically would be to attribute to him a fractal ontology. This discussion returns to the opening lines above with regard to the

<hr>

[9] For more elaboration on this paradox, see Alain Badiou's *Being and Event* and its sequel *Logics of Worlds*. See also Markus Gabriel, who develops this point much more explicitly in his *Mythology, Laughter and Madness* and *Warum es die Welt nicht gibt*. See also Stephen Mulhall in his wonderful book *Inheritance & Originality: Wittgenstein, Heidegger, Kierkegaard*: "The world is not a possible object of knowledge, because it is not an object at all—not an entity or set of entities. It is that within which entities appear, a field or horizon of assignment-relations; it is the condition for the possibility of any intra-worldly relation, and so is not analysable in terms of any such relation. In short, the Cartesian conception of subject and world opens the door to scepticism because it interprets both subject and world as entities (or sets of entities)—as if the world were a great big object, a totality of possible objects of knowledge, rather than that wherein all possible objects of knowledge are encountered." Stephen Mulhall, *Inheritance & Originality: Wittgenstein, Heidegger, Kierkegaard* (Oxford: Oxford University Press, 2003), 238.

[10] One can access the interview at the following link. David Foster Wallace and Michael Silverblatt, "*Infinite Jest* Interview," http://www.kcrw.com/etc/programs/bw/bw960411david_foster_wallace.

"interpretive key" to identifying what's happening structurally in the novel, namely recursive structures. Fractals are one kind of recursive structure, that is, they are geometrical, self-similar objects. For example, stories inside stories, Russian dolls, movies inside movies, or dreams within dreams. Think, for example, of Las Vegas' replicas of famous cities: Paris, New York City, Venice (Italy). Imagine, though, if builders constructed in Vegas a fully functioning model or Las Vegas! Vegas in Vegas. However, within the new Vegas, they also constructed a Vegas within Vegas within Vegas.[11] This is an example of recursion. A fractal demonstrates recursive structure insofar as a basic pattern is iterated such that each individual part resembles the whole. Indeed, we encounter a number of naturally occurring fractals in everyday life! Think, for example, of snowflakes, coral reefs, and nervous systems. We won't explore this here, but there are non-fractal objects that are self-similar, namely line-segments. Note that an important difference exists between abstract and real fractals. The former's iterative structure continues *ad infinitum*, while the latter's doesn't. At some point in the analysis of a natural fractal, the part does not resemble that whole. It's not necessary to analyze in detail the intricacies of fractal geometry here; I do think the preceding definition and discussion will suffice however to follow the argumentation presented below.

What is a Sierpinski Triangle? Let's avoid the mathematical explanation, and focus more on what the triangle looks like and how it can be informally constructed. We'll then speculate a bit on its ontological and metaphysical consequences. A Sierpinski Triangle is an elementary, pyramidical fractal. Its construction involves, first, drawing a triangle; then, within the triangle one draws three triangles and within those three triangles another three triangles, and so on *ad infinitum*. The fractal nature of the triangle consists in its self-similar repetition. [See Figure 1]

The world is standardly taken to denote the totality of all spatiotemporally extended things governed by the physical laws of nature. It treats the world, in the words of Martin Heidegger, *ontically*; that is, the world is treated as an *empirical object*. The Sierpinski Triangle, one could say, exhibits this totality: everything that exists appears inside the triangle and inside the sub-triangles and sub-sub-triangles.

I've argued that we shouldn't limit *the world* to law-governed, spatio-temporal coordinates. Rather, we should expand our notion of the world to a transfinite proliferation of domains in which things exist, appear and perform various roles depending on the nature and rules of that domain. Numbers do very different things depending on the nature of the domain in which they appear; hands perform distinct roles depending on the domain in which

---

[11] For a filmic example of this, see Charlie Kaufman's wonderful *Synecdoche, New York*.

they appear. For example, it's doubtless true that a hand is a collection of sub-atomic particles arranged hand-wise; however, this doesn't exhaust the true descriptions and properties of a hand. It's important to note that I don't want to conflate "horizons" or "perspectives" and what I'm calling worlds. Phenomenology would treat these different descriptions of a particular object as gestalt switches or changes of perspective. However, I want to claim that with what I'll call an objective phenomenology and a metaphysical pluralism the worlds or domains in which things exist and perform various roles *themselves exist*. It amounts, then, to realism *about* domains.[12] We do not project them onto the world; rather, they exist independently of our projective activity.

Each individual triangle composing a Sierpinski Triangle represents, on my reading, a particular domain or world. Furthermore, the number of domains can incessantly extend to the infinitesimally small given that the triangles within triangles continue to proliferate *ad infinitum*. Thus, there are an infinite number of domains. Most importantly, however, we began the triangular construction process by drawing a large triangle, subsequently engendering the "internal" infinite regress. But, we could also include this initial triangle within a much larger, more encompassing triangle, and could proceed outward into the transfinitely large. In other words, the regress extends inward as well as outward.[13]

It's important to note that when I claim that we occupy many domains or worlds, I'm not claiming that our physical spatiotemporal coordinates occupy two *universes*; that is, this position doesn't imply the multiverse view currently gaining traction in contemporary physics. Again, this is because the universe is not *the* world. The universe, rather, is *a* world.

---

[12] I'm convinced more than ever that so-called "idealism" *simpliciter* doesn't exist. That is, all idealists are realists about something. Thus, *idealism is always a local realism about something*. For example, Berkeley is often called an idealist. However, it doesn't follow that nothing is real for Berkeley. On the contrary! God, for example, is real. Ideas, for example, are real. However, there is no "realism" *simpliciter*; *realism is always a realism about something*. For example, realism about the external world, realism about reasons, realism about abstract objects, etc.

[13] For those familiar with debates regarding the foundations of mathematics, it is perhaps easy to see the parallels between the argumentation employed here concerning the plurality of worlds and Gödel's first and second incompleteness theorems. An obvious difference consists in the fact that Gödel's theorems concern formal systems of arithmetic and the existence of truths that aren't provable formally within an arithmetical system. The regress in Gödel commences once we construct a formal system to account for the truth of the previous unprovable, but true proposition; but, once we construct a new formal system, this system itself contains a true, but unprovable proposition and so on.

Think of a world as a domain of objects or a field[14] of objects collected in accordance with axiomatic laws, rules and algorithms. Imagine a table on which you find some cubes. Suppose someone asks you, "How many objects are on the table?" Common sense may claim that there are three cubes on the table. However, suppose Stephen Hawking emerges in the room and says to Common Sense Man, "Sorry. There aren't three objects on the table. Rather, the precise amount is impossible to determine, as these cubes are merely subatomic particles arranged cube-wise." Then, German painter Neo Rauch saunters into the room: "given that the cubes are different colors. We're forgetting to count the colors. So, in addition to the three common sense cubes, I count seven different colors, giving me ten objects."

This example can be a bit misleading for my purposes, though.[15] It can be used not to prove an ontological point, but to support the epistemological claim that the *concept* of existence is plural and, thus, we project different models of counting upon the world. I think this is wrong. I propose that we think of worlds as domains of objects collected according to some rules or laws, as existing independently of human projectile activities. That is, we find ourselves operating, living, acting, and thinking within structures whose nature exists independently of us. One needs to step away from the epistemological position *toward the ontological*. What does this have to do with *Infinite Jest*? I want to suggest that the model Wallace employs to compose his novel, the Sierpinski Triangle, takes this ontological step; that is, *Infinite Jest* explores proliferating domains and worlds and their constitutive laws.

---

[14] Markus Gabriel has developed a *field of sense ontology* from which I pilfer a number of insights. While I have a number of disagreements with this model as it's hitherto formulated, I find the fundamental elements of the theory convincing. For further elaboration of what a field of sense ontology entails, see the following texts: Markus Gabriel, *Transcendental Ontology* (London & New York: Bloomsbury Academic, 2013). Markus Gabriel, *Warum es die Welt nicht gibt* (Berlin: Ullstein, 2013).

[15] For an elaboration of the cube example, see Hilary Putnam, *Ethics of Ontology* (Cambridge, MA: Harvard University Press, 2004), 33.

Objective phenomenology:
Wallace's moral meta-fiction

The ignoramus *is the fundament of transcendence.*

—Hans-Georg Gadamer

However much we come to know or think we know about the world it is
possible and sometimes desirable to try to stand back from it and take a
more reflective attitude toward our conception of the way things are.

—Barry Stroud

It is common knowledge that Wallace emerged out of an influential
movement within post-World War II American fiction, namely meta-
fiction. Meta-fiction seeks to make explicit within traditional fictional
narrative the normally merely implicit structures, mechanisms, and tropes
that are the conditions for the possibility of fiction. Readers of meta-fiction
encounter constant reminders throughout the text that what they're reading
is mediated by an Author whose particular narrative devices can service basic
manipulative goals. In other words, meta-fiction sought the *initially* radical
aim of exposing the degree to which reality and narrative are essentially and
fundamentally mediated. Thus, narrative structure, language, and the Author
of the story become essential characters of the story. Wallace developed his
fictional interests within this tradition; however, he later found its incessant
self-referentiality empty and its use of irony, which had emerged as a form of
radical social critique, had been co-opted by the-powers-that-be.[16] It had, as a
result, lost all its radical potential insofar as its self-referential moves exhibited
all the solipsistic proclivities Wallace grew to abhor. In fact, he struggled most
of his post-*Infinite Jest* career to develop a viable alternative to the empty
formalism of postmodern meta-fiction and succeeded, I think, in performing
what I call a *moral meta-fiction.* The methodology of a moral meta-fiction is
what the title of this section of the chapter calls "objective phenomenology."

Phenomenology consists in the investigation into the nature and logical
structure of human intentionality, and what appears within this intentional
structure—that is, our conscious acts are always *about* something in
particular. I can think, fear, or desire particular empirical or abstract objects,
think about states of affairs in the world, etc. Mental acts and states, that is

---

[16] For his influential take on this, see the wonderful essay in Wallace, "E Unibus Pluram:
Television and U.S. Fiction," in *A Supposedly Fun Thing I'll Never Do Again: Essays and
Arguments* (Boston: Little, Brown & Co., 1997), 21.

intentionality, though, must be directed *at* something; they must be *about* something. Thus, phenomenology pivots around this investigation into the logical structure of intentionality and *ipso facto* there emerge philosophical problems of "inside"/"outside." That is, how do I get from in here to out there? It's not difficult to see where meta-fiction pilfered many of its conceptual tools. Out of phenomenology emerge many of the perennial philosophical problems.[17] For example, consider the problem of the relation of thought and reality, related of course to the discussions above concerning the linguistic and metaphysical turns as well as being a central concern of Wallace's work.[18] How much of the structure of the world and its constituents is a projection of the conceptual and linguistic structure of human beings? Furthermore, how can we even know where our projection begins and ends?

Don Gately, a central character in *Infinite Jest*, relays an interesting joke during an AA meeting that functions as an important analogy to a fundamental problem operative within Wallace's fiction. Two fish are swimming along when they encounter another fish, who/which asks them, "Morning Boys! How's the water?!" Once the fish achieves a sufficient distance from them, one of the two fish asks the other, "What in the hell is water?" Among other things, the joke illuminates the fact that human conceptual calisthenics has infiltrated and permeated reality to such an extent that the "real intellectual adventure" consists in demarcating where precisely, or even approximately, reality begins and conceptual thought ends. But, one must first escape the cave of first-order ignorance in order to achieve the higher-order reflection on the

---

[17] It's important to note here that phenomenology has a rich and complex tradition that can't be given its due justice in the chapter. Many may in fact justifiably object that I've misrepresented phenomenology as being inherently idealist. I will bypass this issue here. Suffice it to say, however, that I do think that a majority of phenomenology does in fact lead implicitly to a weak form of idealism insofar as, whenever ontological questions emerge regarding, say, external objects, the phenomenologist plays the "bracket" card; that is, ontological questions (or questions or truth) or bracketed from the investigation into the transcendental structure of intentionality.

[18] I'm certainly not claiming that Wallace doesn't address solipsism in the phenomenological key discussed here. He most certainly does; furthermore, it forms an important thematic of his entire corpus. But, the point of this chapter seeks to underscore that Wallace also developed, if implicitly, an ontological position the methodology for which can be called an objective phenomenology of worlds. For a more traditional "inside"/"outside" problematic see the following from *Infinite Jest* in which a main character has the following reflection on a statue of Bernini, which appears in a (fictional) film called *Pre-Nuptial Agreement of Heaven and Hell*: "The whole film was from the alcoholic sandwich-bag salesman's POV [point of view], and . . . his head . . . was on-screen every moment . . . except for the four narrative minutes the alcoholic sandwich-bag salesman stood in the Vittorio's Bernini room, and the climactic statue filled the screen and pressed against all four edges. The statue, the sensuous presence of the thing, let the alcoholic sandwich-bag salesman escape himself, his tiresome ubiquitous involuted head, she saw, was the thing. The four-minute still shot maybe wasn't just a heavy-art gesture or audience-hostile herring. Freedom from one's own head, one's inescapable POV" (*IJ*, 742).

water/world—"Morning Boys! How's the world?" Objective phenomenology asks precisely this question.

Objective phenomenology operates a bit differently from orthodox phenomenology. It—objective phenomenology—investigates the logical structure of domains, worlds and states of affairs *in general*. So, while phenomenology thematizes the structure of intentionality, that is, the *aboutness* of *human mental states*, objective phenomenology thematizes the logical structure of the many domains or worlds in which humans appear and engage in activities of various sorts. As we've seen we live and move and have our being in what seems to be an infinitely complex number of domains: there's the domain of Language, Society, Government, Fiction, Physical Reality, State Fairs, Lobster Festivals, Math and Logic Classes, Relationships, University Life, Digital Worlds, Art Museums, Dentist Offices, Bathrooms, Libraries, etc. While of course each particular domain or world is describable within the language of the natural sciences, most particularly and successfully in theoretical and experimental physics, it's not the case that the mathematical language of contemporary physics exhausts the complexities and rules of these respective domains. For example, while the physics of color or the physical laws governing fluid dynamics doubtless explicate many of the complexities composing a Jackson Pollock painting, other equally as important elements of the painting slip through the clutches of physics' mathematical language. It would be strange indeed if MOMA replaced all their museum guides with physicists from NYU since the meaning of a painting is not exhausted by its inclusion or appearance within one particular domain, namely the domain of physics or the domain of art museums. Paintings can appear in what seems like an infinite number of domains, and, most importantly, these domains comprise rules, laws, expectations, norms, etc. that are *not* mere projections of human creatures. Instead, the human finds himself participating in domains the laws of which are already there and function, if you will, as the riverbed through and in which our actions flow.[19]

To get a better feel for this argumentation, let me provide something like a analogical compass, which should make it clearer what I'm getting at. Take, as an example, Duchamp's so-called "ready-mades."[20] Most art critics and Europe-in-seven-days-museum-visitors conceive of Duchamp's aesthetic motivation as something like a democratic gesture; that is, *any particular*

---

[19] I borrow this metaphor from Wittgenstein's late work *On Certainty*. Ludwig Wittgenstein, *On Certainty* (New York: Harper Perennial, 1972).

[20] Let it not go unacknowledged that, in Hilary Putnam's definition of metaphysical realism, he defines realism as the commitment to a "ready-made" world. That is, a world already constituted in such and so a manner. The task of philosophical investigation consists in identifying the one true regimented discourse that adequately ascertains this constitutive structure. See his "Why There Isn't a Ready-Made World," *Synthese* 51 (1982): 141–67.

object, regardless of its status, can be an object of art. However, I think this epistemological interpretation misses a crucial *ontological* feature of Duchamp's radicality. Here's what I mean. Duchamp's "ready-mades" are everyday objects placed within a particular physical space, an art museum, and the apparent radicality of Duchamp's Gesture, placing a toilet within an art museum, *seems* to concern the object itself; that is, anything can be a piece of art. I think this is only partly true. A more interesting thesis is the following: the true radicality of Duchamp's Gesture consists in the toilet's placement within an art museum drawing attention to the domain in which the toilet appears. What counts as "art" or what's included or excluded from the halls of an art museum is governed by stringent inclusion conditions. Duchamp's reflexive move makes explicit the constitutive rules governing the inclusion criteria within the space of an art museum. More importantly, his radical gesture makes explicit the contingency of any and all constitutive rules governing such a space. Duchamp's Gesture is ontological inasmuch as it calls attention to a domain in which things *exist* and *appear* and *perform* various functions given that space's constitutive rules. It's not merely the boring, epistemological insight that we all have different views of the same object.

Objective phenomenology then is a *logics of worlds*. Here we see that objective phenomenology also has an "inside/outside" problematic of its own. Instead of it being a problem of consciousness, however, it's more a problem of, say, configuration spaces or domains. "Configuration space" refers to the abstract space *represented* in experimental and theoretical physics. Simply stated, and indeed, not doing justice to its complexity, it goes something like this: in order to study a particular real event that occurs in the universe, the physicist represents the real time event with a mathematical model or structure that isolates certain variables, the configuration of the system. The experiment seeks to decrease the number of influences operating on the event at the time in question. In order to measure and determine the facts of the event, this configuration space is represented by mathematical models. Suppose one develops a *massive* model to represent a particular state of affairs in the universe. Let's say that model represents the physical universe at war. Now, suppose one uses a tennis court to model a real-time event in the fictional war in question. What if it starts snowing?! Does it snow on the model? Or does it snow in reality? Wallace explores this wonderful example in the famous "Eschaton" event in *Infinite Jest* (321–42). But, while configuration spaces and configurations are, of course, human inventions, highly successful ones at that, we should nonetheless not shy away from advocating their reality. That is, they exist. In fact, to my mind, theories and models about reality, given that they exist, are a way reality is.

It's important to note that *Infinite Jest* begins with Hal Incandenza, arguably the novel's main character, a tennis and intellectual prodigy who also develops a circular drug addiction, telling the Reader, "I am in here".[21] He goes on to describe in detail the situation or domain in which he's "in," the (academic) context, the room, the expectations, etc. composing the situation as such. The end of the novel, by contrast, concludes "out there," presumably reflecting Don Gately's—who's a former drug addict who plays an essential role in the novel's exploration of AA communities—escape from the cycle of Demerol addiction.[22]

---

[21] See the wonderfully comedic opening section of *Infinite Jest*, which in the novel's chronological time is actually the end (*IJ*, 3). See also a parallel passage in *The Pale King* where Lane Dean Jr., an IRS accountant working what appears to be the single most boring job ever conceived, regards his existence both in and out of work as "just going through the motions" (Wallace, *The Pale King* [New York: Little, Brown & Co., 2011], 157). The job, though, while mechanical and thoughtless in its nearly fatal boredom, offers something interesting. "One thing you learn in Rote Exams is how disorganized and inattentive most people are and how little they pay attention to what's going on outside of their sphere" (160). He describes taking Obetrol, a kind of sense- and self-awareness-inducing drug, which has the following effect: "it did make me more self-aware. If I was in a room, and had taken an Obetrol or two with a glass of water and they'd taken effect, I was now not only in the room, but I was aware that I was in the room. In fact, I remember I would often think, or say to myself, quietly but very clearly, '*I am in this room*'. It's difficult to explain this. At the time, I called it 'doubling', but I'm still not entirely sure what I meant by this, nor why it seemed so profound and cool to not only be in a room but be totally aware that I was in the room, seated in a certain easy chair in a certain position listening to a certain specific track of an album whose cover was a certain specific combination of colors and designs—being in a state of heightened enough awareness to be able to consciously say to myself, *I am in this room right now. The shadow of the foot is rotating on the east wall. The shadow is not recognizable as a foot because of the deformation of the angle of the light of the sun's position behind the sign. I am seated upright in a dark-green easy chair with a cigarette burn on the right armrest*'" (184).

[22] Circularity and geometrical structures heavily populate most of Wallace's fiction. I focus in this chapter on structural circularity or structural, geometrical shapes that impact the nature of human thought and action. For Wallace's non-fiction book on infinity and other related matters, see *Everything and More: A Compact History of* ∞. A number of pages in the book explicate the dangerous of abstraction and the tendency to become entangled in the revolving door of circularity. For example: "The dreads and dangers of abstract thinking are a big reason why we now all like to stay so busy and bombarded with stimuli all the time. Abstract thinking tends most often to strike during moments of quiet repose. As in for example the early morning, especially if you wake up slightly before your alarm goes off, when it can suddenly and for no reason occur to you that you've been getting out of bed every morning without the slightest doubt that the floor would support you. Lying there now considering the matter, it appears at least theoretically possible that some flaw in the floor's construction or its molecular integrity could make it buckle, or that even some aberrant bit of quantum flux or something could cause you to melt right through. . . . The abstract question you're lying there considering is whether you are truly justified in your confidence about the floor. [This has] happened over and over before. The principle involved is really the only way we can predict any of the phenomena we just automatically count of without having to think about them. And the vast bulk of daily life is composed of these sorts of phenomena; and without this confidence based on past experience we'd all go insane, or at least we'd be unable to function because we'd have to stop and deliberate about every last little thing. It's a fact: life as we know it would be impossible without this confidence" (Wallace, *Everything and More: A Compact History of* ∞ [New York: Norton, 2003], 14).

Wallace's fiction attempts to present and explore incomplete fictional worlds—kinds of locally structured worlds of inexhaustible reality—the completion of which requires the participation of his readers. The completion process is outsourced to his readers who, lost within an informational overload, seek to be reflectively at home in a world.[23] Most of Wallace's work, I believe, can be placed within the ancient tradition of spiritual exercises, where the goal of physics, poetry, and philosophy was to enable those who embark on the life of understanding to achieve a harmonious and reflective existence within the complex infinities of space and time. However, in the ancient tradition, the preferred means of reflection on the secrets of nature and the infinite complexity constitutive of the world consisted in thought's cosmic exile from the physical strictures of mortal life. Hence, in almost all ancient traditions, we read of exiles into the heavens where, stationed away from the riff-raff of everyday life, one can contemplate in a state of purity the wonders of the world and its peculiar occupants, human beings.[24] Wallace prevents cosmic escapades into contemplative heaven by preventing a bird's-eye view of the whole, or what Thomas Nagel called *the view from nowhere*.[25] How to combine the perspective of a particular person inside the world with an objective view of that same world, the person and his viewpoint included? How is it possible to develop a theory of totality when one's position of enunciation is *within* that totality? Human thought cannot achieve a position from which the whole and its constituent parts and interrelations gradually

---

[23] See Wallace's comments in D. T. Max's biography: "There is an ending as far as I'm concerned. Certain kind of parallel lines are supposed to start converging in such a way that an end can be projected by the reader somewhere beyond the right frame. If no such convergence or projection occurred to you, then the book's failed for you." D. T. Max, *Every Love Story is a Ghost Story* (New York: Viking, 2012), 321n19.

[24] Indeed, such a position isn't limited to the ancient world. Bertrand Russell made the following romantic remark about thought: "Remote from human passions, [the mathematical realm is a place] where pure thought can dwell as in its natural home, and where one, at least, of our nobler impulses can escape from the dreary exile of the actual world." (Bertrand Russell, *Mysticism and Logic and Other Essays [1918]* [New York: Rowman and Littlefield, 1988], 61).

[25] See Thomas Nagel, *The View from Nowhere* (Oxford: Oxford University Press, 1989). Nagel dubs this "a problem that faces every creature with the impulse and capacity to transcend its particular point of view and to conceive of the world as a whole." Nagel thinks that an objective view cannot include everything and will always be incomplete. "Reality," Nagel asserts, "is not just objective reality." For Nagel, objectivity is not a property of things. Rather, objectivity consists in an *attitude toward things*. That is, the manner of understanding things and their relations such that one seeks to describe any kind of experience or thought "from the outside," and include it in a wider account of things in which that experience or thought occupies no privileged position. Nagel claims, if I'm reading him correctly, that some things remain unaccounted for within an objective account: some things will have been left out within the account. Debussy once said of Maeterlinck that he had a "passion for the beyond," a kind of "synoptic ambition."

develop into a high-definition picture of reality. Wallace keeps us moored *within* a world, or within a domain, in all their labyrinthine complexity, stitching together what seem to be patterns and interrelations without the psychological or ontological release of definitive answers. Whether those patterns are *really* there and constitutive of reality, or whether those patterns are simply projections of a 1,360-gram meat machine, serves as a fundamental *aporia* within Wallace's fiction, and kind of, say, metaphysical skepticism.

Wallace's big TOE

The exploration of an author's contemporary reality and its seemingly herculean, interconnected patterns, and the attempt to capture and represent these underlying patterns in some kind of fictional intuition constitutes one of the aims of a form of literary fiction, namely theory of everything (TOE) or encyclopedic fiction. At 1,079 pages, 97 of which comprise 388 footnotes, *Infinite Jest* fits snugly into this tradition alongside the sprawling novels of his heroes—Thomas Pynchon's *Gravity's Rainbow*, William Gaddis's *The Recognitions*, and *JR*, James Joyce's *Ulysses* and *Finnegans Wake*—but not without the following caveat: where most TOE novels explore the effect and possibility of the mythological and metaphysical impulse of totalization, *Infinite Jest*, while being a TOE, shows the impossibility of TOEs. TOE novels are expansive in reach and seek to capture reality's infinite complexity within a particular model.[26] Unlike most encyclopedic novels, Wallace enacts a fictional critique of the metaphysics of totality, what we above called "domain reductionism." Metaphysics can be understood in this sense as *a reaching for a conception of totality*.

According to Immanuel Kant, the nature of human reason consists in its desire to propel itself out of a finite situatedness toward the "idea of absolute totality."[27] In short, *Infinite Jest* shows its readers that *the* World doesn't exist; rather, reality comprises a transfinite proliferation of domains. Worlds are

---

[26] There is perhaps an important distinction constitutive of the TOE (Theory of Everything) genre. I'm most familiar with the American TOE tradition; however, that's just an *ad hoc* feature of this chapter. One could certainly identify a LITTLE TOE genre, one in which Borges would play a prominent role. I'm focusing in this essay on the BIG TOE genre, and the American one more particularly, one in which books like *Infinite Jest*, *Gravity's Rainbow*, *Gold-Bug Variations*, *The Recognitions*, *JR*, *Something Happened*, *You Bright and Risen Angels* would most certainly appear.

[27] See Immanuel Kant, *Critique of Pure Reason* trans. Norman Kemp Smith (New York: St. Martin's, 1965), A vii. "Human reason has the peculiar fate that in one species of its knowledge it is burdened by questions which, as prescribed by the very nature of reason itself, it is not able to ignore, but which, as transcending all its powers, it is also not able to answer."

infinitely complex and transfinitely proliferating.[28] But there are certain dangers implicit within infinity and infinite regresses, dangers that were certainly not alien to Wallace. In fact, he consistently explored the concept of infinity both in his nonfiction and his fiction. Below, we'll explore two types of infinity, "bad" and "good" infinity, operative within Wallace's *Infinite Jest*.

Good and bad infinity: Morning Boys! How's the world?

He would find a way to access all of himself. He possessed nothing that anyone could ever call doubt, inside.

—David Foster Wallace

I would like to connect metaphysical pluralism to a couple of themes that occupied Wallace's work perhaps more than any other: solipsism and human freedom. The aforementioned infinite loops, recursions, and addictions in *Infinite Jest* chronicle the degree to which excessive data-gathering, addiction, annular fusion technology, and athletic training lead to a dizzying circularity from which there appears to be no escape.[29] However,

---

[28] In an important passage early in *Infinite Jest*, tennis coach Schtitt introduces a recursive tennis strategy that takes advantage of Georg Cantor's set-theoretical "paradise." The narrator claims that "Schtitt, whose knowledge of formal math is probably about equivalent to that of a Taiwanese kindergartner, nevertheless seemed to know what Hopman and van der Meer and Bollettieri seemed not to know: that locating beauty and art and magic and improvement and keys to excellence and victory in the prolix flux of match play is not a fractal matter of reducing chaos to pater. Seemed intuitively to sense that it was a matter not of reduction at all, but—perversely—of expansion, the aleatory flutter of uncontrolled, metastatic growth—each well-shot ball admitting of n possible responses, n^2 possible response to those responses, and on into what Incandenza would articulate to anyone who shared both his backgrounds as a Cantorian continuum of infinites of possible move and response, Cantorian and beautiful because *in*foliating, *contained* this diagnate infinity of infinities of choice and execution, mathematically uncontrolled but humanly *contained* bounded by the talent and imagination of self and opponent, bent in on itself by the containing boundaries of skill and imagination that brought one player finally down, that kept both from winning, that made it, finally a game, these boundaries of self" (*IJ*, 82).

[29] The development of the narrative pivots around what seems like an endless number of circularities, regresses, double binds, infinites, etc. Here's just a short list: Orin (the brother of Hal Incandenza, arguably the main character of the novel) tracing "∞"on the backs of his female sexual conquests; annular fusion ("a type of fusion that can produce waste that's fuel for a process whose waste is fuel for the fusion" [*IJ*, 572]); the film "Infinite Jest," which lulls its viewers into the fatal act of watching said film over and over again; drug addiction (most of which occurs in the novel's two main settings, Enfield Tennis Academy and Ennet House, a rehabilitation center for drug and alcoholic addiction), which explores the constant relapses and regresses of mechanical drug behavior where choice seems irrelevant; tennis coach Schtitt's mention of logician and mathematician Georg Cantor's set-theory during an exploration of his (Schtitt's) tennis strategies.

Wallace offers liberation from the vortex of circularity. I want to suggest that, in Wallace's work, liberation from "bad" infinite regresses consists in the higher-order act of *choosing* what one does and doesn't pay attention to within the operative domains in which we're participating. We can be robotically manipulated by the rules and laws of whatever world we find ourselves in; or, we can tarry with the infinite complexity by breaking the cyclical loop of infinite regresses and self-referentiality by means of higher-order detachment from the world that frees us so that we can thematize its structures and laws.[30] These "bad" infinities are represented in the aforementioned loops, recursions, addictions, mechanical training, and circular themes littered throughout *Infinite Jest*.

The film "Infinite Jest" propels viewers into a regressive feedback loop of incessant viewing until the viewer simply dies. This is the revolving door of solipsism. However, there's another *Infinite Jest*, namely the novel itself, which represents a "good" infinity, an outward expansion beyond mechanical repetition. Moreover, answers to fundamental questions of the novel take place *outside* the temporal boundaries of the novel and force the Reader to enter the space of reasons and connect the dots. Wallace's moral meta-fiction absorbs the Reader not into his (Wallace's) own consciousness in order to alert the Reader to the fact and structure of subjective or authorial mediation; rather, while remaining within the orbit of meta-fiction, Wallace sublimates its narcissism and all-encompassing repetitive vortex of signifiers, into a *moral meta-fiction*, one concerned with inviting the Reader into particular domains not of his (the author's) making. Once the Reader inhabits a particular world, Wallace issues an imperative, "Pay attention!" or "Look around! See the extra-ordinariness and infinite complexity of the ordinary and finite." In this sense Wallace embodies a nuanced version of Socrates, not because he engages discursively with interlocutors to discover the *logoi* of concepts and definitions, but rather the *logoi* of what Wittgenstein called "forms of life."

Wallace's ontology was a regional ontology. Yet, within the regional were both an infinitesimal depth and a transfinite breadth. He invited you, the Reader, into domains already constituted in such and so a manner, and begged you to pay attention to their abyssal complexity. In his now famous commencement address to the Kenyon College graduates in 2005, now titled

---

[30] In *The Pale King*, "What it felt like was a sort of emergence, however briefly, from the fuzziness and drift of my life in that period. As though I was a machine that suddenly realized it was a human being and didn't have to go through the motions it was programmed to perform over and over. It also had to do with paying attention . . . what became more intense was my awareness of my own part in it, that I could pay real attention to it" (184).

This Is Water, Wallace explored this idea. He reminds the audience repeatedly that the goal of any education worthy of the name "isn't really about the capacity to think, but rather about the choice of what to think about"[31]; "that education can reveal a (properly) Copernican revolution in which humans, immediate experience to the contrary, are *not* the center of the universe. The opposite view, that we are the center of the universe and existence, is our default setting, hardwired into our boards at birth. Think about it: There is no experience you've had that you were not at the absolute center of." He goes on to underscore the difficulty involved in avoiding lapsing into solipsism, that is, the tendency to attribute everything to a function of one's projectile cognition: "it is extremely difficult to stay alert and attentive instead of getting hypnotized by the constant monologue inside your head" (47). Education, then, consists in teaching students that learning how to think "really means learning how to exercise some control over *how* and *what* you think. It means being conscious and aware enough to *choose* what you pay attention to and to *choose* how you construct meaning from experience. Because if you cannot or will not exercise this kind of choice in adult life, you will be totally hosed . . . how to keep from going through your comfortable, prosperous, respectable adult life dead, unconscious, a slave to your head and to your natural default setting of being uniquely, completely, imperially alone, day in and day out" (47, 48). He later claims, "But, if you've really learned how to think, how to pay attention, then you will know you have other options. It will actually be within your power to experience a crowded, hot, slow, consumer-hell-type situation as not only meaningful, but sacred, on fire with the same force that lit the stars—compassion, love, the subsurface unity of all things" (57).

Wallace's use of Ludwig Wittgenstein concerns not merely the focus on "meaning as use" or the construction and analysis of logical space. Rather, this passages show that he takes seriously the idea of *showing* versus *saying*. To speak or say what's wonderful spoils the wonder; Wallace can only invite you and gesture toward the infinite complexity of the domains he explores.[32] He sometimes seems to function as a philosophical tour guide of the various domains he chose to explore.

---

[31] Wallace, *This Is Water: Some Thoughts, Delivered on a Significant Occasion, about Living a Compassionate Life* (New York: Little, Brown, & Co., 2009), 41.

[32] A good example of this occurs at the conclusion of Terrence Malick's 2012 film, *To the Wonder*, in which Marina (Olga Kurylenko), wandering in a field sensing the presence of an unidentified observer, invites the viewer (us) to follow her and explore the extraordinariness of the ordinary. The film concludes with another reference to Cathedral Saint-Michel in Normandy, or "The Wonder." Also, see the conclusion of Wallace's short story "Forever Overhead" in *Brief Interviews with Hideous Men*.

Philosophy and fiction, for Wallace, appear to be therapeutic activities; however, not because, as Wittgenstein thought, philosophy cures the hubris and gullibility of human reason to mistake linguistic and grammatical complexities for metaphysical entities. On the contrary, philosophy and fiction can provide the "kick" to propel the person into a reflexive relation to his or her default settings, both epistemological and ontological, in order that the worlds and situations in which we find ourselves, and their constitutive rules and laws, are thematized and made an object of reflection. Most importantly, higher-order reflection on the structure and laws of domains exposes the contingency of those constitutive rules. Philosophy and fiction can illuminate the contingency of the formal structures and laws governing all domains. This is precisely what makes philosophy and fiction so radical.

Perhaps it's a stretch, but I think it's at least interesting to think of Wallace's implicit metaphysics as "quantum," that is, a kind of *quantum fiction*. As contemporary theoretical physicists improve and develop the standard model, we're seeing radical alternatives emerging concerning what's most constitutive of physical reality. Some propose that the most fundamental reality is not in fact particles or individuals things; rather, the most fundamental level of reality is intangible: fields, relations, or waves. I'm proposing that we extend this quantum logic to domains in the sense defined above. Both the "manifest" and "scientific" images posit individual things, whether macroscopic or microscopic respectively, as the most fundamental constituents of reality. However, some avant-garde views posit fields or waves in which individual objects appear. However, these fields aren't in any sense of the word *things*. Likewise, what is most fundamental metaphysically, on the account sketched above, are not the individual objects that appear in domains but rather the domains themselves.

Domains comprise interdependent individuals interfacing according to evolving rules and laws whose governance function as the rails along which society moves. The most fundamental components are not the elements, the individuals, nor the particles; rather, the worlds, fields, relations, networks, etc. in which they appear and perform are what's most fundamental in the many worlds of Wallace's fiction. It's important again to stress that worlds are not empirical objects. Physicists like to think of the physical universe as an empirical object, most recently as a wave-function. However, worlds on this conception are no things, they are *no-thing* perhaps "less than nothing." To conclude with the conclusion of the film *Now You See Me*, Wallace could have said this to you as well: "Come in close. Closer. Now you know the secret . . . on the count of three open your eyes and tell me what you see. 1, 2 . . . [Fade to black: No-thing]."

14

Does Language Fail Us? Wallace's Struggle with Solipsism

Patrick Horn

We all suffer alone in the real world; true empathy is impossible.

—David Foster Wallace[1]

A solipsism of sorts

A struggle with solipsism haunts much of David Foster Wallace's writings, interviews, and speeches. In a 1993 interview with Larry McCaffrey, he lamented the inadequacy of language for any genuine compassionate exchange and pronounced the consequences: "true empathy is impossible."[2] In this same well-known and oft-quoted early interview, Wallace offered an account of Wittgenstein's *Tractatus* as a kind of acceptance of the truth of solipsism ("Which divides us, metaphysically and forever, from the external world").[3] Then, he said to McCaffrey that in later writing the *Philosophical Investigations* Wittgenstein provided us with "the single most comprehensive and beautiful argument against solipsism that's ever been made."[4] And yet, Wallace bemoaned that a sort of communal solipsism persists:

> Wittgenstein argues that for language even to be possible, it must always be a function of relationships between persons (that's why he spends so much time arguing against the possibility of a "private language"). So he makes language dependent on human community, but unfortunately

---

1   Larry McCaffrey, "An Expanded Interview with David Foster Wallace" (1993), in Stephen J. Burn (ed.), *Conversations with David Foster Wallace* (Jackson, MS: University Press of Mississippi, 2012), 22.
2   Ibid.
3   Ibid., 44.
4   Ibid.

we're still stuck with the idea that there is this world of referents out there that we can never really join or know because we're stuck in here, in language, even if we're at least all in here together.[5]

We may not have the external world, suggested Wallace, but at least we have each other. Or, at least we have language, which allows us to gesture toward one another. But we only have gestures, or hauntings, of reality. We can never experience or encounter real empathy, for example. The best that we can hope for in art is thus to share, through "a sort of *generalization* of suffering," a haunting connection with that suffering.[6] Wittgenstein's "beautiful argument" then is an ultimately futile attempt to solve the perennial problem of solipsism; for Wallace, the inadequacy of language cannot be overcome. We must accept that, because we are "stuck in here, in language," sureness about anything ultimately eludes us. And Wallace is clever enough to appreciate that this lack of certainty is as applicable to ironic perspectives as it is to simple and sincere perspectives. Our connection to both irony and sincerity is hauntingly tenuous. And so, in an age in which only irony seems real, Wallace set out to show us that the experience of irony is only a haunting and that we are still able to experience the hauntings of sincere moral and religious language.

Missing the Wittgensteinian point

While Wallace wants to utilize the work of Wittgenstein, there are aspects of Wittgenstein's work that he seems to ignore. In what follows, I will suggest that Wallace neglected two central features of Wittgenstein's work, and in so doing failed to appreciate that his own writing did considerably more than haunt us with sincere moral and religious language. Here is a brief look at what will be dealt with more fully in what follows.

First, Wallace overlooked the distinctive way in which Wittgenstein approached the question of solipsism, leading Wallace to a conclusion that Wittgenstein himself would have been unable to make sense of, namely, that language ultimately fails to connect us to reality. The first feature that Wallace neglected is Wittgenstein's emphasis (both early and late) that he is not practicing philosophy per usual; he is not offering an argument, a doctrine, or a theory against solipsism. He did not think that it would make sense to offer a counter argument to solipsism because he did not think that

---

[5] Ibid.
[6] Ibid., 22.

the problem of solipsism could be sensibly posed in the first place.[7] Solipsism runs into the logical problem that people live and speak together in a shared world. If one accepts this speaking together in shared lives as constitutive of any language use, then it follows that any attempt to state the problem of solipsism, that is, that I can only be certain of the existence of my own mind and nothing else of the world around me, is already a logical muddle. What is this world in which our minds are said to be metaphysically severed from if not that in which we live and speak together and attempt to state philosophical problems using our minds? If we counter solipsism with a theory or an argument, we only perpetuate the muddle that requires us to reject the very ground that makes possible its own statement. Wallace failed to recognize that Wittgenstein's approach to solipsism never ventured into that muddle because his work never took the form of offering a counter theory; Wittgenstein focused instead on the logical difficulties in trying to state the problem of solipsism. Wallace thus accepted the sense of a problem that Wittgenstein tried to show could never be sensibly stated.

The second feature neglected by Wallace is the later Wittgenstein's attempts to show us that cogent language is not limited to object language. The early Wittgenstein excluded religious and moral language from his investigations because he assumed that logic is by definition the logic of objects and cannot be sensibly applied to moral and religious language, which is not about objects. While the early Wittgenstein never denied the importance of moral and religious language, he did seem to think that these language uses were struggles to say what, logically speaking (and, philosophically speaking, for the early Wittgenstein), cannot be said. He later came to see that this early attempt to limit the logical use of language to the language of objects was confused because ordinary language itself is not limited to simple object-talk. Ordinary moral and religious language is used and understood in our lives without having to prove the objective presence of some other reality outside of our own, and thus it is not a struggle to say what cannot be said. Moral and religious language can be perfectly cogent as it stands. Wallace, however, shared the early Wittgensteinian perspective that moral and religious language is not object language. Wallace took this to mean that such language use must necessarily fall short of communicating anything real because we are stuck in language; he never appreciated that, for the later Wittgenstein, the attempt to speak of some sort of reality that is independent of what we understand through language is nonsense. This

---

[7] "The reason why these problems are posed is that the logic of our language is misunderstood" (Ludwig Wittgenstein, *Tractatus Logico-Philosophicus*, trans. C. K. Ogden (London: Routledge and Kegan Paul Ltd., 1922), 3.

deficiency in Wallace's appreciation of the later Wittgenstein meant that skepticism concerning moral and religious language went unchecked in his work, though Wallace nonetheless wanted us to experience the hauntings of moral and religious language.

These observations of Wallace's neglect of Wittgenstein will bring us to the main task of the chapter, that is, to demonstrate that Wallace's short story, "Good Old Neon," does not simply haunt us with sincere empathy but rather robustly connects us to the reality of the moral virtue of empathy. I will thus demonstrate that in this story Wallace displayed the true empathy that he thought was impossible, and through this story we can come to a better appreciation of the nature of moral and religious concepts. Furthermore, Wallace made other remarks about religious and moral ways of living. These remarks help us to see that the reality of moral virtues such as empathy, though not justified or explained by knowledge and the intellect, is not a haunting ethereal reality that lies just beyond the human grasp. In both "Good Old Neon" and these general remarks, Wallace's use of moral and religious language shows that moral and religious reality is seen and fully understood in the very language in which Wallace claims that we are stuck, cutoff from reality. And thus I will show that Wallace's own work demonstrates the invalidity of his solipsistic thesis that language fails to connect the community to reality.

Wallace's challenge to solipsism

For all his admiration of the later Wittgenstein, Wallace seems to have been much more influenced by the early Wittgenstein. Nonetheless, I think that Wallace, like many analytic philosophers, did not grasp the peculiar role of philosophy in Wittgenstein's early work. A short foray into Wittgenstein's work is needed to make this point.

A Wittgensteinian interlude

In the preface to the *Tractatus*, Wittgenstein wrote that he had no interest in whether his thoughts in the work agreed with past philosophers, and in proposition 4.112 he says:

> Philosophy aims at the logical clarification of thoughts.
>
> Philosophy is not a body of doctrine but an activity.
>
> A philosophical work consists essentially of elucidations.

Philosophy does not result in "philosophical propositions", but rather in the clarification of propositions.[8]

His work is thus not a doctrine or a proposed theory that you can either agree or disagree with. It is an activity, an exercise in clarification, that is more or less successful in its efforts to clarify but it is never a set of propositions that one can either prove or disprove, assent to or not. For Wittgenstein, the only proper judgment to be made of the *Tractatus* is the degree to which its propositions successfully elucidate the nature of speaking about objects in the world. The work's special elucidatory propositions were intended to be self-evident so that their truth, like a tautology, is incontrovertible. It wouldn't make any sense to contradict them. (He even admitted that they are "nonsensical" in the special sense that you cannot *determine* whether they have sense.)[9] Their purpose is to remind us of the nature of language, which is self-evidently displayed whenever we say something about objects (things) in the world. The logic of language is the logic of things in the world. And thus the very activity of speaking about things in the world entails the reality of that world. If the world is not accessible to us, then speaking can never make any sense. Therefore, solipsism can never properly be posed as a problem without dislocating the logic of language itself. Even so, these observations are not a theory of the nature of reality. They are intended to be incontrovertible, logical elucidations of language and reality.

Wittgenstein emphasized again in his later work this understanding of the nature of philosophy as an exercise in elucidation: "Philosophy just puts everything before us, and neither explains nor deduces anything.—Since everything lies open to view, there is nothing to explain."[10] And: "The work of the philosopher consists in marshaling recollections for a particular purpose."[11] Thus in both the early and late works, Wittgenstein rejected the traditional philosophical approach of tackling a perennial problem as a puzzle to be solved. Instead, he investigated the conditions and assumptions that give rise to these problems and tried to show the reader that they are not puzzles awaiting brilliant solutions: "the reason why these problems are posed is that the logic of our language is misunderstood."[12] Wittgenstein

---

[8] Ibid., 49, § 4.112.
[9] Ibid., 151, § 6.54: "My propositions serve as elucidations in the following way: anyone who understands me eventually recognizes them as nonsensical, when he has used them—as steps—to climb up beyond them."
[10] Ludwig Wittgenstein, *Philosophical Investigations*, trans. G. E. M. Anscombe, eds. P. M. S. Hacker and Joachim Schulte, revised 4th edn (Chichester, West Sussex: Wiley-Blackwell, 2009), 55e, § 126.
[11] Ibid., 55e, § 127.
[12] *Tractatus*, 3.

wanted philosophers to see the logic of our language, or as he later put it, "the grammar" that we employ in our various language games. If we pay attention to this grammar, we can readily see that certain traditional metaphysical problems, like the traditional problem of solipsism, are flights of fancy that have left the ordinary contexts in which language use has its home. We can come to see that posing these perennial philosophical problems takes us away from understanding what is said in ordinary contexts.

The later Wittgenstein also began to appreciate the sense in which all ordinary uses of language, not just language about objects, are in perfect logical order without having to prove the existence of some external referent. Religious and moral speaking is thus not an attempt to say something illogical, or to say what cannot be said, as he seemed to think in his early work. In their ordinary contexts, religious and moral terms have a home, though admittedly, the fact that language is not one thing makes for complications and great potential for misunderstanding. Yet, because for Wittgenstein the fact that language is notoriously elusive and that a single word can mean many different things (sometimes even the opposite thing) in different contexts, it does not follow that language as a whole fails (or falls short) of some intended goal of accurately and dependably communicating every feature of reality, independent of personal and cultural mores and preferences. Language logically cannot have such a goal, no matter how badly we may want it to. We, and our language, are a part of reality, so language logically cannot serve the role of independently communicating to us a reality that is independent of ourselves and our language. Wallace seems to have appreciated that there is a confused dualism in Modernism's attempted bifurcation of language and reality. But he was unable to escape the procrustean choice: either language is adequate or it is inadequate.

What Wallace struggled to bring into relief (along with many other postmodern writers and philosophers) are the philosophical observations that follow from the recognition of a confused dualism in these expectations of language. If philosophical dualism is confused (not wrong but, rather, nonsensical), then language has never sensibly had the metaphysical goal of conveying the whole of reality. Some postmodernists acted as if they had made some new discovery about language but if the "discovery" is correct, then it cannot be a new fact about language. The child's exclamation in *The Emperor's New Clothes* is not a discovery. It is simply the statement of the obvious when people would prefer to maintain certain pretensions. If these postmodern observations are correct, then language has *never* been about communicating some reality beyond the human one. And thus language's "failure" to do so is not a failure that we can make sense of. It is a failure that is more akin to "failed" contemporary attempts to prove and to disprove the existence of God. These are not failures in any meaningful sense. They "fail" only because they are themselves confused efforts.

Wallace's reading of Wittgenstein thus stopped short. He embraced the notion from the early Wittgenstein of a realm beyond our grasp but he did not seem to appreciate that Wittgenstein's work, early and late, was not an argument against solipsism. Had he embraced this radical feature of Wittgenstein's philosophical work as elucidatory, he would have realized that Wittgenstein was trying to show us that the skeptical problem of solipsism never gets off the ground. Wittgenstein does not mean to suggest that the struggle is not genuine; rather, the struggle is peculiarly the struggle that it is because it entails confusions and entanglements that have muddled our thinking. His work is an effort to clear up the confusion and disentangle our thoughts: "What is your aim in philosophy?—to show the fly the way out of the fly-bottle."[13] This is quite different from claiming to have provided an argument or theory that solves the problem of solipsism. A theory proposed as a solution to a problem assumes that the problem has a logical sense. In Wittgenstein's approach, the problem is not assumed to have a sense. On the contrary, an investigation into the use of language reveals that the skeptical gap between the mind and the external world, the gap needed to make sense of the problem of solipsism, is seen to be an illusion. The notion of a mind separated out from the world is an illusory picture. The word "mind" is inextricably linked to the concept of a world. In fact, there is no ordinary use of the word "mind" that does *not* entail a world with people perceiving things and relating to one another in various ways. Thus, strictly speaking, there can be no problem of solipsism because the statement of the problem requires imagining a concept (a mind without a world) that is not found in the ordinary course of our lives.

Wallace, solipsism, and "Good Old Neon"

Wallace, by contrast, struggled with solipsism as a problem to be confronted and overcome by producing, at best, haunting moments of sincerity. "Good Old Neon" is perhaps his most concentrated effort to tackle the problem of solipsism, and we find there, inimical to Wittgenstein, the clear expression of skepticism about our capacity to connect with one another:

> You already know the difference between the size and speed of everything that flashes through you and the tiny inadequate bit of it all you can ever let anyone know. As though inside you is this enormous room full of

---

[13] *Philosophical Investigations*, 110ᵉ, § 309.

what seems like everything in the whole universe at one time or another and yet the only parts that get out have to somehow squeeze out through one of those tiny keyholes you see under the knob in older doors. As if we are all trying to see each other through these tiny keyholes.[14]

Poignantly revealing the nature of his personal, life-long, philosophical struggle with solipsism, Wallace tells us the story of Neal. Neal was a guy that Wallace purportedly knew in high school, and this story was an attempt "to reconcile what this luminous guy had seemed like from the outside with whatever on the interior must have driven him to kill himself in such a dramatic and doubtlessly painful way."[15] The tale is thus a sort of experiment in empathy, a test to see if the loneliness of solipsism can be lessened. If Wallace could successfully connect what he knew about Neal to a plausible account of Neal's emotional struggles, then he would have made accessible that generalized notion of suffering that he spoke about with McCaffrey. The problem for Wallace is that empathy involves a sentimental relation to another. In order for this effort to be successful, Wallace would need to delve into the trustworthiness of sentimentality: Is it possible to share in Neal's suffering when Wallace's own understanding of Neal necessarily labors beneath an unknowing and uncertain sentimentality? Will sentimentality enable him to make that connection or will it make impossible any connection to a generalized notion of suffering?

Two basic sorts of sentimentality are addressed in "Good Old Neon." The first is the sentimentality expressed in the word "happy" when used to describe the yuppie that has everything but isn't "happy." Neal is keenly aware of the skewered sentimentality in this notion:

I was in regional advertising at the time in Chicago, having made the jump from media buyer for a large consulting firm, and at only twenty-nine I'd made creative associate, and verily as they say I was a fair-haired boy and on the fast track but wasn't happy at all, whatever *happy* means, but of course I didn't say this to anybody because it was such a cliché—"Tears of a Clown", "Richard Cory", etc.—and the circle of people who seemed important to me seemed much more dry, oblique and contemptuous of clichés than that, and so of course I spent all my time trying to get them to think I was dry and jaded as well, doing things like yawning and looking at my nails and saying things like, "*Am I happy?* is one of those questions that, if it has got to be asked, more or less dictates its own answer."[16]

---

[14] Wallace, "Good Old Neon," in *Oblivion* (New York: Little, Brown & Co., 2004), 178.
[15] Ibid., 181.
[16] Ibid., 142.

This is a sort of typical postmodern target. The plight of the modern bourgeois consciousness is relentlessly ironized with wit and razor sharp logic: The man who has everything he ever wanted is not happy; isn't he the most pitiful man of all. The irony multiplies through the clever Neal, who, with impressive mental ferocity, thoroughly and mercilessly deconstructs his own pathetic plight of deceitful living:

> The fraudulence paradox was that the more time and effort you put into trying to appear impressive or attractive to other people, the less impressive or attractive you felt inside—you were a fraud. And the more of a fraud you felt like, the harder you tried to convey an impressive or likable image of yourself so that other people wouldn't find out what a hollow, fraudulent person you really were. Logically, you would think that the moment a supposedly intelligent nineteen-year-old became aware of this paradox, he'd stop being a fraud and just settle for being himself (whatever that was) because he'd figured out that being a fraud was a vicious infinite regress that ultimately resulted in being frightened, lonely, alienated, etc. But here was the other, higher-order paradox, which didn't even have a form or name—I didn't, I couldn't.[17]

In passages like this one, we see that Wallace was a postmodernist like so many other authors, though perhaps more thoroughly so because his characters often engage in the arduous work of a hyper-intensive self-deconstruction.

But, of course, Wallace furnished an additional twist, the sort of move that he often made, leading some critics to accuse him of being guilty of the very sort of sentimentality that he ironized. Wallace revealed in the story that Neal's story is one that he (Wallace) imagined so that we are made explicitly aware that the relentless mental ferocity used to deconstruct "Neal's" fraudulence was really Wallace's own mental ferocity and not Neal's. This meta-fictive move is a familiar literary trope among postmodern writers used to remind readers that all language use is recursive, that is, that all speaking and writing is the product of a conscious self. But, interestingly, Wallace used this consciously revealed self, the author himself, to issue (and here is the twist) a moral rebuke at the end of the story:

> David Wallace trying, if only in the second his lids are down, to somehow reconcile what this luminous guy had seemed like from the outside with whatever on the interior must have driven him to kill himself in such a dramatic and doubtlessly painful way—with David

[17] Ibid., 147.

Wallace also fully aware that the cliché that you can't ever truly know what's going on inside somebody else is hoary and insipid and yet at the same time trying very consciously to prohibit that awareness from mocking the attempt or sending the whole line of thought into the sort of inbent spiral that keeps you from ever getting anywhere (considerable time having passed since 1981, of course, and David Wallace having emerged from years of literally indescribable war against himself with quite a bit more firepower than he'd had at Aurora West), the realer, more enduring and sentimental part of him commanding that other part to be silent as if looking it levelly in the eye and saying, almost aloud, "Not another word."[18]

Wallace rebuked the very part of himself that had provided this clever and vicious undoing of Neal. And the part that does the rebuking is the part of himself that Wallace wrote is more "enduring and sentimental," the second sort of sentimentality.

The result turns the whole project of ruthless, brutal, and endless irony upon its head. Irony becomes an object of irony. But the most profound feature of this ironizing of irony is that it rests, in Wallace's story, not on cleverness and mental ferocity, but on the enduring and sentimental ordinary self. Wallace posited a nonmetaphysical basis for moral speaking. He participated in, but did not remain with, the clever and rational deconstruction of the established (or metaphysical) self. Rather than reveling in the solipsistic trope of endless play, the ordinary self speaks authoritatively, but only after the metaphysical self has been unmasked as an illusion. We shall return to the question of whether Wallace simultaneously deconstructed the ordinary self with the double entendre, "Not another word," but for now let us contemplate the fact that this more enduring self was allowed to speak an authoritative word, rebuking the insensitive and glib imaginings that Wallace provided of the mental struggles of Neal.

This seems to me to accomplish at least two things. First, irony without end (solipsism without a hint of sincerity) is shown to be itself a kind of sentimentality that is not entirely unlike the sentimentality of the yuppie who is not "happy." The underlying assumption of the yuppie's sentimentality is that the self can, with an appropriate amount of vim and vigor, create a life full of assured meaning. The modern self is said to do this by virtue of any number of metaphysical assumptions about the nature of reality. Reality and Truth are held in place firmly enough by these assumptions to enable the individual to be certain about the nature of the world and the truth of

---

[18] Ibid., 181.

her values and thus confidently live a life of meaning. Yuppie "happiness" involves trusting a picture (the rational self who works hard, applies a rational set of moral values to that work, and thus deserves and receives social and economic success, good physical health, and psychological peace and contentment) that is assumed to have rational justification. But the picture lacks rational justification because it is an illusion; there are numerous examples of people who work hard, are morally responsible, have common sense, and yet who never enjoy contentment. Wallace does not overthrow the fundamental revelation of the postmodern era, that is, that the emperor of Western Metaphysics wears no clothes (or more specifically, that metaphysical assumptions require one to embrace an all-encompassing illusion about the nature of reality), but he does show that the endless irony of mainstream postmodernism itself depends upon a sentimental trust in the nature of the clever and rational author (an illusory metaphysical self) to deconstruct, without end, the nature of human life and its attempts to posit meaning. Endless irony not only fails as a source of assured meaning and certainty, as indeed its suppliers happily admit, but it fails as an approach to the question of meaning by its own standards: it logically cannot do what it purports to do, that is, decisively deconstruct human meaning making without sentimental reliance upon human faculties, that is, the distant, metaphysical, and rational self.

Wallace's second accomplishment with this ending, "Not another word," is that moral sincerity arrives on the scene in the form of an empathetic connection to the beleaguered Neal. Ultimately, Wallace used solipsistic irony (the clever and distressing picture of Neal) to make possible the haunting response of sincerity. And this is Wallace's challenge to solipsism: solipsism does not have enough ground to eradicate the hauntings of sincerity. However, as we have already seen, Wallace arrived at this position without an appreciation for Wittgenstein's attempt to show us that solipsism does not have any ground (or sense) at all. This lack of appreciation for the groundlessness of solipsism, as we shall see in the next section, leaves the door open for skepticism about moral and religious language.

Wallace's skepticism about moral language

"Not another word" does indeed serve as a double entendre that expresses both the moral authority described above and the inadequacy of language, that is, that no words can be said in this attempt to empathetically connect with Neal. Wallace thereby reaffirmed that, even in the presence of a haunting sincerity, solipsism, too, still haunts us. The moral rebuke in "Not another word" is for Wallace, at best, a *gesture* toward sincerity that is unable to connect us to real empathy. The limits of language help us to understand "why it feels so good to break down and cry in front of others, or to laugh, or speak in tongues, or chant in Bengali—it's not English anymore, it's not getting squeezed through any hole."[19] And so Wallace was unable to posit the ordinary self without a simultaneously clever undermining (deconstruction) of the ordinary self. The "realer self" was unable to address the less real self without also including some doubts about the adequacy of moral language.

But what did Wallace want moral language to do? Did he want it to assert authority the way that gravity asserts its factuality? Did he want some sort of independent experiment that would resolve the matter of whether real empathy is possible? Are we really in a perpetual state of uncertainty concerning our moral values without this independent verification? Do we genuinely doubt whether the kidnapping and torture of children in Ohio is immoral? Are moral values, always and forever, uncertain because we can never conduct an independent check to see if our moral judgments are really describing reality? This insistence that language must be either adequate or inadequate rests on the illusion of a gap between language and reality. In those places in our lives where moral values have their purchase, the question of whether the moral statement reaches reality is absurd. The absurdity is clearest in those cases where raising doubts about a moral judgment is itself seen to be immoral, as in cases of abuse, oppression, and genocide: "Can we really say it was absolutely immoral?" In the face of such horrors, that question is an immoral denial of reality. And, of course, Wallace would have agreed because his characterization of language as inadequate depends not on how we actually speak and live but upon philosophical language, a metaphysical picture, that is, a world of objects that language can reference. It is a picture that his works thoroughly undermine, and yet, the persistence of solipsistic skepticism in his philosophical reflections needs this picture.

Wallace said that "true empathy is impossible" but what he is trying to say here is not possible; it is illogical, an illusion created by a confused use of language. His use of the phrase is supported only by a modern Cartesian dualism in which the skeptical thesis is accepted that unless there is some way in which I experience the same experience of the sufferer, then I cannot truly be empathetic to the sufferer's suffering. True empathy is distorted when it is thought of in this way as forever and metaphysically separated from us. If Cartesian dualism is rejected as an illusion, as well it should be because in this case the ordinary use of "empathy" never in any circumstance suggests that the body of the empathetic one is the same body as the sufferer, then the

[19] Ibid., 179.

skeptical thesis must also be rejected as nonsensical. And thus the ordinary use of "true empathy" retains its full force in the community of language users. True empathy recognizes that under different circumstances another's sufferings could be your own and in that experience of recognition one may express sympathy and/or compassion for the sufferer. True empathy is not just an enduring ghost; we see examples of it in our ordinary lives and in the literature that is all around us (arrestingly present in Wallace's own works). When we turn it into a metaphysical problem and suggest that we can only gesture at its reality, we distort it. We become obsessed with the question of how we can *speak* of true empathy so that our attention shifts from talk of true empathy to talk of how we can talk of true empathy. Such a discussion, as we have seen, led Wallace to deny the very possibility of true empathy.

Wallace, faced with the seeming conclusion that the only way to avoid falling into skepticism, nihilism, or solipsism, is to resign oneself to *gestures* at empathy, failed to appreciate that the response of resignation is parasitic on the illusion that the primary relation between a person and moral reality is an independent and rationally determined connection between language and reality. If one accepts that our relation to reality is not an independent, rational investigation delineated according to the human capacity to systematize names and objects, then we are free to subject our rational processes to other values. The subjugation of the intellect to love, for example, is not necessarily a choice made through rational deliberation; we may describe it as a calling, or a religious mission, or a moral demand, or a passionate love, or a childlike trust. A person who lives this way may not even be able to offer an intellectual defense of their lives and their commitment to certain values. An intellectual account of this way of living may describe the source of such values as Mystery (a placeholder for those who give intellectual accounts of religious and moral living but appreciate that sociological and cultural explanations are often unable to fully account for a practitioner's motivations).[20] Wittgenstein spoke of a

---

[20] I do not mean to suggest that history, sociology, cultural studies, etc. have no contribution to make in our understanding of religion and morality. I am merely pointing out that these intellectual accounts do not necessarily serve as explanations or justifications for the practitioners. An intellectual account that does justice to *that* fact will need to note that the source of the practice for the practitioner (such as "God" or "Truth") is mysterious from an intellectual perspective. In the following pages I use "Mystery" with a capital "M" as a sort of general placeholder for the source of people's religious and moral practices. I am not entirely comfortable with this term. I am trying to use it as a conceptual/intellectual holding place to help nonreligious people understand something about religious devotion. Mystery is reflective of the human condition, not an object to be investigated. I don't think that it makes sense to worship Mystery (at least in the way I am using this term); one can only worship God (or Allah or the Wiccan Goddess) in and in response to Mystery. My use of the term here risks re-instantiating the very solipsistic skepticism (with all of its endless irony) that I am trying to show is an illusion.

language-game in this context: "it is not based on grounds. It is not reasonable (or unreasonable). It is there—like our life."[21] Practitioners thus may be unable to explain feelings and acts of empathy, but their lives may nonetheless show that they extol these values above knowledge and intelligence. Further, one may come to appreciate that the intellect cannot offer a justification for this extolling. If love, for example, is said by such a person to be the source of empathy and all other values, then love is the condition and ground of all attempts at justification and can hardly be an object of justification itself. This would mean that the extolling of love above all else, from an intellectual perspective, is a mysterious occurrence, neither reasonable nor unreasonable.

The fact that deep commitments to moral and religious values can be a mysterious occurrence tempts us to think that these values lie beyond our ability to authentically communicate in language. Further, the postmodern fascination with the "limits" of language places confused expectations on our language, expectations which can only be supported by the very metaphysics that postmodernism is supposed to have driven away.[22] When the illusions are accepted as illusions, then ordinary language is allowed to retain the force it has in the community; there is no need to haltingly apply our words on the perception that language is inadequate, since the general skeptical thesis is shown to be itself a product of metaphysical illusions. Our seeing "only in part" the nature of the world and reality is not a failure of language; it is not a failure of anything. Talk of that which lies beyond our grasp is not a dead end when we appreciate that what is communicated is so by means of indirect communication in language. "In part" expresses *in language* a central Mystery of human existence, a condition of our existence, not a shortcoming of what we might have otherwise had. There is no denying the fact that we use language ("heaven," "the transcendent," "the eternal forms") that tempts us to think that our religious and moral truths exist more purely in another nonhuman dimension. But the sense of such talk ("we know in part," "Mystery," "the unknown") is found in the way that it is mediated in the context of human life. We can then begin to appreciate the nature of moral and religious language. For example, justice is not present (*Dike* leaves earth to live beside her father *Zeus* on Mount Olympus) when war and disease permeate the earth. In Plato's words it is "the other side of the sky." In such cases justice is not present, but its reality is understood in and through the language that calls for an end to wars and disease. Its reality is a longing that may come to birth—a longing

---

[21] Ludwig Wittgentein, *On Certainty* (New York: Harper & Row, 1969), 72ᵉ, § 559.

[22] The most thorough philosophical account of this phenomenon can be found in D. Z. Phillips's writings on Richard Rorty in D. Z. Phillips, *Faith After Foundationalism: Plantinga-Rorty-Lindbeck-Berger–Critiques and Alternatives* (Boulder: Westview Press, 1995), chs 10–12.

for an absolute good.[23] Language does not fail us, nor does our intellect, but rather we see in the language and in the context a reality that we do not relate to as an object or a presence.

That reality is not an object to which language corresponds is the second feature of Wittgenstein's work that Wallace failed to appreciate. The later Wittgenstein demonstrated in *Philosophical Investigations* that, just as there are many different sorts of activities called games, language is not reducible to any one sort of activity, certainly not the linking of words to objects: "It is as if someone were to say: 'Playing a game consists in moving objects about on a surface according to certain rules . . .'—and we replied: You seem to be thinking of board-games, but they are not all the games there are."[24] Wallace's skepticism about moral and religious language rests on the notion of language as one sort of activity, the linking of words to reality (or objects). The main problem with this assumption, as Wittgenstein thoroughly demonstrated, is that language consists of all sorts of activities:

Giving orders, and obeying them –

Describing the appearance of an object, or giving its measurements –

Constructing an object from a description (a drawing) –

Reporting an event –

Speculating about an event –

Forming and testing a hypothesis –

Presenting the results of an experiment in tables and diagrams –

Making up a story: and reading it –

Play-acting –

Singing catches –

Guessing riddles –

Making a joke; telling it –

Solving a problem in practical arithmetic –

Translating from one language to another –

Asking, thanking, cursing, greeting, praying.[25]

When one assumes that all language must be of the same sort, some practices, such as those employing moral and religious language, get distorted. When one cannot demonstrate that words and actions of empathy connect to the

---

[23] Phillips, *Faith After Foundationalism*, 275.
[24] *Philosophical Investigations*, 6ᵉ § 3.
[25] Ibid., 15ᵉ, § 23.

intended recipient like the names of objects connect to their intended target, skepticism is introduced into the language of empathy. Wallace thus accepted this skepticism about moral and religious language without understanding the later Wittgenstein's elucidation of the nature of language.

But perhaps Wallace only meant to suggest that true empathy cannot be a matter of direct communication. There is, of course, great depth and importance in the distinction between direct and indirect communication, which may help to account for the suggestion that Wallace's "Not another word" implies that language has exhausted its options. However, in such a case it is not *language* that has exhausted its options but rather *direct communication* that has run out of options. The morally good thing, for example, is not done when one directly says, "Don't speculate about a person's troubles"; the morally good thing is done when one stops speculating about a person's troubles. I think this is communicated very clearly, though indirectly, in the forceful rebuke, "Not another word." If Wallace had chosen instead to write, "I really should stop speculating about this person's troubles," it would have been consistent with the less real, and less sentimental, self, playing this evil game. "Not another word" communicates a robust, moral authority that greatly exceeds a hint or a haunting. And this formidable, moral phrase was said in language.

True empathy in Wallace's "Good Old Neon"

"Not another word" was said in a language shared by a community. In that community, people might recognize in the phrase the voice of a father or a mother or a teacher, an authoritative voice, establishing moral boundaries. It is a phrase in a context, as Wallace wrote, "commanding" and "looking it levelly in the eye." Many of us will understand what is being communicated here. It is the voice of moral authority. It is a voice that some postmodernists assumed would disappear when people realized that metaphysics is an illusion. But if metaphysics is an illusion, then the voice of moral authority never depended upon it. Whether there is sense in what the voice of moral authority says depends upon the community in which it is said, not the philosopher's metaphysics. Postmodernism has successfully, in my opinion, demonstrated that metaphysics is an illusion, but it has not thereby demonstrated that the moral and religious claims of a community are illusions. As long as there are mothers in our language communities who teach moral lessons to their children, the voice of moral authority will have a sense in our language. If one asks, as some have, "Where do mothers get their authority?," an honest, intellectual answer might have something to say about the role of Mystery in our lives, but the realer, more sentimental answer will be: "Don't ask silly questions." Wallace thus successfully demonstrated that the metaphysics of the self remains intact in much of postmodern literature insofar as the trope of endless irony depends upon the infinite cleverness of the author:

> MTV-type co-optation could end up a great prophylactic against cleveritis—you know, the dreaded grad-school syndrome of like "Watch me use seventeen different points of view in this scene of a guy eating a Saltine." The real point of that shit is "Like me because I'm clever"— which of course is itself derived from commercial art's axiom about audience-affection determining art's value.[26]

He attributed this cleverness for cleverness sake to the phenomenon of "crank turners" who capitalize on original and genuine contributions to art that become fashionable. Consequently, he argues that the unfashionable and the naïve may become the new rebels:

> The next real literary "rebels" in this country might well emerge as some weird bunch of *anti*-rebels, born oglers who dare somehow to back away from ironic watching, who have the childish gall actually to endorse and instantiate single-entendre principles. . . . The new rebels might be artists willing to risk the yawn, the rolled eyes, the cool smile, the nudged ribs, the parody of gifted ironists, the "Oh how *banal*."[27]

This lack of cleverness, though it rebels against endless irony, does not resort to metaphysical defenses or illusions of the self. I think this may be Wallace's point: If empathy is going to have a chance against the terror of solipsism, sentimentality will need to come from somewhere else other than external illusions about the self, even those (or perhaps especially those) sophisticated literary pictures of the self as extremely clever, rational, and self-recursive because such pictures depend upon a sentimental trust in the illusory security of the distant, rational self.

Sam Adler-Bell has noted that this clever and distant self also resists the community needed to lessen our loneliness:

> What the postmodern posture reveals is not a deficit of belief, but rather an unwillingness to open ourselves up to the kind of vulnerability entailed in betraying true belief. There is a sick cycle at work in our culture,

---

[26] "Interview with David Foster Wallace," 29.
[27] Wallace, "E Unibus Pluram: Television and U.S. Fiction," in *A Supposedly Fun Thing I'll Never Do Again* (New York: Little, Brown & Co., 1997), 81.

which Wallace's fiction has identified: (stay with me here) as Americans, we share a basic and formative fear of being alone, but we exist in a culture that compels us to be ironic and cynical to earn inclusion, so we adopt a posture of ironic distance, which itself, by diminishing the meaning and limiting the possibility of real, open, mutually-vulnerable communication, precludes the formation of the kinds of community that would actually assuage our loneliness.[28]

I think this is right, but I would add that the culture of irony and cynicism is fed by the confused notion found among highly educated people that any attempt to speak with genuine sincerity is to assume that language can bridge an enormous metaphysical gap between the speaker and the hearer. Wallace seemed to be saying, "Language can't do it, but it is important to speak with genuine sincerity, anyway." We have grown into this modern assumption concerning the role of language, that is, that genuine expressions expect to make a miraculous connection to others, enabling one person's personal feelings to be felt and experienced by another. Since it is obvious that language does not do this, it is assumed that any attempt to express a genuine connection to another person is to naïvely and ignorantly believe that language *can* bridge the distance between two brains and their respective bodies. By perpetually speaking in ironic and cynical tones, we demonstrate our cleverness to others that we know that language cannot be trusted to do this. Wallace agreed that language fails us, but he tried to get us to see that it doesn't matter whether we demonstrate cleverness or not. He nonetheless participated in this logical confusion, failing to appreciate that what connects us, what has always connected us, to others and to the world is our lives, not language.

As we have seen, Wallace haunts us in "Good Old Neon" with genuine sentimentality. He does this by holding in tension the ordinary self who asserts a genuine connection to the character Neal with the self that knows that language is inadequate for making any real connection. But Wallace's solipsistic skepticism has underestimated the power of the words uttered by his ordinary unassuming self, as he says, "the realer, more enduring and sentimental" self. The command, "Not another word," does not attempt to traverse some imagined metaphysical distance between Wallace and Neal; neither does it rest upon the foundation of rational thought and justification.

---

[28] Sam Adler-Bell, "Some Writing about Writing about David Foster Wallace," *Wag's Revue*, 57. This is an excellent little article in which Adler-Bell convincingly argues that Wallace's writings have much in common with those of the later Derrida. I think that Adler-Bell is correct, and for this reason, some of the criticisms that I raise of Wallace in this chapter are applicable to the later Derrida as well.

It is simply the self-asserting moral truth, thereby elucidating the nature of moral assertions. It is not an attempt to arrive at moral truth through rational reflection (the metaphysical system). Moral truth, having been learned in some community, is simply believed and lived. This is sentimentality in the sense that it is trust without rational justification, but it is not trust in an illusion about the nature of the self or about what the clear-thinking rational self deserves.

Elsewhere, Wallace hinted that morality rooted in a trust in something other than the self is the only sort of morality there can be, a lived faith in moral principles that are sustained by that which is worshipped and submitted to:

> In the day-to-day trenches of adult life, there is actually no such thing as atheism. There is no such thing as not worshiping. Everybody worships. The only choice we get is *what* to worship. And an outstanding reason for choosing some sort of God or spiritual-type thing to worship—be it J.C. or Allah, be it Yahweh or the Wiccan mother goddess or the Four Noble Truths or some infrangible set of ethical principles—is that pretty much anything else you worship will eat you alive.[29]

Wallace seemed here to appreciate that living a life entails trust. The question is whether he appreciated that his remarks here are themselves religious and spiritual. Living a spiritual life is not simply a matter of rationally and independently seeing that spirituality is best among all the options, choosing the spiritual option, and then constructing one's life around it. What will and will not eat a person alive is itself a moral and/or spiritual distinction. Wallace arrived at this observation through his own spiritual/moral journey. His observation thus does not, external to that journey, justify why we should worship something spiritual rather than other alternatives.

What is missing from Wallace's recommendation is the recognition of the role of Mystery in these ways of living, or at least the recognition that moral and spiritual responses are neither reasonable nor unreasonable. Spiritual ways of living are rooted in heart, passion, and desire; this makes them mysterious occurrences. They have no intellectual ground that is independent of the living of life itself. The existentialists understood this: there is no substitute for the individual's life response. Without an appreciation for the mysteriousness of spiritual living, Wallace's response suggests that it just makes rational sense to live a spiritual life because worship of this sort takes you away from a selfish orientation that destroys the self. But this notion

[29] Wallace, *This Is Water* (New York: Little, Brown & Co., 2009), 98–102.

of the self is itself a religiously informed one, and Wallace's appeal is not an independent justification of spirituality. Notions of Truth and Absolute Justice and God's Will are not formed in resigned acceptance of something less valuable than rational thought, but rather in a passionate abandonment to that which cannot be justified by rational thought: "To accept the mystery is not a matter of being content with ignorance where knowledge would be had, but, rather, a matter of coming to accept a spiritual truth."[30] We oglers, writers, and philosophers who struggle to give justified accounts of reality must learn how to recognize these spiritual truths in the details of people's everyday lives. In our culture, it is extremely difficult to recognize such Mystery, even when it is right in front of our noses. I have tried to demonstrate in this paper that Wallace's "Good Old Neon" gives us a robust picture of the virtue of empathy that belies his struggle with solipsism. And further, Wallace's struggle rests on the devaluation of our moral and religious vocabulary on the illusory assumption that language is inadequate to express Mystery. We have too often assumed in our culture that the only sort of mystery in life is one that can be potentially or theoretically solved. Walker Percy wrote in several places about this problem, and summarizes the issue well:

> What has happened is not merely the technological transformation of the world but something psychologically even more portentous. It is the absorption by the layman not of the scientific method but rather of the magical aura of science, whose credentials he accepts for all sectors of reality. . . . Such a man could not take account of God, the devil, and the angels if they were standing before him, because he has already peopled the universe with his own hierarchies.[31]

Religious and moral language often speaks of things which are said to lie beyond humanity's reach—an absolute justice, a transcendent God—but grasping the sense of these terms depends upon seeing how they illuminate our everyday, ordinary lives. This is the sense in which such language revolves around Mystery. Mystery is not at some great distance from us, incomprehensible to our finite minds and inaccessible to our narrow language. Mystery shows up each day in mundane human activities in which people strive to do the right thing, showing us the sense of an absolute justice, and in which people worship and pray to God for their daily bread, showing us the sense of a transcendent God who is said to be with us.

---

[30] Phillips, *Faith After Foundationalism*, 282.
[31] Walker Percy, "A Novel about the End of the World," in *The Message in the Bottle* (New York: Picador, 2000), 113.

We are not doing justice to moral and religious concepts if we simply rest content with Wallace's resignation that in our use of language "we're at least all in here together."[32] We must see and feel the full weight and force of the reality that is there like our lives. We must see that when people live and speak, as when Wallace rebukes himself in "Good Old Neon" and empathetically connects to Neal, they demonstrate their trust that language makes sense. We oglers have no ground upon which to undermine that trust, and when we properly observe language and life, we see the power of both irony and sincerity, the breadth of both playfulness and solemnity, the depth of both Beauty and Truth. The language makes sense to these users because it is part and parcel of the lives they lead.

I think that Wallace knew this when he made his remark about JC, Allah, Yahweh, the Four Noble Truths, and the Wiccan Goddess. However, the remark itself is slathered in the postmodern cynicism that he seemed unable to escape. The whimsical nature of the remark and the suggestion that these religious figures and principles are like grocery items that we could take off the shelf, take home with us, and cook up in the boiling pot of our daily lives utterly fails to do justice to the roles that these religious figures/principles play in the lives of their respective worshipers. Religious devotion is not simply a matter of choice; it is existential struggle with (and in) the Mystery of Life and in the deepest recesses of the human psyche. Language *about* religious language must reflect this if it is to do justice to the role such religious language plays in the lives of believers.

Of course, when I write something like this I fear that I sound like a fundamentalist Christian apologist, or, at least, an apologist for the Christian apologist. That is not my intention at all. My concern is that, as scholars and readers and writers of literature, we do intellectual justice to the variety of religious commitments that we ogle, to borrow Wallace's term yet again. This means that we have to do justice to how such language is not ironic to those believers. And further, it means that we have to jettison the remnants of those metaphysical illusions that we continue to obliviously trade on when we claim that language is not trustworthy. When Joe Christian sings, "A Mighty Fortress is Our God," language does not fail him even though what is expressed is mostly about Mystery, and our intellectual accounts of those words must reflect this fact. When Jane Buddhist speaks of clearing her mind of negative thoughts, she is not chasing some metaphysical pipe dream; she is participating, along with her Buddhist community, in a practice that has ordinary parameters, criteria, and expectations that will either be met or not. In order for us oglers to see the sense of these practices and phrases, we must

---

[32] "Interview with David Foster Wallace," 44.

appreciate the fundamental respects in which they arise from commitments that are deep, reverential, and non-ironic.

I am not arguing that religious practitioners are immune to ironic ridicule. They often are legitimate objects of ridicule. But whether or not they are will depend on what they do and say in the communities of language in which they participate. They are not ridiculous simply because they trust God or follow the Noble Path, what I have in this paper called expressions of Mystery, or by virtue of non-ironically holding to beliefs that arise in the face of Mystery. Neither am I arguing that trust in these expressions somehow solves the Mystery of Life, thus providing the solution to the rational question of whether life has a sense. I hope that I am elucidating Wallace's remark about all those religious figures and principles. Worship and devotion are responses to the Mystery that surrounds us, expressing a sense to life that is neither a rational solution to the existential question of existence nor a justification of all that happens in life. These religious responses are expressions of faith/trust that are an orientation to life, holding life and language together. They cannot be rationally justified nor can they provide rational justification for life because such expectations are confusions that continue to trade on metaphysical illusions about life and rational thought. This is why such religious and moral beliefs are not metaphysical; they do not await intellectual justification nor do they assume that intellectual justification will be forthcoming when the conditions are right. They express features of reality that are not dependent in any way upon justification by some consciousness.

So Wallace's "Good Old Neon" ends with a sentimentality that is not deluded about what the rational self can provide, but neither does it need to fall to the confused notion that the self can assert nothing authoritatively whatsoever. What the self asserts authoritatively is not rooted in the self and is not tied to an illusion about what will or will not happen to the self. Wallace's attempt in this story to make accessible a generalized notion of suffering, by haunting us with genuine empathy, thus depends for its success on an ordinary nonmetaphysical self that asserts moral authority. The problem, as I have tried to show, is that Wallace thought this to be the best response to solipsism, a resigned acceptance of the inadequacy of language, which nonetheless enables us to gesture toward something akin to real empathy. It is the best "solution" to solipsism, though he knows that it is no solution at all. Thus he felt "stuck."

Wallace felt "stuck" because he continued to hold on to some version of the dualism that he and his patriarchs so thoroughly attacked. But, as we have seen, both his fiction and his remarks about spiritual ways of living betray the dualism that he clung to. Feeling stuck by the limits of language is an illusion. Language does not "fail" when Wallace's realer self says to the self with a penchant for endless ironizing, "Not another word." The phrase clearly communicates: "Shut up! Your incessant speculations and mental gymnastics serve only to perpetuate an evil that one ought to resist." Does language fail us when we say, "Words cannot express my gratitude"? Is this a failure of language? Is this a failure to communicate gratitude? No, of course not. And likewise, "Not another word" is not a failure of language on any level. It clearly and forcefully expresses the moral command to love one's neighbor.

One might reasonably ask, "If this moral authority does not rest in the self and it is not metaphysical, where is it and how can language possibly communicate its reality?" Moral and religious language necessarily involves trusting in something that cannot be clearly delineated and justified by the intellect, trusting in something whose source is inherently Mystery to the intellect. It does *not* follow from this that what one trusts lies beyond human knowledge, beyond language, and thus is ultimately inaccessible to human life. What follows from this observation is that many features of our lives involve speaking to one another about things that we have some understanding of but cannot intellectually justify: goodness, love, grace, justice, God, and so on. How then do we make sense of this language? How can we be certain that it has a sense if we can't provide an intellectual foundation for this sort of language? Language makes sense if living makes sense.[33] That is, making rational sense of the use of our language cannot be separated from the sense that we make of our own lives. That sense logically cannot be secured or guaranteed by rational thought because the sense of rational thought (and language use) depends on what we take to be the sense of the life in which the language is spoken. That sense is secured by our existential commitments to live in the ways that we do, not by our rational justification of those ways of living.

Wallace's philosophical struggle with solipsism made it difficult for him to fully appreciate the nature of morality and spirituality. He struggled deeply with solipsism and the question of whether we can ever truly say anything about reality. I have tried to show that he was never able to completely free himself from the horror of solipsism because he continued to approach it as an intellectual problem to be solved, a struggle to experience the "click"

---

[33] D. Z. Phillips, "Editor's Introduction" in Rush Rhees and D. Z. Phillips (eds), *Wittgenstein and the Possibility of Discourse* (Cambridge: Cambridge University Press, 1998), 6.

that he spoke of in doing philosophy and writing fiction.[34] As we have seen, his writings demonstrate (to some extent) that he understood that solipsism itself is a pseudo-problem that logically can never get off the ground. But he also recognized that this means that the old metaphysical problem of a Cartesian "I", separate from the world (and its solution requiring some form of metaphysical realism), never gets off the ground and that we will never be able to experience the "click" of a solution to that problem because it is a pseudo-problem. It is like being given a puzzle that logically has no solution, or a Zen koan with the expectation as a puzzle lover that you will eventually figure out the answer and then coming to realize that the puzzle cannot be solved. The puzzle is not really a puzzle at all. And this disappoints and depresses because a solution (and the feelings of euphoria that accompany) will not be forthcoming. The difference is that the stakes are raised because this was supposed to be a puzzle about life and whether speaking has any meaning. And thus "Good Old Neon" expresses the disappointment of not being able to experience the satisfaction of solving a puzzle that turns out not to be a legitimate puzzle, after all. The work is genuine and reflective of the age but thus also expressive of a debilitating condition: a depressing state in which moral and spiritual truths are said to be the best we can do, given the inadequacy of language.

The irony here is that some postmodernists and successors to post-modernism, like Wallace, experience the disappointment even though at least one central component of postmodernism is to show that metaphysics cannot provide a rational foundation for our morality. The postmodernist experiences a "loss," which she knows is not really a loss. The confusion is that the loss is associated with the stability or certainty of claims about religion and morality, whereas the emotional disappointment is really more akin to

---

[34] "For most of my college career I was a hard-core syntax wienie, a philosophy major with a specialization in math and logic. I was, to put it modestly, quite good at the stuff, mostly because I spent all my free time doing it. Wienieish or not, I was actually chasing a special sort of buzz, a special moment that comes sometimes. One teacher called these moments 'mathematical experiences'. What I didn't know then was that a mathematical experience was aesthetic in nature, an epiphany in Joyce's original sense. These moments appeared in proof-completions, or maybe algorithms. Or like a gorgeously simple solution to a problem you suddenly see after half a notebook with gnarly attempted solutions. It was really an experience of what I think Yeats called 'the click of a well-made box'. Something like that. The word I always think of it as is 'click'. . . . At some point in my reading and writing. . . . I discovered the click in literature, too. It was real lucky that just when I stopped being able to get the click from math logic I started to be able to get it from fiction. The first fictional clicks I encountered were in Donald Barthelme's *The Balloon* and in parts of the first story I ever wrote, which has been in my trunk since I finished it. I don't know whether I have that much natural talent going for me fiction wise, but I know I can hear the click, when there is a click." ("Interview with David Foster Wallace," 35).

needing the feeling of euphoria which comes with solving an intellectual puzzle. The postmodernist comes to realize that she can't even enjoy the experience of a solution because the "solution" lies in being able to see that it's not really an intellectual puzzle, and that the proper response to the pseudo-problem of solipsism is to say, "It doesn't make sense to bifurcate language and reality like that." Like many intellectuals of the last three decades, we have seen that Wallace, too, assumed that moral virtues like empathy are always a bit shaky, just out of our grasp. But we have also seen that that assumption rests on a metaphysical illusion. The voice of moral authority does not stand, and has never stood, on the foundation of rational thought. It stands, as it always has, on that which is Mystery to our intellects and toward which our relation is something akin to a child's trust. Many in our culture have assumed that the rational backing for morality is necessary, even if they could not explain it themselves, like the technology and engineering of computers and microwave ovens. The "discovery," or observation, that religion and morality do not have that kind of backing is tantamount, for some, to a loss of authority; whereas, this observation ought to have led intellectuals to investigate what associations are found where religion and morality actually *do* exercise authority: tradition, community, family, ritual, integrity, consistency, and so on. Such an investigation, of course, would not provide a rational justification of religious and moral authority, but it would provide an elucidation of the nature of religious and moral authority.

Language is not struggling to reach reality; whatever articulable understanding we possess about reality, we do so in and through language. This means that language is not a limited tool that gets us to a certain point and then breaks or fails. Language does exactly what it does. When we reach a point at which we can't provide a rational justification for our language, it is not language, or anything for that matter, that fails. We simply reach Mystery and we tell stories *in language* that give expression to our relations to Mystery and we give various accounts of the role that Mystery plays in our lives and we talk about the variety of ways that humans have responded to Mystery. This is not a *failure* of language; this *is* language, and the reality of human existence. This means that our lives are not lived with reality on one side and inaccessible Mystery on the other. We live with and in Mystery. One neighbor suffers with incurable cancer; another enjoys a long and healthy life. One region suffers drought or some other natural disaster; another prospers. Mystery is all around us and grows along with our knowledge of empirical reality. Mystery grows when people continue to act in moral (and immoral) and religious (and irreligious) ways without explanation or justification. When we attempt to describe these features of reality as if our primary orientation and relation to them is one of understanding (such as we would for questions of fact), we are engaging in illusory talk. Such talk is illusory because we are trying to force these features of reality to be what they are not. When Wallace spoke of language as a limited tool, he participated in this illusory talk, wishing or wanting these features to be objects of understanding. When we come to understand that they are not objects of understanding, we come to understand that language is not limited with respect to these features of reality. Language is not a limited tool; human existence, experience, and understanding are lived in a reality that includes Mystery. Language gives expression to our relation to Mystery, seen in responses to acts of grace in which we say things like, "Words cannot express my gratitude," or to acts of horror, "I will never understand why this happened," or to immoral speculations about another's sufferings, "Not another word." These are not failures of language and human understanding; these are expressions of life lived in relation to Mystery.

Index

9 781441 162656